Fraud: A Practitioner's Handbook

Fraud: A Practitioner's Handbook

Adrian Eissa
Barrister at 25 Bedford Row

Colin Wells
Barrister at 25 Bedford Row

Nathaniel Rudolf
Barrister at 25 Bedford Row

Foreword by

His Honour Judge **Alistair McCreath**
Honorary Recorder of the City of Westminster
Resident Judge, Southwark Crown Court

Bloomsbury Professional

Bloomsbury Professional Ltd, Maxwelton House, 41–43 Boltro Road, Haywards Heath, West Sussex, RH16 1BJ

© Bloomsbury Professional Ltd 2014

Bloomsbury Professional, an imprint of Bloomsbury Publishing Plc

All rights reserved. No part of this publication may be reproduced in any material form (including photocopying or storing it in any medium by electronic means and whether or not transiently or incidentally to some other use of this publication) without the written permission of the copyright owner except in accordance with the provisions of the Copyright, Designs and Patents Act 1988 or under the terms of a licence issued by the Copyright Licensing Agency Ltd, Saffron House, 6–10 Kirby Street, London EC1N 8TS. Applications for the copyright owner's written permission to reproduce any part of this publication should be addressed to the publisher.

Warning: The doing of an unauthorised act in relation to a copyright work may result in both a civil claim for damages and criminal prosecution.

Crown copyright material is reproduced with the permission of the Controller of HMSO and the Queen's Printer for Scotland. Any European material in this work which has been reproduced from EUR-lex, the official European Communities legislation website, is European Communities copyright.

A CIP Catalogue record for this book is available from the British Library.

Every effort has been taken to ensure the accuracy of the contents of this book. However, neither the authors nor the publishers can accept any responsibility for any loss occasioned to any person acting or refraining from acting in reliance on any statement contained in the book.

ISBN: 978 1 78043 137 6

Typeset by Phoenix Photosetting, Chatham, Kent
Printed and bound in the United Kingdom by CPI Group (UK) Ltd, Croydon, CR0 4YY

Dedication

Nathaniel Rudolf writes for Leah Lin Pearl
Colin Wells writes for James and Patricia
Adrian Eissa writes for his children

Acknowledgments

The three of us thank all the practitioners at 25 Bedford Row, London for their support, encouragement and assistance in our understanding of criminal fraud litigation. The clerks' room at 25 has allowed us the time and space to complete this book.

A big thank you to all at Bloomsbury Professional who have made this book, and its publication on time, possible. Thank you too for the additional proofreading support provided by Catherine Wells and Klaxon C Wilson.

Thanks as well to our families who have shown support and understanding.

Adrian Eissa
Colin Wells
Nathaniel Rudolf

Foreword

The process of trying fraud is a difficult one for all who are involved in it. The imperative of doing justice to all parties whilst at the same time keeping these trials within limits of time and complexity is not always easy to achieve but is central to the effectiveness of the trial process. The critical role of knowledgeable lawyers in this field should never be underestimated. This is something recognised in the 2005 Protocol on the Control and Management of Heavy Fraud Cases. Above all, the part played by such practitioners is hugely valued by the judges who try these cases.

The exercise of good judgment at all stages of the trial process is critical. Which allegations will the prosecution proceed with? What evidence will they call in an attempt to prove them? Where do the real issues in the case lie? To what extent and in what way will the defence assist in identifying the issues? Which prosecution witnesses need to attend for cross-examination? What admissions can be made? What documents should be adduced in evidence? What disclosure should be made? What disclosure should be sought? These questions – and many, many more – have to be faced and answered by the lawyers. If they are not addressed or are addressed but answered wrongly, the risk to the effectiveness of the trial process is likely to be high, in terms of unjustifiable cost and, of obvious importance, in terms of potential injustice. A good prosecution case can be lost under an avalanche of excess information just as a good defence case can be lost by a failure to insist on the disclosure of material, the relevance of which to the defence case may not always be obvious to the prosecutor.

The ability to exercise good judgment is the product of many factors, one of which, a sound knowledge base, is obvious and important. It is easily said that this kind of knowledge cannot be obtained from a book. If there ever was a truth in this kind of assertion, the publication of this Handbook goes a long way to undermine it, although this excellent book does a very great deal more than provide a basic knowledge of the subject.

It is the product of considerable industry and of a great deal of skill and experience.

It is filled with information valuable to practitioners at all levels of knowledge and experience. For those who are less experienced, there are descriptions of common frauds (for example, Ponzi, boiler room, MTIC) of outstanding clarity. For those who are preparing themselves for journeys into the as yet uncharted territory of Deferred Prosecution Agreements, there is an extremely helpful explanation of the scheme and two appendices containing the relevant parts of the Criminal Procedure Rules and the Code of Practice. For practitioners at all

Foreword

levels of experience there is an abundance of valuable information, including source materials, practical information and guidance, informed discussion of the different topics dealt with, and much more.

Practitioners in this field need to access a wide range of material, including sentencing guidelines, Criminal Procedure Rules, provisions under many statutes, codes of practice and guidelines issued in relation to many different aspects of the process. All of this material is obtainable but much of it is only found at the end of long and sometimes difficult journeys, whether in a paper or an electronic environment. To have all of it available in this single volume is a very considerable bonus.

This invaluable handbook will – and certainly should – find its way into the library of all who conduct criminal litigation in fraud cases, amongst them the judges on whom the duty of trying these cases fall.

His Honour Judge Alistair McCreath
Honorary Recorder of the City of Westminster
Resident Judge, Southwark Crown Court
August 2014

Introduction

Considering the breadth of cases that come under the 'umbrella' of fraud the practitioner is often faced with a dizzying array of legal principles, management protocols, disclosure rules, factual scenarios and sentencing/confiscation authorities that seem at times to be endless and ever changing.

It is with credit then that Colin Wells, Adrian Eissa and Nathaniel Rudolf, all highly experienced and respected practitioners within the field of fraud have produced a publication that is of great value not only to seasoned practitioners, but also to those embarking upon a practice in the field of fraud. I have no doubt that this book will also be of great assistance to the judiciary.

The authors have sought to place fraud offences in their historical context whilst explaining to the reader the need for change within the context of fraud as a whole. For example, Chapter 1 commences with the history of the Fraud Act 2006, putting it in the context of past and current practice. Equally at Chapter 2, the rationale behind retaining conspiracy to defraud as an offence is explained.

One extremely impressive feature of the book is the accessible form in which various types of fraud are explained whilst pointing the practitioner to much of the reference material they will need. For example, at Chapter 3, Prevalent Types Of Fraud, the authors set out a guide to each type of mortgage fraud – false accounting, Ponzis, boiler room frauds, MTIC, carbon credits, cheating the public revenue, insider trading, money laundering and fraudulent trading. Within each category they set out the legislation in relation to that type of fraud, the historical context of the fraud and the characteristic features. In addition, they illustrate the point with practical examples and set out the consequences of conviction both in terms of sentencing and confiscation. The guide to each type of fraud is clear and concise.

For those of us who practice in the field of fraud it goes without saying that case management and disclosure have become more and more important. Proper case management from an early stage, and the willing engagement of both the prosecution and defence, can lead to sometimes extremely complex issues becoming digestible and understandable for the jury, leading to a trial that is hopefully smooth running and efficient. This book educates those that are unfamiliar with the Criminal Procedure Rules 2014 or the Protocol On The Control and Management of Heavy Fraud as to what is expected of them. It is also a useful reminder and guide to those familiar with such principles as to why they exist and their practical application. The subject is covered in detail at Chapter 6 and moves smoothly and sensibly into the subject of abuse

Introduction

of process at Chapter 8, abuse arguments of course often being the result of failures in disclosure.

Again the subject is set out with clarity and a practical twist. Having set out the well-known principles in relation to abuse of process the chapter then goes on to demonstrate the point by reference to cases such as *Vitric*, *Venison* and *Gnawed*, illustrating how failures in disclosure may lead to a case being stayed. There is, as one would expect, full reference to and consideration of the relevant authorities weighed up against the real issues that may be apparent in any trial.

Other areas covered include alternatives to prosecution at Chapter 5, including a detailed analysis of deferred prosecution agreements, search seizure and investigation at Chapter 4 and sentencing at Chapter 9, this being extremely important bearing in mind the new guidelines coming into use as of October 2014.

I referred at the start of this introduction to the fact that this book will point the practitioner towards much of the reference material they need. It does this by way of the many footnotes and authorities cited in the main body of the work; however, much more helpfully it sets out a series of appendices at the back of the publication that act as an excellent resource for the most important rules and protocols affecting the conduct of fraud cases. For example, at Appendix 1 the Sentencing Guidelines Council's 2014 guidelines in relation to fraud are set out. At Appendix 3, the Criminal Procedure Rules 2014, Pt 3 relating to case management are set out, at Appendix 4 Pt 3 of the Criminal Procedure and Investigation Act 1996, and inevitably at Appendix 9 the protocol for the Control and Management of Heavy Fraud Cases.

There is no question that this publication adds a new dimension to the study and practice of fraud, combining a scholarly approach with a practical sensibility. I am sure it will soon be recognised as a great asset to all of those who practice in the field of fraud.

Tom Price QC
25 Bedford Row
London

Contents

Foreword	*vii*
Introduction	*ix*
Table of Statutes	*xvii*
Table of Statutory Instruments	*xxv*
Table of Cases	*xxvii*
Bibliography	*xliii*

Chapter 1 The Fraud Act 2006	**1**
Introduction	1
Fraud	2
Fraud by false representation	3
Fraud by failing to disclose information	4
Fraud by abuse of position	5
Gain and loss	6
Possession of articles for use in fraud	6
Making or supplying articles for use in fraud	7
Fraudulent trading by non-corporate offenders	8
Obtaining services by dishonesty	9
Liability of company officers for offences committed by a company	10
Chapter 2 Conspiracy to Defraud	**11**
Overview	11
Jurisdiction	12
The offence	14
Chapter 3 Prevalent Types of Fraud	**15**
Introduction	15
Mortgage fraud	15
Context	15
Prevalence	16
The commission of mortgage fraud	16
Common misrepresentations	16
The investigation of mortgage fraud	19
The link between mortgage fraud and money laundering	19
The Fraud Act 2006	20
The Theft Act 1968	24
The role of the professional	28
Avenues of investigation	31
Sentencing	32
Civil recovery and mortgage fraud	35

Contents

Ponzi frauds	36
Overview	36
Charges	37
Conspiracy to defraud	37
Fraud	37
The regulatory position	38
Defences	40
Boiler room fraud	41
Overview	41
Charges	44
Conspiracy to defraud	44
The regulatory position	45
Defences	49
Missing Trader Intra-Community (MTIC) fraud	50
Introduction	50
The fraud	50
Badges of MTIC fraud	55
Potential charges	61
Disclosure	63
Sentencing	71
Confiscation proceedings	72
Carbon credit fraud	75
Introduction	75
Environmental background	75
Carbon credits	76
Carbon credit trading	77
Cheating the Public Revenue	78
Overview	78
The offence	78
Unlicensed money lending (aka 'loan-sharking')	78
Overview	78
The offence	79
Insider trading	89
Background	89
The purpose of the legislation	89
Instituting proceedings	91
The commission of the offence	91
Contracts for difference	96
Spread betting	96
The role of professionals	97
The reverse burden	98
Typical defences	99
Expert evidence	99
Proving the offence	99
Summary of key ingredients	100
Sentence	101

Fraudulent trading	103
Definition	103
Typical cases	103
Ingredients of the offence	104
Unincorporated entities	107
Penalties and sentence	107
Directors disqualification	108
Money laundering	108
Introduction	108
The approach to inferences and submissions of no case to answer	118
Evidence of the underlying crime	120
Pecuniary advantage	123
The principal offences	124
Authorised disclosures	128
Proving the case in practice	129
Joinder with predicate offences	130
Sentencing	131
An overview of the reporting obligations in POCA 2002, ss 330–332	133
Penalties	134
Chapter 4 Search, Seizure and Investigations	**135**
The Police and Criminal Evidence Act 1984	138
Privileged material	139
General power to seize	140
Electronic material	141
Criminal Justice and Police Act 2001, s 50	141
Retention of material	142
Post-arrest powers	142
Admissibility issues	143
Production of material	143
The Proceeds of Crime Act 2002	143
Serious Fraud Office	145
HM Revenue and Customs	150
Department of Business, Innovations and Skills	151
Financial Conduct Authority	151
Chapter 5 Alternatives to Prosecution	**153**
Cautions	153
Introduction	153
Simple police cautions	153
Conditional police cautions	156
Deferred Prosecution Agreements	157
Schedule 17 of the Crime and Courts Act 2013	158
The behaviour to which a DPA can relate	158
The offences to which a DPA can relate	158

Contents

The operation of a DPA	159
The content of a DPA	162
The Code on DPAs	163
Part 12 of the Criminal Procedure Rules 2014	172
The First-tier Tribunal	173
Introduction	173
Practice and procedure at First-tier Tribunals	174

Chapter 6 The role of the Preparatory Hearing, Case Management and Interlocutory Appeals — 177

Preparatory hearings under the Criminal Justice Act 1987 and case management	177
Introduction	177
Ordering a preparatory hearing	178
Pre-trial rulings and case management	179
Part 3 of the Criminal Procedure Rules 2014	180
Sections 7–10 of the Criminal Justice Act 1987	181
Criminal Procedure and Investigations Act 1996	186
Appeals	187
Interlocutory appeals after terminating rulings by the prosecution under the Criminal Justice Act 2003	187
Which rulings are included?	187
Prosecutor's responsibilities	191
Appeals	192

Chapter 7 Disclosure — 193

Introduction	193
Common law	194
Statutory basis: Criminal Procedure and Investigations Act 1996	195
E-disclosure	198
Encryption	201
Sifting/examination, keeping of records and scheduling	201
Disclosure in practice	203
Effective disclosure	205
Attorney-General's Guidelines on Disclosure 2013	206
Third party disclosure	209
Overseas third party disclosure	211
Public interest immunity	212
Sentencing material disclosure	216

Chapter 8 Abuse of Process — 217

Introduction	217
Common law discretion	217
Definition	218
The test	219

Abuse of process issues	219
Delay	219
Disclosure issues	223
Judicial trial control mechanisms	224

Chapter 9 Sentencing — **225**

Introduction	225
Sentencing Guidelines	226
Corporate offending	231
Ancillary Orders	233
Financial reporting order	233
Serious crime prevention order	234
Disqualification as a company director	237
Appendix 1 Fraud, Bribery and Money Laundering Offences: Definitive Guideline	239
Appendix 2 Reduction in Sentence for a Guilty Plea: Definitive Guideline	291
Appendix 3 The Criminal Procedure Rules 2014, Part 3	301
Appendix 4 Criminal Procedure and Investigations Act 1996, Part III	323
Appendix 5 Simple Cautions for Adult Offenders	335
Appendix 6 National Decision Model: Cautions	357
Appendix 7 Criminal Procedure Rules 2014, Part 12	359
Article 8 Deferred Prosecution Agreements: Code of Practice	371
Appendix 9 Control and Management of Heavy Fraud and Other Complex Criminal Cases	395
Appendix 10 Crown Prosecution Guidance: Proceeds Of Crime Act 2002 Part 7 – Money Laundering Offences	411
Appendix 11 Attorney General's Guidelines for Prosecutors on the Use of the Common Law Offence of Conspiracy to Defraud	427
Index	431

Table of Statutes

A

Accommodation Agencies Act 1953 .... 3.211

B

Bankers' Books Evidence Act 1879 .... 4.48
Banking Act 1979
  s 1(3) 3.79
Bribery Act 2010
  s 1, 2 .... 5.22, 9.33
  6, 7 .... 5.22, 9.33

C

Commissioners for Revenue and Customs Act 2005 .... 3.101
Companies Act 1948
  s 332 .... 3.254
Companies Act 1985 .... 4.54
  s 431 .... 7.67
  434 .... 7.67
  441 .... 7.67
  447 .... 4.54
  448 .... 4.54
  450 .... 5.22
  451A 7.67
  453A 4.54
  458 .... 1.28, 1.29, 3.251, 3.255
  718 .... 1.28
Companies Act 1980 .... 3.212
Companies Act 1989 .... 4.54
Companies Act 2006
  s 658 .... 5.22
  680 .... 5.22
  993 .... 1.28, 3.247, 3.250, 3.257
  (2) 3.249
  (3) 3.259

Companies Directors Disqualification Act 1986
  s 1 .... 9.39
  2 .... 9.39
  (3) 3.261
Company Securities (Insider Dealing) Act 1985 .... 3.212
  s 10 .... 3.223
Computer Misuse Act 1990
  s 1 .... 1.21
Consumer Credit Act 1974 .... 3.186, 3.187, 3.193
  s 8 .... 3.200
  (2) 3.200
  9 .... 3.200
  16 .... 3.202
  16A 3.203
  16B 3.203
  16C 3.203
  17 .... 3.204
  Pt 3 (ss 21–42) 3.187, 3.188
  s 21(1) 3.198, 3.199
  39 .... 3.190
  (1) 3.188, 3.194, 3.195, 3.199
  167 .... 3.195
  189 .... 3.199
  (1) 3.198, 3.200, 3.201
  (2) 3.201
  Sch 1 .... 3.195
  Sch 2 .... 3.195
Consumer Credit Act 2006 .... 3.198
Coroners and Justice Act 2009
  s 120 .... 9.2
Crime and Courts Act 2013
  s 45 .... 5.20
  Sch 17 .... 5.18, 5.20, 5.47, 5.48, 5.49, 5.64
  Pt 1 (paras 1–14) 5.23

Table of Statutes

Crime and Courts Act 2013 – *contd*	
Sch 17 – *contd*	
Pt 1 (paras 1–14) – *contd*	
para 1	5.24
2	5.25
3	5.25
3(2)	5.25
4(1)	5.20
5(1)	5.27, 5.43
(3)	5.29
(4)	5.29
(5)	5.27, 5.45
6	5.31
7(1)(b)	5.29
8(1)(b)	5.29
9	5.55
12	5.52
13	5.39, 5.41
(4)–(6)	5.41
Pt 2 (paras 15–31)	5.21
para 15–20	5.22
Pt 3 (paras 32–39)	5.21
para 31	5.23
39	5.21
Crime (International Co-Operation) Act 2003	4.48
s 13	4.48
14	4.48
15	4.48
(2)	4.48
16	4.48
17	4.48
18	4.48
19	4.48
Sch 1	4.48
Criminal Appeal Act 1968	5.55
s 1	6.2
9	6.2
33(1)	6.21, 6.29
Criminal Attempts Act 1981	3.28
Criminal Justice Act 1967	
s 10	5.41
Criminal Justice Act 1972	
s 36	6.2
Criminal Justice Act 1987	6.1, 6.18, 7.16
s 1(1)	4.38
(3)	4.38
2	4.39, 4.41
(1)	4.38

Criminal Justice Act 1987 – *contd*	
s 2(2)	4.42
(3)	4.38
(4)	4.4, 4.39, 4.42
(5), (6), (6A)	4.39
(9)	4.46
(10)	4.39, 4.47
(13)	4.39
3	4.40
(5)	4.41
7	6.13, 6.14, 6.15, 6.19
(1)(a)–(d)	6.15
8	6.5, 6.13, 6.14
9	6.13, 6.14, 6.15
(1)	6.2
(3)(aa)–(d)	6.16
(11)	6.20
9A	6.14
10	6.13, 6.14
12	3.137
Criminal Justice Act 1988	
s 71	3.173
Criminal Justice Act 1993	
Pt I (ss 1–6)	2.6
Pt V (s 52–64)	3.212
s 52	3.218, 3.219
(3)	3.217
53	3.239
(a)–(c)	3.239
55	3.222
(1)	3.227
(4), (5)	3.227
56	3.220
(1)(b)	3.221
(c)	3.241
(d)	3.221
57	3.224
(1)(a), (b)	3.226
(2)(a), (b)	3.225
59(1)–(3)	3.229
61	3.245
(2)	3.216
62	3.230
(1)(a), (c)	3.230
(2)(a), (b)	3.230
Sch 2	3.231, 3.232

Table of Statutes

Criminal Justice Act 2003	3.143, 3.146, 3.305, 6.22, 7.3, 7.5, 7.6, 7.9, 7.10, 7.11, 7.12
s 23A	5.17
43	6.4
44	6.4
58	3.290, 6.3, 6.22
(4), (8)	6.26
59	6.22
(2)	6.27
(3)(b)	6.27
60	6.22
61	6.22
(3)	6.28
(7)	6.28
62	6.23
74	6.22
(1)	6.23
144	9.10
(1)	9.11
164	9.23
174	9.11
240A	9.18
Sch 37 para 1	7.7
Criminal Justice and Police Act 2001	4.16, 4.22, 7.16, 7.25
s 33	9.38
50	4.21, 4.25, 4.54, 4.56, 7.21
51	4.21, 4.25, 7.21
52	4.21
53	4.25, 7.23
54	4.25, 7.23
55	4.25, 7.23
56	4.25
57	4.25
58	4.25
Sch 1	4.21
Criminal Justice (International Co-Operation) Act 1990	4.48
s 14	3.211
Criminal Law Act 1977	
s 3	3.89
12(3)	2.1
Criminal Law Act 1997	
s 5(1)	2.1

Criminal Procedure and Investigations Act 1996	3.143, 3.145, 3.146, 3.156, 3.160, 4.24, 6.13, 6.18, 6.19, 7.3, 7.5, 7.6, 7.7, 7.10, 7.11, 7.16, 7.33, 7.36, 7.46, 7.56
s 1(2)(g)	5.33
3	3.150, 7.7
(2)	3.142, 7.38
5	7.7
6A	7.11
6E(2)	7.12
7	3.150
8	7.8, 7.30, 7.37
9	7.8
11	7.8, 7.13
15	7.9
16	7.45
23	7.7
29	6.9, 6.19
30	6.19
31	6.19
32	6.19
33	6.19
39	6.9, 6.10
40	6.5, 6.9, 6.10
Criminal Procedure (Attendance of Witnesses) Act 1965	
s 2	7.44
Customs and Excise Management Act 1979	5.22
s 50	9.2
161	4.53
161A	4.53
118C	4.53
170	9.2, 9.19
170B	9.2

D

Drug Trafficking Offences Act 1986	
s 23A	3.211

F

Finance Act 1991	4.53
Finance Act 2007	4.9, 4.49
Financial Services Act 2012	3.189, 3.191

xix

Table of Statutes

Financial Services and Markets Act 2000	3.83, 3.85, 3.97, 3.99, 3.188, 4.55
s 19	3.70, 3.88, 3.89, 3.189
21	3.89, 3.95
22	3.71, 3.90, 3.191
(1A)	3.191
23	3.85, 3.88, 3.89, 3.187, 3.189, 3.189, 5.22
(3)	3.78
25	3.88, 3.89, 5.22
90	1.16
167	4.55
176	4.56
346	5.22
397	5.22
398	5.22
418(1), (5)	3.72
Fire Precautions Act 1971	
s 23	1.33
Forgery Act 1861	5.5
Forgery Act 1913	
s 4(1)	3.253
Forgery and Counterfeiting Act 1981	5.22
Fraud Act 2006	1.1, 1.6, 1.23, 2.4, 2.6, 3.1, 3.19, 3.20, 3.30, 3.31, 3.33, 3.34, 3.35, 3.38, 3.68, 5.22, 9.2, 9.3, 9.4, 9.5, 9.36
s 1	1.6, 1.9, 9.19, 9.33, 9.36
1(2)(a)	1.6
(b)	1.6
(c)	1.6
(3)	3.57
(a), (b)	1.7
2	1.6, 1.10, 1.13, 1.14, 1.21, 2.9, 3.15, 3.20, 3.303
(1)(a)	1.10
(b)(i)	1.10
(ii)	1.10, 3.22
(2)(a)	1.11, 2.9
(b)	1.11, 2.9, 3.24
(c)	2.9
Fraud Act 2006 – *contd*	
s 2(3)(a), (b)	1.12
(4)	1.12, 3.24
3	1.6, 1.15, 1.17, 1.21, 3.20, 3.25
(a)	1.15, 3.26
(b)(i), (ii)	1.15
4	1.18, 1.20, 1.21, 3.20
(1)	3.35
(a)	1.18
(b)	1.18
(c)(i), (ii)	1.18
(2)	1.18
5(2)(a), (b)	1.21
(3)	1.21
(4)	1.21
(6)	2.9
6	1.22, 1.24, 1.27, 9.19, 9.36
(1)	1.22
(2)(a), (b)	1.24
7	1.25, 1.26, 1.27, 3.27, 9.19, 9.36
(1)	3.28, 9.36
(a), (b)	1.25
(2)(a), (b)	1.26
8(1)(a), (b)	1.27
9	1.28, 1.30, 3.258
(1)	1.28
(2)(b)	1.28
(6)(a), (b)	1.30
11	1.31, 1.32, 9.33
(1)(a)	1.31
(2)(a), (b)	1.31
(c)(i), (ii)	1.31
(3)(a), (b)	1.31
12	1.33
14(2)	3.29
16(1)	3.30
17	9.19
Sch 2	3.29

H

Human Rights Act 1998	4.9, 4.27
s 1(2)	8.3
Sch 1	8.3

I

Identity Act 2006	5.5

Table of Statutes

Identity Documents Act 2010 ..... 5.5
Insolvency Act 1986 .... 3.247

M

Magistrates Court Act 1980
  s 97 .... 7.44

P

Police and Criminal Evidence Act 1984 .... 7.16
  s 8 .... 4.12, 4.49, 4.50, 4.52
  9 .... 4.49
  10 .... 3.50, 4.13, 4.51
    (2) 4.14
  11 .... 4.12
  13 .... 4.12
  14 .... 4.12
  15 .... 4.9, 4.34, 4.49, 4.56
    (2) 4.10
    (6) 4.10
  16 .... 4.9, 4.34, 4.49, 4.56
  17 .... 4.49
  18 .... 4.26, 4.49, 4.52
  19 .... 4.16, 4.49
  20 .... 4.17
  21 .... 4.34, 4.49
  22 .... 4.24, 4.34, 4.49
  24 .... 4.49
  32 .... 4.26, 4.49, 4.52
  37A 5.14
  54 .... 4.49
  55 .... 4.49
  62 .... 4.49
  63 .... 4.49
  66 .... 4.49
  78 .... 4.27, 8.18, 8.22
  82(2) 4.27
  114 .... 4.9, 4.49
    (2)(b) 4.20
  Sch 1 .... 4.49
Police (Property) Act 1897 .... 4.2
Prevention of Terrorism (Temporary Provisions) Act 1976
  s 10 .... 3.211
Proceeds of Crime Act 2002 .... 3.111, 3.173, 3.208, 3.265, 4.29, 5.22

Proceeds of Crime Act 2002 – *contd*
  s 10 .... 3.168, 3.169
  13 .... 9.1
  75 .... 3.296
  Pt V (ss 240–316) 3.62, 3.290, 3.291
  s 240 .... 3.289
  242 .... 3.289
  Pt VII (ss 327–34) 3.290
  s 327 .... 3.262, 3.280, 3.295, 3.296, 3.297, 3.298, 3.308
    (1)(c) 3.298
    (2)(A) 3.298
  328 .... 3.262, 3.295, 3.296, 3.328, 3.301, 3.308
    (1) 3.289, 3.299
    (3) 3.298
  329 .... 3.137, 3.205, 3.207, 3.211, 3.262, 3.277, 3.284, 3.285, 3.295, 3.302, 3.308, 9.33
    (1) 3.296
      (a) 3.276, 3.303
      (c) 3.262
    (2)(c) 3.211
      (A) 3.298
    (3) 3.209, 3.211
  330 .... 3.278, 3.309, 3.310, 3.311, 3.314
    (6)(a) 3.310
    (12) 3.264
    (14) 3.310
  330A 3.310
  331 .... 3.278, 3.309, 3.311, 3.312, 3.314
    (6) 3.311
      (A) 3.311
  332 .... 3.278, 3.309, 3.312, 3.314
  333 .... 3.278, 3.314
  333A 3.313
  334 .... 3.205
  338 .... 3.304
  339 .... 3.309
  339A 3.304
    (2), (3) 3.304
  340 .... 3.211, 3.269, 3.270, 3.273, 3.290

Table of Statutes

Proceeds of Crime Act 2002 – *contd*
s 340(2)(a), (b) 3.269
    (3) 3.208, 3.266, 3.280
        (a) 3.266, 3.267, 3.273
        (b) 3.277, 3.280
    (4)(a)–(c) 3.269
    (5) 3.266, 3.273, 3.275
    (6) 3.273, 3.292, 3.293, 3.294
    (9) 3.268
        (a)–(c) 3.268
    (10)(a), (d) 3.276
  345 .... 4.29
  346 .... 4.29
  347 .... 4.29
  348 .... 4.29
    (6), (7) 4.30
  349 .... 4.29, 4.31
  350 .... 4.29, 4.32
  351 .... 4.29
    (1)–(3) 4.33
  352 .... 4.34
    (1) 4.7
    (4) 4.34
    (6)(b) 4.7
  353 .... 4.34
    (4)(a)–(c) 4.34
  354 .... 4.34
  355 .... 4.34
  356 .... 4.34
  357 .... 4.35
    (4)(a)–(c) 4.35
  358(2)(a), (b) 4.35
    (3), (4) 4.35
  359 .... 4.35
  361 .... 4.35
  363 .... 4.36
  364 .... 4.36
  365 .... 4.36
  370 .... 4.37
  371 .... 4.37
  372 .... 4.37
  373 .... 4.37
  374 .... 4.37
  375 .... 4.37
Sch 2 .... 3.205, 3.296, 9.33
Sch 9 .... 3.264, 3.309
Prosecution of Offences Act 1985 .... 5.25, 9.36, 9.38
  s 19(2) 9.37, 9.38

Protection of Freedoms Act 2012 .... 4.2, 4.9

R

Regulation of Investigatory Powers Act 2000
  Pt III (ss 49–56) 7.26
Rehabilitation of Offenders Act 1974 .... 5.12
Rent Act 1968
  s 13 .... 3.211

S

Senior Courts Act 1981
  s 29(3) 5.55
Serious Crime Act 2007
  s 6–15 .... 9.35
    19 .... 9.35
  Sch 1 .... 4.50
  Pt 1 .... 9.38
Serious Organised Crime and Police Act 2005 .... 3.304, 4.9
  s 73 .... 9.9
    74 .... 9.9
    76(1) 9.32
    102 .... 3.269
    104 .... 3.310
Social Security Administration Act 1992
  s 111A 9.2

T

Taxes Management Act 1970
  s 20BA 4.50
    106A 9.2
  Sch 1AA 4.50
    para.5 .... 4.51
Theft Act 1968 .... 1.1, 2.3, 3.19, 3.23, 3.29, 3.34, 5.22
  s 15 .... 1.1, 3.19, 3.35, 3.39
    (1) 3.35, 3.36
    15A 1.1, 3.19, 3.30, 3.35, 3.37, 3.38, 3.60, 3.303
    16 .... 3.30
    17 .... 3.32, 3.137, 9.2
        (2)(b) 3.33

Table of Statutes

Theft Act 1968 – *contd*	
s 20(2)	1.1, 3.39
22(1)	3.280
25	1.22, 1.23
34(1)	3.35
116	1.1
Sch 1	1.1
Theft Act 1978	1.1, 2.3
s 1	1.1
(1)	3.39

Theft (Amendment) Act 1996	1.1, 2.3
s 1	3.37

V

Value Added Tax Act 1994	4.52
s 70	9.19
72	3.137, 3.139, 5.22, 9.2
77A	3.111

Table of Statutory Instruments

C

Consumer Credit Act 2006 (Commencement No. 3) Order 2007, SI 2007/3300
 art 3(2).................................. 3.198
 Sch 2...................................... 3.198
Crime (International Co-Operation) Act 2003 (Exercise of Functions) Order 2009, SI 2009/3021... 4.48
Criminal Justice Act 2003 (Conditional Cautions: Financial Penalties) Order 2013, SI 2013/615............. 5.17
Criminal Procedure Rules 2013, SI 2013/1554.......... 3.142, 4.48, 6.4
 Pt 5... 4.3
 Pt 6... 4.3
 r 6.1–6.22 .... 4.37
 6.29 .... 4.37, 4.43
 6.30 .... 4.37, 4.43
 (10).................................... 4.11
 6.31–6.33 .... 4.37, 4.43
 6.34–6.36 .... 4.37
 Pt 12 .... 5.18, 5.31
 Pt 22 .... 7.62
 r 22.2 .... 7.62
 22.3(3)............................... 7.62
 Pt 76
 r 76.1(1)(c) 5.56
Criminal Procedure Rules 2014, SI 2014/1610
 Pt 1 .... 6.11
 Pt 3 .... 6.9, 6.11, 7.15
 r 3.2(3).................................. 6.12
 3.14–3.18 .... 6.13, 6.18
 Pt 12 .... 5.18, 5.48, 5.49, 5.64
 r 12.2(c)............................... 5.54
 (3)(b), (c) 5.65
 Pt 50 .... 9.35

F

Financial Services and Markets Act 2000 (Carrying on Regulated Activities by way of Business) Order 2001, SI 2001/1177 .... 3.74
 art 2 .... 3.78
 (1)(a), (b).......................... 3.78
Financial Services and Markets Act 2000 (Financial Promotion) Order 2001, SI 2001/1335............... 3.96, 3.100
Financial Services and Markets Act 2000 (Regulated Activities) (Amendment) (No 2) Order 2013, SI 2013/1881................................ 3.188
 art 20(10)............................... 3.188
Financial Services and Markets Act 2000 (Regulated Activities) Order 2001, SI 2001/544 .... 3.74, 3.91, 3.96, 3.192
 art 5 .... 3.72
 (1)(b) 3.72
 14 .... 3.91, 3.94
 18 .... 3.93
 21 .... 3.91, 3.94
 Pt 14A (arts 60B–60M)........... 3.192
 art 60B.................................... 3.192
 (3).................................... 3.192
 60C–60M 3.193
 72 .... 3.94
 87 .... 3.91
 89 .... 3.91

I

Insider Dealing (Securities and Markets) Order 1994, SI 1994/187
 Sch 2................ 3.228, 3.244

Table of Statutory Instruments

M

Money Laundering Regulations
    2007, SI 2007/2157 .... 3.8
    reg 45 .... 5.22

P

Police and Criminal Evidence
    Act 1984 (Application to
    Revenue and Customs)
    Order 2007, SI 2007/3175 .. 4.9, 4.49

T

Tribunal Procedure (First-tier
    Tribunal) (Tax Chamber)
    Rules 2009, SI 2009/273 ..... 5.69

V

Value Added Tax Regulations
    1995, SI 1995/2518
    reg 25 .... 3.103

Table of Cases

A

Adams v Queen, The [1995] 1 WLR 52, [1995] BCC 376, [1995] 2 BCLC 17, [1995] 2 Cr App R 295, [1995] Crim LR 561, (1995) 92(4) LSG 33, (1995) 139 SJLB 13, PC (NZ)	1.19
Attorney General v District Court at Hamilton [2004] 3 NZLR 777	8.21
Attorney General's Reference (No 1 of 1982), Re [1983] QB 751, [1983] 3 WLR 72, [1983] 2 All ER 721, (1983) 77 Cr App R 9, (1984) 148 JP 115, [1983] Crim LR 534, (1983) 127 SJ 377, CA	2.7
Attorney General's Reference (No 1 of 1988), Re [1989] AC 971, [1989] 2 WLR 729, [1989] 2 All ER 1, (1989) 5 BCC 625, [1990] BCLC 172, [1989] PCC 249, (1989) 89 Cr App R 60, [1989] Crim LR 647, (1989) 139 NLJ 541, HL	3.213
Attorney General's Reference (No 1 of 1990), Re [1992] QB 630, [1992] 3 WLR 9, [1992] 3 All ER 169, (1992) 95 Cr App R 296, (1992) 156 JP 593, [1993] Crim LR 37, (1992) 156 JPN 476, (1992) 89(21) LSG 28, (1992) 142 NLJ, CA	8.14
Attorney General's Reference (No 2 of 2001), Re [2003] UKHL 68, [2004] 2 AC 72, [2004] 2 WLR 1, [2004] 1 All ER 1049, [2004] 1 Cr App R 25, [2004] HRLR 16, [2004] UKHRR 193, 15 BHRC 472, [2004] Crim LR 574, (2004) 101(4) LSG 30, (2004) 148 SJLB 25, HL	8.12, 8.13, 8.16
Attorney General's Reference (Nos 7 and 8 of 2013), Re; sub nom R v Kallakis (Achilleas Michalis); R v Williams (Alexander Martin); R v Levene (Nicholas David) [2013] EWCA Crim 709, [2014] 1 Cr App R (S) 26, [2013] Lloyd's Rep FC 417, [2013] Crim LR 776, CA	2.2, 3.67, 9.8, 9.13
Attorney General's Reference (Nos 88, 89, 90 and 91 of 2006), Re; sub nom R v Meehan (Brian John); R v McCallister (Gerard Martin); R v Sangha (Bhovinder Singh); R v Burch (David William) [2006] EWCA Crim 3254, [2007] 2 Cr App R (S) 28, CA	3.165
Augustus Barnett & Son Ltd, Re (1986) 2 BCC 98904, [1986] PCC 167, Ch D	1.29

B

Barker v Wingo (1972) 407 US 514	8.15
Barlow Clowes Gilt Managers Ltd, Re [1992] Ch 208, [1992] 2 WLR 36, [1991] 4 All ER 385, [1991] BCC 608, [1991] BCLC 750, (1991) 141 NLJ 999, [1991] NPC 73, Ch D	7.68
Bates v Chief Constable of Avon and Somerset [2009] EWHC 942 (Admin), (2009) 173 JP 313, [2009] Po LR 186, DC	4.12
Bell v DPP of Jamaica [1985] AC 937, [1985] 3 WLR 73, [1985] 2 All ER 585, [1985] Crim LR 738, (1985) 82 LSG 2161, (1985) 129 SJ 448, PC (Jam)	8.15

Table of Cases

Berry (Linton) v Queen, The [1992] 2 AC 364, [1992] 3 WLR 153, [1992] 3 All ER 881, (1993) 96 Cr App R 77, (1992) 89(27) LSG 34, (1992) 136 SJLB 183, PC (Jam).. 7.51
Bilta (UK) Ltd (In Liquidation) v Nazir; sub nom Jetivia SA v Bilta (UK) Ltd [2013] EWCA Civ 968, [2014] Ch 52, [2013] 3 WLR 1167, [2014] 1 All ER 168, [2014] 1 All ER (Comm) 176, [2014] 1 Lloyd's Rep 113, [2013] STC 2298, [2013] BCC 655, [2014] 1 BCLC 302, [2013] Lloyd's Rep FC 620, [2013] STI 2677, CA 3.247
Bond House Systems Limited v HMRC, *See* Optigen Ltd v HMRC (C-354/03)
Bowman v Fels [2005] EWCA Civ 226, [2005] 1 WLR 3083, [2005] 4 All ER 609, [2005] 2 Cr App R 19, [2005] 2 CMLR 23, [2005] 2 FLR 247, [2005] WTLR 481, [2005] Fam Law 546, (2005) 102(18) LSG 24, (2005) 155 NLJ 413, (2005) 149 SJLB 357, [2005] NPC 36, CA 3.301
Bristol & West Building Society v Mothew (t/a Stapley & Co) [1998] Ch 1, [1997] 2 WLR 436, [1996] 4 All ER 698, [1997] PNLR 11, (1998) 75 P & CR 241, [1996] EG 136 (CS), (1996) 146 NLJ 1273, (1996) 140 SJLB 206, [1996] NPC 126, CA.. 1.19

C

Chemists (A Firm) v HMRC [2009] UKFTT 66 (TC), [2009] STC (SCD) 472, Sp Comm 7.59
Chief Constable of Humberside Police v Information Commissioner [2009] EWCA Civ 1079, [2010] 1 WLR 1136, [2010] 3 All ER 611, [2009] Info TLR 123, (2009) 106(42) LSG 20, (2009) 153(40) SJLB 35, CA 5.12
Chief Constable of Merseyside v Owens [2012] EWHC 1515 (Admin), (2012) 176 JP 688, DC 4.24
Connelly v DPP [1964] AC 1254, [1964] 2 WLR 1145, [1964] 2 All ER 401, (1964) 48 Cr App R 183, (1964) 128 JP 418, (1964) 108 SJ 356, HL 8.2, 8.10
Crown Prosecution Service (Nottinghamshire) v Rose [2008] EWCA Crim 239, [2008] 1 WLR 2113, [2008] 3 All ER 315, [2008] 2 Cr App R 15, [2008] 2 Cr App R (S) 80, [2008] Lloyd's Rep FC 206, [2008] Crim LR 650, CA 3.276, 3.284
Customs and Excise Commissioners v Total Network SL [2008] UKHL 19, [2008] 1 AC 1174, [2008] 2 WLR 711, [2008] 2 All ER 413, [2008] STC 644, [2008] Lloyd's Rep FC 275, [2008] BPIR 699, [2008] BTC 5216, [2008] BVC 340, [2008] STI 938, (2008) 152(12) SJLB 29, HL 3.112

D

D v National Society for the Prevention of Cruelty to Children (NSPCC) [1978] AC 171, [1977] 2 WLR 201, [1977] 1 All ER 589, 76 LGR 5, (1977) 121 SJ 119, HL 7.64
DD Jewellers Ltd v HMRC [2013] UKFTT 462, TC 3.139
DPP of Mauritius v Bholah [2011] UKPC 44; [2012] 1 WLR 1737, [2012] Lloyd's Rep FC 406, PC (Maur)... 3.291
DPP v Agyemang [2009] EWHC 1542 (Admin), (2009) 173 JP 487, DC 8.22
DPP v Alexander [2010] EWHC 2266 (Admin), [2011] 1 WLR 653, (2010) 174 JP 519, [2011] RTR 8, [2010] ACD 98, DC 8.6
DPP v Gomez (Edwin) [1993] AC 442, [1992] 3 WLR 1067, [1993] 1 All ER 1, (1993) 96 Cr App R 359, (1993) 157 JP 1, [1993] Crim LR 304, (1993) 157 JPN 15, (1993) 137 SJLB 36, HL 1.3, 1.8

Table of Cases

DPP v Humphrys (Bruce Edward) [1977] AC 1, [1976] 2 WLR 857, [1976] 2 All ER 497, (1976) 63 Cr App R 95, [1976] RTR 339, [1977] Crim LR 421, (1976) 120 SJ 420, HL	8.6
Dare v Crown Prosecution Service [2012] EWHC 2074 (Admin), (2013) 177 JP 37, [2012] Lloyd's Rep FC 718, [2013] Crim LR 413, QBD	3.300
Director General of Fair Trading v Pioneer Concrete (UK) Ltd; sub nom Supply of Ready Mixed Concrete (No 2), Re [1995] 1 AC 456, [1994] 3 WLR 1249, [1995] 1 All ER 135, [1995] ICR 25, (1995) 92(1) LSG 37, (1995) 145 NLJ 17, [1995] 139 SJLB 14, HL	5.75
Dragon Futures Ltd v HMRC [2006] V & DR 348, [2007] STI 373, VDT	3.136, 5.75
Dyer v Watson [2002] UKPC D 1, [2004] 1 AC 379, [2002] 3 WLR 1488, [2002] 4 All ER 1, 2002 SC (PC) 89, 2002 SLT 229, 2002 SCCR 220, [2002] HRLR 21, [2002] UKHRR 542, 2002 GWD 5-153, PC (Scot)	8.12

E

Eckle v Germany (A/51) (1983) 5 EHRR 1, ECtHR	8.12
Edwards v United Kingdom (13071/87) (1993) 15 EHRR 417, ECJ	8.3
Entick v Carrington, 95 ER 807, (1765) 2 Wils KB 275, Ct of KB	4.1

F

Ferrel v Queen, The [2010] UKPC 20, [2011] 1 All ER 95, PC (Gribraltar)	3.306, 3.307
Fitt v United Kingdom (29777/96) (2000) 30 EHRR 480, [2000] Po LR 10, ECJ	7.63

G

Gerald Cooper Chemicals Ltd, Re [1978] Ch 262, [1978] 2 WLR 866, [1978] 2 All ER 49, (1977) 121 SJ 848, Ch D	1.29, 3.249
Gittins v Central Criminal Court [2011] EWHC 131 (Admin), [2011] Lloyd's Rep FC 219, QBD	4.42
Gough v Chief Constable of the West Midlands [2004] EWCA Civ 206, [2004] Po LR 164, (2004) 148 SJLB 298, CA	4.24
Greener Solutions Ltd v HMRC [2012] UKUT 18 (TCC), [2012] STC 1056, [2012] Lloyd's Rep FC 235, [2012] BVC 1551, TC	5.75

H

H v France (A/162) (1990) 12 EHRR 74, ECtHR	8.11
Halifax Plc v HMRC (C-255/02) [2006] Ch 387, [2006] 2 WLR 905, [2006] STC 919, [2006] ECR I-1609, [2006] 2 CMLR 36, [2006] CEC 690, [2006] BTC 5308, [2006] BVC 377, [2006] STI 501, ECJ	3.136
Hampshire Land Co (No 2), Re [1896] 2 Ch 743, Ch D	5.75
HM Advocate v R [2002] UKPC D 3, [2004] 1 AC 462, [2003] 2 WLR 317, 2003 SC (PC) 21, 2003 SLT 4, 2003 SCCR 19, [2003] UKHRR 1, 2002 GWD 39-1280, Pc (Scot)	8.13
Hogan v DPP [2007] EWHC 978 (Admin), [2007] 1 WLR 2944, (2008) 172 JP 57, (2008) 172 JPN 341, DC	3.210
Holt v Attorney General [2014] UKPC 4, [2014] 2 All ER 397, [2014] Lloyd's Rep FC 335, PC	3.279
House Systems Ltd v HMRC (C-484/03). *See* Optigen Ltd v HMRC (C-354/03)	

Table of Cases

I

Integral Resources (UK) Ltd v HMRC [2010] UKFTT 167, TC 3.136

J

Jasper v United Kingdom (27052/95) (2000) 30 EHRR 441, [2000] Po LR 25, [2000] Crim LR 586, ECJ.. 7.63
Jennings v Crown Prosecution Service [2008] UKHL 29, [2008] 1 AC 1046, [2008] 2 WLR 1148, [2008] 4 All ER 113, [2008] 2 Cr App R 29, [2008] Lloyd's Rep FC 421, (2008) 152(21) SJLB 29, HL 3.173
Jetivia SA v Bilta (UK) Ltd. *See* Bilta (UK) Ltd (In Liquidation) v Nazir

K

Kanaris v Governor of Pentonville Prison [2003] UKHL 2, [2003] 1 WLR 443, [2003] 1 All ER 593, [2003] 2 Cr App R 1, [2004] Crim LR 69, (2003) 147 SJLB 146, HL 6.5
Kittel v Belgium (C-439/04) [2008] STC 1537, [2006] ECR I-6161, [2008] BTC 5439, [2008] BVC 559, [2006] STI 1851, ECJ................. 3.136, 3.139, 5.75
Kuwait Airways Corp v Iraqi Airways Co (Disclosure: Fraud Exception) [2005] EWCA Civ 286, [2005] 1 WLR 2734, [2005] CP Rep 32, (2005) 102(21) LSG 33, (2005) 155 NLJ 468 CA 4.14

L

Laythoarp v Bryant, 132 ER 283, (1836) 2 Bing NC 735 .... 3.211
Lees v Solihull Magistrates' Court [2013] EWHC 3779 (Admin), [2014] Lloyd's Rep FC 233, DC 4.2
Livewire Telecom Ltd v HMRC [2009] EWHC 15 (Ch), [2009] STC 643, [2009] BTC 5173, [2009] BVC 172, [2009] STI 190, Ch D 3.136, 3.139, 5.75

M

Maidstone Building Provisions, Re [1971] 1 WLR 1085, [1971] 3 All ER 363, (1971) 115 SJ 464, Ch D... 1.29, 3.252
Marcel v Commissioner of Police of the Metropolis [1992] Ch 225, [1992] 2 WLR 50, [1992] 1 All ER 72, (1992) 4 Admin LR 309, (1991) 141 NLJ 1224, (1991) 135 SJLB 125, CA 4.24, 4.41
Matto v Wolverhampton Crown Court [1987] RTR 337, [1987] Crim LR 641, DC 4.27
Mawji v Queen, The [1957] AC 126, [1957] 2 WLR 277, [1957] 1 All ER 385, (1957) 41 Cr App R 69, (1957) 101 SJ 146, PC (EA) 2.9
McGreevy v DPP [1973] 1 WLR 276, [1973] 1 All ER 503, [1972] NI 125, (1973) 57 Cr App R 424, [1973] Crim LR 232, (1973) 117 SJ 164, HL.... 3.286
McInnes (Paul) v HM Advocate [2010] UKSC 7; 2010 SC (UKSC) 28, 2010 SLT 266, 2010 SCL 462, 2010 SCCR 286, [2010] HRLR 17, [2010] UKHRR 287, 2010 GWD 8-136, SC.. 8.21
McNicholas Construction Co Ltd v HMRC [2000] STC 553, [2000] BTC 5225,[2000] BVC 255, [2000] STI 889, QBD... 5.75
Meridian Global Funds Management Asia Ltd v Securities Commission [1995] 2 AC 500, [1995] 3 WLR 413, [1995] 3 All ER 918, [1995] BCC 942, [1995] 2 BCLC 116, (1995) 92(28) LSG 39, (1995) 139 SJLB, PC (NZ).... 5.75
Mills (Kenneth Anthony) v HM Advocate (No 2) [2002] UKPC D 2, [2004] 1 AC 441, [2002] 3 WLR 1597, 2003 SC (PC) 1, 2002 SLT 939, 2002 SCCR 860, [2002] HRLR 44, [2002] UKHRR 1074, 13 BHRC 549, 2002 GWD 26-886, PC (Scot).. 8.11

Table of Cases

Mobilx Ltd (In Administration) v HMRC; Calltel Telecom Ltd v HMRC; HMRC v Blue Sphere Global Ltd [2010] EWCA Civ 517, [2010] STC 1436, [2010] Lloyd's Rep FC 445, [2010] BVC 638, [2010] STI 1589, CA 3.139, 5.75, 5.76

Morphitis v Bernasconi [2003] EWCA Civ 289, [2003] Ch 552, [2003] 2 WLR 1521, [2003] BCC 540, [2003] 2 BCLC 53, [2003] BPIR 973, (2003) 100(19) LSG 30, (2003) 147 SJLB. 300, CA 3.249

Morris v Bank of India [2005] EWCA Civ 693, [2005] BCC 739, [2005] 2 BCLC 328, [2005] BPIR 1067 CA 5.75

Mungroo v Queen, The [1991] 1 WLR 1351, (1992) 95 Cr App R 334, (1991) 135 SJLB 197, PC (Maur) 8.20

O

Optigen Ltd v HMRC (C-354/03); Fulcrum Electronics Ltd v HMRC (C-355/03); Bond House Systems Ltd v HMRC (C-484/03) [2006] Ch 218, [2006] 2 WLR 456, [2006] STC 419, [2006] ECR I-483, [2006] 2 CMLR 18, [2006] CEC 509, [2006] BTC 5050, [2006] BVC 119, [2006] STI 162, ECJ 3.136, 3.139, 5.75

Oxford v Moss (1979) 68 Cr App R 183, [1979] Crim LR 119, QBD 1.21

P

PG v United Kingdom (44787/98) (2008) 46 EHRR 51, [2001] Po LR 325, [2002] Crim LR 308, ECJ 7.63

Phillips v United Kingdom (41087/98) 11 BHRC 280, [2001] Crim LR 817, ECJ 3.169

POWA (Jersey) Ltd v HMRC [2012] UKUT 50 (TCC), [2012] STC 1476, [2012] BVC 1596, TC 3.136

R

R v Acton Crown Court, ex p Layton [1993] Crim LR 458, DC 4.11
R v Adams. *See* Adams v Queen
R v Ahmad (Shakeel) [2012] EWCA Crim 391, [2012] 1 WLR 2335, [2012] 2 All ER 1137, [2012] STC 1239, [2012] 2 Cr App R (S) 85, [2012] Lloyd's Rep FC 413, [2012] Crim LR 468, [2012] STI 546, CA 3.173
R v Akpom (Azu) [2013] EWCA Crim 2662, CA 1.27
R v Alibhai (Akbal) [2004] EWCA Crim 681, CA 7.47, 7.52
R v Allad and Umerji [2014] EWCA Crim 421, CA 3.110
R v Allen (Brian Roger) [2001] UKHL 45, [2002] 1 AC 509, [2001] 3 WLR 843, [2001] 4 All ER 768, [2001] STC 1537, [2002] 1 Cr App R 18, [2002] HRLR 4, 74 TC 263, [2001] BTC 421, 4 ITL Rep 140, [2001] STI 1348, HL 3.137
R v Anderson (William Ronald) [1986] AC 27, [1985] 3 WLR 268, [1985] 2 All ER 961, (1985) 81 Cr App R 253, [1985] Crim LR 651, HL 2.10
R v Anwar (Nasar) 2013] EWCA Crim 1865, CA 3.272, 3.274
R v Anwoir (Ilham) [2008] EWCA Crim 1354, [2009] 1 WLR 980, [2008] 4 All ER 582, [2008] 2 Cr App R 36, [2008] Lloyd's Rep FC 554, CA 3.288, 3.305
R v Aujla (Ajit Singh) [1998] 2 Cr App R 16, CA 8.22

Table of Cases

R v Bagnall (Darren John); R v Sharma (Nirmal Kumar) [2012] EWCA Crim 677, [2013] 1 WLR 204, [2012] Lloyd's Rep FC 614, CA 3.168, 3.169, 3.173
R v Bayliss (Roy Alfred) (1994) 98 Cr App R 235, (1993) 157 JP 1062, [1994] Crim LR 687, (1993) 157 JPN 522, CA 4.1
R v Beckford (Ian Anthony) [1996] 1 Cr App R 94, (1995) 159 JP 305, [1995] RTR 251, [1995] Crim LR 712, CA 8.2, 8.8
R v Bembridge, 99 ER 679, (1783) 22 St Tr 1, (1783) 3 Doug KB 327, Ct of KB 3.185
R v Bestel (Jean Pierre) [2013] EWCA Crim 1305, [2014] 1 WLR 457, [2013] 2 Cr App R 30, [2014] 1 Cr App R (S) 53, [2014] Crim LR 607, CA 3. 28
R v Birdi (Anita Kaur) [2014] EWCA Crim 780, CA 1.27
R v Boal (Francis Steven) [1992] QB 591, [1992] 2 WLR 890, [1992] 3 All ER 177, [1992] BCLC 872, (1992) 95 Cr App R 272, (1992) 156 JP 617, [1992] ICR 495, [1992] IRLR 420, (1992) 156 LG Rev 763, (1992) 136 SJLB 100, CA 1.33
R v Boness (Dean) [2005] EWCA Crim 2395, [2006] 1 Cr App. R (S) 120, (2005) 169 JP 621, [2006] Crim LR 160, [2006] ACD 5, (2005) 169 JPN 937, CA 9.38
R v Brady (Paul Clement) [2004] EWCA Crim 1763, [2004] 1 WLR 3240, [2004] 3 All ER 520, [2005] BCC 357, [2005] 1 Cr App R 5, [2004] BPIR 962, [2005] Crim LR 224, (2004) 101(29) LSG 29, (2004) 148 SJLB 1149, CA 8.22
R v Briggs-Price (Robert William) [2009] UKHL 19, [2009] 1 AC 1026, [2009] 2 WLR 1101, [2009] 4 All ER 594, [2009] HRLR 21, [2009] Lloyd's Rep FC 442, [2010] Crim LR 139, (2009) 153(18) SJLB 27, HL 3.169
R v Brown (Charles) [2014] EWCA Crim 695, CA 1.28
R v Brown (Toni) [2010] EWCA Crim 2832, [2011] 2 Cr App R (S) 11, CA ... 9.9
R v Bryant (Patrick) [2005] EWCA Crim 2079, CA 7.12
R v Buffrey (Paul Edward) (1993) 14 Cr App R (S) 511, [1993] Crim LR 319, CA 9.13
R v Burger (Craig) [2013] EWCA Crim 2601, CA 1.9
R v Butt (Asif Nazir) [2006] EWCA Crim 137, [2006] 2 Cr App R (S) 44, CA 3.234, 3.246
R v Buzalek [1991] Crim LR 115, [1991] Crim LR 116, CA 8.19
R v Cadman (Paul Martin) [2012] EWCA Crim 611, [2012] 2 Cr App R (S) 88, CA 9.42
R v Cairns (Alison Louise) [2002] EWCA Crim 2838, [2003] 1 WLR 796, [2003] 1 Cr App R 38, [2003] Crim LR 403, (2003) 100(3) LSG 31, CA.... 3.150
R v Caley (David) [2012] EWCA Crim 2821, [2013] 2 Cr App R (S) 47, (2013) 177 JP 111, [2013] Crim LR 342, CA 9.11, 9.12, 9.13
R v Castillo (German Esparcia) [2010] EWCA Crim 658, CA 3.166
R v Central Criminal Court, ex p Adegbesan [1986] 1 WLR 1292, [1986] 3 All ER 113, (1987) 84 Cr App R 219, [1986] Crim LR 691, (1986) SJ 821, QBD 4.10
R v Central Criminal Court, ex p AJD Holdings [1992] Crim LR 669, DC..... 4.9, 4.11
R v Central Criminal Court, ex p Francis & Francis (A Firm) [1988] 2 WLR 627, ~[1988] 1 All ER 677, (1988) 87 Cr App R 104, [1988] Crim LR 305, (1988) 138 NLJ Rep 14, DC 4.13, 4.14
R v Cheltenham Justices, ex p Secretary of State for Trade [1977] 1 WLR 95, [1977] 1 All ER 460, (1977) 121 SJ 70, DC 7.67

Table of Cases

R v Chief Constable of Lancashire, ex p Parker; R v Chief Constable of Lancashire, ex p McGrath [1993] QB 577, [1993] 2 WLR 428, [1993] 2 All ER 56, (1993) 97 Cr App R 90, [1992] COD 356, (1992) 89(20) LSG 36, (1992) 142 NLJ 635, (1992) 136 SJLB 136, QBD	4.9
R v Chief Constable of the West Midlands, ex p Wiley [1995] 1 AC 274, [1994] 3 WLR 433, [1994] 3 All ER 420, [1995] 1 Cr App R 342, [1994] COD 520, (1994) 91(40) LSG 35, (1994) 144 NLJ 1008, (1994) 138 SJLB 156, HL	7.64
R v Chief Constable of Warwickshire, ex p F [1999] 1 WLR 564, [1998] 1 All ER 65, [1998] Crim LR 290	4.9
R v Clarke (Martin Paul) [2007] EWCA Crim 2532, [2008] 1 Cr App R 33, CA	6.23, 6.24
R v Clowes (Peter) (No 1) [1992] 3 All ER 440, [1992] BCLC 1158, (1992) 95 Cr App R 440, CCA	7.68
R v Cole (Solomon) [2011] EWCA Crim 2993, CA	3.35
R v Cook [1997] CLR 436..	3.39
R v Cornelius (Benjamin Jason) [2012] EWCA Crim 500, [2012] Lloyd's Rep FC 435, [2012] PNLR 23, CA	1.12
R v Cox (Peter Nevill) (1982) 75 Cr App R 291, [1983] Crim LR 167, CA	1.29, 3.255
R v Cox and Railton (1884) 14 QBD 154..	4.14
R v Crocker (Ian) [2013] EWCA Crim 1176, CA	3.59
R v Crown Court at Snaresbrook, ex p DPP [1998] 1 All ER 315	4.14
R v Crown Court at Southwark, ex p HMRC [1990] 1 QB 250.......................	4.24
R v Crown Prosecution Service (Interlocutory application under sections 35/36 CPIA) [2005] EWCA Crim 2342, CA..	7.40
R v Da Silva (Hilda Gondwe) [2006] EWCA Crim 1654, [2007] 1 WLR 303, [2006] 4 All ER 900, [2006] 2 Cr App R 35, [2007] Crim LR 77, CA	3.278
R v Davis (Michael George) (No 1) [1993] 1 WLR 613, [1993] 2 All ER 643, (1993) 97 Cr App R 110, (1993) 137 SJLB 19, CA	7.63
R v Derby Crown Court, ex p. Brooks (1985) 80 Cr App R 164, [1985] Crim LR 754, (1984) 148 JPN 573, QBD...	8.4
R v Derby Magistrates Court, ex p B [1996] AC 487, [1995] 3 WLR 681, [1995] 4 All ER 526, [1996] 1 Cr App R 385, (1995) 159 JP 785, [1996] 1 FLR 513, [1996] Fam Law 210, (1995) 159 JPN 778, (1995) 145 NLJ 1575, (1995) 139 SJLB 219, HL..	7.47
R v Dimsey (Dermot Jeremy) (Appeals against Sentence) [2000] 2 All ER 142, [2000] 1 Cr App R (S) 497, [2000] Crim LR 199, CA	3.293
R v Director of Serious Fraud Office, ex p Saunders [1988] Crim L R 837.......	4.1
R v Director of the Serious Fraud Office, ex p Johnson (Malcolm Keith) [1993] COD 58, QBD...	4.43
R v Dixon (Sarah Jane) [2012] EWCA Crim 815, [2012] 2 Cr App R (S) 100, CA	3.186, 3.196
R v Dosanjh (Sandeep) [2013] EWCA Crim 2366, [2014] 1 WLR 1780, CA...	3.141, 3.175
R v Duru (Ignatius Chima) [1974] 1 WLR 2, [1973] 3 All ER 715, (1974) 58 Cr App R 151, [1973] Crim LR 701, (1973) 117 SJ 7, CA	1.3
R v Early (John) [2002] EWCA Crim 1904, [2003] 1 Cr App R 19, (2002) 99(39) LSG 38, CA..	3.150, 7.66

Table of Cases

R v Edwards (Stewart Dean); R v Gray (Rosalind; R v Enright (Kevin James); R v Smith (David Reginald); R v Smith (David Reginald); R v McLean (Michael); R v Rowlands (Tony) [2005] EWCA Crim 3244, [2006] 1 WLR 1524, [2006] 3 All ER 882, [2006] 2 Cr App R 4, [2006] Crim LR 531, (2006) 103(5) LSG 28, CA 8.22
R v Ellames (Charles John) [1974] 1 WLR 1391, [1974] 3 All ER 130, (1974) 60 Cr App R 7, [1974] Crim LR 554, (1974) 118 SJ 578, CA 1.23
R v Elwell (Harry) [2001] EWCA Crim 1320, CA 4.27
R v Epton (John Alan) [2009] EWCA Crim 515, [2009] 2 Cr App R (S) 96, CA 3.76
R v Fazal (Mohammed Yassen) [2009] EWCA Crim 1697, [2010] 1 WLR 694, [2010] 1 Cr App R 6, [2009] Lloyd's Rep FC 626, [2010] Crim LR 309, CA 3.295, 3.298
R v Flook (Robert Daniel) [2009] EWCA Crim 682, [2010] 1 Cr App R 30, [2010] Crim LR 148, CA 7.58
R v Flore (Ioana) [2014] EWCA Crim 465, CA... 1.27
R v Forrest (Nathan); R v Hogg (Michelle); R v Forrest (Elizabeth); R v Hogg (David James) [2014] EWCA Crim 308, CA 1.9, 1.14, 1.17
R v Gabriel (Janis) [2006] EWCA Crim 229, [2007] 1 WLR 2272, [2007] 2 Cr App R 11, [2006] Crim LR 852, CA 3.271, 3.272, 3.273, 3.277, 3.294
R v Geary (Michael) [2010] EWCA Crim 1925, [2011] 1 WLR 1634, [2011] 2 All ER 198, [2011] 1 Cr App R 8, [2010] Lloyd's Rep FC 599, [2011] Crim LR 321, (2010) 107(32) LSG 16, CA 3.296, 3.299
R v Ghosh (Deb Baran) [1982] QB 1053, [1982] 3 WLR 110, [1982] 2 All ER 689, (1982) 75 Cr App R 154, [1982] Crim LR 608, (1982) 126 SJ 429, CA 1.8
R v Gibbons [1997] 2 NZLR 585 .... 8.12
R v Gill (Sewa Singh) [2003] EWCA Crim 2256, [2004] 1 WLR 469, [2003] 4 All ER 681, [2003] STC 1229, [2004] 1 Cr App R 20, [2003] BTC 404, [2003] Crim LR 883, [2003] STI 1421, (2003) 100(37) LSG 31, (2003) 147 SJLB 993, CA 4.1
R v Gillies (Ryan) [2011] EWCA Crim 2140, [2011] Lloyd's Rep FC 606, CA 3.288, 3.289, 3.290
R v Goodenough (Alan John) [2004] EWCA Crim 2260, [2005] 1 Cr App R (S) 88, [2005] Crim LR 71, CA 3.169
R v Governor of Pentonville Prison, ex p Osman (No 1) [1990] 1 WLR 277, [1989] 3 All ER 701, (1990) 90 Cr App R 281, [1988] Crim LR 611, (1990) 87(7) LSG 32, (1990) 134 SJ 458, QBD 4.14
R v Gray (David John) [1995] 2 Cr App R 100, [1995] Crim LR 45, (1994) 91(39) LSG 38, (1994) 138 SJLB 199, CA 3.243
R v Greaves (Claude Clifford) [2010] EWCA Crim 709, [2011] 1 Cr App R (S) 8; [2010] Lloyd's Rep. FC 423, [2010] Crim LR 650, CA................... 3.75, 3.86, 3.89, 3.308
R v Griffiths (Douglas Anthony) [1966] 1 QB 589, [1965] 3 WLR 405, [1965] 2 All ER 448, (1965) 49 Cr App R 279, (1965) 129 JP 380, (1965) 109 SJ 312, CCA 2.13
R v Guildhall Magistrates Court, ex p Primlaks Holdings Co (Panama) Inc [1990] 1 QB 261, [1989] 2 WLR 841, (1989) 89 Cr App R 215, [1989] Crim LR 448, [1989] COD 359, (1989) 133 SJ 628, DC 4.12

Table of Cases

R v H (Interlocutory Application: Disclosure) [2007] UKHL 7, [2007] 2 AC
  270, [2007] 2 WLR 364, [2007] 3 All ER 269, [2007] 2 Cr App R 6,
  [2007] Crim LR 731, (2007) 151 SJLB 332, HL 6.15, 6.17
R v H; R v C [2004] UKHL 3, [2004] 2 AC 134, [2004] 2 WLR 335, [2004]
  1 All ER 1269, [2004] 2 Cr App R 10, [2004] HRLR 20, 16 BHRC 332,
  (2004) 101(8) LSG 29, (2004) 148 SJLB 183, HL 3.143, 7.2, 7.40,
  7.59, 7.63
R v Halai [1983] Crim LR 624, CA 1.3
R v Hancox (Dennis) [2010] EWCA Crim 102, [2010] 1 WLR 1434, [2010]
  4 All ER 537, [2010] 2 Cr App R (S) 74, [2010] Lloyd's Rep FC 307,
  [2010] Crim LR 431, CA 9.38
R v Hashash (Amiram) [2006] EWCA Crim 2518, [2008] STC 1158, [2008]
  BTC 5173, [2008] BVC 298, [2006] STI 2455, CA 3.136, 3.139
R v Hinks (Karen Maria) [2001] 2 AC 241, [2000] 3 WLR 1590, [2000] 4 All
  ER 833, [2001] 1 Cr App R 18, (2001) 165 JP 21, [2001] Crim LR 162,
  (2000) 97(43) LSG 37, (2000) 144 SJLB 265, HL 1.8
R v Hollinshead (Peter Gordon) [1985] AC 975, [1985] 3 WLR 159, [1985]
  2 All ER 769, (1985) 81 Cr App R 365, [1985] Crim LR 653, (1985) 82
  LSG 2739, (1985) 135 NLJ 631, (1985) 129 SJ 447, HL 1.27
R v Hulbert (Peter) [2014] EWCA Crim 712, CA 1.9
R v Hunt (Michael John) [1995] STC 819, (1995) 16 Cr App R (S) 87, 68 TC
  132, [1994] Crim LR 747, CA 3.163
R v I [2009] EWCA Crim 1793, [2010] 1 WLR 1125, [2010] 1 Cr App R 10,
  [2010] Crim LR 312, CA 6.4, 6.8,
  6.12
R v Ike (Peace Nnenna) [1996] STC 391, [1996] Crim LR 515, CA 3.140
R v Inman [1967] 1 QB 140, [1966] 3 WLR 567, [1966] 3 All ER 414, (1966)
  50 Cr App R 247, (1966) 130 JP 415, (1966) 110 SJ 424, Ct of Cr App 3.247
R v Inner London Crown Court, ex p Baines & Baines (A Firm) [1988] QB
  579, [1988] 2 WLR 549, [1987] 3 All ER 1025, (1988) 87 Cr App R 111,
  [1988] Crim LR 50, (1987) 137 N.J 945, (1988) 132 SJ 418, DC 4.10, 4.12
R v James (Michael) [2011] EWCA Crim 2991, [2012] 1 WLR 2641, [2012]
  2 Cr App R (S) 44, [2012] Lloyd's Rep FC 168, [2012] Crim LR 307,
  CA 3.173
R v Jefferies (William Charles) [1969] 1 QB 120, [1968] 3 WLR 830, [1968]
  3 All ER 238, (1968) 52 Cr App R 654, [1968] Crim LR 497, (1968) 112
  SJ 783, CA 6.2
R v Jones (James) [2010] EWCA Crim 925, [2010] 3 All ER 1186, [2010] 2
  Cr App R 10, CA 4.27
R v JW [2013] NICA 6, Ca (NI) 8.18
R v K [2006] EWCA Crim 724; [2006] 2 All ER 552 (Note), [2006] Crim LR
  1012, (2006) 103(16) LSG 24, CA 7.34
R v K [2007] EWCA Crim 491, [2007] 1 WLR 2262, [2008] STC 1270, [2007]
  2 Cr App R 10, [2007] WTLR 817, [2007] Crim LR 645, [2007] STI 1771,
  (2007) 151 SJLB 399, CA 3.273
R v Kausar (Rahila) [2009] EWCA Crim 2242, [2010] Lloyd's Rep FC 353,
  CA 3.211, 3.303
R v Keane (Stephen John) [1994] 1 WLR 746, [1994] 2 All ER 478, (1994) 99
  Cr App R 1, [1995] Crim LR 225, (1994) 144 NLJ 391, (1994) 138 SJLB
  75, CA 7.4

Table of Cases

R v Kemp (Peter David Glanville) [1988] QB 645, [1988] 2 WLR 975, (1988) 4 BCC 203, [1988] BCLC 217, [1988] PCC 405, (1988) 87 Cr App R 95, (1988) 152 JP 461, [1988] Crim LR 376, (1988) 152 JPN 538, (1988) 132 SJ 461, CA 1.29, 3.256

R v Khan (Sultan [1997] AC 558, [1996] 3 WLR 162, [1996] 3 All ER 289, [1996] 2 Cr App R 440, [1996] Crim LR 733, (1996) 93(28) LSG 29, (1996) 146 NLJ 1024, (1996) 140 SJLB 166, HL 4.27

R v King (Hugo Allen) [1992] QB 20, [1991] 3 WLR 246, [1991] 3 All ER 705, (1991) 93 Cr App R 259, [1991] Crim LR 906, (1991) 141 NLJ 1071, (1991) 135 SJLB 76, CA 1.3

R v L [2007] EWCA Crim 764, CA 7.34

R v Lancaster (Paul) [2010] EWCA Crim 370, [2010] 1 WLR 2558, [2010] 3 All ER 402, [2010] 2 Cr App R 7, [2010] HLR 40, [2010] Crim LR 776, CA 3.33

R v Laverty (Charles) [1970] 3 All ER 432, (1970) 54 Cr App R 495, [1971] RTR 124, CA 3.34

R v Lee (Paul) [2013] EWCA Crim 657, [2013] Lloyd's Rep FC 453, CA 3.173, 3.174

R v Lindsay, 18 May 2005, Blackfriars Crown Court, Indictment No T2004–7470 .... 3.147

R v Linegar (Scott Anthony) [2009] EWCA Crim 648, CA 3.197, 3.205, 3.206

R v Looseley (Grant Spencer) [2001] UKHL 53, [2001] 1 WLR 2060, [2001] 4 All ER 897, [2002] 1 Cr App R 29, [2002] HRLR 8, [2002] UKHRR 333, [2002] Crim LR 301, (2001) 98(45) LSG 25, (2001) 145 SJLB 245, HL .. 4.27

R v Louizou and Others [2004] EWCA 1579 .... 3.277

R v Maguire (Anne Rita) [1992] QB 936, [1992] 2 WLR 767, [1992] 2 All ER 433, (1992) 94 Cr App R 133, CA 7.51

R v Maguire (Martin Peter); R v Heffernan (John Stephen) [2009] EWCA Crim 462, CA 8.22

R v Mahmood (Shaukat) [2013] EWCA Crim 325, [2013] 1 WLR 3146, CA .. 3.174

R v Majid (Taher) [2012] EWCA Crim 1023, CA 3.170

R v Manchester Crown Court, ex p Rogers [1999] 1 WLR 832, [1999] 4 All ER 35, [1999] 2 Cr App R 267, [1999] Crim LR 743, (1999) 96(10) LSG 31, QBD 4.13

R v Manjdadria [1993] Crim LR 73, CA 1.3

R v Marshall (Roy) (1990) 90 Cr App R 73, CA 3.193, 3.201

R v Martin (Alan) [1998] AC 917, [1998] 2 WLR 1, [1998] 1 All ER 193, [1998] 1 Cr App R 347, (1998) 95(3) LSG 24, (1998) 148 NLJ 50, (1998) 142 SJLB 44, HL 8.5, 8.9

R v Mavji (Ramniklal Nathoo) [1987] 1 WLR 1388, [1987] 2 All ER 758, [1986] STC 508, (1987) 84 Cr App R 34, [1987] Crim LR 39, (1987) 131 SJ 1121, CA 3.137

R v May (Raymond George) [2008] UKHL 28, [2008] 1 AC 1028, [2008] 2 WLR 1131, [2008] 4 All ER 97, [2009] STC 852, [2008] 2 Cr App R 28, [2009] 1 Cr App R (S) 31, [2008] Lloyd's Rep FC 453, [2008] Crim LR 737, (2008) 105(21) LSG 21, (2008) 158 NLJ 750, (2008) 152(21) SJLB 29, HL 3.173

R v Maybery (John) [2003] EWCA Crim 782, CA 8.18

R v Mayers (Jordan) [2008] EWCA Crim 2989, [2009] 1 WLR 1915, [2009] 2 All ER 145, [2009] 1 Cr App R 30, [2009] Crim LR 272, CA 3.76

Table of Cases

R v McCrae (John) [2012] EWCA Crim 976, [2013] 1 Cr App R (S) 1, CA..... 3.248, 3.260
R v McIntosh (Leroy Samuel) [2011] EWCA Crim 1501, [2011] 4 All ER 917, [2011] STC 2349, [2012] 1 Cr App R (S) 60, [2011] Lloyd's Rep FC 577, [2011] Crim LR 814, [2011] STI 1940, CA 3.174
R v McQuoid (Christopher) [2009] EWCA Crim 1301, [2009] 4 All ER 388, [2010] 1 Cr App R (S) 43, [2009] Lloyd's Rep FC 529, [2009] Crim LR 749, CA 3.215, 3.237, 3.246
R v Mee (Jason David) [2004] EWCA Crim 629, [2004] 2 Cr App R (S) 81, [2004] Crim LR 487, (2004) 148 SJLB 267, CA 9.38
R v Miles [1992] Crim LR 657, CA 1.29, 3.251
R v Millard (Ray) (1994) 15 Cr App R (S) 445, [1994] Crim LR 146, CA 9.42
R v Mitchell [1993] Crim LR 788, CA.. 1.3
R v MK [2009] EWCA Crim 952, CA 3.289
R v Moore (Mia) [2013] EWCA Crim 85, [2014] Crim LR 364, CA............... 4.27
R v Morrisey (Ian Patrick) [1997] 2 Cr App R 426, [1997] Crim LR 825, (1997) 94(21) LSG 32, (1997) 141 SJLB 106, CA 3.223
R v Munteanu (Leonard) [2012] EWCA Crim 2221, [2013] 1 Cr App R (S) 107, [2013] Crim LR 84, CA 1.27
R v Napoli (John Francis) [2012] EWCA Crim 1129, [2012] Lloyd's Rep FC 599, CA 3.74, 3.78, 3.79
R v Ngyuen [2008] EWCA Crim 585, [2008] 2 Cr App R 9, [2008] Crim LR 547,CA 8.22
R v NT [2010] EWCA Crim 711, [2010] 1 WLR 2655, [2010] 4 All ER 545, [2010] 2 Cr App R 12, [2010] Crim LR 711, CA 6.6, 6.26
R v O [2007] EWCA Crim 3483, CA... 3.153
R v O [2010] EWCA Crim 2233, [2011] 1 WLR 2936, [2011] 2 All ER 656, [2011] 2 Cr App R 33, (2010) 174 JP 529, [2011] Crim LR 403, CA.... 3.31, 3.33
R v O'Farrell (Sean Paul) [2014] EWCA Crim 170, CA 1.9
R v Okafor (Stephen) [1994] 3 All ER 741, (1994) 99 Cr App R 97, [1994] Crim LR 221, (1993) 137 SJLB 244, CA 4.1
R v Olu (Nicholas Andreas) [2010] EWCA Crim 2975, [2011] 1 Cr App R 33, (2011) 175 JP 1, CA... 7.42
R v P (Telephone Intercepts: Admissibility of Evidence), Times, 23 May 2000... 8.22
R v P [2007] EWCA Crim 2290; [2008] 2 All ER 684, [2008] 2 Cr App R (S) 5, [2008] Crim LR 147, (2007) 151 SJLB 1438, CA 9.9
R v Pace (Martin Edward) [2014] EWCA Crim 186, [2014] 1 Cr App R 34, (2014) 178 JP 133, [2014] Lloyd's Rep FC 319, CA 3.280, 3.281, 3.282, 3.285
R v Patel [2002] Crim LR 304, CA 7.66
R v Pennock (Angela) [2014] EWCA Crim 598; [2014] 2 Cr App R 10, CA.. 1.9, 1.19
R v Petkova (Perunika Todorova) [2011] EWCA Crim 109, CA 3.61
R v Philippou (Christakis) (1989) 5 BCC 665, (1989) 89 Cr App R 290, [1989] Crim LR 585, [1989] Crim LR 559, CA... 3.257
R v Preddy (John Crawford) [1996] AC 815, [1996] 3 WLR 255, [1996] 3 All ER 481, [1996] 2 Cr App R 524, (1996) 160 JP 677, [1996] Crim LR 726, (1996) 160 JPN 936, (1996) 93(31) LSG 29, (1996) 146 NLJ 1057, (1996) 140 SJLB 184, HL 1.3, 3.19, 3.30, 3.36, 3.37, 3.39
R v Randhawa (Jagprit) [2012] EWCA Crim 1, [2012] STC 901, [2012] 2 Cr App R (S) 53, [2012] Lloyd's Rep FC 283, [2012] STI 140, CA............... 3.167

xxxvii

Table of Cases

R v Ravjani (Dilawar) [2012] EWCA Crim 2519, CA 3.185
R v Reading Justices, ex p Berkshire CC [1996] 1 Cr App R 239, [1996] 1 FLR 149, [1996] 2 FCR 535, [1996] Crim LR 347, [1995] COD 385, [1996] Fam Law 84, DC 7.47
R v Redford (David) [1988] STC 845, (1989) 89 Cr App R 1, [1989] Crim LR 152, CA 3.137
R v Rezvi (Syed) [2002] UKHL 1, [2003] 1 AC 1099, [2002] 2 WLR 235, [2002] 1 All ER 801, [2002] 2 Cr App R 2, [2002] 2 Cr App R (S) 70, [2002] HRLR 19, [2002] UKHRR 374, [2002] Crim LR 335, (2002) 99(10) LSG 29, (2002) 146 SJLB 37, HL 3.169
R v Rochford (Gavin) [2010] EWCA Crim 1928, [2011] 1 WLR 534, [2011] 1 Cr App R 11, CA 7.11
R v Rollins (Neil) [2010] UKSC 39, [2010] 1 WLR 1922, [2010] 4 All ER 880, [2010] Bus LR 1529, [2011] 1 Cr App R 4, [2010] Lloyd's Rep FC 585, (2010) 154(30) SJLB 34, SC 3.295
R v Rollins (Neil) [2011] EWCA Crim 1825, [2012] 1 Cr App R (S) 64, [2011] Crim LR 896, CA 3.246
R v Rossouw [2006] EWCA Crim 2980 .... 7.65
R v S (Stephen Paul) [2006] EWCA Crim 756, [2006] 2 Cr App R 23, (2006) 170 JP 434, [2007] Crim LR 296, (2006) 170 JPN 760, CA 8.17
R v Saik (Abdulrahman) [2006] UKHL 18, [2007] 1 AC 18, [2006] 2 WLR 993, [2006] 4 All ER 866, [2006] 2 Cr App R 26, [2006] Crim LR 998, (2006) 103(20) LSG 24, (2006) 150 SJLB 603, HL 2.10, 3.283
R v Saleh (Aziz) [2012] EWCA Crim 484, CA 3.286
R v Sanders, unreported, 13 February 2012, Southwark Crown Court 3.229
R v Sang (Leonard Anthony) [1980] AC 402, [1979] 3 WLR 263, [1979] 2 All ER 1222, (1979) 69 Cr App R 282, [1979] Crim LR 655, HL 4.27
R v Smith (Wallace Duncan) (No 1) [1996] 2 BCLC 109, [1996] 2 Cr App R 1, [1996] Crim LR 329, (1995) 92(44) LSG 31, (1996) 140 SJLB 11, CA.... 3.255
R v South Western Magistrates Court, ex p Cofie [1997] 1 WLR 885, (1997) 161 JP 69, (1996) 160 JPN 1046, DC 4.10
R v Starmer (Richard Gordon) [2010] EWCA Crim 1, CA 3.272
R v Stratford Justices, ex p Imbert [1999] 2 Cr App R 276, (1999) 163 JP 693, (1999) 163 JPN 771, QBD 8.3
R v Takkar (Harjit Singh) [2011] EWCA Crim 646, [2011] 1 WLR 3062, [2011] 3 All ER 340, [2011] Lloyd's Rep FC 361, [2011] STI 737, CA ... 3.106
R v Tarcuta (Ionut Alexandra) [2014] EWCA Crim 823, CA 1.27
R v Tirado (Emilio) (1974) 59 Cr App R 80, CA 3.34
R v Turner (Paul David) [1995] 1 WLR 264, [1995] 3 All ER 432, [1995] 2 Cr App R 94, CA 7.66
R v Twaites (Jacqueline Anne) (1991) 92 Cr App R 106, [1990] Crim LR 863, CA 4.1
R v Uddin, Ali, Baig, Chandoo, Golechha, 25 May 2005, Southwark Crown Court, T2002–7012, T2002–7222, T2002–7507 .... 3.149, 3.157
R v Vocaturo, Brown, Drewery, Roden, Saunders, Edwards-Sayer, Sharma and Pathak (Indictment No T2002/7170) Nottingham Crown Court 3.153
R v W [2008] EWCA Crim 2, [2009] 1 WLR 965, [2008] 3 All ER 533, [2008] Lloyd's Rep FC 163, [2008] Crim LR 900, CA 3.290
R v Waqanika (Joeli) [2014] EWCA Crim 902, CA 1.20

Table of Cases

R v Ward (Judith Theresa) [1993] 1 WLR 619, [1993] 2 All ER 577, (1993) 96
  Cr App R 1, [1993] Crim LR 312, (1992) 89(27) LSG 34, (1992) 142 NLJ
  859, (1992) 136 SJLB 191, CA 7.4, 7.49
R v Ward (Noel) [2005] EWCA Crim 1972, CA 3.7, 3.40
R v Ward (Roger) [2003] EWCA Crim 814, [2003] 2 Cr App R 20, (2003) 147
  SJLB 384, CA 6.20
R v Weerdesteyn (Gerritt Johannes) [1995] 1 Cr App R 405, [1995] Crim LR
  239, CA 4.1
R v Wharam and others indictment number T2004-0685 .... 3.148
R v White (Anthony Alan) [2014] EWCA Crim 714; [2014] 2 Cr App R 14,
  (2014) 158(17) SJLB 37, CA 1.9, 3. 26, 3. 30
R v White (Anthony) [2011] EWCA Crim 2280, [2012] 1 Cr App R (S) 100,
  CA 3.60
R v William (Venus Rose) [2013] EWCA Crim 1262, CA 3.267, 3.293
R v Wilmot (Tomas George) [2012] EWCA Crim 1424, [2013] 1 Cr App R (S)
  61, CA 3. 81, 3.85
R v Wooley (Raymond) [2003] EWCA Crim 3458, CA 3.164
R v Woollin (Stephen Leslie) [1999] 1 AC 82, [1998] 3 WLR 382, [1998] 4 All
  ER 103, [1999] 1 Cr App R 8, [1998] Crim LR 890, (1998) 95(34) LSG
  32, (1998) 148 NLJ 1178, (1998) 142 SJLB 248, (1998) 142 SJLB 230,
  HL 1.10, 1.14
R v Wright (Brian) [2008] EWCA Crim 3207, [2009] 2 Cr App R (S) 45;
  [2009] Lloyd's Rep FC 256, [2009] Crim LR 373, CA 9.34
R v Wright (Robert) [2014] EWCA Crim 382, CA 1.14
R v Y; R v ZSB; sub nom R v YDG [2012] EWCA Crim 2437, [2013] 1 WLR
  2014, [2013] 2 All ER 121, [2013] 1 Cr App R 21, [2013] Crim LR 415,
  CA 6.9
R v Yates (Nicholas John) [2010] EWCA Crim 1028, [2011] 1 Cr App R (S) 15,
  CA 3.15, 3.61
R v Zinga (Munaf Ahmed) [2012] EWCA Crim 2357, [2013] Lloyd's Rep
  FC 102, [2013] Crim LR 226, CA 4.11
R (on the application of AB) v Huddersfield Magistrates' Court [2014] EWHC
  1089 (Admin), (2014) 178 JP 265, QBD 4.3, 4.11
R (on the application of Amand) v HMRC [2013] Lloyd's Rep FC 278, DC 4.11,
                                                                                                            4.42
R (on the application of Bhatti) v Croydon Magistrates' Court [2010] EWHC
  522 (Admin), [2011] 1 WLR 948, [2010] 3 All ER 671, (2010) 174 JP
  213, [2010] Lloyd's Rep FC 522, DC 4.9
R (on the application of Dulai) v Chelmsford Magistrates' Court; R (on the
  application of Essex CC) v Chelmsford Crown Court [2012] EWHC 1055
  (Admin), [2013] 1 WLR 220, [2012] 3 All ER 764, [2012] 2 Cr App R 19,
  [2013] Crim LR 86, [2012] ACD 76, DC 4.11
R (on the application of Energy Financing Team Ltd) v Bow Street Magistrates
  Court [2005] EWHC 1626 (Admin), [2006] 1 WLR 1316, [2005] 4 All ER
  285, [2006] ACD 8, DC 4.42, 4.43
R (on the application of G) v Commissioner of Police of the Metropolis [2011]
  EWHC 3331 (Admin), DC 4.2
R (on the application of Glenn & Co (Essex) Ltd) v HMRC [2011] EWHC
  2998 (Admin), [2012] 1 Cr App R 22, (2012) 176 JP 65, [2012] Lloyd's
  Rep FC 115, [2012] Crim LR 464, [2012] ACD 5, DC 4.2

Table of Cases

R (on the application of Global Cash & Carry Ltd) v Birmingham Magistrates
  Court [2013] EWHC 528 (admin), [2013] ACD 48, DC 4.2
R (on the application of Golfrate Property Management Ltd) v Southwark
  Crown Court [2014] EWHC 840 (Admin), [2014] 2 Cr App R 12, [2014]
  Lloyd's Rep FC 431, QBD.. 4.3, 4.7, 4.8
R (on the application of Hallinan Blackburn-Gittings & Nott (A Firm)) v
  Middlesex Guildhall Crown Court [2004] EWHC 2726 (Admin), [2005]
  1 WLR 766, DC 4.14
R (on the application of Hicks) v Commissioner of Police of the Metropolis
  [2012] EWHC 1947 (Admin), [2012] ACD 102, DC.................................. 4.11
R (on the application of Hoque) v City of London Magistrates' Court [2013]
  EWHC 725 (Admin), [2013] ACD 67, DC.. 4.2, 4.11
R (on the application of Horne) v Central Criminal Court [2012] EWHC 1350
  (Admin), [2012] 1 WLR 3152, [2012] Lloyd's Rep FC 546, QBD........ 4.34, 4.42
R (on the application of Miller Gardner Solicitors) v Minshull Street Crown
  Court [2002] EWHC 3077, QBD... 4.13
R (on the application of Paul Da Costa & Co) v Thames Magistrates Court
  [2002] EWHC 40 (Admin), [2002] STC 267, [2002] BTC 5605, [2003]
  BVC 3, [2002] Po LR 14, [2002] Crim LR 504, [2002] STI 112, (2002)
  152 NLJ 141, DC 4.11
R (on the application of Power-Hynes) v Norwich Magistrates' Court [2009]
  EWHC 1512 (Admin), (2009) 173 JP 573, [2009] Lloyd's Rep FC 619,
  [2009] Po LR 264, DC 4.9, 4.12, 4.42
R (on the application of Rawlinson and Hunter Trustees SA) v Central Criminal
  Court (Costs); R (on the application of Tchenguiz) v Serious Fraud Office
  (Costs) [2012] EWHC 3218 (Admin), [2013] 1 Costs LR 122, [2013]
  Lloyd's Rep FC 176, DC 4.2, 4.45
R (on the application of Redknapp) v Commissioner of the City of London
  Police [2008] EWHC 1177 (Admin), [2009] 1 WLR 2091, [2008] 1 All
  ER 229, (2008) 172 JP 388, [2008] Lloyd's Rep FC 466, [2008] Po LR
  106, (2008) 172 JPN 548, (2008) 105(24) LSG 24, (2008) 158 NLJ 861,
  DC 4.2
R (on the application of S) v Chief Constable of the British Transport Police
  [2013] EWHC 2189 (Admin), [2014] 1 WLR 1647, [2014] 1 All ER 268,
  (2014) 178 JP 221, [2014] ACD 19, QBD.. 4.5
R (on the application of Stratton) v Chief Constable of Thames Valley [2013]
  EWHC 1561 (Admin), [2013] ACD 110, QBD.. 5.13
R (on the application of T) v Chief Constable of Greater Manchester [2014]
  UKSC 35, [2014] 3 WLR 96, SC.. 5.12
R (on the application of Thompson) v Metropolitan Police [1997] 1 WLR
  1519, QBD 5.9
R (on the application of Uberoi) v Westminster Magistrates' Court [2008]
  EWHC 3191 (Admin); [2009] 1 WLR 1905, [2009] Bus LR 1544, [2009]
  Lloyd's Rep FC 152, [2009] Crim LR 445, DC 3.216, 3.246
R (on the application of Van der Pijl) v Kingston Crown Court [2012] EWHC
  3745 (Admin), [2013] 1 WLR 2706, [2013] Lloyd's Rep FC 287, [2013]
  ACD 29, DC.. 4.5, 4.11, 4.42
R (on the application of Vuciterni) v Brent Magistrates' Court [2012] EWHC
  2140 (Admin), (2012) 176 JP 705, [2012] CTLC 171, [2012] ACD 113,
  DC 4.11

Table of Cases

R (on the application of Wilkinson) v DPP [2006] EWHC 3012 (Admin) 3.285
R (on the application of Wood) v North Avon Magistrates' Court [2009] EWHC
    3614 (Admin), (2010) 174 JP 157, DC.. 4.2

S

Sarflax Ltd, Re [1979] Ch 592, [1979] 2 WLR 202, [1979] 1 All ER 529,
    (1979) 123 SJ 97, Ch D.. 3.249
Saunders v Soper [1975] AC 239, [1974] 3 WLR 777, [1974] 3 All ER 1025,
    (1974) 118 SJ 863, HL... 3.211
SCF Finance Co Ltd v Masri (No 2) [1987] QB 1002, [1987] 2 WLR 58, [1987]
    1 All ER 175, [1986] 2 Lloyd's Rep 366, [1986] Fin LR 309, (1987) 84
    LSG 492, (1987) 131 SJ 74, CA.. 3.79
Serious Organised Crime Agency v Gale [2011] UKSC 49, [2011] 1 WLR
    2760, [2012] 2 All ER 1, [2012] 1 Costs LR 21, [2012] HRLR 5, [2012]
    Lloyd's Rep FC 1, (2011) 155(41) SJLB 31, SC.. 3.169
Serious Organised Crime Agency v Pelekanos [2009] EWHC 2307 (QB),
    [2010] Lloyd's Rep FC 177, (2009) 106(40) LSG 20, QBD....................... 3.62
Serious Organised Crime Agency v Perry [2012] UKSC 35, [2013] 1 AC 182,
    [2012] 3 WLR 379, [2012] 4 All ER 795, [2012] 5 Costs LO 668, [2013]
    1 Cr App R 6, [2013] Lloyd's Rep FC 59;, SC... 4.35
Sevenoaks Stationers (Retail) Ltd, Re [1991] Ch 164, [1990] 3 WLR 1165,
    [1991] 3 All ER 578, [1990] BCC 765, [1991] BCLC 325, (1990) 134 SJ
    1367, CA... 9.42
Shah v HSBC Private Bank (UK) Ltd [2012] EWHC 1283 (QB), [2013] 1 All ER
    (Comm) 72, [2012] Lloyd's Rep FC 507, [2013] Bus LR D38, QBD 3.278
Spiers v Ruddy [2007] UKPC D2, [2008] 1 AC 873, [2008] 2 WLR 608, 2009
    SC (PC) 1, 2008 SLT 39, 2008 SCL 424, 2008 SCCR 131, [2008] HRLR
    14, 26 BHRC 567, 2007 GWD 40-700, PC (Scot) 8.13, 8.21
Spreadex Ltd v Battu [2005] EWCA Civ 855, CA.. 3.232
Stanford International Bank Ltd (In Receivership), Re [2010] EWCA Civ 137,
    [2011] Ch 33, [2010] 3 WLR 941, [2010] Bus LR 1270, [2011] BCC 211,
    [2010] Lloyd's Rep FC 357, [2010] BPIR 679, CA 4.11
Stogmuller v Austria (A/9) (1979-80) 1 EHRR 155, ECtHR 8.11
Stone & Rolls Ltd (In Liquidation) v Moore Stephens (A Firm) [2009] UKHL
    39, [2009] 1 AC 1391, [2009] 3 WLR 455, [2009] 4 All ER 431, [2010]
    1 All ER (Comm) 125, [2009] Bus LR 1356, [2009] 2 Lloyd's Rep 537,
    [2009] 2 BCLC 563, [2009] 2 CLC 121, [2009] Lloyd's Rep FC 557,
    [2009] BPIR 1191, [2009] PNLR 36, (2009) 159 NLJ 1218, (2009)
    153(31) SJLB 28, HL... 5.75
Supply of Ready Mixed Concrete (No 2), Re. *See* Director General of Fair
    Trading v Pioneer Concrete (UK) Ltd

T

Tchenguiz v Director of the Serious Fraud Office [2013] EWHC 2128 (QB),
    [2014] 1 WLR 1476, QBD... 4.3, 4.4, 4.41, 4.43
Total Network SL v Customs and Excise Commissioners. *See* Customs and
    Excise Commissioners v Total Network SL

U

United Arab Emirates v Allen [2012] EWHC 1712 (Admin), [2012] 1 WLR
    3419, [2013] Lloyd's Rep FC 254, QBD... 1.12

Table of Cases

W

Wai Yu-Tsang v Queen, The [1992] 1 AC 269, [1991] 3 WLR 1006, [1991] 4 All ER 664, (1992) 94 Cr App R 264, [1992] Crim LR 425, (1991) 135 SJLB 164, PC (HK) 3.254

Welham v DPP [1961] AC 103, [1960] 2 WLR 669, [1960] 1 All ER 805, (1960) 44 Cr App R 124, (1960) 124 JP 280, (1960) 104 SJ 308, HL 2.9, 3.253, 2.254

William C Leitch Bros Ltd, Re (No 1) [1932] 2 Ch 71, Ch D............................ 3.253

Bibliography

Articles
Cobain, I and Seager, A 'Revealed: the £5bn-a-year tax fraud', The Guardian, 9 May 2006, pp 1, 7.
Cobain, I and Seager, A 'VAT fraud costing Europe E50bn a year', The Guardian, 11 July 2006, pp 1, 20.
Wells, C 'Systematic disclosure failures at HMRC' Solicitors Journal, 8 January 2008.

Books
Archbold Criminal Pleading, Evidence and Practice, Sweet and Maxwell, 2014.
Farrell QC, S, Yeo, N, and Laddenburg, G, *Blackstone's Guide to the Fraud Act 2006*, Oxford University Press, 2007.
Hynes, P, Furlong, R and Rudolf, N, *International Money Laundering and Terrorist Financing: A UK perspective*, Sweet and Maxwell, 2008.
Ormerod D, *Smith & Hogan's Criminal Law*, 13th edn, Oxford University Press, 2011.
Rees QC, E, Fisher, R, and Thomas, R, *Blackstone's Guide to the Proceeds of Crime Act 2002*, 4th edn, Oxford University Press, 2011.
Stone, R, *The Law of Entry, Search and Seizure*, 5th edn, Oxford University Press, 2013.
Wells, C *Abuse of Process*, 2nd edn, Jordan Publishing Ltd, 2011.
Zander QC, Prof M, *The Police and Criminal Evidence Act 1984*, 6th edn, Sweet and Maxwell, 2013.

Publications
'How to spot VAT missing trader fraud', HM Revenue & Customs, July 2006.
'VAT Notes No. 3 2006', HM Revenue & Customs, September 2006.

Reports
Mr Justice Butterfield, 'Review of Prosecutions conducted by the Solicitor's Office of HM Customs & Excise', HM Customs & Excise, 2003.
HHJ Gower QC and Sir Anthony Hammond QC, 'Review of Prosecutions conducted by the Solicitor's Office of HM Customs & Excise', HM Customs & Excise, 2000.

Bibliography

Web
'Carbon credit trading', www.fca.org.uk/consumers/scams/investment-scams/carbon-credit-trading
Crown Prosecution Service – www.cps.gov.uk
'Do you want to be a millionaire: The missing fraudster' : BBC News Panorama, 17 July 2006, http://news.bbc.co.uk/1/hi/programmes/panorama/5180484.stm
'Do you want to be a millionaire?' BBC News Panorama, 14 July 2006, http://news.bbc.co.uk/1/hi/programmes/panorama/5166584.stm
Financial Conduct Authority – http://www.fca.org.uk
'Investors warn over £24 million carbon credit scam', http://www.actionfraud.police.uk/investors-warned-over-24m-carbon-credit-scam-nov13
Ministry of Justice – www.justice.gov.uk
'Missing VAT customers: Fraud indicators', www.hmrc.gov.uk/manuals/dmbmanual/dmbm875550.htm

Lectures
'Deferred Prosecution Agreements: How will it work in Practice?', Nicola Howard (25 Bedford Row), Sara Harman (Stephenson Harwood) and Joanna Savage (Ministry of Justice).
'Ponzi Fraud', Geoff Payne (25 Bedford Row).

Chapter 1

The Fraud Act 2006

INTRODUCTION

1.1 The Fraud Act 2006 came into force on 15 January 2007 in an attempt to simplify the law relating to fraud offences, by concentrating upon dishonesty as the central concept for criminality and by abolishing the deception offences in the Theft Acts 1968, 1978 and Theft (Amendment) Act 1996.[1]

1.2 The Fraud Act widens the fraud offences available so that prosecuting fraud should become (a) easier, particularly in assessing whether there is a realistic chance of securing a conviction, (b) more comprehensible to juries (c) with less scope for technical objections to indictment counts, as per the Law Commission's Report of July 2002[2] which identifies an important objective being:

> 'to ensure that the scope of the criminal law of fraud is wide enough to enable fraudsters to be successfully prosecuted and appropriately sentenced, without being so wide as to impose unacceptable restrictions on personal freedom, or so vague as to infringe the principle of the rule of law'.[3]

This is against a political backdrop of recognition by government that:

> 'the public has at times felt that those responsible for major crimes in the commercial sphere have managed to avoid justice. Even when fraud is detected, the present procedures are often cumbersome and difficult to prosecute effectively.'[4]

---

1 Theft Act 1968, ss 15 (obtaining property by deception), 15A (obtaining a money transfer by deception), 16 (obtaining pecuniary advantage by deception), 20(2) (procuring the execution of a valuable security by deception), Sch 1 (Abolition of various deception offences) and Theft Act 1978, ss 1 (obtaining services by deception) and 2 (evasion of liability by deception), both Acts being amended by the Theft (Amendment) Act 1996.
2 The Law Commission (Law Com No 276) *Fraud* (July 2002) (Cm.5560), available at http://lawcommission.justice.gov.uk/docs/lc276_Fraud.pdf.
3 The Law Commission Report on Fraud (July 2002) (Cm 5560), p 2, para 1.4.
4 KPMG lecture, 24 June 1998, given by the Lord Chancellor, 'The feasibility of a unified approach to proceedings arising out of major City fraud'.

1.3 *The Fraud Act 2006*

1.3 In the consultation process to the Law Commission 2002 Report, the Crown Prosecution Service favoured the creation of a general offence of fraud based on dishonesty for a number of reasons:

(1) 'because of the flexibility it would offer in prosecuting fraud cases', particularly in developing financial markets and new technologies;[5]

(2) 'because it would cover situations where deceit is not used to commit the fraud, or where it is difficult to establish a link between the deception and the outcome or intended outcome';[6] and

(3) would simplify fraud trials by avoiding complicated and technical legal arguments.[7]

1.4 The Fraud Act retained the offence of conspiracy to defraud, despite proposals to abolish the same by the Law Commission 2002 Report. The retention of the common law offence is helpful to prosecutors for at least two reasons.[8] First, the inexhaustible ingenuity of fraudsters and variety of means they employ, mean that some frauds are difficult or impossible to prosecute for any offence other than conspiracy to defraud. Secondly, there are some cases where the interests of justice can only be served by presenting to the court an overall picture that cannot be achieved by charging a series of substantive offences or statutory conspiracy.

1.5 The Fraud Act is consistent with the UK's anti-fraud international obligations as reflected in the European Union's Convention on the Protection of the European Community's Financial Interests of 1995, its Framework Decision of 28 May 2001, and the Third EU Money Laundering Directive of November 2005, being part of the Government anti-fraud strategy as set out in the Fraud Review of July 2006.

FRAUD

1.6 The Fraud Act 2006 (FA 2006) creates a number of new offences. The main new offence is contained in s 1 (fraud), which can be committed in a number of different ways: s 2 (fraud by false representation); s 3 (fraud by failing to disclose information); and s 4 (fraud by abuse of position) (FA 2006, s 1(2)(a)–(c)).

---

5   A view also expressed by the SFO in particular relating to internet fraud and financial market fraud.
6   The Law Commission Report on Fraud (July 2002) (Cm 5560), p 44, para 5.23.
7   As epitomised in the case of *R v Preddy* [1996] AC 815; see also *R v Duru [1974]* 1 WLR 2 (obtaining mortgage cheque by deception), *R v Halai* [1983] Crim LR 624, *R v King* [1992] QB 20, *R v Mitchell* [1993] Crim LR 788, *R v Manjdadria* [1993] Crim LR 73, *DPP v Gomez* [1993] AC 442.
8   See Attorney-General Hansard HL 14 March 2006 col 1115

1.7 A person who is guilty of fraud is liable:

(a) on summary conviction, to imprisonment for a term not exceeding 12 months or to a fine not exceeding the statutory maximum or to both (s 1(3)(a)); or

(b) on conviction on indictment, to imprisonment for a term not exceeding 10 years or to a fine or to both (s 1(3)(b)).

1.8 The new offence relies on proof of dishonesty[9] without the need to prove an operative deception. The standard of honesty is that of a reasonable and honest person. The defendant is dishonest if considering the defendant's own state of mind he realises he is acting contrary to the *Ghosh* standard.

1.9 Recent prosecutions under s 1 cover a wide range of factual situations including mortgage fraud (see *R v White* [2014] EWCA Crim 714; *R v Forrest and Hogg* [2014] EWCA Crim 308), confidence fraud (*R v Sean O'Farrell* [2014] EWCA Crim 170; *R v Peter Hulbert* [2014] EWCA Crim 712 (on public funds)), unauthorised bank account transfers on property deals (*R v Angela and Richard Pennock* [2014] EWCA Crim 598) and unauthorised payroll, CHAPS payments and company credit card use (*R v Craig* Burger [2013] EWCA Crim 2601).

Fraud by false representation

1.10 A person breaches FA 2006, s 2 if he dishonestly makes a false representation (s 2(1)(a)) and intends[10] by making the representation to make a gain for himself or another (s 2(1)(b)(i)), or to cause loss to another or to expose another to risk of loss (s 2(1)(b)(ii)).

1.11 A representation is false if it is untrue or misleading (s 2(2)(a)) and the person making it knows that it is, or might be, untrue or misleading (s 2(2)(b)). There is no express requirement of materiality in the respect in which it is untrue or misleading, either objectively or subjectively to the defendant. Dishonesty must be present.

1.12 'Representation' means any representation as to fact or law, including a representation as to the state of mind of the person making the representation

---

9 See the two-stage test in *R v Ghosh* [1982] QB 1053: (1) was the defendant's behaviour dishonest by the ordinary standards of reasonable and honest people? If the answer is no, the prosecution fails. If the answer is yes, then (2) was the defendant aware that his or her conduct would be regarded as dishonest by reasonable honest people? Likewise, theft has become defined by dishonesty: see *DPP v Gomez* [1993] AC 442 and *R v Hinks* [2001] 2 AC 241].

10 A person intends something if he acts with the purpose of causing that result or if he knew that it was a highly probable result of his act or virtually certain consequence: see *R v Woollin* [1999] 1 AC 82.

1.13 *The Fraud Act 2006*

(s 2(3)(a)) or any other person (s 2(3)(b)). It does not, however, include a promise as to the future (see *Government of the UAE v Allen* [2012] 1 WLR 3419 DC). A representation may be express or implied (s 2(4)). A representation may be regarded as made if it (or anything implying it) is submitted in any form to any system or device designed to receive, convey or respond to communications (with or without human intervention). Attempted fraud by false representation may be committed where a defendant who dishonestly makes a representation which, contrary to his belief, is true (see *R v Cornelius* [2012] EWCA Crim 500).

1.13 'Phishing' by sending an email falsely representing that it had been sent by a legitimate financial institution, company or person requesting the receipent provide personal information so that the 'phisher' can gain access to bank accounts, is an offence under s 2 (see explanatory notes to the Act).

1.14 Recent prosecutions under s 2 include 'crash for cash' type of insurance fraud (see *R v Robert Wright* [2014] EWCA Crim 382) and mortgage fraud (see *R v White (Anthony Alan)* [2014] EWCA Crim 714; *R v Forrest and Hogg* [2014] EWCA Crim 3080).

Fraud by failing to disclose information

1.15 A person breaches FA 2006, s 3 if he dishonestly fails to disclose to another person information which he is under a legal duty to disclose (s 3(a))[11] and intends, by failing to disclose the information to make a gain for himself or another (s 3(b)(i)), or to cause loss to another or to expose another to a risk of loss (s 3(b)(ii)).

1.16 The legal duty to disclose can arise from:

(a) statute, eg the provisions governing company prospectuses under the Financial Services and Markets Act 2000, s 90;

(b) a transaction of utmost good faith such as an insurance contract;

(c) from the express or implied terms of a contract;

(d) from the custom and practice of a particular market, trade or industry; or

(e) from a fiduciary relationship between the parties such as that of agent and principal.[12]

---

[11] There is no requirement to disclose on moral grounds, only on legal grounds, otherwise s 3 would intrude upon the civil law principle of caveat emptor (being the buyer's responsibility to be aware of what the seller says).

[12] See Law Commission Report on Fraud, (July 2002) (Cm 5560), para 7.28 (Legal Duty of Disclosure).

1.17 Recent prosecutions under s 3 include mortgage fraud (see *R v Forrest and Hogg* [2014] EWCA Crim 308).

Fraud by abuse of position

1.18 A person is in breach of FA 2006, s 4 if he occupies a position in which he is expected to safeguard, or not to act against, the financial interests of another person (s 4(1)(a)), dishonestly abuses that position (s 4(1)(b)) and intends, by means of the abuse of that position to make a gain for himself or another (s 4(1)(c)(i)) or to cause loss to another or to expose another to a risk of loss (s 4(1)(c)(ii)). A person may be regarded as having abused his position even though his conduct consisted of an omission rather than an act (s 4(2)).

1.19 The position of trust covers a wide range of situations including those in a fiduciary relationship with an obligation of loyalty (see *Bristol and West Building Society v Mothew*[13] and *R v Angela and Richard Pennock*[14]). The Law Commission set out the intended scope of the section, which goes beyond that of a fiduciary relationship:

'7.38 The necessary relationship will be present between trustee and beneficiary, director and company, professional person and client, agent and principal, employee and employer, or between partners. It may arise otherwise, for example within a family, or in the context of voluntary work, or in context where the parties are not at arm's length. In nearly all cases where it arises, it will be recognized by the civil law as importing fiduciary duties, and any relationship that is so recognized will suffice. We see no reason, however, why the existence of such duties should be essential. This does not of course mean that it would be entirely a matter for the fact-finders whether the necessary relationship exists. The question whether the particular facts alleged can properly be described as giving rise to that relationship will be an issue capable of being ruled upon by the judge and, if the case goes to the jury, of being the subject of directions.'

1.20 Recent prosecutions under s 4 include *R v Waqanika* [2014] EWCA Crim 902.

---

13 [1998] 1 Ch 1. There are several core liabilities and responsibilities: (a) must act in good faith; (b) must not make a profit out of the trust (see secret profit in *R v Adams* [1995] 1 WLR 52 PC); (c) avoid conflict of interests; and (d) may not act for his own benefit or the benefit of a third party without the informed consent of the principal.

14 [2014] EWCA Crim 598.

1.21 *The Fraud Act 2006*

GAIN AND LOSS

1.21 The references to gain and loss in ss 2 to 4 above refer to gain and loss in money or property (s 5(2)(a)), include any such gain or loss whether temporary or permanent (s 5(2)(b)). 'Property' means any property whether real or personal (including things in action and other intangible property)[15] (s 5(2)(b)). 'Gain' includes a gain by keeping what one has, as well as a gain by getting what one does not have (s 5(3)). 'Loss' includes a loss by not getting what one might get, as well as a loss by parting with what one has (s 5(4)). The offences in ss 2 to 4 require only that there be an intent to gain and loss. There need not be proof of actual gain or loss.

POSSESSION OF ARTICLES FOR USE IN FRAUDS

1.22 A second new offence, possession of articles for use in frauds, is contained in FA 2006, s 6. A person is guilty of an offence if he has in his possession or under his control any article for use in the course of or in connection with any fraud (s 6(1)). The section replaces the offence of going equipped for cheat under Theft Act 1968, s 25, with a wider definition that does not require that the article be with the person when not at his place of abode. The section criminalises the possession of such articles at home.

1.23 In terms of mens rea, case law under Theft Act 1968, s 25, notably *Ellames*,[16] is of relevance, as set out in the explanatory Notes to the Fraud Act 2006:

> 'The intention is to attract the case law on section 25, which has established that proof is required that the defendant had the article for the purpose or with the intention that it be used in the course of or in connection with the offence, and that a general intention to commit fraud will suffice.'

1.24 A person guilty of a s 6 offence is liable:

(a) on summary conviction, to imprisonment for a term not exceeding 12 months or to a fine not exceeding the statutory maximum (or to both) (s 6(2)(a)); or

(b) on conviction on indictment, to imprisonment for a term not exceeding five years or to a fine (or to both) (s 6(2)(b)).

---

15 It does not cover the obtaining of confidential information (see *Oxford v Moss* (1979) 68 Cr App R 183), which can be charged subject to the factual circumstances under Computer Misuse Act 1990, s 1 and/or as a conspiracy to defraud.
16 [1974] 1 WLR 1391

MAKING OR SUPPLYING ARTICLES FOR USE IN FRAUDS

1.25 A third new offence, making or supplying articles for use in frauds, is contained in FA 2006, s 7. A person is guilty of an offence if he makes, adapts, supplies or offers to supply any article knowing that it is designed or adapted for use in the course of or in connection with fraud (s 7(1)(a)) or intending it to be used to commit, or assist in the commission of, fraud (s 7(1)(b)).

1.26 A person guilty of a s 7 offence is liable:

(a) on summary conviction, to imprisonment for a term not exceeding 12 months or to a fine not exceeding the statutory maximum (or to both) (s 7(2)(a)); or

(b) conviction on indictment, to imprisonment for a term not exceeding 10 years or to a fine (or to both) (s 7(2)(b)).

1.27 For the purposes of ss 6 and 7, 'article' includes any program or data held in electronic form (s 8(1)(a)(b)). Examples of items covered by ss 6 and 7 include, but not limited to:

- electricity meter devices ('black boxes'), which reverse the flow of current to reduce the recorded units used;[17]
- credit card skimming devices/Lebanese loops for use at bank ATM machines;[18]
- computer programmes such as 'Credit Master IV' which generate genuine credit card numbers;
- computer template/spreadsheets for identity documents including utility bills;
- fake documents such as false birth certificates issued for use in social security benefit fraud;[19]
- forged bar code labels and blank till receipts;[20]
- stolen bank and credit card details;[21] and
- draft letters for advance fee frauds.

---

17 See *R v Hollinshead* [1985] AC 975.
18 See *R v Munteanu* [2012] EWCA Crim 2221; [2013] 1 Cr App R (S) 107, *R v Tarcuta* [2014] EWCA Crim 823, R v Flore [2014] EWCA Crim 465.
19 See *R v Akpom* [2013] EWCA Crim 2662.
20 See *R v Birdi* [2014] EWCA Crim 780.
21 See *R v Brown* [2014] EWCA Crim 695.

1.28 *The Fraud Act 2006*

FRAUDULENT TRADING BY NON-CORPORATE OFFENDERS[22]

1.28 There is a fourth new offence of participating in fraudulent business carried on by any person (individual or sole trader) under FA 2006, s 9, which mirrors the corporate structure offence under Companies Act 1985, s 458[23] as replaced by Companies Act 2006, s 993.[24] Corporate bodies which are exempt from the provisions of s 458 are not subject to s 9. These are:[25]

- any body incorporated by or registered under any public general act of Parliament;
- non-profit making businesses;
- Secretary of State exemptions; and
- open-ended investment companies.

A person is guilty of a s 9 offence if he is knowingly a party to the carrying on of a business with intent to defraud creditors of any person or for any other fraudulent purpose (s 9(1) and (2)(b)).

1.29 The following principles of case law liability have developed in the corporate s 458 offence:

- dishonesty must be proved;[26]
- a single fraudulent transaction suffices;[27]
- those who are the controlling minds or management of the business are liable;[28]
- an outsider may be knowingly a party to the carrying on of a business by assisting in the fraudulent act; and[29]
- omission is not enough – a positive act must take place.[30]

1.30 A person guilty of a s 9 offence is liable:

---

22 Including sole traders, partnerships, trusts and companies registered overseas.
23 Following a recommendation of the Law Commission, (Law Com No 277) 'The Effective Prosecution Of Multiple Offending' (October 2002) (Cm 5609), Pt VIII: Fraudulent Trading, para.8.11.
24 Retained as an offence with its sentence increased to a maximum of 10 years' imprisonment. Offences committed after 1 October 2007 are covered by Companies Act 2006, s 993.
25 As set out in s 718 of the Companies Act 1985
26 *R v Cox* (1982) 75 Cr App R 291.
27 *Re Gerald Cooper Chemicals Ltd (In liquidation)* [1978] Ch 262
28 *R v Kemp* (1988) QB 645, (1988) 87 Cr App R 95; *R v Miles* [1992] Crim LR 657.
29 *Re Augustus Barnett and Sons Ltd* [1986] BCLC 170 (Ch D).
30 Re Maidstone Building Provisions Ltd [1971] 1 WLR 1085.

(a) on summary conviction, to imprisonment for a term not exceeding 12 months or to a fine not exceeding the statutory maximum (or to both) (s 9(6)(a)); or

(b) conviction on indictment, to imprisonment for a term not exceeding 10 years or to a fine (or to both) (s 9(6)(b)).

OBTAINING SERVICES BY DISHONESTY

1.31 A fifth new offence of obtaining services dishonestly is created under FA 2006, s 11, which replaces dishonestly obtaining services by deception in the Theft Act. A person is guilty of an offence if he obtains services for himself or another by a dishonest act (s 11(1)(a)) and the services are made available on the basis that payment has been, is being or will be made for in respect of them (s 11(2)(a)), he obtains them without any payment having been made for or in respect of them or without payment having been made in full (s 11(2)(b)) and when he obtains them he knows that they are being made available on the basis of payment (s 11(2)(c)(i)) or that they might be (s 11(2)(c)(ii)) but intends that payment will not be made, or will not be made in full. The offence is wider than the Theft Act as there is no need to prove an operative deception. It is the dishonest intention of the fraudster that is important, not the victim being actively deceived. However, s 11 is restricted in its application by the need to prove two essential elements:

(1) a dishonest act must take place, an omission is insufficient to attract liability; and

(2) there must be no intention to make payment for the services obtained.

Although s 11 does not define 'services' Parliament intended the term to have wide application; including the opening of a bank account, the setting up of a company, downloading software or music from the internet.[31]

1.32 A person guilty of a s 11 offence is liable:

(a) on summary conviction, to imprisonment for a term not exceeding 12 months or to a fine not exceeding the statutory maximum (or to both) (s 11(3)(a)); and

(b) conviction on indictment, to imprisonment for a term not exceeding five years or to a fine (or to both) (s 11(3)(b)).

---

31 See 'Fraud Law Reform: Government Response to Consultations' (Criminal Law Policy Unit, The Home Office), para 36.

1.33 *The Fraud Act 2006*

LIABILITY OF COMPANY OFFICERS FOR OFFENCES COMMITTED BY A COMPANY

1.33 If an offence under the Fraud Act 2006 is committed by a body corporate with the consent or connivance of a director, manager, secretary or other similar officer of the body corporate[32] or a person who was purporting to act in any such capacity, he, as well as the body corporate, is guilty of the offence and liable to be proceeded against and punished accordingly (FA 2006, s 12).

---

32 See the earlier decision in *R v Boal* [1992] QB 591, (1992) 95 Cr App R 272 – a case under s 23 of the Fire Precautions Act 1971 that considers the phrase.

Chapter 2

Conspiracy to Defraud

OVERVIEW

2.1   Section 5(1) of the Criminal Law Act 1997 preserves conspiracy to defraud as an offence at common law (abolishing otherwise the offence of conspiracy) and therefore triable only upon indictment. However, unlike most offences at common law where the maximum sentence is life imprisonment, s12(3) of the Criminal Law Act 1977 sets the maximum sentence at 10 years' imprisonment or an unlimited fine or both. It is *not* a Sch 2 offence for the purposes of confiscation.

2.2   In *Attorney General's References (Nos 7 and 8 of 2013) (R v Kallakis and Williams) R v Levene,*[1] the Court of Appeal (Criminal Division) was asked by the Attorney General specifically to reconsider the principles upon which serious conspiracies to defraud were sentenced. The Court refused to so. It said:

> '72. In our judgment, there is no ambiguity in the principles to be applied in sentencing for the most serious offences of fraud, nor in the assessment whether consecutive sentences should be imposed to reflect the overall seriousness of similar offending. No review of the appropriate level of sentencing for serious fraud is required on the facts of the present cases. We acknowledge that in individual cases, of which this is one, the judgment may not be a simple one.'

However this will need to be revisited due to the inclusion of conspiracy to defraud within the sentencing guidelines for fraud, money laundering and bribery (see Chapter 9 for sentencing guidelines).

2.3   In 1994 the Law Commission recommended that the offence be preserved pending a more substantial review.[2] In 2002[3] the Law Commission said:[4]

---

1   [2014] 1 Cr App R (S) 26.
2   Law Commission (Law Com No 228) *Criminal Law Conspiracy to Defraud* (December 1994), at para 1.20.
3   Law Commission (Law Com 276) Fraud (July 2002) (Cm 5560).
4   Law Commission Report on Fraud (July 2002). at para 1.7.

2.4 *Conspiracy to Defraud*

'In line with these conclusions, we recommend that the eight offences of deception created by the Theft Acts 1968–96 should be repealed, and that the common law crime of conspiracy to defraud should be abolished. In their place we recommend the creation of two new statutory offences – one of fraud, and one of obtaining services dishonestly.'

2.4 However the offence was preserved by the Fraud Act 2006. In the Explanatory Notes[5] the Government said:

'The Law Commission's report recommended that conspiracy to defraud should be abolished. The majority of those who responded on this point in the Home Office's consultation were opposed to this on the basis of serious practical concerns about the ability to prosecute multiple offences in the largest and most serious cases of fraud and a desire to see how the new statutory offences worked in practice before abolishing conspiracy to defraud. There were also concerns that limitations on the scope of statutory conspiracy meant that certain types of secondary participation in fraud might still only be caught by the common law charge. So, in the light of the consultation, the Government concluded that immediate abolition of conspiracy to defraud would create considerable risks for the effective prosecution of fraud cases. The Government proposed to reassess whether there is a continuing need to retain conspiracy to defraud in the light of the operation of the new offences and the Law Commission's impending report on encouraging and assisting crime. The Law Commission has now published its report on *Inchoate Liability for Assisting and Encouraging Crime* (Law Com No. 300, Cm 6878, 2006) and is due to publish a second, final, report dealing with secondary liability in late Autumn.'

Notwithstanding that, the offence of conspiracy to defraud still exists.

2.6 The Attorney General has issued updated guidance, dated 29 January 2012, about when it is appropriate to charge conspiracy to defraud as opposed to offences under the Fraud Act 2006 or statutory conspiracies (see Appendix 11).

JURISDICTION

2.7 Conspiracy to defraud is a group B offence for the purposes of jurisdiction and Pt I, ss 1–6 of the Criminal Justice Act 1993. In relation to conspiracy to defraud these may be summarised as follows – it doesn't matter whether:

- a person was a British citizen at any material time;
- a person was in England and Wales at any material time;

---

5   Fraud Act 2006, Explanatory Notes, para 6.

- a person became a party to the conspiracy in England and Wales; or
- any act or omission or other event in relation to the conspiracy occurred in England and Wales,

in relation to Group B offences:

- there is an obtaining of property in England and Wales if the property is either dispatched from or received at a place in England and Wales; and
- there is a communication in England and Wales of any information, instruction, request, demand or other matter if it is sent by any means from a place in England and Wales to elsewhere or from elsewhere to a place in England and Wales.

2.8 If the agreed course of conduct would at some stage involve an act or omission by one or more of the parties or some other event constituting an offence under the law of a different jurisdiction where the act, omission or other event was intended to take place, a person can be guilty of conspiracy to defraud if:

- a party to the agreement or a party's agent do anything in England and Wales in relation to the agreement before its formation; or
- a party to it became a party in England or Wales (by joining it in person or through an agent), or
- a party to it, or a party's agent, did or omitted to do anything in England and Wales in pursuance of it; *and*
- the conspiracy would be triable in England and Wales but for the fraud which the parties to it had in view not being intended to take place in England and Wales.

In such a case the court will presume the condition relating to foreign law satisfied unless the defence serves the appropriate notice upon the prosecution. However, that jurisdiction does not extend to cases where the commission of the fraud would, as a by-product, cause economic loss here (see *Attorney-General's Reference (No 1 of 1982)*).[6]

2.9 As is obvious, though, from the bullet points relating to conduct intended to occur overseas, there is an extension of jurisdiction of the criminal courts to try such allegations of conspiracy to defraud. Great care must also be taken both when prosecuting and defending that the court has in such circumstances the jurisdiction to try the offence.

---

6 (1983) 77 Cr App R 9.

2.10 *Conspiracy to Defraud*

THE OFFENCE

2.10 It is an offence to conspire with one or more others (provided they are not your spouse[7] at the time of the agreement) to defraud others. That means it will be an offence to agree with another or others to do acts that cause economic loss or create the risk of such prejudice. That much has been clear since *Whelham v DPP*.[8]

2.11 The purpose of the agreement must be criminal; that is to say each member must intend by their agreement to further the criminal purpose. In the words of Lord Bridge in *R v Anderson*:[9] 'Nothing less will suffice; nothing more is required'. That is not to be confused with any suggestion that any individual must know what the criminal purpose is or even that it was criminal (see *R v Saik*[10]).

2.12 It has often been said the essence of the conspiracy is the agreement. This is so as, at the point of agreement, the offence is complete, although it may continue as long as two or more persons continue to agree to conclude it. On the basis that people may enter and leave the same conspiracy at different times, all will be liable to conviction on the same count provided the agreement is complete.

2.13 Complexity can arise where the agreement is the achievement of more than a single objective, each of which may, or may not, be a criminal offence in itself. It would appear that the conspiracy is the agreement as a whole and, as a result, failure to prove one or other objective will cause the case to fail. That is not a reason for an indictment for a conspiracy to defraud to lack particularity. Quite the contrary. Particularity, as well as being welcome to defendants in knowing the full allegation they have to face, will also assist in ensuring that only a single offence is charged and that 'rolled up' conspiracies are not evidenced.

2.14 *R v Griffiths*[11] still remains the paradigm authority in relation to the prosecution evidencing more than one conspiracy within a single count charged and should be consulted where the issue arises.

---

7 See *Mawji v Queen, the* [1957] AC 126 (PC). Section 2(2)(a) in relation to statutory conspiracies has been extended to cover spouses and civil partners; s 2(2)(b) and (c) render those under the age of 10 and intended victims of the offence unable to co-conspire respectively. The common law, and its applicability therefore to conspiracy to defraud, appears to stop with spouses as it would appear that s 5(6) applies the rules contained in s 2 only to other 'enactments' – the common law not, it seems, being such.
8 [1961] AC 103 (HL).
9 [1986] AC 27 (HL).
10 [2006] UKHL 18; [2007] 1 AC 18 (HL).
11 [1966] 1 QB 589.

Chapter 3

Prevalent Types of Fraud

INTRODUCTION

3.1 Under the Fraud Act 2006 there is but one offence of fraud that can be committed three ways (together with the miscellaneous offences). There is, however, a fine line between the offence for which a person may be prosecuted and the *type* of offending they are said to have committed. We deal below with some of the more common and serious *types* of fraudulent behaviour. Inevitably these types of fraud can be charged in different ways, but it is the underlying behaviour and allegations that are the subjects of interest.

3.2 Please see Chapter 9 on sentencing for fraud generally. However any 'offence specific' sentencing features are captured in the relevant section below.

MORTGAGE FRAUD

3.3 Mortgage fraud differs in one significant regard to most other frauds. Whereas most frauds involve the immediate obtaining of money or another valuable commodity or service, on one analysis the mortgage fraudster obtains merely a debt, which must be repaid. However this simplistic analysis ignores the real advantages of the fraud.

Context

3.4 It is widely perceived that the UK has one of the highest ratios of home ownership in Europe. Home ownership is widely regarded as a highly desirable alternative to renting accomodation, and for good reason. Provided the mortgage is serviced It provides the owner with far greater security of tenure than the vast majority of tenancies, the opportunity for capital growth and the ability to make most if not all changes to the property without the consent of a third party, the landlord. Depending on interest rates and the levels of supply and demand for rental property, having a mortgage can also work out cheaper than paying rent.

3.5 *Prevalent Types of Fraud*

Prevalance

3.5 Research conducted by financial information services business Experian suggests that of every 1,000 mortgage applications, 43 are fraudulent.[1] These figures represent a 13 per cent increase on 2012 and 26 per cent on 2011. Whether these statistics are wholly reliable or not, as criteria for lending becomes more restrictive and more people are thereby prevented from getting on the property ladder, the temptation to overstate income or withhold information detrimental to credit history inevitably increases.

The commission of mortgage fraud

3.6 The appropriate charges may vary and are considered below at para 3.19 et seq. However charged, the conduct is often the same.

Common misrepresentations

Misrepresentation

3.7 Offences of this nature are very largely committed as a result of misrepresentations contained in the mortgage application. A non-exhaustive list of common misrepresentations and appropriate lines of enquiry is reproduced below in the pictorial box and considered in further detail thereafter.

Typical misrepresentation	Method	Avenues of investigation
Overstating income	False payslips	Mortgage broker HMRC Accountant
Overstating period of employment or tenure of position	False references	Handwriting expert
Application made in wholly false identity	Multiple false documents	All of the above
Misrepresenting the purpose of the mortgage as being for owner occupation whereas it is in fact intended to rented out		Electoral role Utilities Existence of other address or mortgage

---

1   Financial Times Adviser (4 December 2012), available at www.ftadviser.com.

Typical misrepresentation	Method	Avenues of investigation
A dishonestly inflated mortgage valuation		Surveyors files
		Expert evidence to prove the survey was inflated
		Prior reports prepared by the same surveyor to prove a pattern of dishonest inflation

It will be seen that misrepresentations as to identity, means or status or the purpose of the loan all feature in the above table. Multiple misrepresentations might be reflected by the particulars of offence in the count.[2]

Identity of the borrower

3.8 Professional mortgage frauds often have an entirely fictitious borrower. The role of professionals, such as conveyancing solicitors, accountants who prepare accounts on behalf of applicants and mortgage brokers who submit such applications, is important. They are obliged to satisfy themselves as to the identity of the applicant in accordance with their obligations under the Money Laundering Regulations. These are not considered in detail herein, but the essence of the Regulations is that professionals are required to satisfy themselves as to the identity and residence of the applicant and source of the funds.

The property is intended for owner occupation and not buy to let or other investment purposes

3.9 Buy to let mortgages typically have higher interest rates and require a greater deposit than mortgages in respect of property intended for owner occupation. The advantages to the borrower are therefore lower interest rates and a smaller deposit. It is worth noting that the circumstances of genuine applicants may change over time and that if they intend to move to other accommodation, eg because they are relocating for work or moving in a with a partner or spouse, they may wish to rent out the property. Lenders frequently grant permission for this but will often take the opportunity of this change in circumstances to raise the interest rate and/or impose an administration fee.

---

2 For example, in *R v Ward*, [2005] EWCA 1972, the indictment contained 15 particulars which were alleged in the indictment, each relating to the falsity of that which was alleged.

3.10 *Prevalent Types of Fraud*

Rental yield and tenancy

3.10 In both commercial property transactions and residential buy to let applications, the lender will wish to know who is leasing or renting the premises and the amount of rent that they will pay. This is material because the level of income will determine the ability of the applicant to repay the loan. The identity of the proposed lessee is relevant to their likely ability to repay the loan. For example, a long-established high street chain is unlikely to default on rental payments. Misrepresentations as to these matters are made to induce the lender to lend where it might otherwise decline to do so or to lend more money than the property is in fact worth in reliance of a dishonestly inflated rental yield.

Purchase price

3.11 A dishonest surveyor may artificially inflate the price to cause the lender to loan more than the property is worth.

3.12 Aside from fraud by misrepresentation there are however other types of mortgage fraud.

Registration fraud

3.13 This occurs where the details held at the Land Registry are altered so that the property is now registered to an identity used by the fraudster. This will enable the fraudster to take out a mortgage secured against a property which he does not own. This type of fraud is less common than 'misrepresentation' fraud and is professional in nature. Non-resident owners, such as buy to let landlords, are particularly vulnerable to this kind of fraud. Victims are able to claim compensation from the Land Registry.

Multiple frauds in respect of the same property

3.14 Organised fraudsters may seek to repay the original, fraudulently obtained loan by procuring a second fraudulent loan obtained in false identities. The value of the property is likely to have been misrepresented, thereby providing the fraudsters with the ability to repay the first loan and retain both a profit and the property. They use the second loan to repay the first and may repeat this a number of time

Misrepresentation as to income

Case example

3.15 In *R v Yates,* Davis J summarised the facts as follows:[3]

> 'On the application for the mortgage the declared income of the appellant was stated to be £110,199 per annum and his partner's was recorded as £74,000. Those declarations were entirely false. Moreover, forged pay slips and at least one forged bank statement were provided in support of the application. The application was approved and Northern Rock released the money. Northern Rock has since confirmed that it would never have lent the money had it known the true position.[4]
>
> Subsequent enquiries reveal that at the time the legitimate earnings of the appellant were in the region of £42,000 gross per annum. What his partner's income was at the time, if any, is not known. Her last known income was in the region of £21,000.'[5]

The investigation of mortgage fraud

3.16 The existence of documentary evidence enables investigations to take place many years after the event. Investigators looking into the financial assets and lifestyle of a person suspected of ongoing involvement in drug trafficking in 2013 may very well wish to inquire into the historical financial circumstances of the suspect. For example, large-scale drug traffickers have in reality almost certainly been involved in the commission of drug trafficking offences prior to the offence for which they are currently under investigation and may well have laundered the proceeds of their antecedent undetected crimes. Whilst it may very well be that lack of evidence of these crimes means that they cannot be prosecuted for such offences, it may equally be the case that they can be prosecuted for money laundering the proceeds.

The link between mortgage fraud and money laundering

3.17 Consider a drug trafficker or other acquisitive criminal whose activities generate cash. He wants a home to live in, and just, law-abiding members of the community sometimes do perhaps views property as a sound investment. Every mortgage application will ask the origin of the deposit and from which means the debt will be repaid. In the unlikely event that the

---

3   2010 EWCA Crim 1028.
4   The offence would now be charged under s 2 of the Fraud Act 2006 and there would no need to prove that the lender would not have lend the money had it know the true position.
5   At paras 4 and 5.

3.18 *Prevalent Types of Fraud*

application provides honest answers to those questions, the application would inevitably be refused. So the application will contain misrepresentations as to those matters. Criminals are also no doubt acutely aware that prosecutions for acquisitive crime or drug trafficking inevitably result in an inquiry into their assets and the very real prospect that the proceeds of their crimes will be stripped away. So the application may lie about the identity of the applicant and a trusted partner may apply for the mortgage in his name, concealing the fact that the real beneficial owner is a criminal. Trust deeds may be created for no apparent reason other than to conceal the identity of the true beneficial owner. Needless to say, if trust deeds are created, they will not be disclosed to the lender.

3.18 An indictment alleging mortgage fraud will often include allegations of money laundering and other offending such as drug trafficking or another acquisitive crime. In such circumstances, consideration will need to be given as to whether there is a sufficient nexus to justify joinder and if so, whether the defendant is likely to suffer prejudice or if severance is not granted.

The Fraud Act 2006[6]

3.19 The key points to note regarding the Fraud Act 2006 are as follows:

- Under the Theft Act 1968, mortgage fraud was often prosecuted as obtaining property by deception under s 15 or, more latterly under s15A – obtaining a money transfer by deception. It was necessary to prove that the deception had induced the lender to make the loan, ie was an 'operative deception'. Under the Fraud Act 2006 there is no need to prove an operative deception.[7]

- There is no need to prove an actual loss, only that the defendant's actions placed another at risk of economic prejudice.

    This is subject to the need to prove dishonesty. All offences carry a requirement that the defendant has acted dishonestly.

    R v Preddy[8] provides an example of a case in which the fact that misrepresentations were made was not in dispute, but it was argued by the defence that they were not dishonest:

    'In relation to each count, the mortgage application or accompanying documents contained one or more false statements, the applicant knowing the statements to be false. The statements related to, for example, the name of the applicant; his employment and/or income; the intended use of the property; or the purchase price. Some of the counts related to

---

6   See Chapter 1 of this book for a more detailed consideration of the Fraud Act 2006.
7   See the section below entitled 'The Theft Act 1968'.
8   [1996] 2 Cr App R 524.

mortgage applications which were refused, in which event the applicant was charged with an attempt to obtain property by deception.

'Both appellants accepted that the applications were supported by false representations. But they were were confident that the advances would be repaid because, in the economic climate at that time, the houses could and would be resold at a price higher than the purchase price and, even if there were a shortfall, this would be covered by an endowment policy taken out at the time of the advance. Indeed the lenders appear to have been more interested in the value of the property in question than in the personal details of the applicant'.[9]

In the event the jury rejected that defence and convicted the defendants.

Fraud by false representation

3.20 Section 1 of the Fraud Act 2006 creates the offence of fraud, which can be committed in three different ways as defined in ss 2–4. Section 2 states:

'(1) A person is in breach of this section if he—

    (a) dishonestly makes a false representation, and

    (b) intends, by making the representation–

        (i) to make a gain for himself or another, or

        (ii) to cause loss to another or *to expose another to a risk of loss.*

(2) A representation is false if—

    (a) it is untrue or misleading, and

    (b) the person making it knows that it is, *or might be, untrue or misleading.*

(3) *'Representation'* means any representation as to fact or law, including a representation as to the state of mind of—

    (a) the person making the representation, or

    (b) any other person.

(4) A representation may be express or implied.

(5) For the purposes of this section a representation may be regarded as made if it (or anything implying it) is submitted in any form to any system or device designed to receive, convey or respond to communications (with or without human intervention).'

---

9   Paragraph 3 per Lord Goff.

3.21 *Prevalent Types of Fraud*

Analysis of section 2

3.21 A representation may be as to law or to fact.

The risk of loss

3.22 Section 2(b)(ii) provides that an intention to expose another to the risk of loss is sufficient to prove the count; it is not necessary to prove an intention to cause loss or an actual loss. Clearly if the lender is acting under a misapprehension as to the identity of the borrower, the means and liabilities of the borrower and the value of the property the risk of loss is perhaps obvious.

No need for an operative deception

3.23 Unlike offences under the Theft Act 1968, it is not necessary to prove that the offence misrepresentations were 'operative', ie that but for the representations, the loan would never have been forthcoming. Thus, even if the misrepresentations in fact played no part in the lender's decision to make the advance, the count is capable of being made out. In practice, most cases will still feature a statement from an employee of the lender which concludes by saying that the lender would not have made the loan but for the misrepresentation. However this is not now a necessary element of the offence.

3.24 Under s 2(2)(b), a representation is false if it the person making it knows that *it might* be untrue or misleading. For example, a self-employed person who gives inflated forecasts as to his income will be guilty of the offence if the forecasts might be misleading. Subject of course to the onerous requirement of dishonesty, the offence is widely drawn. It is submitted that a reckless or negligent forecast would be insufficient. Under s 2(4), a representation may be express or implied. A misrepresentation may be as to law or fact. Section 2(4) of the Act provides that a misrepresentation may be express or implied. In the context of a mortgage application it is far more likely to be express.

Fraud by failing to disclose information

3.25 A person is in breach of s 3 of the Fraud Act 2006 if he:

(a) dishonestly fails to disclose to another person information which he is under a legal duty to disclose, and

(b) intends, by failing to disclose the information–

    (i) to make a gain for himself or another, or

    (ii) to cause loss to another or to expose another to a risk of loss.

Analysis

3.26 The Act does not define what amounts to a 'legal duty' within the meaning of s 3(a), nor is any assistance to be found in the Explanatory Notes. The Law Commission report on Fraud stated that:

> 'Such a duty may derive from statute (such as the provisions governing company prospectuses), from the fact that the transaction in question is one of utmost good faith (such as a contract of insurance), from the express or implied terms of a contract, from the custom of a particular trade or market, or from the existence of a fiduciary relationship between the parties (such as that of agent and principal)'.

In the context of mortgage fraud it is submitted that it would include a duty to disclose the existence of matters, such as a diagnosed medical condition, which might affect the ability of the mortgagor to repay the loan. In *R v White*,[10] it was held that the appellant was, as a matter of law, not under a duty to disclose to the lender that he was unemployed in a case where he had falsely misrepresented that he was employed. In practice most representations are made in response to questions posed in the application form and a failure to answer them comprehensively arguably amounts to an implied misrepresentation. Ignorance as to the existence of the duty appears to be no defence but once again the requirement to prove dishonesty would in most cases make this a strong factor in favour of the defendant.

Making or supplying articles for use in frauds

3.27 Section 7 of the Fraud Act 2006 states:

'(1) A person is guilty of an offence if he makes, adapts, supplies or offers to supply any article—

    (a) knowing that it is designed or adapted for use in the course of or in connection with fraud, or

    (b) intending it to be used to commit, or assist in the commission of, fraud.

(2) A person guilty of an offence under this section is liable—

    (a) on summary conviction, to imprisonment for a term not exceeding 12 months or to a fine not exceeding the statutory maximum (or to both);

    (b) on conviction on indictment, to imprisonment for a term not exceeding 10 years or to a fine (or to both).

---

10 [2014] EWCA Crim 714.

3.28 *Prevalent Types of Fraud*

(3) Subsection (2)(a) applies in relation to Northern Ireland as if the reference to 12 months were a reference to 6 months.'

Case example

3.28 In *R v Bestel*,[11] Pitchford LJ stated:

'It was alleged that to each of the seven separate financial institutions named in the indictment the applicant falsely represented that he was employed by Ernst & Young LLP as an accountant earning sums in excess of £275,000–£290,000 pa, dishonestly, and with the intention of making a gain for himself or to expose the lender to the risk of loss. He was in fact a former employee of Ernst & Young. In Counts 8–11 the applicant was charged with four offences of making articles for use in fraud, contrary to section 7(1) of the Fraud Act 2006. The articles made or adapted were alleged to be documents created for the purpose of supporting the dishonest applications for mortgage loans by representing that he was employed by Ernest & Young with a salary and benefits of more than £275,000. By this means the applicant had obtained funds for the purchase of many buy-to-let properties.'[12]

The Theft Act 1968

3.29 Prior to 15 January 2007, mortgage fraud offences were charged as offences under the Theft Act 1968. This was repealed by the Fraud Act 2006 as of April 2007. Saving provisions apply (see s 14(2) and Sch 2 of the Fraud Act 2006) and the former legislation applies if the offence was at least partly committed before 15 January 2007. It is therefore still necessary to consider appropriate charges under the Theft Act 1968 for offences committed prior to 15 January 2007.

3.30 *R v White*[13] is a recent example of ongoing problems caused by the inappropriate use of the Theft Act 1968. The mortgage applications made in 2004 contained misrepresentations as to the applicant's employment status and income. He had obtained successive mortgage advances on the same property by claiming he was employed when he was not. He was charged with offences contrary to s 16(1) of the Theft Act 1968 (obtaining a pecuniary advantage by deception), and Fraud Act 2006 offences to cover misrepresentations which took place after the introduction of the Fraud Act 2006. In 2010 the case was reported as an appeal against sentence. At that stage neither counsel nor the Court of Appeal saw any difficulty with the guilty pleas entered by the

---

11 [2013] EWCA Crim 1305.
12 At para 35.
13 [2014] EWCA Crim 714.

appellant. However, in the 2014 appeal, their Lordships reiterated that since the decision on *R v Preddy* in 1996 it was plain that pecuniary advantage did not extend to mortgage advances.[14] The court expected the Director of Public Prosecutions to urgently review the failings of the Crown Prosecution Service and the prosecution to identify and charge such relatively common offences in order to prevent the repeat of indictments proceeding on a basis unjustified in law.[15]

False accounting

3.31 *R v O and H*[16] is a further example of a relatively recently decided case prosecuted under s 17 of the Theft Act 1968. It is illustrative of some of the difficulties which can arise under the Theft Act but which do not arise under the Fraud Act 2006.

3.32 Section 17 of the Theft Act 1968 provides as follows:

'(1) Where a person dishonestly, with a view to gain for himself or another or with intent to cause loss to another,—

  (a) destroys, defaces, conceals or falsifies any account or any record or document *made or required for any accounting purpose; or*

  (b) in furnishing information for any purpose produces or makes use of any account, or any such record or document as aforesaid, which to his knowledge is or may be misleading, false or deceptive in a material particular;

  he shall, on conviction on indictment, be liable to imprisonment for a term not exceeding seven years.

(2) For purposes of this section a person who makes or concurs in making in an account or other document an entry which is or may be misleading, false or deceptive in a material particular, or who omits or concurs in omitting a material particular from an account or other document, is to be treated as falsifying the account or document.'

3.33 In *R v O and H* the prosecution successfully appealed against a terminating ruling by the first instance judge on the basis there was no evidence that the mortgage applications were 'required for an accounting purpose', this being an ingredient of the offence. The Court of Appeal ruled as follows;

'The judge held that there was no evidence that the mortgage lenders required the applications for an accounting purpose. Although the mortgage

---

14 The Court substituted the s16 Theft Act convictions with offences under s 15A of the Theft Act but did not substitute the Fraud Act 2006 conviction with any offence
15 Paragraph 33.
16 [2010] EWCA Crim 2233.

3.34 *Prevalent Types of Fraud*

applications had been produced by employees of the mortgage lenders (who ritually said that the mortgages would not have been granted had it been known that the particularised details were false), none of them explained (nor were asked to explain) how if at all the applications were required for an accounting purpose.'[17]

Having reviewed at length a number of authorities the court in *R v O and H* concluded that:

'It is understandable why, having briefly discussed a number of these cases, the editors of Smith's Law of Theft 9th Edition say (para 4.11): "Unfortunately, the Courts have failed to adopt a consistent approach."

...

'It is very difficult if not impossible to reconcile all the cases on the point.

...

'In our view and without any further direct evidence of the accounting practices of the lender, a jury is entitled to come to the conclusion that an application for a mortgage or a loan made to a commercial institution is a document required for an accounting purpose. We should add that it is important not to overlook the requirement of materiality: see Lancaster, above para 30.[18]

In these circumstances the appeal is allowed and we set aside the ruling made by HHJ Carr finding that there was no case to answer in the absence of direct evidence of the accounting practices of the mortgage company.'[19]

The result is that the jury will have to determine the very issue which their Lordships noted has given rise to an inconsistent approach. This appears to be the unavoidable outcome of proceeding under this section, but equally illustrates the utility of the Fraud Act 2006 in enabling juries to focus on the alleged dishonest conduct.

3.34 Under the Fraud Act 2006, there would be no requirement to prove that the document was required for any such purpose, still less that it operated on the minds of the lender. Under the Theft Act 1968, unless there is good reason for not doing so, it is the prosecution's duty to call the person or persons

---

17 [2010] EWCA Crim 2233, At para 8.
18 In deciding in a non-disclosure case whether there had been an omission within the meaning of the words 'omits a material particular' in the Theft Act 1968 s.17(2)(b), the omission would be material if it had the effect that the document was liable to mislead in a significant way, and that would depend on the nature of the document and the context. The test was objective, and a good way to convey that to the jury would be to say that it was for the jury to judge for themselves, on the facts of the case, whether they thought the omission was significant. Headnote of R v Lancaster 2010 EWCA Crim 370.
19 *R v O and H*, at paras 45, 48–50.

who were alleged to have been deceived by the false representations[20] and for them to prove that deception operated upon his or her mind.[21]

Obtaining property by deception

3.35 Under s 15 of the Theft Act 1968:[22]

'(1) A person who by any deception dishonestly obtains *property belonging to another*, with the intention of permanently depriving the other of it, shall on conviction on indictment be liable to imprisonment for a term not exceeding 10 years.

(2) For purposes of this section a person is to be treated as obtaining property if he obtains ownership, possession or control of it, and "obtain" includes obtaining for another or enabling another to obtain or retain.

[...]

(4) For purposes of this section "deception" means any deception (whether deliberate or reckless) by words or conduct as to fact or as to law, including a deception as to the present intentions of the person using the deception or any other person.'

By s 4(1) of the Act (applied to s 15(1) by s 34(1)), it is provided that property includes money and all other property, real or personal, including things in action and other intangible property.

Analysis

3.36 Mortgage fraud used frequently to be charged as obtaining property belonging by deception. In the landmark decision of *R v Preddy*,[23] the House of Lords held that a mortgage was a 'chose in action' and therefore was 'property' within the meaning of the Act, but the issue was whether this chose in action, at any stage, *belonged to another*. Ultimately, it was solely created for the applicant and accordingly it did not 'belong to another':

'(1) where a payment was made from one bank account to another bank account either telegraphically or electronically, no identifiable property passed from the payer to the payee; thus the payer could not be guilty of

---

20 *R v Tirado* (1974) 59 Cr App R 80 (CA).
21 *R v Laverty* (1970) 54 Cr App R 495.
22 Because ss 15 and 15A of the Theft Act 1968 had been repealed by the Fraud Act 2006 by the time the guidelines were issued. However, the guidelines were 'relevant' to the applicant's case since they applied to the same or similar types of offences which would now come within the Fraud Act 2006: *R v Cole* [2011] EWCA Crim 2993.
23 [1996] 2 Cr App R 524.

3.37 *Prevalent Types of Fraud*

obtaining 'property belonging to another', contrary to section 15(1) of the Theft Act 1968.

'(2) Accordingly, in the instant cases, the appellants, although they had obtained or attempted to obtain the mortgage advances by misrepresentations, had not contravened section 15(1) of the Theft Act 1968, and the position was no different if the advances in question had been transferred to a solicitor acting for both the lending institution and the mortgagor.'[24]

Obtaining a money transfer by deception (Theft Act 1968, s 15A)

3.37 The difficulty caused by the judgment in *Preddy* led to statutory reform and the introduction of s 15A of the Theft Act 1968 which created the offence of obtaining a money transfer by deception. This came into force on 18 December 1996.[25]

3.38 A money transfer occurs when a debit is made to one account, a credit is made to another. Section 15A became the appropriate charge from December 1996 to the introduction of the Fraud Act 2006.

Other available offences

3.39 In *R v Cook*,[26] the convictions for mortgage fraud charged under s 15 of the Theft Act 1968 could not be sustained in the light of *Preddy* (see above), but the court substituted them with the offence of procuring the execution of a valuable security by deception contrary to s 20(2) of the 1968 Theft Act and obtaining services by deception under s 1(1) of the Theft Act 1978.

The role of the professional

3.40 *R v Ward*[27] provides an example of dishonest activity by solicitors, surveyors and mortgage brokers:

'Ward was a mortgage broker, trading as Aaron Associates. ... He also was an authorised introducer, that is he introduced transactions to banks and other lending institutions, doing so for commission.

[...]

One essential source of assistance was, of course, conveyancing. That activity was facilitated for him [WARD] by the use of TI Clough, the solicitors

---

24 Headnote in *R v Preddy*.
25 Introduced by s 1 of the Theft (Amendment) Act 1996.
26 [1997] CLR 436.
27 [2005] EWCA Crim 1972.

firm. In each of these four or five instances as acting for both borrower and lender. That in its turn brought in the second appellant, Brown. Mr Brown was a very experienced long-standing conveyancing clerk with TI Clough and he undertook all that was necessary to bring about these transactions. This involved him in dealing with, if not producing, false applications and turning a blind eye to false information that was being put before him. He acted in all five cases and had clearly a role in, as it were, the engine room for this activity.

Additional to a conveyancer, Ward needed to be able to represent the persons said to be applying for the advances as persons with financial standing. To this end, they were respectively represented to be self-employed and that meant in turn that the lenders needed to see accounts to confirm contentions as to their earnings and social standing. That was systematically provided by the co-accused, Clayton. Clayton was a chartered accountant, who concocted bogus accounts as and when required by Ward.'[28]

Bank managers

3.41 Persons employed within the lending institution may collude in mortgage fraud in order to achieve commission or they may receive covert payment from the applicants.

Brokers

3.42 In self-certification mortgages the applicant need not prove his or her income. This sort of application is obviously ripe for abuse. A broker adds an air of legitimacy to fraudulent application. He or she can vouch for the identity of the applicant and his accounts. If a broker or other professional is suspected of involvement in one mortgage fraud, investigators should consider a thorough trawl of prior applications, as, if the suspicions are well founded, they are unlikely to be a wholly isolated example.

3.43 Defendants charged with making false representations to brokers may often blame the broker for the inaccurate nature of the information. The ability to so is made easier by the fact that information is sometimes supplied via a sales screen on a computer operated by the broker and no paper copy is signed by the applicant. In addition, brokers have a financial incentive to misstate the position since they receive commission from the lender if the application is successful.

---

28   *R v Ward*, at paras 18, 20, 21.

3.44 *Prevalent Types of Fraud*

Accountants

3.44 Accountants can support the provision of false information and confirm anticipated income.

Solicitors

3.45 A dishonest solicitor may collude in deceiving the lender as to the identity, status and/or means of the borrower. The solicitor may provide a false or incomplete Report of Title thereby misleading the lender as to the true value of the property. For example, in a commercial mortgage the lender will want to know whether there is a tenant in occupation and the terms of lease, including the rent. If the solicitor fails to accurately report the situation, he will have colluded in deceiving the lender. However, in this situation it is much more likely that the solicitor was simply relating information provided to him by the applicant and if this is the position then obviously the solicitor will have committed no offence.

3.46 The Council for Mortgage Lenders sets standards of what is expected of conveyancing solicitors acting for a lender; failure to adhere to such standards may be evidence of fraud although breach of terms cannot of itself amount to a crime.

Surveyors

3.47 Surveyors may misrepresent the commercial viability or development prospects of land. They may inflate the true value of the property or may intentionally omit things which adversely affect value of land to enable the applicant to borrow more than the lender would otherwise be prepared to lend. Lenders will almost always have a maximum loan to value ratio, which varies between lenders and their products. For example, if the LTV is 70 per cent, the lender will lend a maximum of £70,000 against a property valued at £100,000.[29] Evidence of 'comparables'[30] are important in assessing whether a valuation was made in good faith or whether it is so grossly overstated that it must have been provided in order to perpetrate a fraud on the lender

---

29 Lending practices before the 'credit crunch' are widely recognised to be more lax than at present and this would include the greater availability of 100 per cent LTV products.
30 Comparables are simply the sale prices of similar properties in the same area at the material time.

Avenues of investigation

3.48 What investigations prove necessary will inevitably depend on the facts of the case. Typical lines of enquiry are set out below

Companies House

3.49 The application may contain a representation that the applicant works for a company. Companies House checks may reveal that no such company is registered or the company returns may contain inconsistencies with what is asserted in the application

Solicitors' files

3.50 Investigators should also apply for the conveyancing files held by the solicitors. These will contain information supplied by the applicant to the solicitor about the purpose of the loan, the source of any deposit, the occupation and earnings, address and identity of the applicant.[31]

Council tax records and utilities

3.51 If the type of fraud alleged is that the defendant applied for an owner occupier mortgage intending in reality to rent it out, then the question of who is in occupation becomes relevant. Equally, if it is alleged that the true identity of beneficial owner is concealed as part of an effort to conceal true ownership of the asset, for example to conceal wealth and assets generated by other criminal conduct, then who is in fact in occupation is also relevant.

Receipts

3.52 Receipts will record expenditure in the name of the defendant or others, and, depending on the circumstances, workmen who have done work at the property. If traceable, they may be able to provide evidence as to who was in occupation and what line of business they understood them to be in.

Seller or agent

3.53 The estate agent or vendor may recall conversations with the purchaser/applicant that disclose how it would be paid for and who would be living in it.

---

31 This material is prima facie privileged: see s10 of PACE 1984 for procedure and test of disclosure.

3.54 *Prevalent Types of Fraud*

Bank account information

3.54 Mortgage repayments are generally made from a bank account in the name of the applicant. A further line of investigation is to obtain the bank account application forms completed at the time of opening the account to look for inconsistencies in stated occupation, income and source of deposit.

HMRC

3.55 Very often the employment and income details provided do not correlate to the tax returns provided by the suspect and it is standard practice to make inquiries of HMRC. In such circumstances it may be appropriate to add a charge of cheating the revenue[32] – if the defendant's income was as stated on the application then he ought to have disclosed it the Revenue and discharged the resulting tax liability. Where appropriate to the circumstances of the case, tax returns should be examined to see if rental income has been declared. If not, a charge of cheating the revenue may be preferred.

Sales screen applications

3.56 Mortgage applications may be completed on sales screen application. Such applications are completed by a broker and submitted to the mortgage lender without being signed by the applicant. It is submitted that this method of applying for a mortgage is highly unsatisfactory as it means that the largest ever financial commitment most people ever undertake can be processed without their signature. Clearly if the application is not signed there may well be an issue as to whether the applicant knew or even had the opportunity to ascertain that details provided in the application were false.

Sentencing

3.57 Section 1(3) of the Fraud Act 2006 states that the term of conviction for anyone found guilty of fraud is, on summary conviction, a term not exceeding 12 months, and after conviction on indictment a maximum of 10 years.

3.58 The sentencing examples below must be read subject to the new Sentencing Council guidelines which came into force in October 2014. They are included to provide some assistance as to the proper approach to sentencing issues that frequently arise in this context.

---

32 This offence is discussed at paras 3.184 and 3.185 below, but the essence of it is made out on proof that the defendant dishonestly evaded a tax liability for which he liable.

Should multiple offences result in consecutive sentences?

Case examples

3.59 In *R v Crocker*,[33] Elias LJ stated:

> 'The three mortgage advance offences related to three separate properties. Count 9 concerned a house in Hitchin. The appellant obtained an advance of £212,000 by deception from the Halifax plc. The application was made in the name of Keith Pardoe, although it was never intended that he would repay the mortgage loan. It stated that he was self-employed and had an income of about £85,000 a year, but that was false. False trading accounts were provided along with a bank statement and a copy of a driving licence in the name of K Pardoe.
>
> Count 10 related to a property in Frithville. There was an advance of £256,000 from Santander bank. Again there was false information provided to secure this.
>
> Count 11 involved the appellant obtaining a mortgage from the Santander bank in the sum of £500,000 to purchase property in Boston, Lincolnshire. This time the application was in his own name. Again false information was given. He claimed to be the owner of a business which did not exist and to be receiving all the net profits from the business which he said was £158,230. In fact, repayments were made on all three mortgages, although the barn in Frithville was repossessed.
>
> [...]
>
> Counsel did not complain about the judge using the Sentencing Guideline Council's fraud guidelines or banking and insurance frauds when passing sentence. The guideline suggests a range of four to seven years for frauds of over £750,000 and the total amount here was in the region of £900,000. But having regard to the fact that there was no loss, it is submitted that the judge ought to have started at the bottom end of that range, whereas he must have started at a figure of six years, which is more than the five-year starting point for frauds of that nature. Indeed, Mr Stein QC submitted to us today that the appropriate point to have begun would have been at the lowest end of that range, it should have been four years.
>
> We accept that it would have been desirable in principle for the judge to have given concurrent sentences in relation to these mortgage frauds rather than consecutive sentences. That of itself is not a matter of great moment but it does mean that the judge then has to take into account considerations of totality, which he did in this case, in order to ensure that the appropriate sentence overall is given. We think that he did not have sufficient regard

---

33 [2013] EWCA Crim 1176.

3.60 *Prevalent Types of Fraud*

for totality. An appropriate sentence for these mortgage frauds, bearing in mind no loss and totality, would in our view have been four-and-a-half years after a trial which would mean three years giving full credit for the plea. We say that because the amount intended to be gained was in excess of the £750,000 which is the figure for the starting point and in addition these were planned and sophisticated frauds. That means that we would reduce the sentence in relation to the mortgage frauds from four years to three years and added to the 18 months for the benefit frauds it would give a total sentence of four-and-a-half years.'[34]

The correct approach where successive mortgages are obtained on the same property

3.60 In *R v White*,[35] the appellant pleaded guilty to two counts of obtaining a pecuniary advantage by deception and two counts of fraud.[36] The appellant made successive false mortgage applications in respect of the same property in which he lied about his income and stated that he employed when in fact he was not. Underhill J noted:

'The judge described the amount obtained as £660,000 and took a starting point of four years, although she proceeded to reduce that somewhat, as we have already identified, to just under three-and-a-half years, in the interests of totality because the appellant was already serving a prison term. Four years—the figure taken by the judge—is the recommended starting point for cases where the amount obtained is £500,000 or more, and in fact the rubric says that the starting-point is based on an amount obtained of £750,000.

[It was submitted that] *[S]ince each offence after the first was a re-financing which involved repayment of the amount previously lent, the appellant never obtained a total of £660,000 or anything like that. The actual amount was that of the last and largest loan—that is, £265,000—and that put the case ... in the next bracket down, for which the recommended range is two to four years and the starting-point, based on an amount advanced of £300,000, is three years.*'

This submission was accepted by the Court. The sentence handed down was 30 months' imprisonment for obtaining a pecuniary advantage by deception and fraud, reduced to two years.[37]

---

34 At paras 5–7, 11, 12.
35 [2011] EWCA Crim 2280.
36 See para 3.30 above, which makes it clear that the charges were misconceived. Nonetheless, it is submitted the principle as to the approach to sentence in the event of re mortgages is unaffected.
37 In the subsequent appeal against conviction in which the appeal was in part allowed and three of the four counts substituted with offences contrary to s 15A of the Theft Act 1968, the sentence was unaltered.

Mortgage fraud **3.62**

The effect on sentence where no loss is sustained and other factors affecting sentence?

3.61 It may be that the lender suffers no loss as a result of the mortgage fraud.[38] Although *Petkova* (below) was decided before their introduction, the current Sentencing Guidelines make clear that cases in which there is no loss are less serious than those in which loss occurs or is intended.[39] The other factors referred to in the extract below are also likely to remain relevant to sentence. The following passages are extracts from the decision in *R v Petkova*:[40]

> 'In the course of his written submissions, our attention was drawn to the case of *R v Yates* [2010] EWCA Crim 1028, where at paragraph 12, Davis J giving the judgment of this court said that:
>
>> "... we would suggest that — and subject always to the Definitive Guidelines— in the case of a loan or loans obtained by fraud of this kind some of the potentially relevant features may be (in no particular order) as follows: first, whether one or several transactions are involved; second, whether the fraud is committed by a professional person or is otherwise committed in breach of trust; third, the nature of the fraud will need to be considered and the means by which it is carried through; fourth, whether the fraud was an isolated incident or involved ongoing deception; fifth, the amount of money sought and obtained; sixth, the amount of actual loss, so far as it can be identified, to the lender; seventh, whether the offender has involved others, or is involved with others, in the fraud; and eighth, whether at the time there was an intention to repay (and, if so, the anticipated means of repayment) or whether there was no intention to repay. There may well be other factors, and regard will of course need to be had in the usual way to matters such as a guilty plea, relevant previous convictions or lack of previous convictions, and so on. In particular, regard must, of course, always be had to the relevant Definitive Guidelines."
>
> [...]
>
> 'Actual loss is however a factor, and moreover one that the guidelines make clear regard must be had to.'[41]

Civil recovery and mortgage fraud

3.62 In *Serious Organised Crime Agency v Pelekanos*,[42] Mr P was investigated by police for drug trafficking offences but was not charged. The

---

38 This absence of loss is specifically recognised as a mitigating feature.
39 See p 7 of the Fraud Bribery and Money Laundering Guidelines
40 2011 EWCA Crim 109.
41 At paras 19 and 22.
42 [2009] EWHC 2307 (QB).

3.63 *Prevalent Types of Fraud*

police referred the case to SOCA who investigated Mr P's financial affairs. The civil recovery action under Pt V of the Proceeds of Crime Act 2002 (POCA) failed in respect of the allegation of drug trafficking. However, the investigation uncovered false representations in various mortgage applications submitted by Mr P which resulted in the making of a recovery order. Hamblen J ruled that:

'This began as a case about drug trafficking. It has ended up as a case about mortgage fraud. As such, it illustrates the breadth of application of the civil recovery legislation. As the law stands, any person, however otherwise law abiding, may be the subject of a civil recovery order if he makes a deliberately false statement in a mortgage application form. It is important that this be more widely known, and it is desirable that mortgage providers spell out this possible consequence of a misstatement in their application forms.'

As to the practice and procedure of Pt V of POCA 2002, see Eissa and Barber.[43]

PONZI FRAUDS[44]

Overview

3.63 In 1920 the eponymous Charles Ponzi used a scheme of promising high returns to persuade people to invest with him. It was a fraud. There were no profits on investments to pay people that which was promised. Peter was being robbed to pay Paul so that promises to previous investors were made good by using a new person's investments rather than lawful profit created by genuine business. So it is that this sort of investment fraud is known as a Ponzi fraud. In recent times huge schemes have been perpetrated, most famously in the United States by Bernie Maddoff and Allen Stanford.

3.64 Although there are numerous variations on the theme, there will be classic 'badges' that tend to appear. First, schemes offer unrealistically high rates of return. When compared to high street banks or even the greatest risk investments undertaken by City traders and others, the percentage returns offered are very high indeed. Meaningless phrases such as 'high yield investment programmes' will be employed to sound attractive but no more than that. Secondly, the mechanics of the scheme are kept away from the investors. It is true that there will be in all likelihood glossy brochures, websites – even lectures and presentations – but the detail of the nature of the investment is unlikely to be revealed. The reasons given usually relate to commercial confidentiality.

---

43 Adrian Eissa and Ruth Barber, *Confiscation Law Handbook* (Bloomsbury Professional, 2011).
44 With gratitude to Geoff Payne of 25 Bedford Row for his input and assistance.

3.65 Thirdly, investors – once the initial investment is made and the first return is paid out – are persuaded to 'roll over' their original investment rather than receive the capital back. This has the advantage to the fraudster of not having to find further money to pay out, and gimmicks, such as further percentage increases on returns in exchange for extended 'lock in' of capital, once the first returns are paid give the scheme an increasingly shiny veneer of respectability. If an investor does want his capital then this is paid back; this also ensures that to the outside world things look legitimate and the scheme profitable. Fourthly, they almost always come to a disastrous end with the 'investments' being lost. The fraudster will nearly always have persuaded family members to invest with him but the reality is that unless new money is continually pumped into the scheme to pay the ever-increasing number of returns the scheme cannot survive.

Charges

3.66 There are a number of different charges that Ponzi schemes can be indicted as. Sometimes it will depend on the size of the scheme, other times it will depend on the prosecution's assessment of the roles of the defendants that it has managed to charge. For example, 'pyramid' schemes are often Ponzi frauds in disguise. A person who manages to persuade 10 people to invest in another's scheme will obtain a reward, and be asked to find others who are prepared to do the same. In this way the scheme spreads, with the organisers spreading the workload and, to a degree, insulating themselves, by being one step removed, from the investment process.

Conspiracy to defraud

3.67 Large schemes and senior defendants can be charged with conspiracy to defraud. Self evidently this is an offence of dishonesty treated extremely seriously. Chapter 2 for an analysis of this offence generally. For an example of sentencing in a Ponzi fraud see *Attorney General's References (Nos 7 and 8 of 2013) (R v Kallakis and Williams) (R v Levene)*,[45] where Levene's sentence was reduced from 13 to 12 years' imprisonment.

Fraud

3.68 Alternatively substantive counts of fraud under the Fraud Act 2006 can be brought. Self evidently this is an offence of dishonesty treated extremely seriously. See Chapter 1 for an analysis of this offence generally.

---

45 [2014] 1 Cr App R (S) 26.

3.69 *Prevalent Types of Fraud*

The regulatory position

Breach of the general prohibition on carrying out regulated activity

3.69 As well as the traditional offences of dishonesty referred to above, there are also some regulatory offences where liability does not depend on dishonesty, but behaviour. These are used to prosecute people lower down the 'food chain' who have assisted in the gathering of investments but whom the prosecution are not convinced they will be able to persuade a jury of any dishonesty.

3.70 Investment frauds of this variety almost always involve the taking of deposits. That is an activity regulated by the Financial Services and Markets Act 2000 (FSMA) in the following way:

'19(1) No person may carry on a regulated activity in the United Kingdom, or purport to do so, unless he is—

 (a) an authorised person; or

 (b) an exempt person.

(2) The prohibition is referred to in this Act as the general prohibition.'

[…]

'23(1) A person who contravenes the general prohibition is guilty of an offence and liable—

 (a) on summary conviction, to imprisonment for a term not exceeding six months or a fine not exceeding the statutory maximum, or both;

 (b) on conviction on indictment, to imprisonment for a term not exceeding two years or a fine, or both.

(2) In this Act "an authorisation offence" means an offence under this section.

(3) In proceedings for an authorisation offence it is a defence for the accused to show that he took all reasonable precautions and exercised all due diligence to avoid committing the offence.'

Thus there is a 'general prohibition' upon certain types of regulated activity, breach of which general prohibition is a criminal offence, known as an 'authorisation offence', punishable by up to two years in prison. The offence itself is breaching the prohibition; that can be committed in a number of ways, of which this is but one example.

3.71 An activity is regulated if it is of a specified kind as set by s 22:

Ponzi frauds **3.73**

'22(1)   An activity is a regulated activity for the purposes of this Act if it is an activity of a specified kind which is carried on by way of business and—

  (a)   relates to an investment of a specified kind; or

  (b)   in the case of an activity of a kind which is also specified for the purposes of this paragraph, is carried on in relation to property of any kind.

(2)   Schedule 2 makes provision supplementing this section.

(3)   Nothing in Schedule 2 limits the powers conferred by subsection (1).

(4)   "Investment" includes any asset, right or interest.

(5)   "Specified" means specified in an order made by the Treasury.'

3.72   'Accepting deposits' is a specified kind of activity according to the Financial Services and Markets Act 2000 (Regulated Activities) Order 2001:

'5(1)   Accepting deposits is a specified kind of activity if—

  (a)   money received by way of deposit is lent to others; or

  (b)   any other activity of the person accepting the deposit is financed wholly, or to a material extent, out of the capital of or interest on money received by way of deposit.

(2)   In paragraph (1), "deposit" means a sum of money, other than one excluded by any of articles 6 to 9, paid on terms—

  (a)   under which it will be repaid, with or without interest or premium, and either on demand or at a time or in circumstances agreed by or on behalf of the person making the payment and the person receiving it; and

  (b)   which are not referable to the provision of property (other than currency) or services or the giving of security.'

Thus by reg 5(1)(b), if the money received, by way of business, is used to further a scheme, which it is, then the accepting of the deposits will be a specified activity which will in turn place a person in breach of the general prohibition provided as s 418(1) and (5) of FSMA 2000 mandates that where a person who is carrying on a regulated activity does not have his head office in the United Kingdom he will nonetheless be regarded as so doing if he uses an establishment maintained by him in the United Kingdom.

3.73   Needless to say people engaged in these schemes are not, ordinarily, authorised or exempt persons (and to that end no more is said about it save that, evidentially there will be statements from the Financial Conduct Authority proving that).

3.74 *Prevalent Types of Fraud*

3.74 In *R v Napoli*,[46] the Court of Appeal (Criminal Division) considered with some care the 'complex' legislative provisions in this area and the interrelationship between the provisions of FSMA 2000 and those of the Financial Services and Markets Act 2000 (Regulated Activities) Order 2001 and the Financial Services and Markets Act 2000 (Carrying on Regulated Activities by way of Business) Order 2001 holding that the offence, in that case, was properly made out.

3.75 In terms of sentence each case will depend upon its own facts, bearing in mind the maximum is up to two years. Such cases will often have money-laundering offences alongside, with a maximum of 14 years. In *R v Greaves*[47] the Court of Appeal held that the question was whether the money laundering 'added anything further' to the other offences. If it did, then further punishment, consecutively if necessary, was appropriate. If it didn't add anything then a person was not to be punished for the same offending twice.

3.76 In *R v Epton*,[48] 15 months, after a plea of guilty, was upheld for a 65-year-old man who had been drawn into a scheme due to his own greed and who had himself been ruined. The Court held that the vulnerability of the financial system and investors to scams on a much larger scale had been highlighted by recent events and the subversion of controls on investments represented a public danger. See also *R v Powell & Hinkson*.[49]

Defences

3.77 Traditionally most people convicted of Ponzi schemes deny dishonesty by asserting they believe the scheme to be true. If that is so, or may be so, then of course they will not be guilty of an offence of dishonesty. However, it tends to run into difficulty when such persons are asked to detail how the investment scheme would legitimately make such levels of return. Additionally the lifestyle of the person being tried has tended to become more extravagant during the currency of the scheme.

3.78 Such people will, more often than not, be guilty of breaches of the general prohibition in any event, although those who 'serve' under people who swear that a scheme is lawful will try to rely on the 'due diligence' defence in s 23(3) of FSMA 2000 (see above). There is, however, a statutory defence by way of exception provided by the Financial Services and Markets Act 2000 (Carrying on Regulated Activities by way of Business) Order 2001), Art 2, namely:

---

46   [2012] Lloyd's Rep FC 599; [2012] EWCA Crim 1129.
47   [2011] 1 Cr App R (S) 8.
48   [2009] 2 Cr App R (S) 96.
49   [2009] 1 Cr App R 30.

'(1) A person who carries on an activity of the kind specified by article 5 of the Regulated Activities Order (accepting deposits) is not to be regarded as doing so by way of business if—

  (a) he does not hold himself out as accepting deposits on a day to day basis; and

  (b) any deposits which he accepts are accepted only on particular occasions, whether or not involving the issue of any securities.

(2) In determining for the purposes of paragraph (1)(b) whether deposits are accepted only on particular occasions, regard is to be had to the frequency of those occasions and to any characteristics distinguishing them from each other.'

The prosecution must disprove at least one or other of one of Art 2(1)(a) or (b) (as they are expressed conjunctively).[50]

3.79 This will be a matter for the jury to determine whether or not such behaviour is 'day to day' or 'occasional'. In *R v Napoli*,[51] the Court of Appeal was 'more helpfully' referred to *SCF Finance v Masri (No 2)*,[52] where Slade LJ said, in relation to the words 'holds himself out to accept deposits on a day to day basis' in relation to s 1(3) of the Banking Act 1979:

'The Act gives no guidance as to the construction of section 1 (3) beyond that afforded by the wording of the sub section itself. In our judgment, however (without attempting any comprehensive definition of the phrase), on the ordinary meaning of the words, a person 'holds himself out to accept deposits on a day to day basis' only if (by way of express or implicit invitation) he holds himself out as being generally willing on any normal day to accept such deposits from those person to whom the invitation is addressed who may wish to place money with him by way of deposit'.

BOILER ROOM FRAUD

Overview

3.80 Allegations of boiler room fraud are known about by the public thanks to films such as the eponymous Vin Diesel vehicle 'Boiler Room' and, more recently, Leonardo Di Caprio's 'Wolf of Wall Street'. At their most basic they involve the sale of non-existent or effectively worthless shares to unsuspecting individuals who pay large sums of money for them. They are categorised by 'high pressure' (hence 'boiler room') tactics from salesmen who target those

---

50 *R v Napoli* [2012] Lloyd's Rep FC 599; [2012] EWCA Crim 1129.
51 [2012] Lloyd's Rep FC 599; [2012] EWCA Crim 1129.
52 [1987] 1 QB 1002 at 1022E.

3.81 *Prevalent Types of Fraud*

vulnerable to purchasing such shares by, for example, using electoral rolls to discover more elderly people, using share registers from legitimate companies to discover who has bought shares in the past or 'repeat' calling those they have sold to before.

3.81 The courts are taking these cases very seriously as they tend to involve very large amounts of money and vulnerable victims. In *R v Wilmot*,[53] the Court of Appeal, presided over by the Lord Chief Justice, said:

> '6. The shares were sold to members of the public by telephone sales in which high-pressure selling techniques were deployed. As the boiler rooms were based overseas, they were not registered with the Financial Services Authority and were therefore outside the scope of the protection otherwise afforded to members of the public under the FSA protection scheme.
>
> 7. On the Crown's case approximately 36.8 million shares in the companies were sold by boiler rooms for an estimated sum of £13.97 million.
>
> [...]
>
> 13. The applicant was the mastermind of a complex and sophisticated fraud on a massive scale. It was conducted over a considerable period of time and was directed at elderly, gullible and therefore vulnerable victims, some of whom could ill afford their losses. It involved the creation of documentation designed "to obfuscate the issues in this case and confuse the investors". It also involved the extensive use of forged documents, including official documents to be sent to Companies House, and the dishonest use of the identity of others, including friends of the Wilmots, without their knowledge. The proceeds of the fraud were processed through offshore companies in a manner designed to distance the applicant and his sons from their criminal activity'.

In that case a sentence of nine years was upheld for four conspiracies to defraud and, but for the health of the applicant, the sentence would have reached into double figures.

3.82 The Financial Conduct Authority says:[54]

> 'Share scams are often run from "boiler rooms" where fraudsters cold-call investors offering them worthless, overpriced or even non-existent shares. While they promise high returns, those who invest usually end up losing their money.
>
> Boiler rooms use increasingly sophisticated tactics to approach investors offering to buy or sell shares in a way that they say will give investors a

---

53 [2013] 1 Cr App R (S) 61.
54 http://www.fca.org.uk/consumers/scams/investment-scams/share-fraud-and-boiler-room-scams.

huge return. But in the end, victims are often left out of pocket – sometimes losing all of their savings or even their family home.

We have found that victims of share fraud lose an average of £20,000 to these scams, with as much as £200m being lost in the UK each year. Even seasoned investors have been caught out, with the biggest individual loss recorded by the police being £6m'.

3.83 There are two common types of share sale. First, there are sales of shares in UK companies that the purchaser is told is likely to list on a stock market within a short period of time (usually a junior market such as the Alternative Investment Market ('AIM') and that if they don't purchase now they are going to miss out on a quick and large profit. Recently, due to changes in the UK legislation affecting regulation of those who provide financial services under the Financial Services and Markets Act 2000 ('FSMA'), many salesmen are based abroad, traditionally in Spain. However, depending on the sophistication of the scheme, a purchaser may think they are dealing with a UK-based office with a UK telephone number and so forth. Once 'sold', the purchaser will have paid for their shares and is likely to receive a certificate showing their ownership. The problem is that either the companies do not exist or, if they do, the shares are virtually worthless, as the company is not going to list on any market and may or may not have no product to sell whatsoever.

3.84 The second, commonly encountered share, is the 'Regulation S' share from the United States. The Financial Conduct Authority says:[55]

'Many reports we receive about share scams or boiler rooms involve the sale of restricted or controlled US shares. While the sale of these shares is not always a scam, it is often not made clear to investors that they can be very difficult or expensive to trade.

Restricted or controlled shares are also known as 'Regulation S shares'. This comes from a US ruling that allows firms there to sell stocks that do not meet listings standards (and therefore have tight restrictions on their sale in the US) to investors outside the US.

These shares are often issued at a discount to their normal US price, but most of this discount is kept by the broker.

How it works

If you buy these shares you will have to keep them for a set period, usually six months or one year. You cannot sell them back to buyers in the US during this time without paying to lift the restriction. Once the holding period has passed you still have to pay a US lawyer to remove the legal restriction

---

55 http://www.fca.org.uk/consumers/scams/investment-scams/share-fraud-and-boiler-room-scams/restricted-us-shares.

3.85 *Prevalent Types of Fraud*

from the share certificate before selling the shares, which could cost more than your shares are worth. For this reason, investors holding restricted or controlled shares are often targeted by fraudsters that offer to get the restriction removed or say they will minimise the loss on the investment. But this is often a scam run from a boiler room and you are unlikely to ever receive the money from the sale of the shares'.

Charges

3.85 Charges in such cases tend to be one of two types. In the more serious cases, and in relation to those said to be higher up the chain, conspiracy to defraud is considered appropriate. As has already been seen from *R v Wilmot*,[56] this was successfully prosecuted in relation to four companies from which shares had been sold. For less serious behaviour, or as alternative to conspiracy to defraud, offences under FSMA 2000 are prosecuted. As is seen elsewhere in this book, the offence under s 23 of FSMA 2000 of breaching the 'general prohibition' in s 19 of FSMA 2000 encompasses many different kinds of financial conduct if such is a 'regulated activity'.

Conspiracy to defraud

3.86 This is considered generally in Chapter 2. Given that the 'boiler rooms' themselves are often located outside the jurisdiction, careful consideration should be given to whether or not a prosecution is able to be mounted in the UK. Normally the targeting of people within the UK will be sufficient to meet this hurdle however. Otherwise charges will usually be particularised by reference to the dishonest selling of shares based upon a number of features such as misleading information being imparted about listing on markets. An example is that in *R v Greaves*.[57] There the indictment read:

> 'Henrik Botcher Claude Greaves Phillipa Greaves Fraser Jenkins Paula Jno-Baptiste and Roozbeh Yazdanian between the 10/10/2005 and 15/12/2006 conspired together and with other persons unknown to dishonestly defraud such persons as could be induced to part with money by way of cheque and credit transfers in reliance on false representations that:
>
> 1/ they acting in the course of business, were lawfully allowed to communicate invitations or inducements to engage in investment activity to UK investors or prospective investors.
>
> 2/ they were lawfully allowed to offer, to sell and advise on shares to UK investors or prospective investors or to agree to do so

---

56 [2013] 1 Cr App R (S) 61.
57 [2011] 1 Cr App R (S) 8.

3/ they genuinely believed what they told prospective UK investors about the nature value and prospects of the shares they advised on, offered and sold to those investors.

4/ Pantera Oil and Gas PLC, had applied for its shares to be listed on a UK investment exchange.

5/ Pantera Oil and Gas PLC and its officers expected its shares to be imminently listed on a UK investment exchange.

6/ the shares in

Pantera Oil and Gas Plc.

Northern Lynx Plc.

ParOs Plc.

ValiRX Plc'.

The regulatory position

Breach of the general prohibition on carrying out regulated activity

3.87 As indicated the selling of shares is a 'regulated activity'. What follows is a very basic indication of the sorts of pitfalls and regulatory twists and turns that might exist. The basic position is straightforward. However, the various exceptions that exist can be exploited (or be attempted to be exploited) by some people to try to avoid being captured by the Financial Conduct Authority's regulatory framework in relation to investments.

3.88 In the context of boiler room frauds, the basic framework arises by reference to the Financial Services and Markets Act 2000 (FSMA) in the following way:

'19(1) No person may carry on a regulated activity in the United Kingdom, or purport to do so, unless he is—

(a) an authorised person; or

(b) an exempt person.

(2) The prohibition is referred to in this Act as the general prohibition.'

'23(1) A person who contravenes the general prohibition is guilty of an offence and liable—

(a) on summary conviction, to imprisonment for a term not exceeding six months or a fine not exceeding the statutory maximum, or both;

3.89 *Prevalent Types of Fraud*

>   (b)   on conviction on indictment, to imprisonment for a term not exceeding two years or a fine, or both.
>
> (2) In this Act 'an authorisation offence' means an offence under this section.
>
> (3) In proceedings for an authorisation offence it is a defence for the accused to show that he took all reasonable precautions and exercised all due diligence to avoid committing the offence.'

Thus the general prohibition is the carrying on of a regulated activity without authorisation or if exempt. Section 25 of FSMA 2000 provides the maximum sentence is two years' imprisonment (as it would be for a conspiracy to contravene the general prohibition).

3.89 The legislative landscape was described by the Court of Appeal in *R v Greaves*[58] as follows:

> '3. Section 19 of the Financial Services and Markets Act 2000 provides that only authorised persons may carry on a regulated activity in the United Kingdom. The sale of the shares was a regulated activity and was not being carried on by authorised persons. Section 21 of the Act provides that persons who are not authorised must not in the course of a business communicate an invitation to engage in investment activity unless the invitation has been approved by an authorised person. The salesmen were not authorised and their communications were not approved by an authorised person. Sections 23 and 25 make breach of ss.19 and 21 punishable with up to two years imprisonment. Applying s.3 of the Criminal Law Act 1977 the maximum sentence for conspiracy to contravene these sections is the maximum provided by the sections themselves.'

3.90 An activity is regulated if it is of a specified kind as set by s 22:

> '(1) An activity is a regulated activity for the purposes of this Act if it is an activity of a specified kind which is carried on by way of business and—
>
>   (a)   relates to an investment of a specified kind; or
>
>   (b)   in the case of an activity of a kind which is also specified for the purposes of this paragraph, is carried on in relation to property of any kind.
>
> (2) Schedule 2 makes provision supplementing this section.
>
> (3) Nothing in Schedule 2 limits the powers conferred by subsection (1).
>
> (4) "Investment" includes any asset, right or interest.

---

58   [2011] 1 Cr App R (S) 8.

(5) "Specified" means specified in an order made by the Treasury.'

It is at this point that the framework begins to get more complicated. As already stated this is not an analysis that deals with every single conceivable factual aspect, but we have tried to hit the common 'highspots'.

3.91 Thus specifically, 'dealing in investments as principal' and 'dealing in investments as agent' are 'specified kinds of activity' according to the Financial Services and Markets Act 2000 (Regulated Activities) Order 2001 ('the Order'). That states:

'Dealing in investments as principal

14. Buying, selling, subscribing for or underwriting securities or contractually based investments (other than investments of the kind specified by article 87, or article 89 so far as relevant to that article) as principal is a specified kind of activity.'

and

'Dealing in investments as agent

21. Buying, selling, subscribing for or underwriting securities or relevant investments (other than investments of the kind specified by article 87, or article 89 so far as relevant to that article) as agent is a specified kind of activity.'

Articles 87 and 89 can usually be dispensed with relating, as they do, to funeral plans and pensions.

3.92 Consulting the Order is important as there are a number of further exclusions within it. This is a lengthy and difficult topic and the position should always be considered depending on the facts of the case. Two examples however are instructive.

3.93 First, Art 18 of the Order deals with the 'the issue by a company of its own shares' and is, prima facie, excluded from the ambit of a regulated activity. 'Private placement memorandums' are an often-encountered aspect of boiler room fraud allegations, whereby a company 'places' its own shares in order, it is said, to specifically defeat the regulation of the undertaking of investment activity. Whether it is dishonest or not or effective or not will depend always on the facts.

3.94 Secondly, there is the exclusion in Art 72 for the 'overseas person'. In relation to Arts 14 and 21 above this means:

'Overseas persons

72.(1) An overseas person does not carry on an activity of the kind specified by article 14 by—

3.95 *Prevalent Types of Fraud*

    (a) entering into a transaction as principal with or though an authorised person, or an exempt person acting in the course of a business comprising a regulated activity in relation to which he is exempt; or

    (b) entering into a transaction as principal with a person in the United Kingdom, if the transaction is the result of a legitimate approach.

(2) An overseas person does not carry on an activity of the kind specified by article 21 by—

    (a) entering into a transaction as agent for any person with or through an authorised person or an exempt person acting in the course of a business comprising a regulated activity in relation to which he is exempt; or

    (b) entering into a transaction with another party ('X') as agent for any person ('Y'), other than with or through an authorised person or such an exempt person, unless—

      (i) either X or Y is in the United Kingdom; and

      (ii) the transaction is the result of an approach (other than a legitimate approach) made by or on behalf of, or to, whichever of X or Y is in the United Kingdom.'

In other words if the person overseas engages in investment activity as principal or agent, provided the person he is selling to is in the UK and he is overseas, the activity is not regulated if it is the result of a 'legitimate approach', as set out in Art 72(7):

'(7) In this article, 'legitimate approach' means—

    (a) an approach made to the overseas person which has not been solicited by him in any way, or has been solicited by him in a way which does not contravene section 21 of the Act; or

    (b) an approach made by or on behalf of the overseas person in a way which does not contravene that section.'

3.95 Section 21 of FSMA 2000 states (in pertinent part):

'**Restrictions on financial promotion**

(1) A person ('A') must not, in the course of business, communicate an invitation or inducement to engage in investment activity.

(2) But subsection (1) does not apply if—

    (a) A is an authorised person; or

    (b) the content of the communication is approved for the purposes of this section by an authorised person.

(3) In the case of a communication originating outside the United Kingdom, subsection (1) applies only if the communication is capable of having an effect in the United Kingdom.'

Thus it would appear, provided that the communication 'is capable of having an effect' in the UK, that persons involved in investment activity are considered to be in breach of the general prohibition.

3.96 However the position may not end there. The Financial Services and Markets Act 2000 (Financial Promotion) Order 2001[59] imposes 'financial promotional restrictions' but is itself subject to exceptions, for example with 'solicited real time communications' by overseas communicators and other areas besides, which also may need consideration in the appropriate case as this may – depending on the facts – be part of the case for or against an accused.

3.97 As already indicated, this is a highly technical area and, in any relevant case, FSMA 2000, the Order, other regulation and even European directives[60] may need to be considered with some care.

Defences

3.98 In relation to conspiracy to defraud, in one sense the defences to such are likely to involve the traditional claims by defendants that they either (1) didn't participate in any agreement, and/or (2) they were not dishonest. Each case will of course need considering on its merits.

3.99 In relation to offences under FSMA 2000, dishonesty is, of course, not an element of the offence. The particular behaviour of any defendant must be scrutnised with utmost care to see whether or not they have in fact fallen foul of the general prohibition or whether, for example as discussed above, they are not for whatever reason to be considered to be carrying on a regulated activity.

3.100 Questions as to 'high net worth' individuals and 'sophisticated individuals' may also need to be considered if such people have purchased shares and they have certified themselves in this way. The Financial Services and Markets Act 2000 (Financial Promotion) Order 2001[61] also deals with these topics.

---

59 SI 2001/1335.
60 Eg Markets in Financial Instruments Directive (Directive 2004/39/EC) OJ [2004] L145/1 ('MIFID').
61 SI 2001/1335.

3.101 *Prevalent Types of Fraud*

MISSING TRADER INTRA-COMMUNITY (MTIC) FRAUD

Introduction

3.101 The state system of Value Added Tax (VAT) collection in the United Kingdom obliges VAT registered traders (individuals and company traders) to act as collectors of VAT on goods and services that they supply and then to pay the VAT that they charge over to HM Revenue and Customs (HMRC), previously HM Customs and Excise (HMCE).[62]

The fraud

3.102 In its simplest form, HMRC[63] describe missing trader intra-community (MTIC) fraud in the following terms:

> 'the fraud involves a fraudster obtaining a VAT registration number in the UK for the purposes of purchasing goods free from VAT in another EU member State, selling them at VAT inclusive purchase price in the UK and then not paying the output tax due to HMRC. The goods are then sold through a number of UK businesses and finally sold outside the UK free from VAT. The final UK business claims a VAT repayment from HMRC that, if paid, crystallises the loss at the start of the UK supply chain.'

3.103 MTIC fraud initially involves a UK VAT registered trader acquiring (or purporting to acquire) goods[64] from a EU Member State supplier, without payment of VAT, as the goods coming from the EU supplier are zero-rated. The UK importing trader then sells the goods on to another UK VAT registered

---

62 Until 2005 the Inland Revenue and HM Customs & Excise were separate government departments. As a consequence of this historical separation, the legislation creating offences against the public revenue is contained in different Acts of Parliament. The Commissioners for Revenue and Customs Act 2005 created a new department, HM Revenue and Customs (HMRC), which exercised the functions previously exercised by those two departments, and which has now be subsumed within the Crown Prosecution Service.

63 See HMRC publication Notice 726: 'Joint and several liability for unpaid VAT' (March 2008, replacing that of August 2003) at p 4.

64 The list of specified goods that the Revenue viewed as commonly used to perpetrate MTIC fraud, can be found in the Notice 726: for supplies made from 10 April 2003 onwards telephones and computers and equipment, parts or accessories, made or adapted for use in connection with telephone, telecommunications, computers or computer systems; for supplies made on or after 1 May 2007 other equipment (such as telephone chargers, computer chips, memory and game cards, electronic equipment for use by individuals for leisure or entertainment (including digital cameras, camcorders, iPods, portable DVD players, Playstation Portables, 'satnavs', but not any screws or wires used in the adaption of the equipment!). Other items, according to some commentators, that have been targeted include a diverse range of goods from soft drinks, razors, medical (dialysis) equipment, luxury cars to soap powder. MTIC fraud began in the clothing 'rag' trade in the 1970s.

trader, adding VAT (output tax) onto the sale price. Any subsequent sale within the UK is also liable to VAT at the standard rate. This VAT (output tax) should be paid to the Revenue at the end of the trader's tax accounting period (varying from monthly to quarterly returns).[65] The fraud involves a UK trader that either goes missing without payment of their VAT liability ('missing trader') or simply fails to pay their VAT liability ('defaulting trader'). The goods are often sold and resold in a series of transactions, involving 'buffer companies', which are often 'back to back' sales (usually the same day, with instant banking money transfers). VAT is charged and paid over between the traders. The audit trail of deals is deliberately obscured by fraudsters passing goods through a succession of 'buffer' traders (sometimes splitting consignments of goods) to create the appearance on paper of legitimate trade. Each buffer trader makes a profit, charges VAT and subsequently reclaims the VAT it was charged by its supplier.

3.104 By having buffer companies between the original importer of the goods and the eventual exporter, distance is created between the importer and exporter traders in an attempt to frustrate attempts by HMRC to detect the fraud. Buffer companies are designed to make it more difficult for HMRC to detect and demonstrate circularity in the transactions chains. Buffer companies distance and insulate the eventual substantial claimant of a VAT repayment from the original missing trader, making it more difficult for HMRC to justify an input tax denial based on grounds of non-economic activity. However, in reality the buffer traders do not fulfil any genuine economic purpose.

3.105 The goods are then exported out of the UK and the VAT is reclaimed by the exporting broker trader. The exporter maintains that they had made genuine taxable supplies by purchasing goods on the home market and legitimately selling them on for export. The original UK trader importer, having reclaimed and retained the VAT, then goes missing. In order to make the fraud harder to detect the fraudster may also use, or take over, by 'cloning' or 'hijacking', the identity of a genuine VAT registered company trader.

3.106 In short, there are a number of variations on what might be described as an MTIC fraud; the term embraces a number of different factual and legal circumstances – including missing traders (who make no VAT returns), defaulters (who furnish VAT returns but do not pay their liability), acquisition[66] and carousel fraud and even where the importing trader does not go 'missing'

---

65 See reg 25 of the VAT Regulations 1995. Most VAT registered traders are on quarterly three-monthly accounting return periods, but monthly returns are also possible.

66 MTIC acquisition fraud involves a VAT registered UK trader acquiring zero-rated goods/supplies from another EU Member State and sells the same in the UK, for domestic consumption, charging and receiving from the UK customer VAT at the standard rate. The importer ('acquirer') trader fails to pay over to HMRC the (output tax) VAT charged on the UK sale. Unlike the carousel fraud there is no need to export the goods back to the EU.

3.107 *Prevalent Types of Fraud*

(for example see *R v Takkar*[67]) the importer trader sends the VAT to various companies and offshore accounts as a result of payment instructions issued by one of the 'buffer' companies.

3.107 In a number of cases it is suspected that the goods, as described on invoices and consignment notes, do not exist and the terms 'purchase' and 'sale' should, more accurately be termed 'purported purchase' and 'purported sale'. Computer generated bogus deal chains of 'virtual carousels' are used in which no goods change hands, but which generate invoices, deal packs and Microsoft Excel spreadsheets in order to reclaim VAT.

3.108 In a more sophisticated variation of the fraud, 'contra-trading'[68] is used to disguise a 'dirty chain' of MTIC deals. The VAT repayment due to a broker trader in a chain with a tax loss is offset to another broker trader in a deal chain where there is no tax loss. A contra-trade transaction is a means by which brokers create output tax (VAT generated on sales) to offset (or contra) the input tax (VAT paid on purchases) claimed on traders' VAT returns; the reclaim being the difference between the two amounts. This has the effect of masking the VAT loss at the start of an MTIC transaction chain, in an attempt to avoid the attention of HMRC. The purpose of the contra trading is to disguise the broker traders' UK purchases. Large VAT repayment claims of input tax are made by brokers involved in MTIC dirty chains. The contra transaction chain results in the VAT repayment claim being submitted by a broker trader who, at first sight, appears to be legitimate and not participating in a transaction chain that commences with a missing trader. When the repayments are made to the traders, because it appears the brokers are acting legitimately and there being no obvious grounds to withhold the VAT repayment claim, the Revenue suffers the loss. The contra-trading involves the UK acquirer importer in the contra transaction chain being the broker exporter in the dirty transaction chain commencing with a missing trader. The missing trader's default is offset in the contra chain by the repayment claim made by the second broker to mask the loss from Customs.

3.109 Considerable ingenuity is frequently employed to commit the fraud, including the recycling of goods, hence the expression 'carousel' fraud, the use of carefully prepared paperwork trades to conceal the fact that goods do not actually exist and the use of complex deal chains and banking transactions to mask the disposal of the proceeds of the cheat.

3.110 In providing a trial jury with an overview of how MTIC fraud works, the prosecution are entitled to call evidence from customs officers as to the

---

67 [2011] EWCA Crim 646.
68 Identified by Customs in July 2005 as a counter-measure introduced by fraudsters in response to Customs MTIC strategy of withholding VAT repayment claims that were subject to extended verification process.

Missing Trader Intra-Community (MTIC) fraud **3.111**

mechanics of the fraud but the officers are not entitled to opine on whether or not the accused had knowingly participated in the fraud. In *R v Allad and Umerji*,[69] an appeal against a MTIC fraud conviction, Roderick Stone, HMRC officer and a regular feature in MTIC prosecutions, was criticised for 'overstepping the mark and trespassing into an area of forbidden opinion'. He gave evidence not as an expert but to provide the jury with an overview of how MTIC fraud works. Such witnesses should stick with primary facts and not move into prohibited second inference.

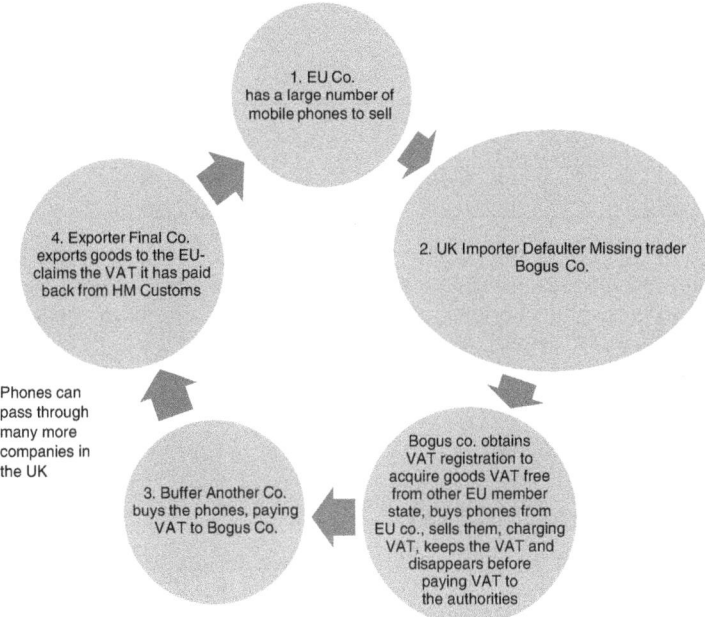

In this example most of the companies are acting legally but in some cases all companies are criminal and the goods are entirely fictional.

Extent of MTIC fraud

3.111 The estimated loss to the Revenue runs into billions of pounds.

---

69 [2014] EWCA Crim 421.

3.111 Prevalent Types of Fraud

Tax year	Estimated[70] losses (amount in £ billion)
2000–1	1.3–2.4
2001–2	1.7–2.5
2002–3	1.5–2.3
2003–4	1.0–1.7
2004–5	1.1–1.9
2005–6	3.0–4.0
2006–7	2.0–2.5
2007–8	1.0–1.5
2008–9	1.0–1.5
2009–10	1.0–1.5
2010–11	0.5–1.0

Two points are obvious from the figures in the table. First, MTIC frauds typically involve significant sums of money. Secondly, the losses sustained have reduced in recent years. One reason for the diminishing loss is that HMRC have been proactive in taking measures to refuse repayment of suspicious VAT claims, including the use of:

- reverse charging;[71] and
- service of HMRC Reference Notice 726 (dated March 2008) 'Joint and several liability for unpaid VAT'.[72]

If the VAT reclaim money is not paid out there is of course no loss to the Revenue. A trader, business or individual who is denied a VAT repayment has recourse to the VAT Tribunal.[73] Further, the number of officers investigating MTIC fraud has increased over the years, including the setting up of specialised

---

[70] Source: *The Guardian*, 9 May 2006 and HMRC 'Provisional VAT gap estimates; Official Statistics Release' (29 November 2011).

[71] From 1 June 2007, where the VAT exclusive value of specified goods (mobile phones and computers) supply is £5,000 or more, it is the responsibility of the customer (rather than the supplier) to account to HMRC for the VAT on the supply of goods (the reverse of the usual tax liability). The EU allowed the UK this derogation because MTIC fraud was perceived (a view expressed by the EU Tax Commissioner Laszlo Kovacs) as the EU's number one tax problem. See 'Business Brief' published by Customs 2006.

[72] The joint and several liability rules are found in s 77A of the Value Added Tax Act 1994 operative from 1 May 2007, with notification letters to traders informing them who HMRC consider to be jointly and severally liable for the unpaid VAT. A liability notice can be sent by HMRC to traders demanding payment of VAT for which HMRC considers the trader jointly and severally liable for.

[73] See 'The First-tier Tax Tribunal' in Chapter 5 of this book 'Alternatives to Prosecutions'.

Missing Trader Intra-Community (MTIC) fraud **3.113**

MTIC teams of assurance officers and investigators,[74] with a MTIC strategy which has led to VAT registrations being refused for new traders (involving pre-registration compliance visits to premises), de-registrations[75] taking place, VAT assessments being carried out, extended verification programme[76] of repayment returns by brokers, and using POCA 2002 (eg for account monitoring and early restraint of funds) to disrupt money flows and recover lost revenue (including the use of civil recovery measures through insolvency proceedings and appointment of receivers).

3.112 Judicial concern about MTIC fraud is illustrated by Lord Hope's description of MTIC fraud as a 'sophisticated attack on the VAT system', a 'pernicious stratagem', being of the view that EU Member States were justified in making use of 'every means at their disposal within the scope of the Sixth Directive[77] to eradicate it': *Total Network SL v HMRC*.[78]

Badges of MTIC fraud

3.113 A number of 'badges' (indicators) of MTIC fraud have been identified by the Revenue:

(a) no or poor due diligence carried out by traders on suppliers and customers. HMRC[79] cite a number of checks and obtaining of documents which may assist with due diligence in establishing the integrity of the supply chain:

    (i) obtain copies of Certificates of Incorporation and VAT registration certificates;

    (ii) verify VAT registration details with Customs;

    (iii) obtain signed letters of introduction on headed paper;

    (iv) obtain some form of written and signed trade references;

    (v) obtain credit or background checks from an independent third party (eg Veracis);

---

74 With MTIC technical teams being established as part of HMRC Specialist Investigations Directorate.
75 HMRC tries to notify relevant traders – by way of a 'veto letter' – when the VAT registration of a 'missing' trader has been cancelled or when a legitimate trader's VAT registration has been hijacked.
76 Involved (a) obtaining the details of each sale and purchase transaction, (in the form of 'deal sheets') including payment details, in respect of the supply chain which the trader (broker) has made an EU export.,the purpose being to establish whether the trading chain can be traced back to a missing trader; and (b) assessing the extent of the trader's commercial knowledge and corporate governance, including due diligence checks on customers and suppliers.
77 The Sixth Directive (77/388/EEC) has, since 1 January 2007, been replaced by the 'Principal VAT Directive' 2006/112/EC of 28 November 2006.
78 [2008] UKHL 19, [2008] STC 644.
79 See Notice 726 at p 11.

3.113 *Prevalent Types of Fraud*

- (vi) have personal contact with a senior officer of the prospective supplier, making an initial visit to their premises whenever possible; and
- (vii) obtain the prospective supplier's bank details, to check whether payments would be made to a third party;

(b) back to back transaction deals, within a short time span;

(c) no price negotiations between the trading parties;

(d) no formal contracts of sale;

(e) no insurance taken out on the goods;[80]

(f) no inspection of goods prior to purchase;

(g) no deal packs kept of purchase orders, invoices, delivery notes, CMRs,[81] packing lists, allocation notification, inspection reports (counting, inspecting, scanning serial numbers);

(h) no records kept of identification marks, stock or serial numbers of the goods traded (eg IMEI in mobile phone cases[82]);

(i) purchase of EU specification products (which require adaption for use in UK);

(j) no actual goods transacted or transported by freight forwarders;

(k) false travel documentation, eg CMR's consignment notes;

(l) quantity of goods traded too high (sometimes above levels of manufacturers annual global production figures);

(m) no history of similar trades by the UK traders;

(n) speedy circular banking money transfers within the deal chains, often by use of internet banking; and

(o) third party payments for traded goods.

---

[80] Between 14 January 2005 and July 2007 the Insurance Mediation Directive meant that freight forwarders had to be registered with the Financial Services Authority to be able to insure their clients' cargo under 'All Risks' policies. During that period cargo owners (broker trader) had to find alternative cargo insurance cover.

[81] Convention Merchandises Routiers – CMR forms contain 20 information boxes detailing sender's name and address, sender's reference, Customs reference, consignee name and address, carrier's name and address, place and country of delivery and taking over the goods, shipping marks and description of goods, gross weight in kilos, volume in cubic metres, carriage charges, sender's instructions, reservations, documents attached, special agreements, goods received, company completing the note, place, date and signature.

[82] From 1 February 2006 Customs has had a live database – NEMESIS – which involved storing scanned bar codes, including IMEI numbers, from goods examined in UK warehouses and at ports used for exports. NEMESIS is able to report in 'real time' whether the goods have been reported lost or stolen or previously scanned by Customs. Access to the system is restricted to Customs staff who have a business need to see the data.

'Back to back'

3.114 The deals are often carried out on a 'back to back' basis on or around the same day, meaning that customers and suppliers were contacted, terms agreed, goods sourced and dispatched all on or around the same day. HMRC argue that, in reality, a reasonably conscientious business carrying on a commercial venture, would, if it was buying goods to then sell on, often end up holding unsold stock. Alternatively, if the trader was first contacted by a customer and instructed to source the goods, one would expect there to be a delay between obtaining the order and finding someone able to supply the precise quantities and specifications of goods required by the customer. The fact that these requirements could be instantly matched suggests, to HMRC, that the deals were artificially contrived.

No written contract

3.115 There is no evidence that the trader entered into any formal written contracts containing clauses, terms and conditions with its supplier or customer despite the high value of the goods. Commercial deals ordinarily are covered by contractual terms and conditions covering (a) formal returns or exchange policy for either party should any of the goods be found to be faulty, (b) transfer of title, and (c) payment and delivery terms. In the absence of a written contract there is a possible inference that the deal was a paper exercise sham.

No insurance

3.116 In terms of insurance, a genuine business has a valid insurance policy in place before carrying out high value transactions. The absence of insurance cover is a possible indicator that no genuine commercial purposes were involved as neither loss or theft were ever likely to arise.

No stock records

3.117 There is no evidence that trader kept serial numbers/stock reference for the products. Without keeping the serial numbers/stock reference the trader cannot guarantee that any products returned to them are the same as the ones they sent to their suppliers for replacements in case of faulty goods. If the trader did not keep the serial numbers/stock reference an inference can be drawn that they are not concerned about faulty goods and replacements as the deals were being undertaken for the purposes of MTIC fraud rather than genuine commercial purposes, so no faulty or replacement issues were ever likely to arise.

3.118 *Prevalent Types of Fraud*

No price negotiations

3.118 There is also no evidence of price negotiations and goods bought and sold at identical mark ups, irrespective of commodity or quantity. In respect of a 'dirty' transaction chain commencing with a VAT loss, the following pricing features are usually present:

- the acquirer importer is able to purchase the goods for less than the exporter broker;
- the acquirer importer incurs no costs of selling and delivering the goods;
- the buffer traders are able to purchase the goods for less than the exporter broker;
- the buffer traders undertake no process to add additional value to the goods;
- the exporter broker fails to maximise his profit by purchasing the goods from the cheapest UK source (the importer missing trader); and
- the exporter broker has customers in other EU Member States but does not maximise his profit by sourcing goods from an EU supplier and delivering them direct to his EU customers.

High speed banking

3.119 The trader along with its customer and supplier used an internet banking account with the same banking institution (eg FCIB[83]) for the transactions without any commercial risk to the trader as the company was paid by its customer before it pays its supplier. This HMRC argues does not represent commercial reality.

No or insufficient due diligence

3.120 This is a failure by the trader to carry out any, or any sufficient due diligence checks on its supplier and customer. Such checks involve obtaining information directly from the supplier such as a valid VAT certificate, bank details, business premises address, banking/business references and Companies House enquiries (eg annual returns and certificate of incorporation). Where insufficient financial or credit checks are carried out by the trader on the supplier and/or customer, HMRC argue that this suggests that the checks were carried out purely as 'window dressing' – a box ticking exercise to satisfy

---

83 The FCIB bank's activities were suspended in October 2006 as a result of a joint Anglo-Dutch state investigation into MTIC fraud and money laundering.

HMRC verification procedures as opposed to informing a real commercial decision.

No trading history

3.121 No history of similar trades. Some MTIC fraudsters take over a VAT registered business and immediately embark on very high value deals trading goods in which they have no experience, knowledge or expertise.

Third party payments

3.122 Third party payments are sometimes used to avoid Customs use of freezing orders in civil recovery actions against missing traders. In some MTIC dirty chains the missing trader will instruct the first line buffer trader to pay the purchase price (including output tax) not to him, the supplier, but to a third party who is usually based outside of the UK jurisdiction, beyond the reaches of Customs. As a result, when Customs become aware that the missing trader is defaulting on his obligation to account for the output VAT, the missing trader is unlikely to have any assets liable to meet the liability, the monies having gone outside the UK. Third party payment instructions are frequently moved further up the chain of buffer traders: for instance between first and second buffers.

Defence points

3.123 In relation to the badges of MTIC fraud, noted above, there are a number of points that may be used to counter and explain the suspicious indicators of particular deals/trades. Generally, a trader defendant, with hindsight, having considered the prosecution evidence, accept that the deals/trades were contrived and linked with fraudulent tax losses. However, the defendant trader may have unwittingly been caught up in a tainted chain, but did not contrive trades to commit fraud. At the time of the trades the defendant trader understood his company was taking part in legitimate business activity as part of a genuine vibrant wholesale market. The defendant trader did not know anything about the alleged defaults by traders listed by the prosecution as defaulters. In particular the defendant trader may not have trade directly with the missing or defaulting trader. This 'confess and avoid' type of defence can, subject to the prosecution approach, greatly simplify and shorten the length of the trial process, reducing the length of the prosecution case in terms of court time, with the use of agreed schedules covering such topics as deal lists, freight movements, banking and VAT returns.

3.124 In relation to the specific badges of fraud a number of defence points can be made.

3.125 *Prevalent Types of Fraud*

3.125 There is nothing inherently commercially wrong in back to back deals. Many defendant traders are independent dealers, whose business model involves matching demand and supply in real time for a given trade/deal opportunity. Independent dealers operate in a deal-centric environment in which they typically do not know any party of the distribution chain other than the ones they deal with directly.

3.126 The deal chain must, as a matter of necessity, have begun with a manufacturer. There may not be any evidence available to the defendant trader, as to whether or not the deals involved authorised distributors, retailers or end users. Such evidence is beyond the ability and resources of the defendant trader to obtain. Further, prosecution investigations often seek to go beyond European suppliers or customers. Defendant traders' business models are often such that the trader can only know the buyer and supplier (+1 and −1 on the deal chain).

3.127 The defendant trader's long established business model may have been to trade easily transportable high value, popular goods (such as computers/mobile telephones), which made those market sectors a target for fraudulent traders. Fraudulent targeting of those trade sectors was known to genuine traders who undertook precautions to avoid trading with fraudsters and unwittingly becoming involving in 'dirty' trading chains of deals. The defendant trader carried out proper due diligence checks on suppliers and customers and there were no negative indicators which would have led the defendant to discover the suppliers and customers connection to VAT fraud.

3.128 The defendant trader relied on a trusted freight forwarding company to have adequate insurance, with an efficient stock tracking system, which provides protection for goods supplied, up until the goods are purchased by and delivered to the trader's customer, after which, having been inspected, the goods are the customers' concern and liability.

3.129 The defendant trader did not and would not buy any stock that had been exported previously, which could be identified by a Customs stamp: this was a requirement that the defendant trader placed upon the inspection of the goods by all the freight forwarders. The defendant was unaware of any previously exported stock. Without access to the Revenue NEMESIS computer system, there is little available useful information the defendant trader can obtain from identification stock reference/serial numbers (eg IMEI numbers on mobile telephones).

3.130 The defendant relied upon the freight forwarders to view the stock. Sample (sometimes 10 per cent) inspection is good practice to ensure the genuine nature of a deal. The goods were often insured by freight forwarders and/or customers. If freight forwarders did not insure the goods, the defendant would take commercial decisions not to insure goods as it was difficult to secure reasonably priced insurance cover for certain high value goods.

Available insurance was expensive, the probability of harm appeared low and the restrictions were severe on traders to qualify for any claim on such insurance policies.

3.131 Errors in the paperwork of freight movements such as CMRs and underlying paperwork, for which other companies were responsible, should not be attributed to the defendant trader. The defendant trader believed the deals to be genuine and goods to have existed.

3.132 The defendant trader undertook price and delivery negotiations with suppliers and customers in relation to prices and deliveries. These negotiations generated a range of price mark-ups, which were reasonable for a competitive business.

3.133 The defendant trader did not suspect nor became aware of any possibility that funds were being manipulated in a circular fashion by use of internet banking transfers.[84]

3.134 The defendant trader's business turnover of goods was not extraordinary, neither in terms of actual turnover nor percentage growth.

3.135 The defendant trader was unaware and had no means of knowing that Company A was a contra- trader (there being no direct trade with that company) and that Company B and C were connected companies. The defendant would have no way of knowing from whom their suppliers obtained the goods.

3.136 In January 2006 the *Bond House*[85] decision clarified the law, so traders became aware that the right to deduct input tax cannot be denied by prior or subsequent fraud in the chain of transactions unless the relevant person knew or ought of have known of the fraud. In that regard the presence or absence of due diligence measures adopted by the defendant trader are important.

Potential charges

3.137 Revenue criminal prosecutions of MTIC defendants have an array of charges available to summons and indict upon:

---

84 By banks such as the FCIB.
85 *Bond House Systems Limited v Customs and Excise Commissioners* [2006] STC 419 and *Axel Kittel v Belgium* (C-439/04) [2006] ECR I-6161; as applied in *Halifax Plc v Customs and Excise Commissioners* [2006] STC 919, *Dragon Futures Ltd v Revenue and Customs Commissioners* [2007] STI 373, *R v Hashash* [2008] STC 1158, *Livewire Telecom Ltd v Revenue and Customs Commissioners* [2009] EWHC 15 (Ch); [2009] STC 643 (Ch D), *Integral Resources (UK) Ltd* [2010] UKFTT 167(TC) and *Powa (Jersey) Ltd v Revenue and Customs Commissioners* [2012] UKUT 50 (TCC).

3.138 *Prevalent Types of Fraud*

Offence	Source and mode	Sentence
Cheating the public revenue	Common law Triable only on indictment and it is a Group A offence for jurisdiction purposes under the Criminal Justice Act 1993, Pt I	Punishable by a fine and/or imprisonment at large
Conspiracy to defraud	Common Law as per Criminal Justice Act 1987, s 12	Punishable by a maximum sentence of 10 years' imprisonment
Fraud offence	Statutory	Punishable by a maximum sentence of 10 years' imprisonment
Money laundering	Proceeds of Crime Act 2002, s 329	Punishable by a fine and/or imprisonment not exceeding a term of 14 years
Fraudulent evasion of VAT	VAT Act 1994, s 72 Triable either way.	Summary conviction: to a penalty of the statutory maximum or of three times the amount of the VAT, whichever is the greater, or to imprisonment for a term not exceeding six months' imprisonment or to both On indictment: unlimited financial penalty and/or to imprisonment for a term not exceeding seven years
False accounting	Theft Act 1968, s 17	On indictment: imprisonment for a term not exceeding seven years

3.138 Cheating the public revenue may be proved by the prosecution adducing evidence of dishonestly making false statements with intent to deceive or prejudice the Revenue. Dishonest failure to declare or make proper VAT returns may also suffice. In *R v Mavji*,[86] Michael Davies J said (at p 1392):

> 'This appellant ... had a statutory duty to make VAT returns and pay over to the Crown the VAT due. He dishonestly failed to do either. Accordingly, he was guilty of cheating ... the public revenue. No further act or omission is required.'

---

86 [1987] 1 WLR 1388.

See also *R v Redford*[87] and *R v Allen*.[88]

3.139 Section 72 of VATA 1994 (fraudulent evasion of VAT) can be committed by participation in a MTIC 'carousel' fraud whereby payment of VAT was avoided by a series of sales passing between different EU Member States.[89] VAT liability is determined by the objective appearance of the transaction, regardless of any fraudulent intent.[90]

3.140 As to the wording of indictments generally see *R v Ike*.[91]

3.141 The offence of conspiracy to cheat the public revenue, in the words of Lady Justice Hallett, in *R v Dosanjh*:[92]

'retains its established and clearly understood role in the prosecution of revenue cases. It is used to supplement the statutory framework and is recognised as the appropriate charge for the small number of the most serious revenue frauds, where the statutory offences will not adequately reflect the criminality involved and where a sentence at large is more appropriate than one subject to statutory restrictions.'

Disclosure

3.142 Disclosure issues feature heavily in MTIC cases. There are two essentials in effecting proper disclosure. First, all Prosecution material (as per CPIA 1996, s 3(2)) must be recorded, retained and indexed in such a way that it is accessible to the prosecution with an effective document handling system, which is properly operated. Secondly, the material set out on the prosecution non-sensitive disclosure schedule must be disclosed to the defence if it falls within the CPIA (as amended).

Sources of disclosure guidance in MTICs

3.143 In MTIC cases there are often linked investigations, traders, companies and individuals who are already known to HMRC. The database of relevant

---

87 (1989) 89 Cr App R 1.
88 [2002] 1 AC 509.
89 See *R v Hashash* [2006] EWCA Crim 2518, the Court of Appeal applying the ECJ decision in *Optigen Limted v Customs and Excise Commissioners* (C-354/03) [2006] ECR I-483, [2006] CH 218, [2006] 2 WLR 456)
90 See also *Bond House Systems Limited v Customs and Excise Commissioners* [2006] STC 419, *Axel Kittel v Belgium* (C-439/04) [2006] ECR I-6161,[2008] STC 1537, *Livewire Telecom Ltd v Revenue and Customs Commissioners* [2009] EWHC 15 (Ch); [2009] STC 643 (Ch D), *Mobilx Limited v Revenue and Excise Commissioners* [2010] EWCA Civ 517 and *DD Jewellers Ltd v Revenue and Customs Commissioners* [2013] UKFTT 462 (TC).
91 [1996] Crim LR 515.
92 [2013] EWCA Crim 2366 at para [33].

3.144 *Prevalent Types of Fraud*

material is accordingly large in MTIC frauds and it is particularly important, in ensuring full, proper and timely disclosure, that defence disclosure requests are focused and clearly formulated, taking account of the following:

- Attorney-General's Guidelines 2005, 2011 and 2013;[93]
- CPIA 1996 (as amended by CJA 2003);
- *R v H and C*;[94]
- The Control and Management of Heavy Fraud and Other Complex Criminal Cases Protocol;[95]
- Disclosure Protocol 2006;[96]
- Criminal Procedure Rules 2013;
- MTIC Information Handling Project (MIHP); and
- Supplementary Attorney General's Guidelines on Disclosure Digitally Stored Material 2011.[97]

Disclosure failures cases[98]

3.144 Much of the prosecution work undertaken by HMRC is of a specialist nature and highly technical, involving international dimensions, with investigations taking a long period of time. There are often disclosure and public interest immunity issues to be considered. Disclosure difficulties are increased by overlaps in some of the investigations, in terms of trading companies and time duration, the involvement of other agencies and undercover operations. Cases often involve several defendants engaged in sophisticated large-scale conspiracies of a cross-border nature. By 2000 the Gower Review reported that in relation to the handling of prosecutions,

> 'the majority of respondents, viewed collectively, presented a depressing and disturbing picture. In recent years the standards of Customs and Excise prosecutions had declined and case preparation and presentation

---

93 See: www.gov.uk/attorney-generals-guidelines-on-disclosure-2005-and-2011. See Attorney General's Guidelines on Disclosure for Investigators, Prosecutors and Defence Practitioners (December 2013) at www.gov.uk/government/publications/attorney-generals-guidelines-on disclosure-2013.
94 [2004] 2 AC 134, [2004] 2 Cr App R 10.
95 http://www.dca.gov.uk/criminal.
96 http://www.hmcourts-service.gov.uk.
97 http://www.attorneygeneral.gov.uk/Publications/Documents/Guidelines.
98 See: HHJ Butler QC, 'Report of an Inquiry into the Prosecution of Regina versus Doran and Others' (8 June 2000); HHJ Gower QC, 'Review of Prosecutions conducted by the Solicitor's Office of H.M. Customs and Excise' (5 December 2000); and Mr Justice Butterfield's 'Review of Criminal Investigation and Prosecutions Conducted by HMCE' (published in July 2003).

had failed to meet expectations. Many respondents, both external to and within Customs and Excise, ascribed the fall in standards and the lowering of efficiency to a lack of resources. The workload had expanded not only in quantity but also complexity and there were additional responsibilities on Custom and Excise lawyers resulting from disclosure requirements. The numbers of staff had not kept pace with this expansion and working conditions were inadequate'.[99]

More worryingly from a disclosure point of view are the Gower Review's observations on the relationship between Customs investigators and Customs solicitors:

'Customs and Excise lawyers and investigators appeared not to work harmoniously together. Some felt that investigators seemed not to trust the Customs and Excise lawyers and that Customs and Excise's unique powers had contributed to a culture of secrecy which led on occasions to the reluctance on the part of the investigating officers to disclose material[100] even to their own lawyers, leading in turn to problems over Public Interest Immunity.'[101]

3.145 The culture of secrecy criticism was also cited in the 2003 Butterfield Review,[102] noting investigations suffered from a 'culture of excessive secrecy with information closely guarded and only disseminated on a "need-to-know" basis'. The Review found (within the *London City Bond* cases) Customs prosecution failures to comply with their disclosure obligations under the CPIA 1996. In recent years a number of Customs prosecutions[103] have been stayed as an abuse, based on disclosure problems, both at first instance and appellate level. Set out below are a number of MTIC prosecution cases which have been stayed as an abuse of process.

Operation Vitric: 'creeping disclosure'

3.146 One potential problem area in MTIC cases involves 'creeping disclosure'. The CPIA 1996 (as amended by the CJA 2003) provides for a continuing mandatory duty on the prosecution to review material for relevance

---

99 See para 5.7 at pp 41–42 of the Report.
100 Including sensitive material – see para 5.24 at p 51.
101 See para 5.12 at p 44.
102 See para 8.21 at p 159.
103 See Butterfield Review of Criminal Investigations and Prosecutions conducted by HM Customs & Excise (May 2003) into the *London City Bond* cases heard by Mr. Justice Grigson in the Liverpool Crown Court. The cases demonstrated systematic and individual Customs prosecution disclosure failings. The system of recording documents seized or created in the course of the investigation was described by the Report as 'slipshod and casual. There was no effective document handling system in place. The absence of an effective system resulted in an inadequate record of what documents actually existed' (see para 8.18 at p 158).

3.147 *Prevalent Types of Fraud*

and disclosure even during a trial. Continuing disclosure is a necessary consequence of this duty. Unforeseen issues may arise during the course of proceedings, which leads to material becoming relevant and disclosable. The defence require time to examine the new disclosure, consider its relevance and have prosecution witnesses recalled for further cross-examination, causing the trial to be delayed.

3.147 In the first instance case of *R v Lindsay and ors*,[104] HHJ Pontius stayed proceedings as an abuse of process because of problems with 'creeping' disclosure. The case involved a Customs investigation into a MTIC VAT 'carousel' fraud, codenamed Operation Vitric. In staying the indictment HHJ Pontius expressed concern about the piecemeal disclosure that took place in the case, described by the defence as 'drip-fed' or 'creeping' disclosure:[105]

> 'Over these proceedings as a whole the ominous and ever-lengthening shadow of disclosure has fallen.
>
> Documents have been discovered and disclosed, in varying quantities, not only in the many weeks and months leading up to the start of these proceedings ... but also throughout the two months and more of court time that they have occupied.'

HHJ Pontius found that in Operation Vitric the Customs disclosure system had failed to produce the degree of efficient, exhaustive disclosure that a large and complex case demands. He concluded that it could justifiably be said that the larger and more complex the case, the greater the burden of responsibility upon the prosecuting authority to ensure that sufficient resources are devoted to the task of full, comprehensive disclosure.

3.148 HHJ Pontius had lost confidence in the prosecution disclosure system, expressing the view:[106]

> 'Given the history of "creeping disclosure" that we have seen during this hearing, together with what preceded it, I have no confidence that all relevant documents have now been disclosed.'[107]

The possible public cost implications of the risk that further disclosure may lead to the trial collapsing or in the event of a conviction a future appeal being sought based on inadequate disclosure, was also considered by HHJ Pontius:

---

104 18 May 2005, Blackfriars Crown Court, Indictment No T2004–7470.
105 At p 30 of the judgment transcript.
106 At p 59 of the judgment transcript.
107 Also see the decision of HHJ Faber in *R v Wharam and others* indictment number T2004-0685 (Operation Carina) at Kingston Crown Court, 4 December 2006. In *Wharam* HHJ Faber stayed proceedings, inter alia, on the basis of prosecution breaches of court orders relating to disclosure. HHJ Faber's confidence in the disclosure process had been undermined by the prosecution breaches.

'I am conscious of the very real prospect of a trial proceeding with the inevitable continuing "drip-feed" disclosure that has led to my decision; sooner or later the trial would be likely to collapse as a result, at far greater – and wholly unjustifiable – cost to the public purse. Worse still is the prospect – just as real – of a lengthy trial resulting in convictions which, many months later and after yet more relevant documents come to light, cannot be sustained on appeal. This court, like Customs & Excise, has a clear responsibility to protect the revenue and thus to keep unnecessary waste of public funds to a minimum and, further, but of equal and obviously related importance, to keep complex and large-scale trials within a manageable compass.'

Proceedings were stayed as the defendants could not be fairly tried and it was unfair in all the circumstances to try them.

Operation Venison: 'kept in the dark'

3.149   *R v Uddin*,[108] is another example of a MTIC VAT carousel fraud prosecution which was stayed as an abuse of process because of disclosure failures by Customs. The case, codenamed Operation Vension, involved five defendants, who faced charges of conspiracy to cheat the public revenue as part of a series of 'carousel' frauds of mobile telephones, with a loss to the Revenue of £100 million. Freight forwarders Hawk Precision Logistics ('Hawk') received the mobile phones in the UK. There were two prosecution witness statements from Hawk. The evidence contained in the Hawk witnesses' statements did not in itself suggest that the defendants were acting fraudulently.

3.150   At a pre-trial hearing, the prosecution announced that they would not be relying on the evidence of the Hawk witnesses. They could not be put forward as witnesses of truth.[109] All the defendants sought a stay of the indictment by reason of abuse of process of the court, placing reliance upon the judgment delivered by Lord Justice Rose in *R v Early*:[110]

'in our judgment, if, in the course of a public interest immunity hearing or an abuse argument, whether on the voir dire or otherwise, prosecution witnesses lied in evidence to the judge, it is to be expected that, if the judges knows of this, or this Court of Appeal subsequently learns of it, an extremely serious view will be taken. It is likely that the prosecution case will be regarded as tainted beyond redemption, however strong the evidence against the defendant may otherwise be.'[111]

---

108   *R v Uddin, Ali, Baig, Chandoo, Golechha*, 25 May 2005, Southwark Crown Court, T2002–7012, T2002–7222, T2002–7507.
109   The prosecution relied upon Lord Justice Keene's observations in *R v Cairns* [2003] 1 Cr App R 38, at paras 36–9.
110   [2003] 1 Cr App R 19.
111   At para 10.

3.151 *Prevalent Types of Fraud*

The trial judge Mr Justice Crane concluded that the prosecution failed to comply with their disclosure duties under CPIA 1996, ss 3 and 7, the Attorney-General Disclosure Guidelines (November 2000), the HMCE disclosure guidance document and the Investigation Handbook. There were deficiencies in the disclosure of material relating to the reliability and credibility of the Hawk witnesses and the exporter witnesses. Both Hawk and the exporters played a part in suspected MTIC trade outside the confines of Operation Venison.

3.151 Mr Justice Crane went on to consider whether there was deliberate malpractice on the part of the prosecution. Having heard live evidence from Customs officers he was not impressed with their performance, being 'driven to the conclusion that the court has not been told the truth'. Mr Justice Crane retained:

> 'very serious concerns about disclosure. The continuing difficulties, even during the hearing, do not inspire confidence that disclosure in relation to the trial itself is complete.... disclosure has been demonstrated to be flawed.'

No real explanation was given for Customs failure to raise the Hawk matters with Counsel on a number of occasions, prompting Mr Justice Crane to observe:

> 'If prosecuting counsel were to be kept in the dark, there must have been a preparedness to keep the defence, the judge and ultimately the jury in the dark ... about was not only the status and reliability of the Hawk documents. .... If the fraudulent activities of Hawk were concealed, whatever might be thought of the exporters, there was a risk that judge and jury would be presented with a distorted picture. Thus this issue of disclosure was not a matter of procedural skirmishing; potentially it went to the heart of the case. I have seen no sign that those within HMCE recognise the seriousness of that possibility.'

3.152 In staying the proceeding Mr Justice Crane observed:

> 'on this crucial aspect of the abuse application the court has been told what witnesses think the court should know, not frankly what is actually the truth. ... There was a lack of frankness towards prosecuting counsel and therefore towards the defence and the court. ... With very considerable regret, I came to the conclusion that the indictment must be stayed. It would not be fair to try these defendants.'

Systematic disclosure failures

3.153 The first instant decision in *R v Vocaturo, Brown, Drewery, Roden, Saunders, Edwards-Sayer, Sharma and Pathak*[112] is a third example of criminal

---

112 At Nottingham Crown Court (Indictment No T2002/7170), by HHJ Teare, 8 October 2007. Quoted in *R v O* [2007] EWCA Crim 3483 at para14. Discussed in John Cooper, 'Disclosure and abuse of process' [2008] 5 Archbold News 5–6.

proceedings being stayed as an abuse of process because of HMRC's failure to make proper disclosure. The case involved allegations of MTIC fraud and money laundering between December 2002 and December 2004. By April 2006 the defendants had been arrested and charged with offences.

3.154 An application was made by one defendant to have the matter stayed as an abuse of process because of the prosecution's refusal to disclose 8,000 pages of his business trading records, despite repeated defence requests over a 12-month period. The trial judge, HHJ Teare, stayed the case against that defendant. The Court of Appeal upheld the ruling, rejecting the prosecution's interlocutory appeal. The remaining defendants applied to the trial judge for stays on two grounds: late service of documents, and the inadequacy of the disclosure regime.

3.155 A second defendant sought disclosure of material (of approximately 10,000 pages) relating to a company to demonstrate his bona fide trader defence, dealing in genuine goods with legitimate businesses for proper consideration. Disclosure was not forthcoming despite prosecution counsel advising that there should be disclosure.

3.156 The intended trial judge HHJ Teare came to the conclusion that the whole business of the disclosure of the company material was '*wretched*', there has been '*muddle*', '*forgetfulness*' and '*oversight*', and he went on to state his concerns about the approach of the prosecuting authority:

> 'Why do RCPO employ a disclosure counsel and not follow her advice? How can they "overlook" the disclosure of significant material and not copy what they have disclosed to disclosure counsel so that she is aware …
>
> … the attitude of the prosecution was one of non-co-operation and inflexibility … giving the defence genuine concern about the way in which their cases have been treated … inability to foresee the consequences of stubbornly remaining within the barricades of the CPIA and (as another example) of refusing to cross-service defence statements and arguments has, in all probability, led to the situation in which the parties and the court now find themselves'.

3.157 Further disclosure problems concerned the freight forwarding company Hawk Precision Logistics, (who featured in the Customs MTIC fraud prosecution case of *R v Uddin* (Operation Vension), noted above). Customs constructed a 'Hawk Disclosure Pack' which was voluntarily disclosed to defendants in similar trials where 'Hawk' freight movement was evident. The disclosure officer in the present case realised the significance of the pack and made a note of it. Unfortunately he forgot about it and nothing further was done. The 'Hawk' material was relevant to the defence case for a third defendant who was asserting that he was an innocent genuine trader, who sought to demonstrate that goods actually existed and that he was an innocent

3.158 *Prevalent Types of Fraud*

among crooks who were being dishonest without his knowledge. The 'Hawk' documentation, inter alia, evidenced pallets of thousands of mobile phones.

3.158 HHJ Teare decided that:

> 'it is highly significant material for the defence and without any doubt should have been disclosed, more especially because material of this type was specifically identified and requested by the defence in their requests for disclosure. The prosecution acknowledged that it had the Hawk material but could not see its relevance'.

3.159 Further, there were additional disclosure problems in relation to the MTIC Information Handling Project (MIHP) database. MIHP had been set up by Customs after the failure of their prosecution codenamed Operation Venison (noted above), in an attempt to ensure that disclosure could be made to the defence when MTIC investigations overlapped.

3.160 MIHP disclosure was requested by the third defendant's team. It was refused by Customs as not being CPIA 1996 admissible. Customs disclosure counsel explained to HHJ Teare that:

> 'the database is only as good as the person who puts in the data, and although the name of the company or individual may occur within the text of a document, that company or individual will not be identified by a search of the database unless logged under an identifying name.'

The database was searched during both primary and secondary disclosure stages but no hits were noted, and therefore no disclosure could take place, leading HHJ Teare to conclude that 'the database is unfit for the task that it is supposed to fulfill'.

3.161 In relation to disclosure, HHJ Teare observed:

> 'material which was disclosable was being withheld, even though the defence knew of its existence ... The failings of the prosecution have been described as systematic, and having listened carefully to argument on both sides in this case I believe that to be true. The prosecution have consistently been in possession of material which was disclosable and which, for poor reason or for thoroughly bad reason, they have not disclosed. I have no confidence that, given the history thus far, I would not be met with similar complaints in four weeks' time if an adjournment were to be granted, or even during the course of the trial.'

HHJ Teare went on to illustrate his concerns by citing the fact that a schedule of unused material had been in the possession of the Customs investigation team 18 months before it was disclosed to the Customs disclosure team. The schedule contained a substantial amount of relevant documentation relating, inter alia, to freight forwarders:

'It is a dreadful situation. Even after present counsel have been in control of this case for 3 or 4 months, material has been kept from them and the disclosure officer until the date of the trial. How can I have any confidence that this is not going to happen again?'

HHJ Teare stayed proceedings. There had been a systemic failure by the prosecution to disclose relevant material.

Sentencing

3.162 As of 1 October 2014, the Fraud, Bribery and Money Laundering Offences Sentencing Council Guidelines[113] will apply to MTIC sentencing cases. Historically the Fraud Sentencing Guidelines 2009 did not apply to sentences for MTIC cheats, however it was open to a court to have regard to the principles expressed in the guidelines for Revenue fraud when sentencing in MTIC cases, as a point of reference. Court of Appeal sentencing cases should be referred to.

3.163 Although sentencing is not an arithmetically scientific process, the following reported cases give some indication of the terms of imprisonment being imposed for cheating the public revenue (with relevant non-MTIC cases cited). In *R v Hunt*,[114] a conspiracy to cheat the public revenue (of £55 million) the court stated that:

'Those who indulge in fraud on anything like this scale are playing for very high stakes. The potential profit is enormous; the punishment if they are caught must be condign. This type of fraud with its complex web on international transactions, overseas banks and trail of false documents is difficult to detect and immensely [expensive] to prosecute. It is inevitable that those who are brought to justice face deterrent sentences'.

3.164 In *R v Woolley*,[115] a conspiracy to cheat the public revenue (£38 million) case, the court stated that 'good character is of limited assistance' in mitigation.

3.165 In *Attorney General's Reference Nos 88–91 of 2006 (R v Brian Meehan and others)*,[116] the court (a) allowed a 15 per cent sentencing discount allowed to take account of delay between arrest and trial, and (b) observed: 'Those who organise such (MTIC) fraudulent activity can and should now expect sentences well into double figures after trial'.

---

113 www.sentencingcouncil.judiciary.gov.uk/guidelines
114 (1995) 16 Cr App R (S) 87.
115 [2003] EWCA Crim 3458.
116 [2007] 2 Cr App R (S); 28 [2006] EWCA Crim 3254.

3.166 *Prevalent Types of Fraud*

3.166 In *R v Castillo*,[117] a conspiracy to cheat the public revenue (MTIC £45 million loss), two co-defendants were given a 15 per cent discount on their sentences as there had been a delay of six years between their arrest and trial. Castillo received a 15 per cent discount on his sentence for the greater burden on him of imprisonment as a foreign national.

3.167 In *R v Randhawa*,[118] a conspiracy to cheat the public revenue (MTIC £18.9 million VAT reclaim), the Court of Appeal looked at the appropriate starting point for sentencing in MTIC cases and emphasised the fact-specific nature of sentencing in this area. Mr Justice Holroyde observed that:

> '[17] … the total value of identifiable VAT reclaims made or intended to be made, and the total amount actually paid out by way of VAT reclaim, will in most cases provide the most reliable starting point for sentencing. It will also provide the most reliable basis for a comparison with sentencing decisions in other cases, though we would emphasis that sentencing decisions are inevitably fact-specific and that a 'like for like' comparison between cases will often be particularly difficult in frauds of this nature. However, it should not be thought that the total value of the transactions is irrelevant: on the contrary, it will assist the court to gauge the overall size, complexity and sophistication of the conspiracy. Nor should it be thought that the total value of reclaims and repayments will always be a reliable indication of the true gain to the fraudsters or the true loss to HM Revenue:…a sophisticated carousel fraud may involve successful VAT reclaims which HM Revenue are unable to identify as linked to the conspirators. There is, plainly, a risk that a focus on the total amount of identifiable VAT reclaims and repayments might understate the true seriousness of a particularly sophisticated conspiracy. As a matter of principle, therefore, it does not seem to us to be possible to say that the courts must invariably focus upon the amount of VAT reclaimed and repaid: there may be circumstances in which that approach will not assist the court in its assessment of the seriousness of the crime. But in general, we are persuaded that such a focus will best assist the court both to assess the seriousness of a particular case and to set it into the context of sentencing decisions in other cases.'

Confiscation proceedings

3.168 In confiscation proceedings, the prosecution are entitled to adduce evidence of a defendant's involvement in MTIC fraud, even though the defendant had not been convicted of such an offence. The information was relevant to the making of assumptions under s 10 of the Proceeds of Crime Act 2002 (POCA) and the Prosecution were not obliged to prove the offences,

---

117 [2010] EWCA Crim 658.
118 [2012] 2 Cr App R (S) 53.

in confiscation proceedings, beyond reasonable doubt: see *R v Bagnall and Sharma*.[119]

3.169 The fact that the prosecution in confiscation proceedings accused Bagnall of specific criminality and adduced evidence to support that accusation did not amount to the bringing of a new charge (see *Phillips v United Kingdom (41087/98)*).[120] Bagnall was not at risk of any further conviction, there was no finding of guilt and the findings reached by the judge on the assumptions under s 10 of POCA merely went to the amount of the order the court was obliged to make. In such a situation the prosecution is obliged to include in its POCA Statement of Information matters relevant with the making of assumptions and the information it had relevant to the fraudulent MTIC activity accusation.

3.170 The usual *May* principles are applied to MTIC fraud confiscation proceedings, as set in *R v Taher Majid*:[121]

> 'Lord Bingham set out in his exposition of principle in the well-known authority of *May* [2008] UKHL 28, there are three questions to be determined: has the defendant benefited from the relevant conduct?; if so, what is the value of the benefit he so obtained?; what is the recoverable sum in question?'

In determining the questions the court must first establish the facts as best it can on the material available, relying where necessary on statutory assumptions. The facts will in many cases be decisive.

3.171 Secondly, a defendant ordinarily obtains property if in law he owns it, whether alone or jointly, which will ordinarily connote a power of disposition or control. In the context of a fraud on the Revenue, once it is found that companies defrauding VAT are jointly owned by a group of people, the property in question is to be regarded as the joint property of those who controlling the company. A sum that a person jointly, with others, owns and which has been fraudulently obtained from the Revenue is in law as much his as if he has acted alone. The intention of the legislation is to deprive defendants of the benefits they have gained from the relevant criminal conduct, whether or not they have retained such benefit, within the limits of their available means. The statutory scheme does not operate to impose a fine, but the benefit gained is the total value of the property or advantage obtained, not the defendant's net profit after deduction of expenses or any amounts payable to co-conspirators.

---

119 [2012] EWCA Crim 677; [2013] 1 WLR 204.
120 11 BHRC 280. As applied in *R v Goodenough* [2004] EWCA Crim 2260, *R v Rezvi* [2002] UKHL 1, *R v Briggs-Price* [2009] UKHL 19 and *Serious Organised Crime Agency v Gale* [2011] UKSC 49.
121 [2012] EWCA Crim 1023 – King J at para 3.

3.172 *Prevalent Types of Fraud*

3.172 In determining realisable assets, the amount that might have been realised at the time a confiscation order is made, is the total value at that time of all realisable property held by the defendant, less, where there are any obligations upon the property at the time, the total amounts payable in pursuance of such obligations. 'Realisable property' means:

- any property held by the defendant; or
- any property held by a person to whom the defendant has directly or indirectly made a 'tainted' gift.

The burden is on the defendant to prove on the balance of probabilities that his realisable property is less than the amount of the benefit as determined by the court.

3.173 In assessing the benefit figure in MTIC confiscation proceedings, helpful guidance is given by the Court of Appeal in *R v Ahmad (Shakeel) and Ahmed (Syed Mubarak)*.[122] In *Ahmed* the fraudulently reclaimed VAT loss to the Revenue was £12 million. The sentencing judge was wrong to rule that the benefit to the offenders was £92 million (which was the total amount of money which passed through bank accounts controlled by the fraudsters in furtherance of the crime). Unless the statutory assumptions applied, the costs of committing the offence would not form part of the benefit for the purpose of confiscation proceedings under s 71 of the Criminal Justice Act 1988. The confiscation appeal was allowed, reducing the benefit figure to £12 million. The Court of Appeal in *Ahmed* noted that it would be surprising if Parliament intended the costs of committing an offence to form part of the benefit of the offence (considering *Jennings v Crown Prosecution Service*[123]). If the total of the confiscation orders made by a judge exceeded the sum of which the Revenue had been cheated then an issue of proportionality arose (see *R v May*[124]). The words 'in connection with' had to be construed with the word 'benefit' in mind: *R v James (Michael)*[125] applied. If any of the statutory assumptions applied, for example the criminal lifestyle provisions of the Proceeds of Crime Act 2002, then the expenditure on committing the fraud would be assumed to be a benefit, being property obtained as a result of general criminal conduct. In the instant case, none of the statutory assumptions applied. The benefit for each of the appellants should have been £12 million, which would be uplifted to reflect inflation as at the date of the orders made in the court below.

---

122 [2012] EWCA Crim 391; [2012] 2 All ER.1137; [2012] 2 Cr App R (S) 85. As applied by the Court of Appeal in *R v Bagnall* [2012] EWCA Crim 677 and *R v Lee* [2013] EWCA Crim 657.
123 [2008] UKHL 29, [2008] 1 AC 1046.
124 [2008] UKHL 28.
125 [2011] EWCA Crim 2991, [2012] 1 WLR 2641.

3.174 If the judgment in *R v McIntosh*[126] had been available to the first instance sentencing judge, it was unlikely that he would have reached the conclusion that the confiscation orders should be in the sum of the total benefit. A confiscation order, which due to its magnitude exceeded the likely assets of an offender, might operate as a disincentive to co-operate.

CARBON CREDIT FRAUD

Introduction

3.175 Carbon credits can feature in a number of different types of fraud including Missing Trader Intra-Community (MTIC) VAT fraud,[127] high pressurised 'boiler-room' sales and tax evasion.[128] Having considered missing trader VAT fraud (above), this section considers how MTIC fraud developed and morphed into financial markets, including tradable carbon credit CO2 emissions permits on the carbon emission allowances exchange. A number of commentators have identified carbon credit fraud as a particular type of MTIC fraud variant.[129]

3.176 Carbon credit MTIC fraud occurred in Europe mainly between the end of 2008 and the beginning of 2009, at a time when state agencies had tackled and closed down a number of mobile telephone and computer MTIC fraudulent traders. Empirical research carried out by a number of authors has quantified the impact missing trader fraud has had upon the European carbon allowances markets, strongly influenced by oil, energy, gas, coal and equities prices. MTIC fraud losses for the 2008–2009 period have been estimated at €1.3 billion on the French carbon credit exchange.[130]

Environmental background

3.177 Following on from the United Nations Framework Convention on Climate Change, the Kyoto Protocol was adopted on 11 December 1997 and

---

126 [2011] EWCA Crim 1501, [2011] 4 All ER 917. As applied in *R v Mahmood* [2013] EWCA Crim 325 and *R v Lee* [2013] EWCA Crim 657.
127 See *R v Sandeep Dosanjh* [2013] EWCA Crim 2366.
128 See also Operation Amazon involving allegations of conspiracy to cheat and money laundering featuring the use of carbon credits in a sideways trade loss tax relief scheme (of over £100 million), in which the prosecution allege non-commercial activity being used to generate a reduction in tax liability.
129 See R T Ainsworth, 'The morphing of MTIC fraud: VAT fraud infects tradable CO2 permits' (2009) Working Paper No 09-35, Boston University School of Law, Boston, MA; Sarah Donald 'Cops and carbon robbers' (2009) (144)1396 Accountancy 84; MC Frunza and DM Guegan, 'Missing trader fraud on the emissions market' (2011) (18)2 JFC 183.
130 Frunza and Guegan (above at fn 129).

3.178 *Prevalent Types of Fraud*

came into force on 16 February 2005. It sets binding targets for 37 countries and the European Union for reducing greenhouse gas (GHG) emissions. These amount to an average of five per cent against 1990 levels over the period 2008–2012. Treaty countries must meet the target reductions through national measures, with the Kyoto Protocol providing three additional market-based mechanisms:

- emissions trading on the 'carbon market';
- clean development, and
- joint implementation.

Carbon credits

3.178 As part of the Kyoto Protocol, market-based solution carbon credits have been introduced. A carbon credit is a permit certificate allowing the right to emit one tonne of carbon dioxide (CO2). Carbon credits are tradable for money, allowing companies to sell them onto general public investors as part of an environmentally friendly green investment scheme; accordingly carbon credits can also feature in boiler room frauds as a investment scheme.[131]

3.179 There are two types of carbon credit certificates:

(1) Voluntary emission reductions (VER) which offset carbon through a number of schemes including forestry and solar panels, which attract general public investors; and

(2) Certified emission reductions (CER), which attract state agencies and large corporations

3.180 The sale and trading of carbon credits has not been regulated by the Financial Conduct Authority.[132] However, if carbon credits feature in a collective investment scheme (CIS) or in a 'futures' exchange contract, the seller of the credits should be authorised and comes under the regulation of the FCA, in order to promote and operate within the United Kingdom. The scheme may be a CIS where:

- investors do not have day-to-day control over managing the property (such as a plot of forest or use of solar panels) that is generating the credit;

---

131 A point identified by the Financial Conduct Authority on their website www.fca.gov.uk/consumers/scams/investment-scams/carbon-credit-trading.
132 Since 1 April 2013, the FSA has been split up into two new bodies – the Financial Conduct Authority and the Prudential Regulation Authority. If the sale of carbon credits falls outside of the CIS or 'futures' contract, the FCA regulator can pass any complaints over to Trading Standards and the Corporate Complaints Team at the Department of Business, Innovation and Skills.

- the scheme involves pooling investor funds; and
- the operator is responsible for managing the scheme as a whole.
- If so, the seller of the credits should be FCA authorised.

Carbon credit trading

3.181 The EU emission trading system (ETS) began in 2005 and became the largest multinational scheme in the world (73 per cent of the value of the global carbon market in 2008). The ETS is a 'cap and trade' system, which aims to cut greenhouse gas emissions by allocating emission allowances which can then be transferred between operators. Phase 3 of the ETS (2013–2020) will incorporate a yearly decrease of the cap of 1.74 per cent per year, arriving at a reduction of 21 per cent below the 2005 emissions. Transfers of allowances between taxable persons are considered as a supply of service and attract VAT, and so are available for MTIC fraud, particularly as the permits are high value and tradable electronically between countries on organised exchanges such as the French BlueNext and Dutch Climex.

3.182 On 8 June 2009 the main European exchange for spot trading of EU carbon emissions permits and Kyoto offsets closed, as MTIC fraud was suspected. When the French BlueNext began trading permits again on 10 June 2009, the certificates, which had previously been subject to French VAT at 19.6 per cent, were exempt, becoming a security. The trading companies allegedly imported large volumes of carbon credits VAT-free from other countries then sold the credits on French carbon market BlueNext, with a VAT inclusive mark up on the price. The purchasers of the permits would then have been able to claim the VAT back from the French Government, but the suspects did not pay over the VAT in classic MTIC fashion. Reuters data shows the French BlueNext exchange handled on average less than 7 million CO_2 credits per day during January–April 2008, with a record 19.8 million metric tons of EU carbon permits on 2 June 2009, beating the previous record of 15.1 million tons on 28 May 2009. The French exchanged volumes felt nearly to zero following the announcement of reverse charge of VAT at the beginning of June 2009. The estimated loss on the BlueNext exchange is between €1.7 and €1.9 billion.

3.183 During 2009, a number of EU Member States, suspecting fraud in the carbon credit market, applied a domestic reverse charge. As a consequence, in June 2009, the governments of France and the Netherlands have removed VAT from carbon permits. On 30 July 2009 the UK Government followed suit. Accordingly, the ability to use carbon credits as a vehicle of MTIC fraud has been reduced. However, the potential for boiler room and tax offsetting fraud remains within carbon credit trading.

3.184 *Prevalent Types of Fraud*

CHEATING THE PUBLIC REVENUE

Overview

3.184 There isn't much to consider in relation to this aged and (bordering on the) obsolete offence. Most if not all of the criminality that is covered by the crime of cheating the public revenue can be found in diverse statutes. However the offence still exists so it is considered here very briefly.

The offence

3.185 In *R v Bembridge*,[133] as long ago as 1783, Lord Mansfield said:

'So long ago as the reign of Edward III, it was taken to be clear that an indictment would lie for an omission or concealment of a pecuniary nature, to the prejudice of the King'.

It remains the case, that at common law, an indictment will still lie for the making of false statements in relation to revenue matters, provided there be an intention to defraud. This is true of income tax, value added tax and any conduct whereby the UK coffers are deprived of due funds or statements made with that intention. The maximum sentence is life imprisonment. The facts of these cases are so varied, however, that sentences range from a few months up to years in double figures. The recent trend has been to put this offence before the jury in carousel frauds (see above) due to the unlimited sentence. An example of that is *R v Ravjani*,[134] where Mr Ravjani, after a trial, received a sentence of 17 years' imprisonment, which was upheld by the Court of Appeal for an MTIC fraud in excess of £100 million.

UNLICENSED MONEY LENDING (AKA 'LOAN-SHARKING')

Overview

3.186 The era of pay-day lending has brought back to the public's attention the issue of the licensed and unlicensed lending of money. Whatever one's views about banks or pay-day lending firms, they are not committing the criminal offence of unlicensed money lending. However there are, it would appear, a lot of individuals and persons running small companies who may

---

133 (1783) 22 St Tr 1 at 156.
134 [2012] EWCA Crim 2519.

Unlicensed money lending (aka 'loan-sharking') **3.188**

well be. The fact of the matter is that a person may not run a money lending business without authorisation from the Financial Conduct Authority (FCA). Even if they do they are then subject to a battery of regulation designed to protect the consumer. The Court of Appeal (Criminal Division) has put it this way:[135]

> 'Legislation has protected vulnerable borrowers from the predations of money lenders for more than a century. The Consumer Credit Act 1974 regulates commercial money lending to individuals. In particular, lenders must be licensed by the Office of Fair Trading. The Act imposes a series of requirements on lenders to ensure consumer protection. Certain information must be provided to borrowers in writing, including interest rates, the duration of loans, all other charges and the total amount repayable. The Act provides for a cooling off period. A failure by a licensed lender to comply with the strict requirements of the Act and its subordinate legislation will ordinarily lead to the loan agreement being unenforceable. A lender who should be licensed but is not is similarly unable to recover the loan in a civil action. Consumer lending is highly regulated because it is those least able to repay debt who are desperate to borrow money and vulnerable to sharp practice. The reality is that people turn to unlicensed lenders, such as the appellant, when they are unable to borrow from orthodox, regulated financial institutions.'

3.187 As can be seen, it was the Consumer Credit Act 1974 that provided the powers to deal with 'loan sharks'. Parliament has however abolished Pt 3 of the Consumer Credit Act 1974 (the part that dealt with enforcement) and prosecutions for this sort of offence will now lie under s 23 of the Financial Services and Markets Act 2000 (FSMA). However given that very recent change, and given that any offence committed before 1 April 2014 will still be prosecuted under the Consumer Credit Act 1974, we discuss both the pre- and post-1 April 2014 position below.

The offence

1 April 2014 and beyond – the Financial Services and Markets Act 2000

3.188 Article 20(10), contained within Pt 5 of the Financial Services and Markets Act 2000 (Regulated Activities) (Amendment) (No 2) Order[136] ('the Order') 'omits' Pt 3 from the Consumer Credit Act 1974 from 1 April 2014. Part 3 includes the offence under s 39(1) (see below). The Order specifies

---

135 *R v Dixon* [2012] 2 Cr App.R (S) 100 at para 3.
136 SI 2013/1881.

3.189 *Prevalent Types of Fraud*

further activities that are to be 'regulated activities' for the purposes of FSMA 2000. The effect of that is that a person who carries out such an activity must be either authorised to do so or exempt from needing to be authorised. Such authority or exemption will, in each case, be fairly easy to know as the prosecution will provide evidence of the lack thereof. Equally the defendant – if he asserts it to be so – should be able to show it.

3.189 Happily the route to consider whether an offence has been committed is not quite as tortured as its predecessor (see below). That, however, means an offence under s 23 of FSMA 2000 can be committed in the following way by a lender who enters into a regulated credit agreement:

'19(1) No person may carry on a regulated activity in the United Kingdom, or purport to do so, unless he is—

(a) an authorised person; or

(b) an exempt person.

(2) The prohibition is referred to in this Act as the general prohibition.'

'23(1) A person who contravenes the general prohibition is guilty of an offence and liable—

(a) on summary conviction, to imprisonment for a term not exceeding six months or a fine not exceeding the statutory maximum, or both;

(b) on conviction on indictment, to imprisonment for a term not exceeding two years or a fine, or both.

(2) In this Act "an authorisation offence" means an offence under this section.

(3) In proceedings for an authorisation offence it is a defence for the accused to show that he took all reasonable precautions and exercised all due diligence to avoid committing the offence.'

This reflects the 'general prohibition' upon certain types of regulated activity that we have noted, for example, in relation to deposit taking and Ponzi frauds, breach of which general prohibition is a criminal offence, known as an 'authorisation offence', punishable by up to two years in prison.[137]

---

[137] The Financial Services Act 2012 will insert the following into s 23 in relation to those who are in fact authorised persons:
  '(1A) An authorised person ("A") is guilty of an offence if A carries on a credit-related regulated activity in the United Kingdom, or purports to do so, otherwise than in accordance with permission—
   (a) given to that person under Part 4A, or
   (b) resulting from any other provision of this Act.

3.190 Whether a person can show he took all reasonable precautions and exercised all due diligence to avoid committing the offence is a matter of fact in every case; however a person who makes no enquiry as to whether he needs to be authorised or have some form of licence to lend money is unlikely to be able to satisfy this requirement. Thus, as the maximum sentence is the same as that contained with s 39 of the Consumer Credit Act 1974, the old authorities on that section are likely to continue to have much in persuasive value.

3.191 As already stated, entering into a regulated credit agreement, which is the activity that is traditionally covered by 'loan sharking' is now a regulated activity. Section 22 still states (there is prospective legislative change not yet in force[138]):

'(1) An activity is a regulated activity for the purposes of this Act if it is an activity of a specified kind which is carried on by way of business and—

    (a) relates to an investment of a specified kind; or

    (b) in the case of an activity of a kind which is also specified for the purposes of this paragraph, is carried on in relation to property of any kind.

(2) Schedule 2 makes provision supplementing this section.

(3) Nothing in Schedule 2 limits the powers conferred by subsection (1).

(1B) In this Act "credit-related regulated activity' means a regulated activity of a kind designated by the Treasury by order.

(1C) The Treasury may designate a regulated activity under subsection (1B) only if the activity involves a person—
    (a) entering into or administering an agreement under which the person provides another person with credit,
    (b) exercising or being able to exercise the rights of the lender under an agreement under which another person provides a third party with credit, or
    (c) taking steps to procure payment of debts due under an agreement under which another person is provided with credit.

(1D) But a regulated activity may not be designated under subsection (1B) if the agreement in question is one under which the obligation of the borrower is secured on land.

(1E) "Credit" includes any cash loan or other financial accommodation.

(1F) A person guilty of an offence under subsection (1A) is liable—
    (a) on summary conviction, to imprisonment for a term not exceeding the applicable maximum term or a fine not exceeding the statutory maximum, or both;
    (b) on conviction on indictment, to imprisonment for a term not exceeding two years, or a fine, or both.

(1G) The "applicable maximum term" is—
    (a) in England and Wales, 12 months (or 6 months, if the offence was committed before the commencement of section 154(1) of the Criminal Justice Act 2003);
    (b) in Scotland, 12 months;
    (c) in Northern Ireland, 6 months.'

138 Financial Services Act 2012 in relation to financial standing and benchmarking (see proposed FSMA 2000, s 22(1A) and beyond).

3.192 *Prevalent Types of Fraud*

(4) "Investment" includes any asset, right or interest.

(5) 'Specified" means specified in an order made by the Treasury.'

3.192 A new Ch 14A is inserted into the Financial Services and Markets Act 2000 (Regulated Activities) Order 2001[139] as Arts 60B to 60M. Section 60B states:

'Regulated credit agreements

60B.—(1) Entering into a regulated credit agreement as lender is specified kind of activity.

(2) It is a specified kind of activity for the lender or another person to exercise, or to have the right to exercise, the lender's rights and duties under a regulated credit agreement.

(3) In this article—

"credit agreement" means an agreement between an individual or relevant recipient of credit ("A") and any other person ("B") under which B provides A with credit of any amount;

"exempt agreement" means a credit agreement which is an exempt agreement under articles 60C to 60H;

"regulated credit agreement" means any credit agreement which is not an exempt agreement.'

As Art 60B(3) states, there follows a wide set of exceptions and exemptions in ss 60C to 60H which should not be ignored if an offence is encountered.

3.193 As to the issue of whether the specified activity is 'carried on by way of a business' it seems likely, although not certain, that *R v Marshall*[140] – decided under the Consumer Credit Act 1974 (see below) – will be applied, although the wording of the relevant section is not identical. Thereafter, if a person is lending money in the course of a business without authority from the FCA then they are, in all probability, committing an offence unless the agreement is exempt by reference to Arts 60C to 60M of the Order.

Pre-1 April 2014 –Consumer Credit Act 1974, s 39(1)

3.194 Prior to 1 April 2014, these sorts of cases are still governed by s 39(1) of the Consumer Credit Act 1974 as they had been since that Act was passed by Parliament.

---

139 SI 2001/544.
140 (1990) 90 Cr App R 73.

The base offence is committed under s 39(1) of the Consumer Credit Act 1974. That states:

> 'A person who engages in any activities for which a licence is required when he is not a licensee under a licence covering those activities commits an offence'.

3.195 Section 167 provides that the penalties for the commission of the offence are found in Sch 1 to the Consumer Credit Act 1974. Schedule 1 states that an offence under s 39(1) is punishable summarily with a fine of up to £400 and on indictment by a sentence of imprisonment of up to 2 years or a fine or both. Section 39(1) is *not* a Sch 2 offence for the purposes of confiscation.

3.196 In *R v Dixon*,[141] the Court of Appeal (Criminal Division) said:

> 'The sentencing of offences of unlawful money lending is especially difficult and must reflect the particular circumstances of each case. There will be cases of loan sharks who prey on the weak and vulnerable in a calculated way, drawing them deeper and deeper in debt. Such cases may involve explicit menaces and threats or coercive action. It is well known that in cases of that nature the lives of the borrowers can be completely blighted'.

3.197 In *R v Linegar*,[142] the Court of Appeal (Criminal Division) made it entirely clear that it may be appropriate for consecutive sentences to be imposed for unlicensed money lending, where the maximum sentence is two years, and money laundering where the maximum sentence is 14 years. Unfortunately the route from those bare statements of offence and revelation of maximum punishment to what is prohibited by way of activity is fairly tortured.

3.198 So what is it that requires a licence to avoid committing the offence referred to above? Section 21(1) of the Consumer Credit Act 1974 states:

> 'Subject to this section, a licence is required to carry on a consumer credit business or a consumer hire business or an ancillary credit business'.

Section 189(1) of the Consumer Credit Act 1974 – the definitions – proscribes that a consumer credit business means:

> 'any business being carried on by a person so far as it comprises or relates to—
>
> (a) the provision of credit by him, or
>
> (b) otherwise his being a creditor
>
> under regulated consumer credit agreements'.

---

141 [2012] 2 Cr App R (S) 100 at para 16.
142 [2009] EWCA Crim 648.

3.199 *Prevalent Types of Fraud*

It should be noted that this definition appears to have been substituted by the Consumer Credit Act 2006 on the 6 April 2008.[143]

3.199   The original definition in s 189 was:

> 'consumer credit business' means any business so far as it comprises or relates to the provision of credit under regulated consumer credit agreements'.

The definition has perhaps narrowed by reference to the 'person'. However, for the purposes of the offence, s 39(1) plainly requires activity by a 'person' and s21 (1) requires the business to have a licence. Providing a 'person' is carrying on the business the difference in definition does not, it would appear, matter.

3.200   Section 9 of the Consumer Credit Act 1974 defines 'credit':

> 'In this Act "credit" includes a cash loan, and any other form of financial accommodation'.

The next question is what is meant by a 'regulated consumer credit agreement'? Section 189(1) states:

> '"consumer credit agreement" has the meaning given by section 8, and includes a consumer credit agreement which is cancelled under section 69(1) or becomes subject to section 69(2), so far as the agreement remains in force'.

Section 8 of the Consumer Credit Act 1974 states:

> '(1)   A consumer credit agreement is an agreement between an individual ("the debtor") and any other person ("the creditor") by which the creditor provides the debtor with credit of any amount.
>
> [...]
>
> (3)   A consumer credit agreement is a regulated agreement with the meaning of this Act if it is not an agreement (an "exempt agreement") specified in or under section 16.'

Section 8(2) was repealed in 2008 and seems to have removed the ceiling of £25,000 for consumer credit agreements.

3.201   There is then the critical issue of what, for these purposes, is a business. Section 189(1) defines 'business' as follows:

> '"business" includes profession or trade, and references to a business apply subject to subsection (2)'.

---

143   SI 2007/3300, Art 3(2) and Sch 2.

Unlicensed money lending (aka 'loan-sharking') 3.204

Subsection (2) states:

> 'A person is not to be treated as carrying on a particular type of business merely because occasionally he enters into transactions belonging to a business of that type'.

Thus the question of whether a person is operating a 'business' providing cash loans or other financial accommodations – which is required for an offence to be committed – is one of fact. The statute excludes 'occasional' transactions. The question ultimately is for a jury. In *R v Marshall*,[144] the Court of Appeal (Criminal Division) said:

> 'At what point "occasionally" lapses into becoming the general practice is a matter of fact and degree for a jury to decide'.

They continued:

> 'The subsection clearly contemplates within its terms that there could be transactions entered into occasionally which belonged to a business of the type in question, namely an ancillary credit business which would not fall foul of the Act. The crucial matter would be whether it was done occasionally or more than occasionally.'

3.202 Thus a consumer credit business, ie an activity that requires a licence, only relates to the provision of regulated consumer credit agreements. Section 16 of the Consumer Credit Act 1974 provides a set of exempt agreements, the provision of which will mean a person is not carrying on a consumer credit business. Section 16 excludes from regulation a whole host of activities most of which are irrelevant for our purposes such as provision by credit by local authorities, charities etc.

3.203 However, since 6 April 2008, ss 16A, 16B and 16C have been inserted into the Consumer Credit Act 1974. This would appear to be an apparent effort to remove a greater number of agreements from the Act's scope. Section 16A exempts agreements were the debtor is a 'high net worth' natural person and provides a framework as to the steps required to disapply the terms of the Consumer Credit Act 1974. Section 16B exempts business agreements where more than £25,000 is lent to a person predominantly for their own business. Again a framework is provided to disapply the terms of the Consumer Credit Act 1974. Section 16C relates to the provision of sums of money for investment properties.

3.204 Section 17 creates the 'small agreement'. In short, single, one-off provisions of credit of £50 or less do not appear to be caught by the Consumer Credit Act 1974.

---

144 (1990) 90 Cr App R 73.

3.205 *Prevalent Types of Fraud*

Possession of criminal property – Proceeds of Crime Act 2002, s 329

3.205 There has been a tendency recently for those responsible for prosecuting 'loan-sharks' to add to the basic offence detailed above a count involving possession of criminal property. By s 334 of the Proceeds of Crime Act 2002 the maximum sentence upon indictment is 14 years' imprisonment or an unlimited fine or both. Section 329 is *not* a Sch 2 offence for the purposes of confiscation. It would seem that there are some who feel that a maximum of two years for the basic offence might not be sufficient. As referred to above, and as a result of and encouraged by *R v Linegar*,[145] the prosecution 'twin' both the basic offence and that under the Proceeds of Crime Act 2002 in order to present the sentencing court with (at least) the possibility of making consecutive sentences.

3.206 In *R v Linegar*, the Court of Appeal (Criminal Division) said (at para 15):

'However, none of this detracts, in our view, from the fact that the Proceeds of Crime Act offences are entirely independent of the Consumer Credit Act offence. As a result of the Consumer Credit Act offence, the appellant was able to obtain from his victims (because that is what they were) both repayment of the principal sum that he had lent and interest on that personal credit that he had advanced to them without a licence. That interest was doubtless charged at 'commercial rates', at the very lowest. The returned principal sum and the interest thereon constitutes the criminal property that the appellant obtained as a result of the crime of providing personal credit agreements without a licence. The principal and interest is the criminal property which, by virtue of his guilty pleas to counts 1, 2, 4 and 5, he has admitted that he possessed and converted.'

3.207 Section 329 of the Proceeds of Crime Act 2002 states:

'Acquisition, use and possession

(1) A person commits an offence if he—

    (a) acquires criminal property;

    (b) uses criminal property;

    (c) has possession of criminal property.

(2) But a person does not commit such an offence if—

    (a) he makes an authorised disclosure under section 338 and (if the disclosure is made before he does the act mentioned in subsection (1)) he has the appropriate consent;

---

145 [2009] EWCA Crim 648.

Unlicensed money lending (aka 'loan-sharking') **3.210**

(b) he intended to make such a disclosure but had a reasonable excuse for not doing so;

(c) he acquired or used or had possession of the property for adequate consideration;

(d) the act he does is done in carrying out a function he has relating to the enforcement of any provision of this Act or of any other enactment relating to criminal conduct or benefit from criminal conduct.

(3) For the purposes of this section—

(a) a person acquires property for inadequate consideration if the value of the consideration is significantly less than the value of the property;

(b) a person uses or has possession of property for inadequate consideration if the value of the consideration is significantly less than the value of the use or possession;

(c) the provision by a person of goods or services which he knows or suspects may help another to carry out criminal conduct is not consideration.'

3.208 In essence it is asserted by those who prosecute that the receipt by the lender of the repayments of capital and profit from the original loan are criminal property because they are 'obtained as a result of or in connection with'[146] criminal offending, ie the running of an unlicensed money lending business. Whether that is so, as a matter of law, remains to be tested by reference to that definition of 'criminal property' within the Proceeds of Crime Act 2002.

Defences

3.209 There is a full defence to a charge of possession of criminal property. Assuming the property is in fact criminal, s 329(3) as set out above says that payment of consideration for the property will be a defence unless he knows or suspects it may help the other carry out criminal conduct.

3.210 In *R (Hogan) v DPP*,[147] the Divisional Court held that once a defendant had raised the issue by way of evidence it was for the prosecution

---

146 Section 340(3) of the Proceeds of Crime Act 2002 defines, for these purposes, 'criminal property' as:
'Property is criminal property if—
(a) it constitutes a person's benefit from criminal conduct or it represents such a benefit (in whole or part and whether directly or indirectly), and (b)the alleged offender knows or suspects that it constitutes or represents such a benefit.'
147 [2007] 1 WLR 2944.

3.211   *Prevalent Types of Fraud*

to prove, so that a jury was sure, that the defendant had not paid adequate consideration for the criminal property. The question in a case involving unlicensed money lending is whether or not the provision of a loan (albeit at usurious rates of interest) can be disproved as being inadequate consideration for its repayment on agreed terms between the defendant and the person he lends to. If it is consideration then there is a full defence to the charge of possessing criminal property. If not then the defendant will be guilty. This too remains to be tested.

3.211   Consideration in the context of s 329 was considered directly by the Court of Appeal (Criminal Division) in the case of *R v Kausar*.[148] In it they said:

> '10 "Consideration" is a well-known legal term of art. Its use in criminal statutes is not unusual: see, for example, the Accommodation Agencies Act 1953, considered in *Saunders v Soper* [1975] AC 239, section 10 of the Prevention of Terrorism (Temporary Provisions) Act 1976, section 13 of the Rent Act 1968, and, closer to the present context, section 23A of the Drug Trafficking Offences Act 1986. See also section 14 of the Criminal Justice (International Co-operation) Act 1990.
>
> 11 It is difficult to see why Parliament should have used a legal term of art in the Proceeds of Crime Act if some other meaning was intended. Section 329 makes perfect sense if the word is given its normal legal meaning. In our judgment it has such a meaning in this provision. We are supported in that conclusion by the note to section 329 in the Current Law Statutes at paragraph 29–301, which reads:
>
>> "This offence consists in acquiring, using or having possession of criminal property. It is essential (and probably something of a relief) to recall that, by section 340, property is only criminal property if the alleged offender knows or suspects that it constitutes benefit from criminal conduct. *Bona fide* possession of property which turns out to be criminal property is not an offence in terms of section 329. It is, by subsection (2)(c) a defence to a charge of committing an offence under this section that the person charged acquired or used the property or had possession of it for adequate consideration. The heart of the offence is, accordingly, acquisition of the property either without consideration or for inadequate consideration. The word 'consideration' is a familiar one (though more so in English Law than in Scots Law) and there is no reason to suppose that the word here has anything other than its ordinary meaning of 'any act of the plaintiff from which the defendant derives a benefit or advantage, or any labour, detriment, or inconvenience, sustained by the plaintiff, provided such act is performed, or such inconvenience suffered, by the plaintiff with consent, either express or implied, of the defendant' (*Laythoarp v*

---

148   [2010] Lloyds Rep FC 353.

Bryant 5 LJCP 220). Note, however, that the adequacy or otherwise of the consideration falls to be judged according to the criteria set out in subsection (3)."

12 Where a contract is in writing, particularly if it is contained in a deed, and that contract is not alleged to be a sham, the consideration given by the parties is identified in the written document. In the present case, that was the mortgage deed. That there was a mortgage deed is not in dispute. It is not before us, but we know that it imposed on the appellant, as borrower, in return for the mortgage advance, an undertaking to repay the advance with interest and conferred on the lender a charge on the mortgaged property. The charge and the undertaking to repay with interest were the consideration for the advance. There is no suggestion that the interest was other than a market rate, or that in any other respect the consideration (as we have defined it) passing from the appellant was inadequate.

13 It is submitted on behalf of the Crown that a promise can never be good consideration in circumstances where the person obtaining the property knows or suspects the property to be the proceeds of crime. In our judgment that submission gives no force to the wording of section 329, where 'inadequacy of consideration' is clearly a separate ingredient of the offence.'

INSIDER TRADING

Background

3.212 Insider trading has been a criminal offence since the Companies Act 1980 (now repealed) was passed. The current offence is created in Pt V of the Criminal Justice Act 1993 (CJA 1993), which replaced the Company Securities (Insider Dealing) Act 1985, which in turn replaced the Companies Act 1980.

The Criminal Justice Act 1993 came into force on 1 March 1994 and supersedes all prior statutory provisions.

The purpose of the legislation

3.213 The White Paper to earlier legislation was cited by Lord Lowry in *Attorney General's Reference (No 1 of 1988)*:[149]

'I draw attention to paragraph 22 of the White Paper entitled The Conduct of Company Directors (1977) (Cmnd 7037):

"Insider dealing is understood broadly to cover situations where a person buys or sells securities when he, but not the other party to the transaction, is in possession of confidential information which affects the value to be

---

149 (1989) Cr App R 60.

3.214 *Prevalent Types of Fraud*

placed on those securities. Furthermore the confidential information in question will generally be in his possession because of some connection which he has with the company whose securities are to be dealt in (*e.g.* he may be a director, employee or professional adviser of that company) or because someone in such a position has provided him, directly or indirectly, with the information. Public confidence in directors and others closely associated with companies requires that such people should not use inside information to further their own interests. Furthermore, if they were to do so, they would frequently be in breach of their obligations to the companies, and could be held to be taking an unfair advantage of the people with whom they were dealing."

'The same White Paper, having dealt with the position of primary insiders, goes on to say in paragraph 28:

"However, in addition to the specific list of persons who are to be treated as insiders, the Government proposes that anyone who receives information which he knows to be price sensitive and not generally available and which he realises has come directly or indirectly from an insider should also refrain from dealing."[150]

3.214 It is submitted that there is a clear public interest in maintaining the integrity of the financial markets. Like it or not, the markets affect the lives of all us. The performance of stocks and funds determine the performance of pensions; it is inimical to public confidence and to investment in the markets if those with inside knowledge of stocks take advantage of it to profit themselves. To be effective, the offence must extend not merely to directors and the like, but to those who receive information from them.

3.215 The approach of the courts may be seen in the following judicial statements:

'The message must be clear: when it is done deliberately, insider dealing is a species of fraud; it is cheating.'[151]

'Those who involve themselves in insider dealing are criminals: no more and no less. The principles of confidentiality and trust, which are essential to the operations of the commercial world, are betrayed by insider dealing and public confidence in the integrity of the system which is essential to its proper function is undermined by market abuse. Takeover arrangements are normally kept secret. Very few people are permitted to have advance knowledge of them. Those who are entrusted with advance knowledge are entrusted with that knowledge precisely because it is believed that they can be trusted. When they seek to make a profit out of the knowledge and trust

---

150 Per Lord Lowry, p 6.
151 *R v McQuoid* [2009] EWCA Crim 1301, per Lord Chief Justice (Lord Judge) at para 9.

reposed in them, or indeed when they do so recklessly, their criminality is not reduced or diminished merely because they are individuals of good character'.[152]

Instituting proceedings

3.216 Section 61(2) of CJA 1993 provides that:

'Proceedings for offences under this Part shall not be instituted in England and Wales except by or with the consent of—

(a) the Secretary of State; or

(b) the Director of Public Prosecutions.'

Despite the apparently mandatory terms of the foregoing section, no consent to a prosecution is required by the FSA.[153]

The commission of the offence

3.217 Insider dealing typically involves being in possession of confidential information and buying and selling shares of companies that are quoted on exchanges, such as the London Stock Exchange or NASDAQ in the United States.[154] However it also extends to spreadbetting and trading in contracts for difference.

3.218 Section 52 of CJA 1993 creates three ways of committing the offence of insider dealing:

- by *dealing* in the security (s 52(1));
- by *encouraging* another to do so (s 52(2)(a)); and
- by *disclosing* inside information to another (s 52(2)(b))

3.219 The section states:

'**The offence**

(1) An individual who has information as an insider is guilty of insider dealing if, in the circumstances mentioned in subsection (3), he *deals* in securities that are price-affected securities in relation to the information.

---

152 *R v McQuoid* [2009] EWCA Crim 1301, per Lord Chief Justice (Lord Judge) at para 8.
153 *The Queen on the application of Matthew Francis Uberoi, Neel Akash Uberoi v City of Westminster Magistrates' Court v The Financial Services Authority, HM Treasury* [2008] EWHC 3191 (Admin) – see para 29 .
154 CJA 1993, s 52(3) – that the dealing take place on a 'regulated market'. Off-market dealing or dealing on a non-regulated market is outside the scope of the legislation.

3.220 *Prevalent Types of Fraud*

(2) An individual who has information as an insider is also guilty of insider dealing if—

  (a) *he encourages another person* to deal in securities that are (whether or not that other knows it) price-affected securities in relation to the information, knowing or having reasonable cause to believe that the dealing would take place in the circumstances mentioned in subsection (3); or

  (b) *he discloses the information*, otherwise than in the proper performance of the functions of his employment, office or profession, to another person.

(3) The circumstances referred to above are that the acquisition or disposal in question occurs on a *regulated market, or that the person dealing relies on a professional intermediary or is himself acting as a professional intermediary*.[155]

(4) This section has effect subject to section 53.'

What constitutes inside information?

3.220 Section 56 of CJA 1993 defines a key concept within the Act, namely that of 'inside information':

'"Inside information", etc.

(1) For the purposes of this section and section 57, *'inside information'* means information which—

  (a) relates to particular securities or to a particular issuer of securities or to particular issuers of securities and not to securities generally or to issuers of securities generally;

  (b) is specific or precise;

  (c) has not been made public; and

  (d) if it were made public would be likely to have a significant effect on the price of any securities.

(2) For the purposes of this Part, securities are *"price-affected securities"* in relation to inside information, and inside information is *"price-sensitive information"* in relation to securities, if and only if the information would, if made public, be likely to have a significant effect on the price of the securities.

(3) For the purposes of this section *"price"* includes value.'

---

155 Ruling on preparatory hearing – these requirements are disjuntive – even if the dealing does not take place on a regulated market it will suffice if a professional inrtemediary is involved.

Analysis

3.221 In summary, in order for information to be 'insider information', it must be specific or precise (s 56(1)(b)). Market rumours are not caught by the Act. It must also be of such import that if it was made public it would be likely to have a significant effect on the price of any securities (s 56(1)(d)). In practice this is something that is likely to be proved by expert evidence. Examples of information which would be likely to have a significant effect on the price of the security include:

- takeovers – when a company is 'taken over' by another, a premium to its current share price is normally paid, thereby enhancing its value to shareholders;
- discovery of major resources such as oil by an exploration company; and
- advance in technology which increases output or speed of delivery of a product or service.

Price sensitive information includes matters that negatively impact on the price of a stock

3.222 Where there is adverse news such as an imminent profits warning, if the defendant was privy to confidential information and sold his shares to avoid a loss before the news became publically available that is also insider trading.[156]

3.223 The information must relate to a particular security or to the issuer of particular issuers of securities and not to securities generally or to issuers of securities generally. However, the requirement that the information be specific has been widely interpreted. In *R v Morrisey*,[157] it was held that it will suffice if the identity of the price-affected security would be relatively easily discoverable on the basis of the information that was made known – it will be a matter for the jury if the information was sufficient to enable the security to be identified.[158] If it was, then so long as the other ingredients are satisfied, the offence is made out.

The insider

3.224 Section 57 states:

"Insiders".

(1) For the purposes of this Part, a person has information as an insider if and only if—

---

156 Section 55 defines dealing as acquiring or disposing of securities.
157 [1997] 2 Cr App R 426.
158 This case was decided under the provisions of the Company Securities (Insider Dealing Act) 1985, s10, but the outcome would be the same under the current legislation.

3.225 *Prevalent Types of Fraud*

      (a) it is, and he knows that it is, inside information, and

      (b) he has it, and knows that he has it, from an inside source.

(2) For the purposes of subsection (1), a person has information from an inside source if and only if—

      (a) he has it through—

      (i) being a director, employee or shareholder of an issuer of securities; or

      (ii) having access to the information by virtue of his employment, office or profession; or

      (b) the direct or indirect source of his information is a person within paragraph (a).'

Analysis

3.225   You need not be in a position of confidentiality in order to be an insider. It is sufficient if you come into possession of the insider information from such a person (directly or otherwise) and *know* that the source is ultimately from a person who occupies a role described in s 57(2)(a) or (b) above. It is possible for a succession of people to be insiders in respect of the same information. A solicitor acting for a takeover target acquires insider information and passes it to his wife who encourages her nephews to take a position in the stock. Each is guilty of insider trading. The solicitor would be referred to as a 'primary insider' the wife and nephews as 'secondary insiders'.

3.226   Section 57(1)(a) and (b) provide the mens rea necessary in order for the offence to have be committed. All that need be proved is knowledge that the information is inside information; there is no further need to prove dishonesty.

Dealing defined

3.227   Dealing is defined by s 55(1) as acquiring or disposing of securities directly or indirectly through an agent.[159] Disposals or acquisitions must either

---

159 '55(4) For the purposes of subsection (1), a person procures an acquisition or disposal of a security if the security is acquired or disposed of by a person who is—
    (a) his agent,
    (b) his nominee, or
    (c) a person who is acting at his direction,
    in relation to the acquisition or disposal.
    (5) Subsection (4) is not exhaustive as to the circumstances in which one person may be regarded as procuring an acquisition or disposal of securities by another.'

be on a 'regulated market' or via a 'professional intermediary', for example a stockbroker. Each scenario is now considered.

Regulated market

3.228 Dealing in a regulated market takes place where the securities are listed in the Schedule to the Insider Dealing (Securities and Markets) Order 1994 (SI 1994/187) ('the 1994 Order') as being a regulated market.

The professional intermediary

3.229 The dealing need not take place on a regulated market if occurred via a professional intermediary:

> 'In my view the statutory intent was to regard reliance on a professional intermediary as a qualifying circumstance, regardless of whether a transaction occurred on a regulated market or the professional intermediary acted in a way which had a specific impact on the market. In this sense the term 'professional intermediary' is a description of an identity rather than of function or role in a particular transaction'. [160]

A professional intermediary is someone who holds himself out to the public or section of the public as someone who is willing to engage in acquiring or disposing of securities or by acting as an intermediary to someone carrying out such activities or by someone who is employed by such a person.[161] Incidental or occasional activity of type described would not make an individual an intermediary within the meaning of the Act.[162]

Territorial scope

3.230 Section 62 deals with the territorial scope of the offence of insider dealing. The offence only occurs if the individual was within the United Kingdom at the time he is said to have done any act forming part of the alleged insider dealing,[163] or if the professional intermediary was within the United Kingdom when he did what is alleged to constitute the offence.[164] A person is not guilty unless, when he disclosed the information or encouraged the dealing, he was within the United Kingdom[165] or the recipient of the information or the

---

160 *R v Sanders* (unreported) 13 February 2012, Southwark Crown Court Ruling of Simon J, para 45.
161 Section 59(1) and (2).
162 Section 59(3).
163 Section 62(1)(a).
164 Section 62(1)(c).
165 Section 62(2)(a).

3.231 *Prevalent Types of Fraud*

encouragement was within the United Kingdom at the time that he received the information or encouragement.[166]

Contracts for difference

3.231 By virtue of Sch 2 to CJA 1993, 'contracts for differences' are included as securities for the purpose of the Act. A contract for difference is defined as:

'(1) Rights under a contract which does not provide for the delivery of securities but whose purpose is to secure a profit or avoid a loss by reference to fluctuations in—

    (a) a share index or other similar factor connected with relevant securities;

    (b) the price of particular relevant securities; or

    (c) the interest rate offered on money placed on deposit.'

Spread betting

3.232 Spread betting is a form of dealing in securities within the meaning of Sch 2 of the CJA 1993.[167] Because it is a form of gambling, profits generated by spread betting are free of all tax thus making it even an even more lucrative way of insider dealing.

Examples of insider dealing

3.233 Case example 1

As a result of his position in the company the director of company A is aware of advanced confidential discussions with a larger competitor, company B, who wish to take over the business. Company B is willing to pay a price of 20p per share to acquire company A. The director believes that the Board is likely to accept the offer. The director tells his wife and best friend of the confidential negotiations and advises them to buy the shares in company A at 10p in the belief that in the coming weeks they will be worth 20p per share. All three do so but the deal falls through and no takeover takes place. Nonetheless

---

166 Section 62(2)(b).
167 A full description of spread-betting is given by Rix LJ in *Spreadex v Battu* [2005] EWCA Civ 855 at [2]–[4]. Essentially it involves betting on the future performance of a security and enables leveraged gambling on either on a rise or fall in the value of the security. Spread betting enables an investor to invest in the fortunes of a certain quoted share without actually buying it. Because it is a leveraged product a small stake can result in very large gains (and of course, losses but these are far less likely where the individual trader has insider information).

subject to proving one of the statutory defences, all three are guilty of insider trading. The act is criminalised not because of any profit or loss but because the effect such behaviour has on market confidence.[168] Takeovers, especially where hostile, are complex and sensitive and like any other commercial venture, may not be successful.

3.234 Case example 2

In *R v Butt*,[169] it was stated that:

> 'the applicant worked for an investment bank, Credit Suisse First Boston, in a particular position of trust, titularly being described as Vice President. His specific job lay in the hub of the secure zone of the bank known as the Compliance Control Room. This existed to ensure the secrecy of dealings. His position gave him privileged access to highly confidential inside information that was price-sensitive or price-affected about the status and performance of companies which the bank were advising. His job, in which he was experienced, carried exceptional responsibility. It was a central feature of his employment that he should not pass on or make use of the information he received in confidence.
>
> Over a period of three years, using secret inside information relating to certain companies, the applicant entered into spread bets, ie commercial bets, on the likely movement of their shares before the secret details to which he was privy became public knowledge. The actual transactions did not take place in his name. He used the co-accused on the outside to trade for him through dealing accounts which they opened in their own names. The profits were shared between them and recorded by one of them on a computer. Significantly, the applicant was allocated the lion's share, averaging nearly 80 per cent of the winnings'.[170]

The role of professionals

3.235 If similar terms are not already within their contracts of employment, professionals engaged to provide services in confidential situations are likely to be required to sign a confidentiality agreement undertaking not to divulge the proposed takeover to any third party and not to acquire stocks in either company during the pending takeover.

Accountants

3.236 Other persons who might acquire price sensitive information (PSI) include accountants and lawyers acting for the companies concerned.

---

168 See *R v Butt* for an example of insider trading which resulted in a loss.
169 [2006] EWCA Crim 137.
170 See paras 4 and 5 of the judgment.

3.237 *Prevalent Types of Fraud*

Accountants are necessary in takeovers to provide up-to-date accounts and evidence of the financial health of a company. Accountants will also be needed to advise on due diligence and tax implications.

Lawyers

3.237 Each side to a takeover will need lawyers to draw up the detailed terms of the proposed acquisition. There may be a number of different bidders for the company, and there may be a 'confidential auction' where each company is invited to make its highest bid in confidence.

Case example involving a solicitor

In *R v McQuoid*[171] it was stated:

> 'The appellant is a solicitor and former General Counsel of TTP Communications Plc. In the course of his employment he became party to inside information about a proposed takeover by Motorola Plc. He passed the information which came to him on 11 May 2006 to Melbourne.[172] Through Melbourne he procured the purchase of just under 154,000 shares in the company at 13 pence per share on 30 May 2006. The sum paid in total was £20,310.60.
>
> On 1 June 2006 the takeover was made public to the market. The offer price stood at 45 pence per share. Accordingly the profit on the purchase of the shares was £48,919.20. On 1 September 2006 a blank cheque for £24,459.60 (precisely half that amount) was given to the appellant by Melbourne. The appellant filled in his own name as the payee and the cheque was paid into his bank account.'[173]

The reverse burden

3.239 Section 53 of CJA 1993 imposes a reverse evidential burden on the defendant to prove matters. The defendant need only prove the matters in s 53 on a balance of probability. In accordance with long-established principle in reverse burden cases he does not need to make the jury sure of them. Section 53 provides that a person is not guilty of insider dealing if he shows that that he did not at the time expect the dealing to result in a profit attributable to the fact that the information in question was price-sensitive information in relation to the securities[174] or that he believed on reasonable grounds that the information had been disclosed widely enough to ensure that there was no prejudice to those taking part in the dealing who were not party to the information[175] or that he

---

171 [2010] 1 Cr App R (S) 43.
172 The appellant's father-in-law.
173 See paras 5 and 6.
174 Section 53(a).
175 Section 53(b).

would have done what he did even if he had not had the information.[176] Section 53 also provides identical defences in relation to committing the offence by way of encouraging or disclosing insider information.

Typical defences

3.240 Many takeovers are the subject of media speculation prior to occurring. In a booming market, mergers and acquisitions are relatively frequent occurences and offer the speculative investor the opportunity of substantial and immediate returns on his investment. The internet is replete with financial investment websites, and individuals are able to offer their own opinion as to the next prospective takeover in blogs and financial discussion forums. Very often an underperforming share with a significantly lower than its historical high and which offers the opportunity for restricting and further growth is a candidate, all the more so if that company is in a popular or fashionable sector. Similarly, if a major company in a given sector takes over a smaller competitor, this generates speculation that other 'big players' in the sector might be inclined to look for takeover candidates so as not to be left behind.

Expert evidence

3.241 Other areas likely to require expert opinion are:

- Expert opinion may be necessary to see precisely what information was or was not in the public domain.[177] Given the proliferation of diverse media sources this is perhaps not as easy as it once was. Many takeovers are preceded some form of speculation of takeover activity. Experts may be instructed to research the internet and social media sites to see what if any comment about the security was prevalent at prior and at the time of the dealing.
- Expert opinion might also be sought as to whether the information would be likely to affect the share price.
- Expert evidence may be needed to prove an 'actual period of price sensitivity'.

Proving the offence

3.242 The offence may be proved by:

- examination of computers to ascertain what searches were conducted by the suspects;

---

176 Section 53(c).
177 Section 56(1)(c) requires the prosecution to prove that the information was not public.

3.243 *Prevalent Types of Fraud*

- telephone records to prove contact with those with insider knowledge;
- transcripts of recorded telephone calls – where calls are made by those who work in financial institutions where telephone recording is permitted, it is admissible in evidence.

3.243 Case example

In *R v Gray*[178] it was stated:

'For a number of years some City firms had taped records of all the telephone conversations made in some of their departments, particularly those made by stockbrokers and dealers. Much of the business of these persons is conducted by telephone and at great speed. Substantial deals are struck by word of mouth. These telephone calls are recorded to ensure that in the event of any dispute as to what was said or agreed there is some way of checking. Clearly the appellants knew that this system was in operation. The evidence includes transcriptions of a large number of telephone calls to some of which it will be necessary to refer later. As will appear, conversations between the appellants are peppered with references to being unable to talk freely; arrangements to see and speak to each other out of office hours; codewords and thinly disguised references to major events concerning the three companies with whose shares this case is concerned.

The Crown case was that there was in effect a network which included these four appellants who were ready and willing to pass "inside information" between themselves. They did so in order to try and make money which they referred to as "personal spice" or "PA spice". The Crown relied particularly on the speed with which they communicated inside information to each other. They relied also on the fact that the buying and selling was on occasions not done through their normal brokers but through unusual channels. Each of the companies for whom the appellants worked had its own rules of confidentiality. Each of the appellants is said to have breached these rules'.

Summary of key ingredients

3.244

- Does the information relate to a publically listed security within the meaning of Sch 2 and the 1994 Order?
- If yes, is it publically available?
- If no, is the information precise or specific?
- If yes, would it have a significant effect on the price of the security were it publically known?

---

178 1995 2 Cr App R 100.

- Has D either dealt in, or encouraged another to deal in the price-affected security?
- Alternatively has D disclosed the price sensitive information?
- Does D know that the information is insider information?

Sentence

3.245 The maximum penalty on conviction for insider dealing is six months' imprisonment in the Magistrates' Court or seven years imprisonment in the Crown Court. The maximum fine in the Magistrates' Court is the statutory maximum, or unlimited in the Crown Court.[179]

3.246 In *R v McQuoid*,[180] the court gave general guidance as to the considerations that may be relevant to sentencing in cases of insider dealing.

'14. ...

(1) the nature of the defendant's employment or retainer, or involvement in the arrangements which enable him to participate in the insider dealing of which he is guilty;

(2) the circumstances in which he came into possession of confidential information and the use he made of it;

(3) whether he behaved recklessly or acted deliberately, and almost inevitably therefore, dishonestly;

(4) the level of planning and sophistication involved in his activity, as well as the period of trading and the number of individual trades;

(5) whether he acted alone or with others and, if so, his relatively culpability;

(6) the amount of anticipated or intended financial benefit or (as sometimes happens) loss avoided, as well as the actual benefit (or loss avoided);

(7) although the absence of any identified victim is not normally a matter giving rise to mitigation, the impact (if any), where proved, on any individual victim; and

(8) the impact of the offence on overall public confidence in the integrity of the market; because of its impact on public confidence it is likely that an offence committed jointly by more than one person trusted with confidential information will be more damaging to public confidence than an offence committed in isolation by one person acting on his own.'[181]

---

179 Section 61.
180 [2010] 1 Cr App R(S) 43.
181 Per Lord Judge, para 14.

3.246 *Prevalent Types of Fraud*

Table of sentences imposed in recent insider dealing prosecutions

Case	Sentence	Relevant factors
R v Uberoi and Uberoi (2009)	Mattthew Uberoi – two years' imprisonment Neel Uberoi – 12 months' imprisonment	Matthew Uberoi acquired insider information working as a summer intern in the corporate broking arm of a bank He passed information to his father Neel Uberoi Trading in three companies resulted in a profit of £110,000 Both defendants were of good character and were convicted after a trial
R v Rollins [2011] EWCA Crim 1825	Total 27 months 15 months and 21 months for insider trading, with six months consecutive for money laundering	R held a managerial position and sold shares in the company to avoid realising a loss caused by their imminent fall in value. Once notified of the FSA's desire to interview him about the sales he transferred the proceeds of sale to bank accounts in his father's name thereby committing the money laundering offences. The offences resulted in the appellant avoiding a loss of between £50,000 and £60,000 Good character father of two Convicted after a trial
R v McQuoid [2009] EWCA Crim 1301	McQuoid – eight months' imprisonment Melbourne – eight months' imprisonment suspended for 12 months (Not challenged on appeal)	Solicitor and former general counsel of a company who was privy to inside information, in which capacity he passed to Melbourne Convicted after a trial £50,000 profit arising from one count of insider trading

Case	Sentence	Relevant factors
R v Butt [2006] EWCA Crim 137	Five years' imprisonment reduced to four years	Convicted after a trial of conspiracy to commit insider dealing Butt acquired inside information in his capacity as vice-president of an investment bank

FRAUDULENT TRADING

Definition

3.247 Under s 993 of the Companies Act 2006, the offence of fraudulent trading is committed by being party to the carrying on of a business with intent to defraud creditors of the company *or* creditors of any other person *or* any other person for any fraudulent purpose.[182] The Act creates one offence, which may be committed in one of two ways: either by defrauding creditors, or for any other fraudulent purpose.[183] As is apparent from the definition, the offence is capable of embracing a wide range of conduct. The equivalent civil provision under the Insolvency Act 1986 has been held to have extra territorial effect,[184] and it follows that the offence under the Companies Act 2006 is likely to be construed in the same way.

Typical cases

3.248 The offence is frequently charged in boiler room frauds, such as land banking cases, or 'long firm' fraud cases. For example, in a boiler room fraud, the creditors are investors who are sold products at a gross overvalue to their true worth or products that do not exist. In a long firm fraud, credit is extended and goods supplied to companies that have no intention of ever paying for them. In both cases creditors are defrauded, but it is also the case that trading in either such manner would also amount to 'any fraudulent purpose'. At the other end of the spectrum is the genuine business which runs into serious financial difficulties and only at that stage resorts to fraudulent trading. Examples of of fraudulent trading are set out below.

---

[182] The offence is committed notwithstanding that the company has been wound up or is in the process of being wound up (s 993(2)).
[183] *R v Inman* [1967] 1 QB140.
[184] *Jetivia SA v Bilta (UK) Ltd* [2013] EWCA Civ 968.

3.249 *Prevalent Types of Fraud*

Case example: land banking

In *R v McCrae*[185] it was stated:

> 'In January 2009 McCrae set up two companies Future Developments Limited and Future Marketing Limited. Over an extended period of time he purchased a number of plots of land for a total of £48,000. The land was on the former site of Holland's Farm in Burnley. Burnley Borough Council indicated that this land was green belt land and was not likely to receive planning permission up to 2021 and was unlikely thereafter to be granted any planning permission'.

Case example: genuine business

In R v Mackey,[186] the appellant ran an estate agency which managed residential and commercial property for landlords. When the business ran into difficulties:

> 'the appellant took funds that entered the company both in the form of rent and tenant deposits. During the period of the fraud, which was between 1st April 2007 and 30th November 2008, she took around £60,000 which was applied thereafter to keep the company going. Numerous landlords contacted the company due to late or missing payments. In the first instance they were given a plethora of excuses, all seemingly offering legitimate reasons for the delay. As the nonpayments continued it became clear that ULCL had problems. Demands made by landlords were ignored. Many terminated their contract with ULCL and attempted to retrieve their tenants' bonds. It then became apparent that the deposits in many cases had not been protected in the necessary manner. The majority of tenants were never reimbursed by ULCL and as a result demands were made to the landlords to pay out'[187]

Ingredients of the offence

'Carrying on a business'

3.249 In *Re Sarflax*,[188] it was held that the expression 'carrying on any business' is 'not necessarily synonymous with actively carrying on trade'.[189] Section 993(2) provides expressly that the offence may be committed notwithstanding that the company has been wound up or is in the process of being wound up. Whether the company is 'carrying on a business' is a question of fact. Accordingly a single large transaction may suffice to fulfil this part of

---

185 2012 EWCA Crim 976.
186 2012 EWCA Crim 2205.
187 Para 6 of the judgment.
188 [1979] 1 AER 529.
189 Per Oliver J at 534

Fraudulent trading **3.253**

the definition,[190] but will not necessarily do so.[191] It is submitted that a company which has been formed but never traded is unlikely to be within the definition. Thus, a shell company, which is formed with intent that it be used for fraudulent purposes, is likely to be outside the ambit of the section.

The extent of participation

3.250 Section 993 requires proof that the defendant is knowingly a party to the carrying on of the business. The extent to which active participation is required has been considered in a number of cases.

3.251 In *R v Miles*,[192] the court reviewed the historical position and concluded that the equivalent provision then in force:[193]

> 'is designed to include those who exercise a controlling or managerial function, or who, in Lord Lane's phrase, are 'running the business'. A salesman who is not a manager and who sells shares he knows are worthless can be charged with offences under the Theft Act or with conspiracy.'

3.252 In *Re Maidstone Building Provisions Ltd*,[194] it was held that a company secretary who failed to advise the directors of the insolvent nature of the company and that it should cease to trade was not, without more, guilty of fraudulent trading.

Intent to defraud

3.253 If there is no prospect of company debts being honoured then an intention to defraud may be inferred.[195] In *Welham v DPP*,[196] a case decided under s 4(1) of the Forgery Act 1913, the court considered the meaning of the words 'with intent to defraud'. The court held that the words were not to be restricted:

> 'to an intent to deprive a person by deceit of an economic advantage or to inflict upon him an economic loss, and further that such an intent could exist where there was no other intention than to deceive a person responsible for a public duty into doing something, or failing to do something, which he would not have done, or failed to have done, but for the deceit. Lord Denning, who delivered the leading speech, rejected the argument that

---

190 *Re Gerald Cooper Chemicals Ltd* [1978] Ch 262 (Ch D).
191 *Morphits v Bernasconi* [2003] Ch 552.
192 [1992] Crim LR 657.
193 Section 458 of the Companies Act 1985.
194 [1971] 1 WLR 1085 (Ch D).
195 *Re William C Leitch Bros Ltd* [1932] 2 Ch 71.
196 (1960) 44 Cr App R 124.

3.254 *Prevalent Types of Fraud*

an intention to defraud involves an intention to cause economic loss. He referred to opinions of academic lawyers to that effect, and said (at p 153 and p 131):

"I cannot agree with them on this. If a drug addict forges a doctor's prescription so as to enable him to get drugs from a chemist, he has, I should have thought, an intent to defraud, even though he intends to pay the chemist the full price and no one is a penny the worse off.'"

3.254 In *Wai Yu Tsang v Reginam*,[197] the Privy Council applied *Welham* and held that:

'The expression "intent to defraud" is not to be given a narrow meaning, involving an intention to cause economic loss to another. On broad terms, it means simply an intention to practise a fraud on another, or an intention to act to the prejudice of another man's right'.

However dishonesty is an essential ingredient of the offence.[198]

Creditors

3.255 The word 'creditor' should be accorded its ordinary meaning and it is not necessary that such a person has an immediate right to sue.

'In our judgment the word creditor in section 458,[199] in its ordinary meaning, denotes one to whom money is owed: whether that debt can *presently* be sued for is immaterial. This is sufficient to decide the present case'.

Moreover:

'we see no reason in principle why other kinds of creditors should not be within the scope of section 458 because such may come into existence after the fraudulent trading has first begun. Such a construction is consonant with the purpose of the first part of the section which is aimed at preventing insolvent trading to the prejudice of those who are induced to do business.'[200]

3.256 In *R v Kemp*,[201] it was held that, since customers are potential future creditors, an intent to defraud them is sufficient.

---

197 [1992] 94 Cr App R 264.
198 *R v Cox* (1982) 75 Cr App R 291, decided under the offence of fraudulent trading decided under s 332 of the Companies Act 1948.
199 Section 458 of the Companies Act 1985 was the predecessor of the current legislation.
200 *R v Wallace Duncan Smith* [1996] 2 Cr App R 1 (CA).
201 [1988] 1 QB 645.

Any fraudulent purpose

3.257 This is behaviour which goes 'beyond the bounds of what ordinary decent people engaged in business would regard as honest'. In *R v Philippou*,[202] it was held that conduct which deceived the Civil Aviation Authority into granting an aviation licence was capable of amounting to a fraudulent purpose within the meaning of s 993.

Unincorporated entities

3.258 Fraudulent trading is now no longer restricted to companies. Sole traders, partnerships, trusts and companies registered overseas are now caught by s 9 of the Fraud Act, which extends fraudulent trading to unincorporated entities. Sentencing powers are as those for companies.

Penalties and sentence

3.259 Section 993(3) provides that the maximum sentence on indictment is imprisonment for a term not exceeding 10 years and on on summary conviction to imprisonment for a term not exceeding 12 months or a fine not exceeding the statutory maximum (or both). It is submitted that the level of sentence will depend on whether the company was a 'bespoke fraudulent scheme',[203] perhaps targeting elderly or otherwise vulnerable investors, or a genuine business which ran into financial difficulty with the result that other companies, and not members of the public, suffered a loss.

3.260 In *R v Mackey* (above), the Court gave the following guidance:

'1. The Sentencing Council Guideline in relation to fraud does not apply to the offence of fraudulent trading — see *McCrae & Ors [2012] EWCA Crim 976*.

2. To the extent to which, nevertheless, it is appropriate to pay some regard to the guideline, the appellant's offence involved a total gain or loss (however viewed) of £60,000 and elements, it seems to us, of both confidence fraud and banking fraud, the relevant starting points for which are 3 years custody and, as the appellant did not trade fraudulently from the outset, 36 weeks custody respectively.[204]

3. Offences of fraudulent trading cover a wide spectrum of offences. At one extreme there may have been deliberate reckless trading on a large scale, aimed at a rapid return with no genuine intention to

---

202 (1989) 89 Cr App R 290.
203 This expression is to be found in the case of *Mccrae* (above) para 17.
204 These are references to the guidelines then in force. Regard should be had to current guidelines where applicable on the facts.

3.261 *Prevalent Types of Fraud*

discharge the company's debts. At the other end there may have been a properly funded business which ran into financial difficulties, out of which the directors attempted to trade themselves in order to save their own and their employee's jobs but reached a point where they became reckless as to the reality.

4. In broad terms, though perhaps more aptly at the bottom end of the scale, it is right to say that a charge of fraudulent trading, resulting in a substantial total deficiency to creditors is less seriously regarded than a specific charge of theft or fraud of an equivalent amount — see Smith & Palk above.

5. The factors that are relevant to sentence include the amount of the fraud; the manner in which it was carried out; the period over which it was carried out; the position of the defendant in the company and his or her measure of control over it; any abuse of trust involved; any effect on public confidence in the integrity of commercial life; any loss to small investors; the personal benefit to the defendant; the plea; and the age and character of the defendant — see *R v Feld [1999] 1 Cr App R(S) 1*.'

Directors disqualification

3.261 Persons convicted of fraudulent trading can expect to be disqualified from acting as directors in the future. Section 2(3) of the Companies Directors Disqualification Act 1986 provides that the maximum period of disqualification is 15 years in the Crown Court and five years in the Magistrates' Court.

MONEY LAUNDERING

Introduction

3.262 The Explanatory Notes to POCA 2002 define money laundering as:

'the process by which the proceeds of crime are converted into assets which appear to have a legitimate origin so that they can be retained permanently or recylcled into further criminal enterprises'.

In fact the money laundering provisions in ss 327–329 in the Act go much further than criminalising the conversion of the proceeds of crime into assets: subject to proof of mens rea, simple possession of the proceeds of crime is a criminal offence.[205] Given the breadth of offending covered by the three principal offences, it is perhaps understandable that a succinct yet exhaustive definition is elusive.

---

205 See s 329(1)(c) below.

3.263 In its simplest form, money laundering can take the depositing of tainted money into a bank account. At the other end of the spectrum, it may involve funds being moved around the globe between a variety of offshore companies so as to conceal its origin.

3.264 A crucial component in the fight against money laundering is the role of the 'regulated sector'[206]– sectors which by their nature are involved in the receipt, handling and movement of money, for example banks, money transfer businesses or solicitors. The onus is firmly on the regulated sector to have effective anti-money laundering systems in place and a failure to report suspicions to the authorities can result in prosecution. In this way, the businesses and professions are made the gatekeepers of the government anti-money laundering strategy.

3.265 A detailed consideration of the offences and money laundering regulations governing the regulated sector is outside the scope of this book, the focus of which is the substantive offences created by the Proceeds of Crime Act 2002 (POCA 2002). However a brief summary is set out herein at paragraph herein .

Criminal property

3.266 A key concept in the scheme of money laundering offences contained in POCA 2002 is that of 'criminal property', which is defined at s 340:

'(3) Property is criminal property if—
  (a) it constitutes a person's benefit from criminal conduct[207] or it represents such a benefit (in *whole or part* and whether directly or indirectly)'.

Focusing on the words in subsection (3)(a) above, 'in whole or in part', if criminal property is mixed with legitimately acquired property the whole of it is 'criminal property':

'The reference to 'in whole or in part' is important because it shows that the whole property is treated as criminal property, even where only part of it represents benefit from criminal conduct.'[208]

---

206 S330 (12) POCA provides that the 'regulated sector is defined by Schedule 9 of the Act
207 By virue of s340(5) A person benefits from conduct if he obtains property as a result of or in connection with the conduct.
208 *R v William (Venus Rose)* [2013] EWCA Crim 1262, para 25.

3.267 *Prevalent Types of Fraud*

What is 'property'?

3.267 Section 340(9) of POCA 2002 defines property as *'all property wherever situated'* and *'all forms of property'*. Section 340 9 (a)–(c) provides that property includes money, real or personal, heritable or moveable property, things in action and other intangible or incorporeal property. Given the purpose of the Act this broad definition is unsurprising.

What is 'criminal conduct'?

3.268 In order to be criminal property, property must have be the result of criminal conduct. Criminal conduct can be either conduct which is unlawful in in any part of the United Kingdom, (as opposed to England and Wales), or conduct which, if it took place in any part of the United Kingdom, would be unlawful there.[209] Accordingly money generated by the commission of offences committed abroad, but which are also offences in any part of the United Kingdom, is criminal property. For example, the proceeds of crime from drug trafficking in South America is criminal property, notwithstanding that no drug trafficking has taken place in this country.

3.269 The wording of s 340 is prima facie wide enough to embrace conduct which is lawful in the country in which it occurs, but would be an offence if it had occurred in the United Kingdom. However the Act has been amended so that if a person knows or believes on reasonable grounds that the conduct was not unlawful in the country in which it occurred no offence is committed.[210] The criminal conduct need not have been committed by the person who is charged with the money laundering offence: s 340(4)(a)-(c) provides that It is immaterial who carried out the conduct, who benefited from it, and whether the conduct occurred before or after the passing of this Act. The effect of the above is that a person can be charged with a money laundering offence where he did not gain from the commission of the offence that generated the property and where the criminal conduct which gave rise to the property in question was committed by a third party prior to the commencement of the Act.

Lawful profits and the failure to pay tax

3.270 Is lawfully earned money on which no tax is paid 'criminal property' within the meaning of s 340 of POCA 2002? The answer appears to be that it may be, but only if the Crown are able to make out a prima facie case of cheating the Revenue[211] or have otherwise led evidence as to what constitutes tax evasion. The issue has arisen in a number of cases where the Crown sought

---

209 Section 340(2)(a) and (b).
210 Section 102 of the Serious Organised Crime and Police Act 2005.
211 See paras 3.184 and 3.185 on cheating the Revenue.

Money laundering **3.273**

to prove its case on the basis of unparticularised criminal conduct and the jury, in notes to the judge, asked whether 'tax evasion', or failing to pay tax on profits from a lawful business, amounted to criminal conduct.

3.271 In *R v Gabriel*,[212] at para 20 the court was apparently emphatic

'we do not agree with his submission that profits made from trading in legitimate goods, without declaring the profits to the Inland Revenue or the Department of Work and Pensions, *could in any circumstances convert the profits into criminal property.*' [emphasis added]

3.272 *Gabriel* was applied in *R v Yip*,[213] which was summarised in *Anwar* as follows:,

'the position was that the Crown had not sought to allege a specific kind or kinds of conduct by the defendant that was unlawful other than by cheating the Revenue. It was held by a constitution of this court, following Gabriel , that if the prosecution wished to rely on criminal conduct involving a failure to disclose to HM Revenue & Customs income or profits it needed to do more than show mere failure to declare a legitimate income *and it would have to prove facts tending to establish the offence of cheating the Revenue. Further, in such a situation it was, as the court there held, incumbent upon the trial judge to instruct the jury at least as to the essential elements of the offence of cheating the Revenue.*' [emphasis added]

3.273 *Gabriel* was distinguished in *R v IK*,[214] in which it was held that since the prosecution had made out a prima facie case in respect of the offence of cheat the offence was capable of being made out:

'Was it open to the jury to find that the £200,000 was "criminal property"? In our judgment, a person who cheats the Revenue obtains a pecuniary advantage as a result of criminal conduct within the meaning of section 340(6) of POCA. ... Accordingly, MR was taken to have obtained a sum equal to the value of the amount of which the Revenue was cheated, again,section 340(6). That sum is a benefit by reason of section 340(5). The question is whether the undeclared takings "constitutes a person's benefit from criminal conduct or it represents such a benefit (in whole or part and whether directly or indirectly)": section 340(3)(a).

To take a simplified paradigm case, let us suppose that over a 2 year period D fraudulently under-declares the takings of his business by £250,000 per annum with the result that he deprives the Revenue of £100,000 in income tax and £25,000 in VAT in each of the 2 years. In each year, D has obtained a pecuniary advantage of £125,000 as a result of his cheating the Revenue.

---

212 [2006] EWCA Crim 229.
213 [2010] EWCA Crim 1.
214 *R v I K* [2007] EWCA Crim 491.

3.274 *Prevalent Types of Fraud*

That is a "benefit" within the meaning of section 340(3)(a) of POCA . The undeclared takings of £500,000 *'represent'* that benefit *'in part'* within the meaning of section 340(3)(a) in the sense that the undeclared takings of £500,000 should have borne tax and a sum representing or equivalent to part of that figure should have been paid in tax.

[…]

If (contrary to our view) the judge was right in holding that Gabriel decided that the mere fact that a business is engaged in a lawful trade is of itself fatal to a successful money laundering prosecution based on takings not declared to the Revenue, then that conclusion was not necessary for its decision, and, for the reasons that we have given, we would respectfully disagree with it. In Gabriel it was not necessary to analyse section 340 closely.

The view that we have expressed as to the scope of the decision in Gabriel appears to accord with that expressed by Professor Ormerod at [2006] Crim LR 854 in his commentary on the decision. He argues that there are 3 potential ways of proving that the property which forms the basis of the charge of money laundering constituted 'criminal property' within the meaning of section 340. The second of these is that the property was acquired as a result of legitimate dealing, but not subsequently declared as trading income for tax purposes. He says property so acquired is not criminal property, since there is no prior offence. D committed none in acquiring the property and at the time that D came into possession of the property, the fact that she had not declared it as trading income did not render it criminal property. There is no offence unless the Crown can prove cheat.

The difference between Gabriel and the present case is that in the present case, as was not disputed, the prosecution had made out a prima facie case of cheat.'[215]

3.274 In *R v Anwar*,[216] the court allowed an appeal in circumstances where the Crown had not called evidence capable of proving that tax evasion was criminal conduct and where the issue was raised for the first time by a note from the jury whilst in retirement. In answering the jury note the trial judge:

'summarised the respective cases and then concluded that "tax evasion is a criminal offence in the United Kingdom so that is the long and short of it". The jury therefore were never told of the legal elements of the offence; nor were they ever reminded of the total lack of evidence on the point. Indeed, it may be noted that the jury, astutely, had not simply asked can tax evasion in the United Kingdom constitute criminal conduct, they had qualified their question by asking if that was so "for the purposes for this case". Had appropriate focus been put on these last words, we would like to think that

---

215 At paras 20, 21, 28– 30.
216 [2013] EWCA Crim 1865.

the answer given to the jury would have been different. At all events, in the clear view of this court, the answer should have been different'.[217]

Indirect benefit

3.275 Under s 340(5), a person benefits from conduct if he obtains property as a result of or in connection with the conduct. It is submitted that the words 'in connection with the conduct' are broad enough to embrace indirect benefit from criminal conduct.

An interest in property is sufficient

3.276 Section 340(10)(a) provides that 'property is obtained by a person if he obtains an interest in it.' In *CPS Nottinghamshire v Kevin Rose and R v Gareth Whitwam*,[218] the Court rejected the submission that Whitwam could not be guilty of an offence of acquiring criminal property under s 329(1)(a), since a thief or handler acquires no 'interest' in stolen property.

> 'The stolen motorcycle was property obtained by the thief, within the meaning of s 340(10)(a), since the thief obtained a right to possession of it and, by s 340(10)(d), an interest includes a right to possession; and it was self-evidently obtained as a result of or in connection with criminal conduct. It therefore constituted the thief's benefit from criminal conduct.'[219]

Mens rea: knowledge or suspicion

3.277 Section 340(3)(b) states that property is criminal property if 'the alleged offender knows or suspects that it constitutes or represents such a benefit. As as result of s 340(3)(b), mens reas is built into the definition of 'criminal property'. Unless the prosecution prove that the defendant knew or suspected that the property represents his or another's benefit from criminal conduct, the property in question is not criminal property. In *R v Gabriel*,[220] it was stated:

> 'The scope of section 329 is wide. It requires proof of no more mens rea than suspicion. The danger is that juries will be tempted to think that it is for the defence to prove innocence rather than the prosecution to prove guilt. In *R v Louizou and Others* [2004] EWCA 1579 the prosecution had set out the factors upon which it relied and from which it submitted the jury could draw proper inferences. In our judgment it is a sensible practice for

---

217 See para 42 per Lord Justice Davies.
218 [2008] EWCA Crim 239.
219 Para 12 per Lord Justice Richards.
220 [2006] EWCA Crim 229.

3.278 *Prevalent Types of Fraud*

the prosecution, as was done in *Louizou*, either by giving particulars, or at least in opening, to set out the facts upon which it relies and the inferences which it will invite the jury to draw as proof that the property was criminal property. In doing so it may very well be that the prosecution will be able to limit the scope of the criminal conduct alleged'.[221]

What is suspicion?

3.278 'In *R v Da Silva*,[222] Longmore LJ stated:

'16. It seems to us that the essential element in the word 'suspect' and its affiliates, in this context is that the defendant must think that there is a possibility, which is more than fanciful, that the relevant facts exist. A vague feeling of unease would not suffice. But the statute does not require the suspicion to be "clear" or "firmly grounded". To require the prosecution to satisfy such criteria would, in our view, be putting a gloss on the section ...

17. The only possible qualification to this conclusion, is whether, in an appropriate case, a jury should also be directed that the suspicion must be of a settled nature; a case might, for example, arise in which a defendant did entertain a suspicion in the above sense but, on further thought, honestly dismissed it from his or her mind as being unworthy or as contrary to such evidence as existed or as being outweighed by other considerations. In such a case, a careful direction to the jury might be required. But in our view, before such a direction was necessary there would have to be some reason to suppose that the defendant went through some thought process as set out above' cited in *Shah v HSBC* 2012 EWHC 1283(QB) a case which concerned ss 330–333 of the money laundering provisions.'

Suspicion is subjective

3.279 The offence does not require the defendant to have reasonable grounds to suspect, only that the defendant did in fact suspect, although if the facts do not lend themselves to a reasonable suspicion, absent an admission, it may in practice be difficult to prove the existence of a subjective suspicion. The Act does however require the prosecution to prove that the defendant did *as a matter of fact* have such a suspicion and not merely that he ought to have done; it is not an objective test:

'It would not be necessary for the appellant to know that the law labelled what occurred a crime, still less which crime, if she knew or suspected facts which amounted to a crime of some kind. But it was necessary for the

---

221 The above was said in the context of appeal in which the Crown unsuccessfully sought to uphold a conviction which may have been obtained on a basis other than that which was opened to the jury. See 'Pecuniary advantage' below.
222 [2007] 1 WLR 303.

prosecution to prove that she had applied her mind to the circumstances in which the money had been produced. Actual knowledge or suspicion that there was criminal conduct of some kind involved is an essential element of the offence. It was not enough to show that she ought to have realised that some crime, such as theft or obtaining by deception, might well have been involved.' [223]

Suspicion and knowledge contrasted with belief

3.280 In *R v Pace*,[224] the defendants were scrap metal dealers who had accepted scrap metal from undercover police officers. The officers told the dealers that the scrap metal was stolen which of course, as a matter of fact, it was not. The Court highlighted the fact that, unlike a prosecution for handling stolen goods, money laundering requires proof of only knowledge or suspicion, not belief. The Court was critical of the decision to use money laundering provisions on the facts of the case:

'It is perhaps surprising, then, that one can find alleged criminality in dealing with (purportedly) stolen scrap metal being prosecuted, as an attempt, by reference to the provisions of s 327. Assuming no available proceedings under the Scrap Metal Dealers legislation were available, one might have thought that other charges – such as, for example, conspiracy to handle or attempted handling – would have been the more obvious charges to bring. Moreover, the legal problems arising in the present case would not have been likely to have arisen had the offences been so charged. So why have they been so charged? It is difficult not to think, by way of an answer, that the decision to charge in this way (viz attempting to convert criminal property) was primarily prompted by the consideration that under s 327 and s 340(3), the state of mind applicable to the substantive offence is "knowledge or suspicion": whereas, of course, in cases of handling it would be, by s 22(1) of the Theft Act 1968, "knowledge or belief". Plainly suspicion involves a lesser state of awareness than belief. Thus it has been judicially observed that 'to suspect something to be so is by no means to believe it to be so: it is to believe only that it may be so'. (A fuller exposition can be found in Archbold 2014 ed. at para 17–49a and Blackstone 2014 ed. at para B4–183.) This distinction thus is a very real one. No doubt, indeed, it was just for that reason – and in the context of money laundering cases in particular, where the facts may be murky and proof potentially difficult – that Parliament had legislated, by the provisions of s 340(3)(b) of the 2002 Act, so as to refer to knowledge or suspicion, rather than just to knowledge or to knowledge or belief'. [225]

---

223 Per Lord Hughes at para 25 of the Privy Council decision in *Holt v HM Attorney General on behalf of the Queen* [2014] UKPC 4.
224 2014 EWCA Crim 186.
225 Paragraph 36.

3.281 *Prevalent Types of Fraud*

Attempted money laundering

3.281 In *R v Pace* (above), the Court considered the meaning and effect of the Criminal Attempts Act 1981 and concluded (at para 78) that:

> 'For the purposes of a count of attempted money laundering proof of a mental element of suspicion (only) does not suffice.'

Attempting the impossible and money laundering

3.282 In *R v Pace*, Davis LJ continued:

> 'As to the pending trials and the forthcoming cases of the present kind, involving substantively impossible attempts to convert scrap metal – impossible, because the scrap metal will not have been stolen – it will be for the Crown to decide how best hereafter to proceed. We apprehend that the effect of this judgment will preclude, in such cases, the efficacy of charges of attempting to convert criminal property if (as here) the Crown considers that it is not in a position to allege more than suspicion on the part of the accused that the property was stolen.
>
> 81 That may or may not create problems for prosecutors. However, we observe that there in any event may well be, in an appropriate case, other charges potentially available: such as, for example, attempted handling. Those necessarily will, we appreciate, require proof of a higher level of mens rea than suspicion: and of course defendants can be expected to be astute to emphasise that to a jury. Even so, as observed by Lord Hope in paragraph 62 of his speech in Saik, the margin between knowledge and suspicion is perhaps not all that great, at all events where the person has reasonable grounds for his suspicion. *Where a defendant can be shown deliberately to have turned a blind eye to the provenance of goods and deliberately to have failed to ask obvious questions, then that can be capable, depending on the circumstances, of providing evidence going to prove knowledge or belief.*' [emphasis added]

Conspiracy to commit money laundering offences

3.283 In *R v Saik*,[226] it was held that in a case of conspiracy, it had to be proved that the conspirator *knew* that the property was in fact the proceeds of crime or intended that it should be. Suspicion would therefore not suffice, notwithstanding that it is sufficient for the purposes of proving the substantive offence.

---

226 [2006] 2 Cr App R 26; [2006] UKHL 18.

The use of money laundering offences

3.284 Money laundering offences carry a maximum term of imprisonment of 14 years, whereas theft carries a maximum of seven years' imprisonment. In *R v Rose and Whitwam* (above), complaint was made by the defence as to the use of a money laundering offence to prosecute matters such as theft and handling. The Court highlighted aspects of the CPS Code for Guidance on the topic:[227]

> 'A Legal Guidance Manual contains a chapter on money laundering and includes general charging advice which stresses that this is an area where careful exercise of prosecutorial discretion is required, particularly with regard to the possession offence under s 329. The legal guidance confirms that money laundering and the underlying criminality are separate offences and that the underlying offence ought normally to be proceeded with, as it represents the conduct which gives rise to the criminal proceedings. An additional money laundering charge should normally be considered where a defendant has actively tried to conceal or transfer criminal proceeds. Specific guidance is given in respect of handling, reminding prosecutors that money laundering offences are not confined to cases involving money and that there will need to be a careful judgment in those cases where the prosecution could charge money laundering based on possession or an offence of handling stolen goods. The guidance states that prosecutors may consider charging a money laundering offence where a defendant has possessed criminal proceeds in large amounts, or in lesser amounts but repeatedly and where assets are laundered for profit.

3.285 A concern about the use of s 329 in circumstances such as these was in fact ventilated in *R (Wilkinson) v Director of Public Prosecutions*,[228] in which it was sought to challenge the decision to prosecute in a case arising out of very similar facts. A mini motorcycle had been stolen in a burglary and the claimant had been found in possession of it, but he was charged with an offence contrary to s 329 rather than with an offence of burglary or handling stolen goods. An application for leave to apply for judicial review to challenge the decision to prosecute was dismissed on grounds of delay, but in giving judgment Maurice Kay LJ went on (at para 8) to make observations on the substance of the application:

> ' ... [H]aving considered the Code for Crown Prosecutors and the CPS's own document on money laundering, I feel unable to say that the decision to proceed under s 329 was arguably vitiated by some public law consideration. The passages to which we have been referred seem to me to be encouragement to crown prosecutors to resort to offences under the 2002

---

227 See Appendices for the full version.
228 [2006] EWHC 3012 (Admin).

3.286 *Prevalent Types of Fraud*

Act in serious cases. They are less obviously expressed as discouragement to resort to offences in less serious cases, of which this is one. The question of who should be charged and with what offence is essentially one for the Crown Prosecution Service. I am bound to say that when I used to preside over criminal trials and indeed during the far more numerous years when I used to appear as counsel in them, it was a regular occurrence for the judge to criticise the prosecution if he thought that a particular defendant had been over-charged and that a different outcome would be preferable by way of charge. I make it clear that if this case had come before me sitting in the Crown Court, I would have taken precisely that course, encouraging the Crown Prosecution Service to substitute a charge of handling stolen goods. But encouragement is where it would stop. It is ultimately a matter for them. Notwithstanding the obvious wider intention of the 2002 legislation, it cannot be said that the conduct sought to be attributed to the claimant does not fall within s 329.

[...]

20 Whilst acknowledging that charging decisions are for the CPS rather than the courts (subject to exceptional cases of unlawfulness where the court will be prepared to intervene on judicial review), we share the concern evidently felt by Maurice Kay LJ about the use of s 329 in Wilkinson's case. The concern applies equally to Whitwam's case. It applies to a much lesser extent to Rose's case, the circumstances of which are described later in this judgment. It is difficult to see why cases such as those of Wilkinson and Whitwam were thought to merit the charging of a money laundering offence rather than a charge of handling (with or without an alternative charge of burglary or theft). That it may have simplified the issues at the trial is certainly an advantage of the course adopted but is not a complete answer. On the other hand, we do not know the full details of the decision-making process in the individual cases and it would be wrong for us to express any final view in relation to them. More importantly, we see nothing wrong with the tenor of the guidance given to prosecutors'[229]

See also the case of *R v Pace* above.

The approach to inferences and submissions of no case to answer

3.286 It is frequently the case that money laundering prosecutions turn on inferences as opposed to direct evidence. Very often the primary facts are not in dispute but it is the conclusions that can be safely drawn from that is. *R v*

---

229 See paras 19–20 of the judgment. See also *R v Pace* above for judicial criticism as the decision to prosecute scrap metal dealers buying what they thought were stolen goods under the money laundering provisions.

Money laundering **3.286**

Saleh[230] is an example of a case in which the Court of Appeal analysed the correct approach to such applications:

'40 The care to be taken before drawing inferences is the same whether at the submission stage or at the stage when the jury comes to consider its verdict. However, *it is necessary to keep well in mind that at the stage of the submission, the question to be asked is whether the inferences, properly considered with care, are such as are capable of permitting a properly directed jury to come to a verdict of guilty. If they are, then subject to any other considerations, the case will or may be fit to be left to the jury. What need not be decided, at the stage of a submission of no case to answer, is that the jury must go on to convict. It is sufficient if there is a proper foundation for a properly directed jury to be capable of going on to convict.*

41 Ultimately we did not understand these principles to be in dispute — but it is worth citing the passage to which Mr Davies drew our attention, as he tells us that the authority does not feature in Archbold and the point is one that arises in a number of cases. The passage, from Morgan (supra), reads as follows:

"The Court's attention had been drawn by the appellant's counsel to the case of Moore (August 20, 1992) in which the Court had commented obiter; 'It may be helpful for the judge to address specifically the question whether the proved facts are such that they exclude every reasonable inference from them save the one sought to be drawn by the prosecution. If the proved facts do not exclude all other reasonable inferences then there must be a doubt whether the inference sought to be drawn is correct.' The case of Moore was, on its facts, quite plainly one in which the submission of no case should have been allowed. The passage upon which reliance had been placed was obiter and was founded on a passage in the speech of Lord Morris in *McGreevy v DPP [1973] 1 WLR 276* at p 285A, which was, however, clearly not directed to the function of the trial judge when a submission of no case was made to him at the close of the prosecution case but to the role of the jury when they came to discharge their duty of returning a true verdict. At the close of the prosecution case, when a submission of no case is made to the judge, it was not his function to decide the case for himself or to ask himself whether the evidence was such that he would feel sure of guilt. Cases were left to the jury because there was evidence fit for the jury to consider and upon which a jury properly directed could return a verdict of guilty. Cases in which the evidence was circumstantial were not in a special category; many cases involved consideration both of direct and circumstantial evidence. *Taken literally, the words relied on from the judgment in Moore would seem to suggest that, where the evidence was purely circumstantial, the judge ought only to leave the case to the jury if the evidence was such as to convince him of guilt and if, following the case being left to the jury, the verdict of acquittal could thereafter be said to be*

---

230 [2012] EWCA Crim 484.

3.287 *Prevalent Types of Fraud*

> *perverse. That could not have been the meaning intended by the Court of Appeal and the passage was not one from which assistance could really be derived in the present case. If there was an inference of guilt which it was reasonably open to the jury to draw then the case could properly be left to the jury, notwithstanding that there might have been an inference, or other inferences, consistent with innocence. It was the jury's task to see whether the inference of guilt was one which they were sure could properly be drawn. For the judge to withdraw the case from the jury simply because at the close of the prosecution case all other inferences had not been excluded would be to usurp the jury's task.'"*

[Emphasis added]

Evidence of the underlying crime

Do the prosecution need to prove the commission a specific offence?

3.287 If the defendant is charged on the same indictment with the offence which is said to give rise to the criminal property, this issue will not arise. However, there are many cases in which the prosecution seek to prove that the property is criminal property but are unable to point to, let alone prove, any particular crime that gave rise to it.

3.288 In *R v Anwoir*,[231] the court reviewed the various authorities and concluded that there were two ways in which the Crown could prove that property derived from crime:

(1) that it derived from conduct of a specific kind or kinds and that conduct of that kind or those kinds was unlawful; or

(2) the evidence of the circumstances in which the property was handled, such as to give rise to the *irresistible inference* that it could only be derived from crime (see para 21 of the judgment of the court delivered by Lord Justice Latham).[232]

Perhaps understandably, no attempt was made to define the term 'irresisitible inference'. It is submitted it cannot mean inevitable inference since it is in the nature of inferences that the jury is not bound to draw them.

3.289 Case example

The facts in *R v Gillies*,[233] are as follows:

---

231 [2008] EWCA Crim 1354; [2008] 2 Crim App R 36.
232 See *R v Gillies* [2011] EWCA Crim 2140 below as an example of circumstances in which guilt could properly be inferred without there being any evidence of the predicate crime.
233 [2011] EWCA Crim 2140.

Money laundering **3.289**

> '4 ... the appellant, driving a white Astra van, entered a car park at the Underground Station at Brent Cross at approximately 9.30 pm. There he met Mr Mohammed Imran. Imran had travelled to Brent Cross in a minicab. He was seen to arrive at the rendezvous empty-handed, to enter the white van and sit in the front passenger seat. A few seconds later he emerged from the van carrying a large Next paper carrier bag. Mr Imran then returned to his cab and travelled to Leytonstone, where he was searched by the police. Inside the Next bag was found €200,050 in notes contained within clingfilm and further plastic carrier bags.
>
> 7 ... He was 21 years old. He had no savings, and he had no assets save for the white van. He was unemployed and in receipt Job Seekers Allowance which he had collected on the very morning of the offence.
>
> 8 The witness stated that no one had come forward to claim the sum of cash seized; no legitimate source for the cash could be identified. On the other hand, he made the inevitable concession that there was no direct evidence of the crime which the police suspected had generated the cash.
>
> 15 ... The jury properly directed could conclude that this large quantity of cash in the Euro denomination represented the proceeds of previous criminal conduct. They could infer that is the only reason why a man in the appellant's position would have been entrusted with it.'

It is sufficient for a trial judge:

> '19 ... [to make it] abundantly clear that the prosecution must prove that the cash represented the proceeds of *earlier crime of some sort,* by someone and that the appellant knew or suspected it. There is nothing of merit in this appeal and it is dismissed.
>
> 20 At the conclusion of our judgment Ms Levett invited the court to reconcile decisions in the civil jurisdiction as to the application for sections 240 and 242 of the 2002 Act. We declined to do so. The meaning and effect of the offence created by section 328(1) of the Act have been authoratively settled. Different provisions relating to civil recovery are not, in our view, relevant to this appeal.'[234]

[Emphasis added]

A factually similar case involving the hand-over of large sums of cash in a car park and also indicted under s 328(1) of POCA 2002 is that *of R v MK, AS*:[235]

> 'We approach this case, therefore, on the basis that it is open to the prosecution to try to prove guilt from the "evidence of the circumstances in which the property was handled" which it is said"'give rise to the irresistible

---

234 Per Lord Justice Pitchford.
235 [2009] EWCA Crim 952.

3.290 *Prevalent Types of Fraud*

inference that it can only be derived from crime". *They do not have to prove the specific kind of crime'.*[236]

In other words, in appropriate circumstances, even the general nature of the crime need not be specified.

The need for particulars

3.290 In *R v NW*,[237] the prosecution appealed the first instance terminating ruling[238] following the trial judge's decsision to accede to submission of no case to answer. The Crown submitted that in a criminal prosecution, there was no need to provide particulars of even the type of offending which gave rise to criminal property. The Court of Appeal reviewed both the civil enforcement authorities decided under Pt V of POCA 2002 and criminal cases decided under Pt VII of the Act and dismissed the appeal:

'We have already referred to the linguistic differences between Part 5 and s 340. In our judgment they are not so pressing as to yield a conclusion that the legislature in enacting Part 7 intended, in the context of *criminal* measures, to strike the balance between civil rights and the protection of the public at a markedly different place from where, as authority shows, it lies in relation to Part 5. *Indeed it would be anomalous, not to say bizarre, if the Crown were not required to identify the class of crime in question in a criminal prosecution while the Director is so required in a civil enforcement suit. Sullivan J's description of the legislative purpose of POCA, adopted by Moore-Bick LJ, is surely no less apt as a guide for the application of Part 7 as it is for that of Part 5.*

In short, we do not consider that Parliament can have intended a state of affairs in which, in any given instance, no particulars whatever need be given or proved of a cardinal element in the case, namely the criminal conduct relied on. It is a requirement, to use Sullivan J's expression, of elementary fairness.'[239]

[Emphasis added]

3.291 In *Director of Public Prosecutions v Bholah*,[240] Privy Counel councerned a prosecution for money laundering offence in which no predicate offence had been identified and the defendant had been convicted on the basis that the money which he transferred must have, in all the circumstances, been

---

236 Paragraph 12 per Lady Justice Hallett.
237 2008 EWCA Crim 2.
238 Brought under s 58 of the Criminal Justice Act 2003.
239 See paras 37–38. But see *R v Gillies* below in which the Court of Appeal paid no regard to civil recovery cases decided under Pt V of POCA 2002 and where the conviction was upheld without any attempt by the Crown to give particulars of even the type of criminal conduct.
240 [2011] UKPC 44.

criminal property. The Court agreed that both the criminal civil recovery authorities decided under PT 5 of POCA 2002[241] did not require that state to prove the commission of a particular criminal offence but that:

> 'The decisions in the English cases are informative beyond their firm conclusion that proof of a specific predicate offence is not required, however. They are unanimous, in the Board's view, in suggesting that where it is possible to give particulars of the nature of the criminal activity that has generated the illicit proceeds, this should be done. Some of the cases appear to suggest that this is an indispensable requirement; others that it is merely required where it is feasible. All are agreed, however, that *where it is possible to give the accused notice of the type of criminal activity that produced the illegal proceeds, fairness demands that this information should be supplied*'[242]

[Emphasis added]

Pecuniary advantage

3.292 Section 340(6) states that:

> 'If a person obtains a pecuniary advantage as a result of or in connection with conduct, he is to be taken to obtain as a result of or in connection with the conduct a sum of money equal to the value of the pecuniary advantage'.

3.293 In *R v William*,[243] the court considered the construction of s 340(6) and stated that:

> 'Section 340(6) is also important in the context of this case:
>
> > "(6) If a person obtains a pecuniary advantage as a result of or in connection with conduct, he is to be taken to obtain as a result of or in connection with the conduct a sum of money equal to the value of the pecuniary advantage."
>
> This means that someone like Isaac William, who cheats the Revenue by failing to pay the tax he should pay, has obtained a pecuniary advantage and therefore is taken to have obtained a benefit within the meaning of subsection (3) which is equal to the pecuniary advantage.
>
> The value of that benefit is the amount of the tax unpaid.[244] In cases where the turnover is falsely represented, the benefit is the tax due on the undeclared

---

241 See A Eissa and R Barber, *Confiscation Law Handbook* (Bloomsbury Professional, 2011).
242 See para 34.
243 [2013] EWCA Crim 1262.
244 This is consistent with the approach of the Courts in confiscation cases see *R v Dimsey and Allen* [2002] 1 Cr App R (S) 467; ordinarily the tax evaded or obtained is the pecuniary advantage and this is the defendant's benefit.

3.294 *Prevalent Types of Fraud*

turnover. However, the criminal property as defined by section 340 is the entirety of the undeclared turnover and not merely the tax due because the benefit is represented in part by that sum.'

Pecuniary advantage and benefit fraud

3.294 In *R v Gabriel* it was said, obiter:

'We can see how benefits obtained on the basis of a false declaration or a failure to disclose a change in circumstances may amount to obtaining a pecuniary advantage, namely the benefits: see section 340(6) of the Act' [subject to the need] 'to prove that the appellant or anyone else in her family had made any false declaration or failed to disclose a change of circumstances'.[245]

The principal offences

General matters

3.295 The key points regarding money laundering offences are:

- if an authorised disclosure is made no offence is committed;[246]
- the three principal money laundering offences are not mutually exclusive;[247] and
- in *FSA v Rollins*,[248] the Court upheld the right of the FSA (now the FCA) to prosecute offences under ss 327 and 328 and presumably s 329.

3.296 Sections 327 and 328 are listed in Sch 2 of POCA 2002, so that persons convicted of such offences are deemed to have a 'criminal lifestyle' within the meaning of s 75 of POCA 2002.[249] Section 329 is not listed in Sch 2. In respect of all three offences, property must have been criminal property before or at the time the offence is alleged to have taken place:

'In each case the natural meaning of the statutory language is that in each case the property in question must have become criminal property as a result of some conduct which occurred prior to the act which is alleged to constitute the offence, whether that be concealing, disguising, converting, transferring or removing it contrary to section 327 or entering into or

---

245 [2006] EWCA Crim 229, see para 22.
246 See 'Authorised disclosures' below.
247 'It is, of course, possible that that an offence under section 327 is also an offence under section 328 and vice versa': see *R v Fazal* [2009] EWCA Crim 1697 para 17.
248 [2010] 1 WLR 1922.
249 This may have profound consequences in the context of confiscation proceedings – see A Eissa and R Barber, *Confiscation Law Handbook* (Bloomsbury Professional, 2011).

becoming concerned in an arrangement which facilitates its acquisition, retention, use or control by another contrary to section 328. We think that the same must be true of acquiring, using or having possession of criminal property contrary to section 329(1). Moreover, it follows from what we have said that the only authorities directly in point on the interpretation of sections 327 and 328 support that conclusion'.[250]

Limitations on the scope of the offences

3.297 The principal offences are not committed if a person knows or believes on reasonable grounds that the conduct was not committed in the United Kingdom and was not criminal in the county in which it took place nor prescribed by an Order of the Secretary of State.[251] The offences are triable either way. The maximum penalty on indictment is 14 years' imprisonment.

Concealing, disguising, converting, transferring or removing criminal property under POCA 2002, s 327

3.298 Section 327 creates one offence, which can be committed in one of five different ways as set out in s 327:

'(1) A person commits an offence if he—

(a) conceals criminal property;

(b) disguises criminal property;

(c) converts criminal property;

(d) transfers criminal property;

(e) removes criminal property from England and Wales or from Scotland or from Northern Ireland.'

This wording is self explanatory, but an illustration of the approach as to what constitutes conversion of property within the meaning of s 327(1)(c) is to be found in *R v Fazal*:[252]

'21 ... A person may lodge, receive, retain and withdraw monies from his account, each of which would amount to a converting of the monies concerned, ...

22 ... When money goes through an account it changes its nature from money likely to be owned by one bank but representing a debt owed to one creditor into money owned by another bank and representing a debt owed

---

250 *R v Geary* [2010] EWCA Crim 1925, para 36.
251 Sections 327(2)(A), 328(3) and 329(2)(A) respectively.
252 2009 EWCA Crim 1697.

3.299 *Prevalent Types of Fraud*

to another creditor. Finally, when that money is withdrawn in cash, if it is withdrawn in cash, it becomes transferred into cash into the hands of the withdrawer. So at each stage, in our judgment, as the property concerned passed through the appellant's account, it was being converted'.

Entering into or becoming concerned in an arrangement to facilitate under POCA 2002, s 328

3.299   Under section 328(1):

'A person commits an offence if he enters into or becomes concerned in an arrangement which he knows or suspects facilitates (by whatever means) the acquisition, retention, use or control of criminal property by or on behalf of another person.'

It should be noted that property must be criminal property prior to the existence of the arrangement:

'In our view the natural and ordinary meaning of section 328(1) is that the arrangement to which it refers must be one which relates to property which is criminal property at the time when the arrangement begins to operate on it. To say that it extends to property which was originally legitimate but became criminal only as a result of carrying out the arrangement is to stretch the language of the section beyond its proper limits'[253].

Acts preparatory to an arrangement do not constitute an arrangement

3.300   An example of a case in which the acts of the defendant were merely preparatory and not sufficient to amount to an arrangement is *Dare v CPS*.[254] The evidence was that the defendant intended to buy a car which was and which he suspected to be stolen and sell it on at a profit. He took it for a test drive and went away to see what money he could raise with a view to making an offer. Having done so he arranged to meet the thief a second time and make his offer to buy the vehicle:

'9 The arrangement in this case on the facts as found by the Justices was not even a contract of sale. It was an arrangement to meet with a view to negotiating a price. Had a price been agreed and the car been handed over, that would have facilitated in the future the acquisition of the car by somebody else.

10 But the section says that the arrangement must be one which the defendant knows or suspects "facilitates" the acquisition by or on behalf of another

---

253 *R v Geary* [2010] EWCA Crim 1925, at para 19.
254 2012 EWCA 2074(Admin).

Money laundering **3.302**

person. It does not say "will facilitate", still less "will probably facilitate" or "may facilitate". It envisages a snapshot being taken at the moment of the arrangement being concluded so that one can say at that moment that it facilitates (present tense) the acquisition by or on behalf of another person, and therefore that that other person must be identified or at least identifiable.

11 In this case, the acts of Mr Dare were too preparatory for that to have taken place, both because a price had not been agreed and because he had taken no steps to identify a prospective purchaser'.

Legal professionals and arrangement within the meaning of s 328

3.301   In *Bowman and Fels*[255] it was stated that:

'83. ... the proper interpretation of s 328 is that it is not intended to cover or affect the ordinary conduct of litigation by legal professionals. That includes any step taken by them in litigation from the issue of proceedings and the securing of injunctive relief or a freezing order up to its final disposal by judgment. We do not consider that either the European or the United Kingdom legislator can have envisaged that any of these ordinary activities could fall within the concept of "becoming concerned in an arrangement which ... facilitates the acquisition, retention, use or control of criminal property".

89. ... it would require much clearer language than is contained in s 328 and its ancillary sections before a Parliamentary intention could be gleaned to the effect that a party's solicitor is obliged, in breach of this implied duty to the court, and in breach of the duty of confidence he owes to his own client as his litigation solicitor, to disclose to NCIS a suspicion he may have that documents disclosed under compulsion by the other party evidence one of the matters referred to in s 328.

90. It follows that on this narrower issue we are satisfied that even if, contrary to our primary view, s 328 is to be interpreted as including legal proceedings within its purview, it cannot be interpreted as meaning either that legal professional privilege is to be overridden or that a lawyer is to breach his duty to the court by disclosing to a third party external to the litigation documents revealed to him through the disclosure processes.'

Acquisition, use and possession under POCA 2002, s 329

3.302   Under s 329:

'(1)   A person commits an offence if he—

---

[255] [2005] EWCA Civ 226, per Lord Justice Brooke.

3.303 *Prevalent Types of Fraud*

    (a)   acquires criminal property;

    (b)   uses criminal property;

    (c)   has possession of criminal property.

The need to prove inadequate consideration

3.303 In *R v Rahila Kausar*,[256] the appellant was wrongly convicted of acquiring criminal property contrary to s 329(1)(a) of POCA 2002. She supplied false information to the lender and thereby obtained a mortgage. It was held that a person cannot be convicted of the offence unless he has given inadequate consideration. This 'is clearly a separate ingredient of the offence' (para 13). A defendant who fraudulently obtains a loan by supplying false information is nonetheless obliged to repay it at a market rate and has not therefore acquired the property for inadequate consideration. The Court in *Kausar* analysed the matter as follows:

> '12 That there was a mortgage deed is not in dispute. It is not before us, but we know that it imposed on the appellant, as borrower, in return for the mortgage advance, an undertaking to repay the advance with interest and conferred on the lender a charge on the mortgaged property. *The charge and the undertaking to repay with interest were the consideration for the advance. There is no suggestion that the interest was other than a market rate, or that in any other respect the consideration (as we have defined it) passing from the appellant was inadequate.*
>
> [...]
>
> 14 It follows, in our judgment, that the appellant should never have been charged with this offence and should not have been convicted of it. Accordingly, the appeal will be allowed and the conviction quashed.'[257]

Authorised disclosures

3.304 Authorised disclosures made within the meaning of s 338 of the Act limit the scope of the offences. If an authorised disclosure is made no offence is committed. In summary a disclosure is authorised if it is made to an officer of Revenue and Customs, a constable or nominated officer. Such disclosure must be made before the suspected act is performed or when the suspect first

---

256 [2009] EWCA Crim 2242.
257 Per Stanley Burnton LJ. The Court observed that 'when she received the proceeds of the mortgage she would have committed what is now the offence of fraud by false representation under section 2 of the Fraud Act 2006 and was at the relevant time the offence of obtaining a money transfer by deception contrary to section 15A of the Theft Act 1968'. See above on mortgage fraud.

suspects that the act concerned criminal property. If the disclosure is not made until after the prohibited act is complete the offence will be made out unless the suspect had a reasonable excuse for not making disclosure earlier. In both the foregoing scenarios where disclosure is not made before the prohibited act, the disclosure must be made on the as soon as practicable and on the initiative of the suspect. In the case of a deposit taking body no offence is committed if it does the act in the course of maintaining an account held with it and the amount is below the threshold amount determined under s 339A of the Act.[258] Such provision was added by Serious Organised Crime and Police Act 2005, s 102(2) (15 May 2006).

Proving the case in practice

3.305 Ways to prove the case in practice may include:

- Incriminating conversation recorded covertly or by an undercover officer as in *R v Anwoir*.[259]
- Accomplice evidence.
- Scientific testing of bank notes. In an appropriate case where the cash itself is seized it is possible to analyse it for the presence of traces of drugs to prove that it is derived from drug dealing. All notes have traces of drugs on them but the question is whether the concentration is markedly higher than average so as to support an inference the cash is derived from drug dealing.
- Banks are part of the regulated sector and have a duty to report suspicion activity. Depositing cash in small sums at various bank branches to avoid suspicion aroused by the depositing of larger amounts on one occasion. This is sometimes referred to as 'smurfing'. CCTV from banks and paying in slips can be obtained to prove the identity of the payee if this is in issue.
- Company accounts and HMRC tax and VAT returns may be inconsistent with the money paid into accounts or otherwise handled or with an extravagant lifestyle which provides some support for the contention that the origin of such property is criminal conduct.
- Expert evidence that the movement of monies between various accounts or individuals has no commercial purpose may give rise to an inference that it is being moved to disguise its origin.

---

258 Under s 339A(2) that amount is £250 although an officer of Revenue and Customs or a constable may specify the threshold amount when giving or refusing consent to the deposit taking body doing an act mentioned in ss 327–329 in opening operating or maintaining an account: see s 339A(3).
259 [2008] EWCA Crim 1354.

3.306 *Prevalent Types of Fraud*

- Expert evidence as to discrepancies in the accounting records of a company which cannot be reconciled.

- In order to keep the true owner hidden, property may be transferred to a trusted accomplice. In that case proof that it was transferred for other than market value may support the prosecution case that the transfer was carried out to facilitate the disguising or concealment of ownership. The creation of trust deeds to divest the legal or paper owner of any beneficial interest may further support this.

- Previous convictions for acquisitive crime if sufficiently probative to be admissible under the gateways of CJA 2003. This may extend to admitting in evidence the character of associates of the defendant if they can be shown to have provided some or all of the funds alleged to have been laundered.

Joinder with predicate offences

3.306 The essence of money laundering presupposes the commission of other criminal offences. Whilst this need not specifically be proved, it is clear that where evidence of specific offences can be proved they are properly joined to the same indictment. In *Ferrel v R*,[260] the Privy Council held that if the position is that there is prima facie evidence as to the source of the tainted money then clearly that criminal conduct should be reflected in a count on the same indictment: in practice it would be not be realistic or desirable for the allegations to be tried separately and such a course would give rise to the possibility of irreconcilably inconsistent verdicts.

3.307 In *Ferrel*, it was held to be permissible for the jury to conclude that cash deposits made *prior to dates averred in drug trafficking counts* must have come from similar drug trafficking activity and accordingly the Privy Council held that the judge was right not to order severance. The facts were that:

> '4. ... since his arrival in Gibraltar in 2000 the appellant had only worked on eighteen days, and had not been in registered employment since November 2003, but he had a bank account with the NatWest Bank into which he had made frequent payments. Between December 2005 and 27 May 2008 he deposited a total of £69,835, always in cash in amounts of under £1,000. The prosecution case was that that was to avoid the need for the bank to report an unusually large deposit. The appellant had also had a total of seven vehicles registered in his name. Counts 7–15 were specimen counts relating to deposits of cash on various dates between 15 August 2006 and 27 May 2008. In evidence at the trial the appellant claimed that he earned the cash by working as a doorman and by smuggling tobacco into Spain.

---

260 [2010] UKPC 20.

Money laundering **3.308**

10 ... Counts 1 to 4, and especially counts 2 and 4, which alleged possession of cocaine with intent to supply, all dealt with the supply of drugs. The drugs would of course have been sold for money, which would then require to be banked and, in all likelihood, laundered. The Attorney General correctly accepted that the prosecution had to show, in the case of each of the money laundering counts 7 to 15 that some at least of the money derived from drug dealing. He submitted, however, that on the facts set out above, it was open to the jury to infer that the money was indeed the proceeds of drug dealing. He accepted of course that all the money laundering counts related to transactions that pre-dated the possession of the drugs in the drugs counts but submitted that, in the absence of a credible explanation to the contrary, it was open to the jury to infer that the appellant had had a system of selling drugs and laundering the money over an extended period.

12. The only question is whether a jury was entitled to infer that it was drugs money. In the opinion of the Board, the answer to that question, at any rate in the absence of a credible explanation to the contrary, is yes. The only suggestion made by or on behalf of the appellant was that the cash came from working as a doorman and from smuggling tobacco into Spain. There was however no support for the evidence that it came from tobacco smuggling. On the other hand, there is evidence that the appellant was a drug dealer, albeit at a later time than he was laundering the money. It was open to the jury to reject his explanation and to conclude that there was no reasonable doubt that the money came from earlier dealing in drugs.'

Sentencing

3.308 The Sentencing Guidelines Council has published new guidelines in force from 1 October 2014. Cases decided before their introduction may therefore have less relevance. However the decision as to whether or not to impose consecutive sentences in money laundering cases as set out in *R v Greaves*[261] will still be relevant:

'24 It is in accordance with principle and the authorities which we have cited that:

(a) Offences contrary to sections 327 to 329 of the Proceeds of Crime Act, are separate, "free-standing", offences to the offences or offences which give rise to the criminal property with which the Proceeds of Crime Act is concerned.

(b) Where the offender responsible for the primary crime is not the offender guilty of the Proceeds of Crime Act offence, the position

---

261 [2010] EWCA Crim 709.

3.308 *Prevalent Types of Fraud*

is more straight forward than when they are the same. We are not concerned with this situation.

(c) Where the offenders are one and the same, if the conduct involved in Proceeds of Crime Act offence in reality adds nothing to the culpability of the conduct involved in primary offence, there should be no additional penalty. A person should not be punished twice for the same conduct. That can be achieved either by imposing 'no separate penalty' on the Proceeds of Crime Act offence or by a concurrent sentence where the primary sentence is imprisonment.

(d) Where conduct involved in a Proceeds of Crime Act offence does add to the culpability of the conduct involved in the primary offence an additional penalty is appropriate: see Brown and Linegar.

(e) Where the primary offence has a maximum sentence, that is the maximum which Parliament has thought appropriate for conduct constituting the offence. In a case where the Proceeds of Crime Act offence does not add to the culpability of the conduct involved in the primary offence, there should not be a consecutive sentence on the latter on the ground that the maximum permitted on the primary offence is too low. Any difficulty posed by a low maximum for the primary offence may possibly be avoided if it is foreseen by the prosecution. Thus in the present case there might have been a number of specimen substantive counts rather than one count of conspiracy.

(f) Where the conduct involved in the Proceeds of Crime Act offence does add to the culpability of the conduct involved in the primary offence, the maximum sentence permitted on the primary offence may be relevant to the sentence on the Proceeds of Crime Act offence because the seriousness of the primary offence reflects on the seriousness of the laundering: see, for instance, Greenwood and Basra . But it does not as a matter of principle provide a limit: see Linegar. If the Proceeds of Crime Act offence merits it, the sentence for it may add to that for the primary offence bringing it above the maximum for the latter, and it may if appropriate itself exceed the maximum on the latter: see Linegar.

(g) We have avoided the use of the expression "gravamen of the offence", which was much used in submissions to us in the context of the Proceeds of Crime Act offences having or not having a different gravamen to the sections 19 and 22 conspiracies. "Gravamen" in its legal context means "the essential or most serious part of an accusation; the part that bears most heavily on the accused" – the New Shorter Oxford Dictionary, We do not think that is necessary for the Proceeds of Crime Act offence to have a different gravamen to that of the primary offence. We prefer to say that the conduct involved in the former must add to the culpability of the conduct involved in the latter. Put shortly, there must be "something more". The offender is not to be sentenced twice for the same conduct. We have referred to the "culpability of the conduct" We might have referred to "the criminality of the conduct", but we prefer culpability because "criminality" simply means "the quality or fact of being criminal" – Oxford English Dictionary.'[262]

An overview of the reporting obligations contained in POCA 2002, ss 330–332

3.309 Sections 330–332 impose obligations on those working in the regulated sector[263] to report suspicious activities.[264]

3.310 Section 330 requires a business operating in the regulated sector to report suspicious activity. The section does not require that money laundering be actually be proved. The requirement to report such activity arises where there is knowledge, suspicion *or* where reasonable grounds for suspicion exist. The section applies only where the person responsible for the laundering, or the whereabouts of the proceeds, can be identified.[265] Disclosure must be made as soon as practicable. The offence is not committed if there is a reasonable excuse for not making the disclosure[266] or if the information is received by a professional legal adviser acting in 'privileged circumstances'[267] or another relevant professional adviser.[268] In deciding whether the offence has been committed the court may take into account any guidance provided by supervisory body of the relevant profession or other appropriate body or guidance provided by the Treasury. No offence is committed if the money laundering takes place outside of the United Kingdom and the offence is not unlawful in that country and is not prescribed by an Order of the Secretary of State.

3.311 Under s 331, if a nominated officer receives a disclosure under s 330 and fails to disclose the matter he commits an offence under this section. This is subject to proof that as a result of the disclosure made to him he either knew or suspected money laundering was taking place or had cause to do so on reasonable grounds and the identity of the launderer or the whereabouts

---

262 Paragraph 24 per Jack J.
263 POCA 2002, s 330 provides that the regulated sector is as defined at Sch 9 to POCA 2002 – see Appendices below.
264 Although s 339 provides that the form and manner of the report may be prescribed by the Secretary of State, to date this has not occurred.
265 POCA 2002, s 330(A) as amended by Serious Organised Crime and Police Act, s 104.
266 POCA 2002, s 330(6)(a).
267 As defined by s330(10) of POCA 2002.
268 Section 330(14) defines a relevant professional adviser as an accountant ,auditor or tax advisor who is a member of a professional body within the meaning provided for in that section.

3.312 *Prevalent Types of Fraud*

of the proceeds could be identified. The disclosure must be made as soon as practicable. No offence is committed if a person has a reasonable excuse for not making disclosure[269] or if the laundering takes place in another country and is not unlawful under the laws of that country and is not prescribed by the Secretary of State.[270]

3.312 Section 332 of POCA 2002 creates a similar offence which applies to nominated officers working outside the regulated sector. The difference compared with the requirements contained in s 331 is that under this section, the nominated must have actual suspicion or knowledge; objective grounds for such suspicion or knowledge will not suffice.

3.313 Section 333A deals with tipping off. This offence is committed if a person in the regulated sector is aware of a disclosure having been made to either a nominated officer or to the appropriate authorities and makes disclosure that is likely to prejudice the investigation.

Penalties

3.314 Offences contained in ss 330–333 incur a maximum of five years' imprisonment in the Crown Court or six months in the Magistrates' Court.

---

269 Section 331(6) of POCA 2002.
270 Section 331(6)(A) of POCA 2002.

Chapter 4

Search, Seizure and Investigations

4.1 English courts are hostile to any power of entry not based on specific and clear authority.[1] State and private investigators[2] need therefore to be able to rely upon statutory or common law[3] authorisation to justify the lawfulness of any search and seizure of items.

4.2 There are, in England and Wales, a vast array[4] of legal rights of entry allowing certain persons to go onto another's property, with associated powers of inspection, search, seizure and retention of items. The exercise of such powers must comply with the European Convention on Human Rights (ECHR) and respect the convention rights therein, in particular Art 8 (the right to privacy).[5] The courts protect the individual from invasion of privacy that the execution of a search represents, treating the matter as a matter of

---

1 This hostility is centuries old see *Entick v Carrington* (1765) 19 State Tr 1065.
2 The PACE Codes of Practice applies to police officers, including police forces such as the British Transport Police and persons charged with the duty of investigating offences or charging offenders including Revenue and Customs officers (*R v Okafor* 99 Cr App R 97, *R v Weerdsteyn* [1995] 1 Cr App R 405 (CA)), officers of the Serious Fraud Office (*R v Director of Serious Fraud Office, ex p Saunders* [1988] Crim L R 837), and Inland Revenue special compliance officers investigating tax fraud (*R v Gill* [2004] 1 (Cr App R 20 (CA)), and store detectives and similar security officers (*R v Bayliss* 98 Cr App R 235). For commercial investigators see *R v Twaites and Brown* 92 Cr App R 106 (CA).
3 Following arrest or breach of the peace.
4 The Home Office identifying, as part of the consultation process in the introduction of the Protection of Freedoms Act 2012, more than 100 different powers of entry existing under UK legislation.
5 Persons who enter without proper legal authority or a lawful entrant who goes beyond the scope of a warrant or permission, become trespassers and civil remedies arise, eg actions in trespass to land and malicious procurement of a search warrant, conversion, replevin, negligence and actions under the Police (Property) Act 1897. Article 3 (inhuman and degrading treatment) and Protocol 1, Art 1 (peaceful possession of property) may also be engaged.

4.3 *Search, Seizure and Investigations*

high constitutional importance. The obtaining of a search warrant is never a formality.[6]

4.3 The practical application of the principle is set out in Pts 5 and 6 of the Criminal Procedure Rules 2013[7] and cases such as *R v Tchenguiz*,[8] *AB & CD v Huddersfield Magistrates' Court & the Chief Constable of West Yorkshire Police*[9] and *R (on application of Golfrate Property Management Ltd) v Southwark Crown Court and Metropolitan Police*.[10]

4.4 In *Tchenguiz*, the Adminstrative Court set out the duties of the Serious Fraud Office when applying for the issue of a search warrant under s 2(4) of the Criminal Justice Act 1987 in cases involving allegations of serious fraud in the financial markets. In short, the SFO had a duty to ensure that what was put before the issuing judge was clear and comprehensive, so that the judge could rely on it and form a judgment on the basis of a presentation which could be trusted in terms of its accuracy and completeness. Not only had the case for reasonable suspicion to be put, but the matters that might undermine that case had to be enumerated.

4.5 In *AB & CD* Mr. Justice Stuart-Smith observed:[11]

'it should by now be clearly appreciated by all who make or decide applications for the issuing of warrants that there is no part of the process that should be regarded as a formality. Each application must be carefully and precisely formulated so as to satisfy both the statutory requirements and the duty of full and frank disclosure; and a decision to issue may only be taken after that level of critical scrutiny that is required when the court

---

6 See *Redknapp v Commissioner of the City of London Police Department* [2008] EWHC 1177 (Admin) [2009] 1 WLR 2091, as applied in *R (Wood) v North Avon Magistrates Court* 174 JP 157 DC; *G v Commissioner of Police of the Metropolis* [2011] EWHC 3331 (Admin); *R (Glenn and Co. (Essex) Ltd) v HM Commrs for Revenue and Customs* [2012] 1 Cr App R 22 DC; *R (on the application of Global Cash & Carry Ltd) v Birmingham Magistrates' Court* [2013] EWHC 528 (search warrant rendered unlawful where the warrant had been served on the occupant company director in an incomplete form, without a relevant schedule of premises attached); *R (on the application of Hoque) v City of London Magistrates' Court* [2013] EWHC 725 (Admin), [2013] ACD 67 (search warrants were declared unlawful as s 15(6)(b) of PACE was not complied with, the warrants were drawn too widely and gave Customs an undue margin to seize); *Lees v Solihull Magistrates' Court* [2013] EWHC 3779 (Admin), [2014] Lloyd's Rep FC 233 (warrant unlawful as Customs had failed to specify with sufficient precision the material sought).
7 As amended and in force on 7 October 2013 the Criminal Procedure Rules 2013 (SI 2013/1554).
8 *R (on the application of Rawlinson and Hunter Trustees) v Central Criminal Court, R(on the application of Tchenguiz v Director of Serious Fraud Office* [2012] EWHC 2254 (Admin) and [2013] EWHC 2128 (QB), [2013] 1 WLR 1634 (DC).
9 [2014] EWHC 1089 (Admin).
10 [2014] EWHC 840 (Admin).
11 At para 13 of the judgment.

is asked to sanction a substantial invasion of fundamental rights. The flow of the authorities[12] tends towards requiring increasing rigour and precision at all stages of the process and nothing we say in this judgment should be taken or interpreted as going against that flow'.

4.6 In *AB & CD*, for example, it was fatal to the Chief Constable's case that the Police failed to disclose to the issuing Magistrates' Court that the residential premises to be searched were occupied by solicitors. That disclosure failure led to the Administrative Court quashing the search warrant.[13]

4.7 In *R v Golfrate Property Management*,[14] the Administrative Court set aside search and seizure warrants issued under ss 352(1) and (6)(b) of the Proceeds of Crime Act 2002 (POCA), in relation to properties, as part of a money laundering investigation directed at the breach of EU sanctions imposed agisnt members of the ZANU-PF ruling party in Zimbabwe. The court emphasised that police officers applying for search and seizure warrants needed to be aware of the obligation to ensure that judges faced with such applications were presented with a full and clear picture of what lay behind them and to be told of matters that might go against them. The duty of candour and of full and frank disclosure was highlighted. The court held that it is impermissible for the party obtaining a warrant on an ex parte basis, to refuse to disclose the material placed before the judge to the party to whom the warrant has been obtained. LCJ Thomas observed that:

'It can only be withheld if the court sanctions the withholding of that material on public interest grounds'.[15]

4.8 In practical terms LCJ Thomas said:

'[26] the HMCTS[16] must make the necessary resources available so that the Resident Judge at the Crown Court can discharge his responsibility for ensuring that arrangements are in place for these difficult and important applications to be dealt with properly. Judges must therefore be provided with the papers promptly, be accorded the time required to read the papers, to hear the application and to provide written reasons'.[17]

---

12 See for example *PCJ Van der Pijl v Crown Court at Kingston* [2013] 1 WLR 2706,[2012] EWHC 3745 (Admin) at paras [53], [61] and [65] per Wilkie J and *R (S and others) v Chief Constable of the British Transport Police* [2014] 1 AER 268, [2013] EWHC 2189 (Admin) at [31].
13 See para 20 of Mr Justice Stuart-Smith's judgment.
14 *R (on the application of Golfrate Property Management Ltd) v Southwark Crown Court* [2014] EWHC 840 (Admin); [2014] 2 Cr App R 12.
15 Ibid at [18].
16 The Court Service.
17 *R (on the application of Golfrate Property Management Ltd) v Southwark Crown Court* at [26].

4.9 *Search, Seizure and Investigations*

THE POLICE AND CRIMINAL EVIDENCE ACT 1984

4.9 Sections 15 and 16 of the Police and Criminal Evidence Act 1984 (PACE)[18] supplemented by Code of Practice B,[19] provides powers to seize and retain anything for which the search warrant has been authorised or after arrest, other than items attracting legal professional privilege. The requirements of ss 15 (warrant content) and 16 (execution) are applied strictly by the courts.[20] The whole process of warrant, entry and search must be PACE compliant for the search to be lawful.[21]

4.10 In applying for a search warrant, information received justifying an application should be checked for its accuracy[22] and the following must be clear on the application:[23]

- the grounds on which the application is being made;[24]
- the statutory provision relied upon;
- the address of the premise to be entered and searched, including the parts of any multiple premises;[25] and
- insofar as it is practicable, the articles[26] or persons sought.

4.11 An applicant must provide all information so that a judge can make an informed decision, as detailed, anxious and intense scrutiny is needed of such applications. A detailed presentation by the applicant should take place,[27]

---

18 As amended by statutes such as the Serious Organised Crime and Police Act 2005 (which radically altered the requirements for obtaining a search warrant, requiring suspicion of an indictable offence) and case law under the Human Rights Act 1998. See also the Protection of Freedoms Act 2012 and its associated Code of Practice regulating non-police powers of entry. Customs officers are covered by SI 2007/3175 as amended by the Finance Act 2007, made under s 114 of PACE.
19 'For the Search of Premises and Seizure of Property', which current code came into force on 6 March 2011: see www.homeoffice.gov.uk.
20 See *R v Central Criminal Court ex p AJD Holdings* [1992] Crim LR 669; *Kent Pharmaceuticals Ltd v Director of the Serious Fraud Office* [2002] EWHC 3024; *Power-Hynes v Norwich Magistrates' Court* [2009] EWHC 1512 (Admin).
21 See *R v Central Criminal Court exp AJD Holdings* [1992] Crim LR 669; *R v Chief Constable of Lancashire ex p Parker and McGraff* [1993] Crim LR 204; *R v Chief Constable of the Warwickshire Constabulary, ex p Fitzpatrick* [1999] 1 WLR 564; *R (Bhatti) v Croydon Magistrates Court* [2011] 1 WLR 948.
22 As the requesting officer must be prepared to answer questions about the accuracy of background information.
23 See s 15(6) of PACE.
24 See s 15(2) of PACE. See *R v Inner London Crown Court ex p Baines and Baines (a Firm)* [1988] QB 579, 87 Cr App.R 111 (DC).
25 See *R v South Western Magistrates' Court, ex p Cofie* [1997] 1 WLR 885.
26 See *R v Central Criminal Court, ex p Adegbesan* (1987) 84 Cr App R 219 (DC).
27 See *R (Paul da Costa & Co (a Firm) v Thames Magistrates' Court* [2002] STC 267 (DC); *R (Hicks) v Commr of Police of the Metropolis; R (Middleton) v Bromley Magistrates' Court and Commr of Police of the Metropolis* [2012] EWHC 1947.

including information which mitigates against granting a warrant. Full and frank disclosure of information should be made by the applicant,[28] putting on their 'defence hat' and considering what representations could be made by the defendant,[29] including:

- whether any ensuing prosecution is, or is likely to be private;[30]
- whether there had been previous visits by investigators to premises;[31]
- the defendant's potential criminal liability;[32] and
- the nature of the investigation.[33]

Privileged material

4.12 Searching officers cannot, under an ordinary warrant, seize items which are subject to three categories:

- legal privileged;
- excluded;[34] or
- special procedure.[35]

---

28 See *R v Central Criminal Court, ex p AJD Holdings* [1992] Crim LR 669 (DC); *R v Acton Crown Court, ex p Layton* [1993] Crim LR 458 (DC).
29 See *Re Stanford International Bank Ltd; Janvey v Westell v Serious Fraud Office v Wastell* [2011] Ch 33 (CA) as applied in *AB v CD Huddersfield Court & CC West Yorkshire Police* [2014] EWHC 1089 (Admin).
30 See *Zinga v R* [2013] Lloyd's Rep FC 102 (CA) and r 6.30(10) of the Criminal Procedure Rules 2013 (SI 2013/1554)
31 See *R (Dulia) v Chelmsford Magistrates' Court and Essex County Council; R (Essex County Council) v Chelmsford Crown Court and Essex Magistrates'Court, Dulai (Interested Parties)* [2012] 2 Cr App R 19 (DC).
32 See *R (on the application of Vuciterni) v Brent Magistrates' Court*, (2012) 176 JP 705 (DC).
33 See *R (Hoque) v City of London Magistrates' Court* [2013] ACD 67 (DC). See also *R (Amand) v HM Revenue and Customs Commrs* [2013] Lloyd's Rep FC 278 (DC) and *R (Vand der Pijl) v Crown Court at Kingston* [2013] 1 WLR 2706.
34 Excluded material is defined in s 11 of PACE as: (a) personal records held in confidence in the course of a trade, business, professional or occupation; (b) human tissue or tissue fluid; and (c) journalistic as defined in s 13 of PACE.
35 As defined in s of 14 PACE covering non-excluded journalistic material and other material held in confidence as the result of an implied or express undertaking by a person or by statutory obligation. See *R v Guildhall Magistrates' Court, ex p Primlaks Holdings Co (Panama) Inc.* [1990] 1 QB 261, 89 Cr App.R 215 (DC); *Bates v Chief Constable of Avon and Somerset Police and Bristol Magistrates' Court* (2009) 173, JP 313 (DC) (no jurisdiction under s 8 of PACE to issue warrant for computers at home of expert witness, who had acted in many cases over a long period of time relating to computer-based material); and *Power-Hynes v Norwich Magistrates' Court* (2009)173 JP 573 (DC) (no s 8 jurisdiction in relation to an accountant who acted as company secretary for several companies, some of which were not under investigation. The warrant was drafted too generally).

4.13 *Search, Seizure and Investigations*

4.13 Section 10 of PACE defines legally privileged documents as those involving:

(a) communications between a professional legal adviser and his client or any person representing his client made in connection with the giving of legal advice to the client; or

(b) the same made in connection with or in contemplation of legal proceedings; and

(c) items enclosed with or referred to in (a) and (b).[36]

4.14 Items held with the intention of furthering a criminal purpose are not items subject to legal privilege.[37]

4.15 It is prudent where legal professional privilege may arise that independent counsel is instructed to attend the search to ensure that if such documents or materials are present such items are not inspected by the searching officers. Such material can be seized but only inspected by the searching officers once independent counsel has verified that any legal professionally privileged material has been excluded/redacted.

General power to seize

4.16 In addition, there is a general power, under s 19 of PACE, to seize anything which is on the premises if there are reasonable grounds to believe that it has been obtained in the commission of an offence, or that it is evidence and that it is necessary to seize it to prevent it being concealed, lost, altered or destroyed.[38]

4.17 Section 20 of PACE provides a related power to require information which is stored in any electronic form (eg derived from computer or web-based files) and is accessible from the premises to be produced in a form in which it

---

36 This section does not cover simply records such as attendance notes, time sheets, fee records, appointment records, conveyancing documents: see *R v Crown Court at Inner London ex p Baines and Baines* [1987] 3 All ER 1025; *R v Central Criminal Court, ex p Francis and Francis* [1988] 1 All ER 677; *R v Manchester Crown Court, ex p Rogers* [1999] 1 WLR 832 which was followed in *Miller Gardner Solicitors v Minshull Street Crown Court* [2002] EWHC 3077 (QB).
37 As per s 10(2) of PACE. See *R v Crown Court at Snaresbrook , ex p DPP* [1998] 1 All ER 315; *Francis & Francis v Central Criminal Court* [1998] 3 All ER 775; *R v Governor of Pentonville Prison, ex p Osman* 90 Cr App.R 281 (DC), *R (Hallinan Blackburn Gittings & Nott (a firm) v Crown Court at Middlesex Guildhall* [2005] 1 WLR 766 (DC) and *Kuwait Airways Corp v Iraqi Airways Co (No 6)* [2005] 1 WLR 2734 (CA). For the common law position see *R v Cox and Railton* (1884) 14 QBD 154.
38 Which covers electronic form material as per Criminal Justice and Police Act 2001.

can be taken away and in which it is visible and legible or from which it can readily be produced in a visible and legible form.

Electronic material

4.18 In relation to fraud investigations, searching officers face a number of practical difficulties as they often come across large quantities of documentary material, often in electronic form (whether on hard drive or portable storage devices), which it is difficult at the time of search to determine the relevance of and whether it is protected by legal professional privilege.

4.19 An image (a forensically sound copy) of the digital material may be taken at the location of the search.[39] Where the investigator makes an image of the digital material at the location, the original need not be seized. Alternatively, when originals are taken, investigators must be prepared to copy or image the material for the owners when reasonably practicable in accordance with PACE 1984, Code B 7.17.

4.20 Where it is not possible or reasonably practicable to image the computer or hard drive, it will need to be removed from the location or premises for examination elsewhere. This allows the investigator to seize and sift material for the purpose of identifying that which meets the tests for retention in accordance with the 1984 Act.[40]

THE CRIMINAL JUSTICE AND POLICE ACT 2001, S 50

4.21 The powers of seizure in ss 50 and 51 of the Criminal Justice and Police Act 2001 (CJPA) only extend the scope of existing PACE and other statutory authorities of search and seizure[41] where the relevant conditions and circumstances apply. Investigators must be careful only to exercise powers under the CJPA when it is necessary and not to remove any more material than is justified.[42] The removal of large volumes of material, much of which may not ultimately be retainable, may have serious consequences for the owner of the material, particularly when they are involved in business or other commercial activities. A written notice must be given to the occupier of the premises where items are seized under sections 50 and 51.[43]

---

39 See para 17 of the Attorney-General's Guidelines on Disclosure of Digitally Stored Material (2011).
40 See para 18 (as above). PACE search provisions apply to Revenue and Customs investigators as per s 114(2)(b) of PACE.
41 Schedule 1 of the Criminal Justice and Police Act 2001 (CJPA) contains a list of over 70 statutory powers of search.
42 As per para 7.7 of PACE Code B.
43 Under s 52 of the CJPA 2001.

4.22 Material seized under the CJPA 2001 must be kept securely and separately from any other material seized. It must be examined as soon as reasonably practicable to determine which elements may be retained and which should be returned. Regard must be had to the desirability of allowing the person from whom the property was seized, or a person with an interest in the property, an opportunity of being present or represented at the examination.[44]

4.23 The provisions do not state who can be compelled to produce the material. As Richard Stone points out:

> 'is it the occupier of the premises, the person who owns the computer on which the material is stored, the internet service provider on whose file-server the information is stored, or all of them?'[45]

The answer varies according to the powers being used and the wording of the statute relied upon.

Retention of material

4.24 Where material is seized under the powers conferred by PACE the duty to retain it under the Code of Practice issued under the Criminal Procedure and Investigations Act 1996 (CPIA) is subject to the provisions on retention under s 22 of PACE. The general principle under s 22 is that seized items may be retained for as long as is necessary in all the circumstances.[46]

4.25 Material seized under ss 50 and 51 of the CJPA 2001 may be retained or returned in accordance with ss 53–58 of that Act. Retention is limited to evidence and relevant material (as defined in the Code of Practice issued under the CPIA 1996). Where either evidence or relevant material is inextricably linked to non-relevant material which is not reasonably practicable to separate, that material can also be retained. Inextricably linked material is material that is not reasonably practicable to separate from other linked material without prejudicing the use of that other material in any investigation or proceedings.

Post-arrest powers

4.26 Sections 18 and 32 of PACE contain specific post-arrest powers of search of premises occupied or controlled by the arrested person or where he

---

44 See para 22 of the Attorney-General's Guidelines on Disclosure of Digitally stored material (2011).
45 *The Law of Entry, Search, and Seizure* 5th Edn (Oxford University Press, 2013), p 27.
46 See *Marcel v Commissioner of Police of the Metropolis* [1992] 1 All ER 72; *Gough v Chief Constable of West Midlands Police* [2004] EWCA Civ 206; *R v Crown Court at Southwark, ex p Customs and Excise Commissioners* [1990] 1 QB 250; *Chief Constable of Merseyside Police v Owens* [2012] EWHC 1515 (Admin).

was arrested for evidence relating to the arrest offence if there are reasonable grounds for believing that there is such evidence, and seizure and retention of the same.

Admissibility issues

4.27 If the prosecution proposes, at trial, to adduce evidence which has been obtained as a result of an unlawful search, the defence may challenge the admissibility of the evidence to exclude the same under common law,[47] s 78 of PACE[48] and/or the Human Rights Act 1998.[49]

Production of material

4.28 There are a number of statutory provisions that cover the state's power to obtain production of items from individuals and companies.

THE PROCEEDS OF CRIME ACT 2002

4.29 In criminal money laundering/confiscation proceedings and civil recovery investigations financial investigators can apply to a Crown Court Judge, under ss 345 to 351 of the Proceeds of Crime Act 2002 (POCA), for a production order of material in the possession of a specified person, supplemented by a search warrant, relevant to financial investigations to ascertain criminal benefit figures and to evaluate available realisable assets of a convicted person/company. Under s 346 of POCA, before a production order is granted there must be reasonable grounds:

- for suspecting that the specified person has benefitted from criminal conduct or the property specified is recoverable property or associated property or has committed a money laundering offence;
- the person specified is in possession or control of the material;
- the material sought is likely to be of substantial value to the investigation; and
- it is in the public interest for the material to be produced.

Section 347 of POCA allows an order to grant entry to be issued by a judge allowing an appropriate officer access to material on any premises.

---

47 As preserved by s 82(3) of PACE.
48 See *R v Sang* [1980] AC 402 as applied in *R v Khan* [1997] AC 558 and *R v Elwell (Harry)* [2001] EWCA Crim 1320. See also *Matto v DPP* [1987] Crim LR 641.
49 See *R v Loosely* [2001] UKHL 53, as applied in *R v Jones* [2010] EWCA Crim 925 and *R v Moore* [2013] EWCA Crim 85.

4.30 *Search, Seizure and Investigations*

A production order does not require a person to produce, or give access to, privileged material, including material to which legal professional privilege applies nor excluded material (as per s 348 of POCA).

4.30 An appropriate officer may take copies of any material which is produced, or to which access is given. Material may be retained for so long as it is necessary to retain in connection with the investigation, which may be until proceedings are concluded (see ss 348(6) and (7) of POCA).

4.31 Access to computer material must be access to material in a form that is visible and legible (as per s 349 of POCA).

4.32 The production order provisions apply to authorised government departments (see s 350 of POCA).

4.33 An application for a production order or an order to grant entry may be made ex parte to a judge in chambers (s 351(1) of POCA). Rules of court may make provision as to the practice and procedure to be followed in production and entry orders (s 351(2) of POCA). An application to discharge or vary the production or entry order may be made to the court by the person who applied for the order or any person affected by the order (s 351(3) of POCA).

4.34 Sections 352 to 356 of POCA cover search and seizure warrants.[50] Section 352 of POCA allows a judge, on an application made to him by an appropriate officer, to issue a search and seizure warrant to enter and search premises and seize and retain material (s 352(4)) where a production order has not been complied with and there are reasonable grounds for believing that the material is on the premises. Section 353 of POCA allows for a search and seizure warrant where a production order is not available because it is not practicable to communicate with any person against whom a production order could be made (s 353(4)(a)) or would be required to comply with an order to gain entry to the premises (s 353(4)(b)) or where the investigation might be seriously prejudiced unless an appropriate person is able to secure immediate access to the specified material (s 353(4)(c)). A search and seizure warrant does not confer the right to seize privileged material (s 354 of POCA). Section 355 allows the Secretary of State to order modifications to ss 15 (search warrants safeguards),16 (execution), 21 (access and copying) and 22 (retention) of PACE to apply to confiscation and money laundering investigations.

4.35 Section 357 of POCA allows a judge to make a disclosure order, in confiscation and civil recovery investigations, requiring a specified person to answer questions (s 357(4)(a), provide information (s 357(4)(b)) and produce documents (s 357(4)(c)) to an appropriate officer, provided there are

---

50 See *R (Horne) v Central Criminal Court* [2012] 1 WLR 3152 (DC).

reasonable grounds for suspecting that the person has benefitted from criminal conduct (s 358(2)(a)) or the property specified is recoverable or associated property (s 358(2)(b), and that the information is likely to be of substantial value to the investigation (s 358(3)) and it is in the public interest (s 358(4)). The authority to make a disclosure order under s 357 can only be exercised in respect of persons within the jurisdiction.[51] Section 359 of POCA creates two offences of non-compliance with a disclosure order. In line with other statutory provisions, a disclosure order does not confer the right to require a person to answer any privileged question, provide any privileged information or produce any privileged document, except that a lawyer may be required to provide the name and address of a client of his (s 361 of POCA).

4.36 Sections 363 to 365 of POCA allows a judge to make, on an application, a customer information order in a confiscation or money laundering or civil recovery investigation, requiring a financial institution to provide customer information it has relating to a specified period, in relation to an individual's or company name, date of birth, current and previous addresses, registered address, account number and details of any person holding an account jointly with the specified person, provided there are reasonable grounds for suspecting benefit from criminal conduct or recoverable or associated property are involved or a money laundering offence has been committed. Further there must be reasonable grounds for believing that the customer information to be provided is likely to be of substantial value to the investigation and it is in the public interest for the customer information to be provided. Section 366 creates two offences of failure to provide customer information. Section 367 deals with the general admissibility of customer information order statement as evidence against financial institutions in criminal proceedings.

4.37 Sections 370 to 375 of POCA provides for account monitoring orders. Section 370 allows for a judge on application to make an order requiring the provision of information relating to an account or accounts held at a specified institution by a specified person for a period not exceeding 90 days. Sections 371 and 372 set out the requirements that must be satisfied before an order can be made and the admissibility of such statements provided, respectively.

The relevant procedural rules can be found at Criminal Procedure Rules 2013 (SI 2013/1554) Pt 6, rr 6.1–6.22 and 6.29–6.36.

SERIOUS FRAUD OFFICE

4.38 The Serious Fraud Office originates from and is constituted by s 1(1) of the Criminal Justice Act 1987 (CJA 1987). Under CJA 1987, s 1(3), the SFO Director has power to ' investigate any suspected offence which appears to

---

51   See *Serious Organised Crime Agency v Perry (No 2)* [2013] 1 AC 182.

4.39 *Search, Seizure and Investigations*

him on reasonable grounds to involve serious or complex fraud'. Section 2(1) provides for the investigation powers of the Director. In this context, s 2(3) provides that:

> 'The Director may by notice in writing require the person under investigation or any other person to produce [at such place as may be specified in the notice and either forthwith or at such time as may be so specified], any specified documents which appear to the Director to relate to any matter relevant to the investigation or any documents of a specified class which appear to him so to relate; and—
>
> (a) if any such documents are produced, the Director may—
>
>   (i) take copies or extracts from them;
>
>   (ii) require the person producing them to provide an explanation of any of them;
>
> (b) if any such documents are not produced, the Director may require the person who was required to produce them to state, to the best of his knowledge and belief, where they are.'

4.39 For these purposes, pursuant to s 2(4) to (6A), the SFO can obtain a warrant authorising a constable to enter (using such force as is reasonably necessary for the purpose) and search premises, and to take possession of documents. Section 2(10) allows obligations owed in respect of banking confidentiality to be overridden in the specific circumstances therein identified. Section 2(13) provides that:

> 'Any person who without reasonable excuse fails to comply with a requirement imposed on him under this section shall be guilty of an offence and liable on summary conviction to imprisonment for a term not exceeding six months or to a fine not exceeding level 5 on the standard scale or to both.'

Accordingly, CJA 1987, s 2 subjects the recipient of a notice to a compulsory obligation to produce the relevant documentation, enforceable by criminal sanction.

4.40 Section 3 of CJA 1987 deals with disclosure of information:

> '3(1) Where any information [to which s 18 of the Commissioners for Revenue and Customs Act 2005 would apply but for s 18(2)] has been disclosed by [Her Majesty's Revenue and Customs] to any member of the Serious Fraud Office for the purposes of any prosecution of [an offence relating to a former Inland Revenue matter], that information may be disclosed by any member of the Serious Fraud Office—
>
>   (a) for the purposes of any prosecution of which that Office has the conduct;

(b) to the [Revenue and Customs Prosecutions Office] for the purposes of any prosecution of an offence relating to a former Inland Revenue matter; and

(c) to the Director of Public Prosecutions for Northern Ireland for the purposes of any prosecution of [an offence relating to a former Inland Revenue matter],

but not otherwise.

[...]

(3) Where any information is subject to an obligation of secrecy imposed by or under any enactment other than an enactment contained in the Taxes Management Act 1970, the obligation shall not have effect to prohibit the disclosure of that information to any person in his capacity as a member of the Serious Fraud Office but any information disclosed by virtue of this subsection may only be disclosed by a member of the Serious Fraud Office for the purposes of any prosecution in England and Wales, Northern Ireland or elsewhere and may only be disclosed by such a member if he is designated by the Director for the purposes of this subsection.'

Subsection (5) provides that:

'Subject to subsections (1) and (3) above and to any provision of an agreement for the supply of information which restricts the disclosure of the information supplied, information obtained by any person in his capacity as a member of the Serious Fraud Office may be disclosed by any member of that Office designated by the Director for the purposes of this subsection—

(a) to any government department or Northern Ireland department or other authority or body discharging its functions on behalf of the Crown (including the Crown in right of Her Majesty's Government in Northern Ireland);

(b) to any competent authority;

(c) for the purposes of any criminal investigation or criminal proceedings, whether in the United Kingdom or elsewhere, and

(d) for the purposes of assisting any public or other authority for the time being designated for the purposes of this paragraph by an order made by the Secretary of State to discharge any functions which are specified in the order.'

4.41 Mr Justice Eder in *Tchenguiz*[52] recognised that:

'... by reason of the nature of the information which the SFO will or may obtain using its powers, and by reason of the compulsory powers themselves,

---

52 [2013] EWHC 2128 (QB) para 10 of judgment.

4.42 *Search, Seizure and Investigations*

> the SFO owes a duty of confidence in respect of the information which it receives [see *Marcel v Commissioner of Police* [1992] Ch 225] ... such duty of confidence is, in effect, overridden in the limited circumstances set out in s 3(5) so as to permit the SFO voluntarily to give disclosure of documents obtained pursuant to its statutory powers to certain third parties in the circumstances there specified ... it is also indisputable that the SFO does not have power to disclose documents voluntarily to the claimants since this would not fall within one of the specific "gateways" in s 3(5): see *Morris v Director of the SFO* [1993] Ch 371. Equally, it was common ground that confidence alone is not a basis for not giving disclosure in civil litigation: *Science Research Council v Nassé* [1980] AC 1028.'

> '... The provisions of the CJA do not preclude the SFO from giving disclosure in this action of material obtained pursuant to its compulsory powers in s 2 of the CJA, nor (should it be so contended) material provided to it voluntarily'.[53]

Mr Justice Eder found that there is no implied restriction in CJA 1987 which overrides the obligation on the SFO to provide disclosure pursuant to the court's order, still less to prevent the court making such order. The SFO is not prevented by the provisions of CJA 1987 from giving disclosure of documents received from third parties in response to notices under s 2 of CJA 1987 and permitting inspection of such disclosed documents.

4.42 Under s 2(2) of the CJA 1987, the Director of the Serious Fraud Office has the power, on notice, to require the person whose affairs are to be investigated or any person who has relevant information to answer questions or otherwise furnish relevant information at a specified place and time. Section 2(4) allows the SFO to obtain a warrant to support the production application. Notice should, wherever possible, be given and consideration given to obtaining documents from alternative untainted sources. The warrant request should be drafted with sufficient precision to enable both those who executed it and those whose property was affected by it to know whether any document or class of document fell within it.[54]

---

53 Ibid at para 11 of judgment
54 See *R (Energy Financing) v Bow Street Magistrates Court* [2006] 1 WLR 1316 [24] as applied in *Power-Hynes v Norwich Magistrates' Court* [2009] Lloyd's Rep FC 619; *Gittins v Central Criminal Court* [2011] Lloyd's Rep FC 219; *R (Horne) v Central Criminal Court* [2012] EWHC 1350 (Admin); *R (Anand) v Revenue and Customs Commrs* [2013] CP Rep 2 and *R (Van der Pijl and Another) v Crown Court at Kingston* [2013] 1 WLR 2706 at [53].

4.43 Where a warrant was issued, the affected party cannot invite the court to reconsider the decision, the remedy is judicial review.[55]

4.44 Before a production order is granted, the SFO have to produce information, on oath, that (a) a person has failed to comply with an obligation to produce documents, or that it is not practicable to serve a notice demanding production, or service might seriously prejudice the investigation, and (b) that the documents are found on the premises specified in the application. The documents sought should be specified with as much precision as possible.

4.45 It is important for the application to contain full and frank disclosure, with detailed information. In *R (Rawlinson and Hunter Trustees SA) v Central Criminal Court* (costs), *R (Tchenguiz) v Serious Fraud Office* (costs),[56] the Serious Fraud Office was ordered to pay costs on an indemnity basis after the court set aside search warrants which it had obtained in the course of an investigation. It had wholly failed to discharge its duty of proper disclosure when applying for the warrants and had failed to acknowledge its errors until a very late stage in the proceedings.

4.46 Documents to which legal professional privilege attaches are covered by s 2(9) of CJA 1987; where such material may be on the premises a lawyer independent of the SFO should be involved in the search to assess whether material is covered by privilege.

4.47 Section 2(10) of CJA 1987 protects confidential information held in the course of a banking business, unless the person to whom the confidence is owed consents, or the Director of the SFO[57] authorises the requirement of disclosure.

4.48 Sections 13–19 (Part 1: Mutual Assistance in Criminal Matters) of the Crime (International Co-Operation) Act 2003[58] allows the above procedures to be used following a foreign government request for assistance in relation to an overseas fraud investigation. Sections 13–14 deal with the procedure to be followed for requests for assistance from overseas authorities and the

---

55 See *R (Energy Financing) v Bow Street Magistrates Court* [2006] 1 WLR 1316 and *R v Director of the Serious Fraud Office, ex p Johnson* [1993] COD 58 QBD. The *Tchenguiz* case has led to new rules 6.29 to 6.33 in the Criminal Procedure Rules 2013 intended to make sure that applications meet fully all the relevant statutory requirements, as interpreted by the courts.
56 [2012] EWHC 3218 (Admin); [2013] 1 WLR 1634; [2013] 1 Costs LR 122.
57 Or a designated member of the SFO.
58 Replaces the Criminal Justice (International Co-Operation) Act 1990.

4.49 *Search, Seizure and Investigations*

powers of the Secretary of State to arrange for the obtaining of such evidence; such requests can be passed onto the Director of the SFO in relation to serious or complex fraud investigations (s 15(2)). Section 16 incorporates the PACE powers of entry, search and seizure for indictable offences. Section 17 allows the issue of a warrant to enter, seize and search and s 19 deals with evidence seized pursuant to the warrant.[59] The court proceedings receiving such evidence is governed by Sch 1[60] which deals with attendance of witnesses and privilege, oaths, persons entitled to appear, exclusion of the public, the forwarding of evidence obtained, the application of the Bankers' Books Evidence Act 1879[61] and costs. Legal professional privilege and the Art 8 right to privacy must also be considered by the court.

HM REVENUE AND CUSTOMS[62]

4.49 Regulations made under s 114 of PACE (SI 2007/3175 as amended by the Finance Act 2007) give Customs investigators largely the same PACE powers of search, seizure and retention of material as Police officers.[63]

4.50 When investigating fraud Customs officers can rely upon the s 8 PACE powers to obtain a search warrant. In addition Customs officers can obtain a production order by way of s 20BA and Sch 1AA of the Taxes and Management Act 1970, by applying to a Crown Court judge, on oath, with information that there are (a) reasonable grounds for suspecting that an offence involving serious fraud[64] has been or is about to be committed, and (b) documents which may be required as evidence in the possession of a specified person.

---

59 The Crime (International Co-Operation) Act 2003 (Exercise of Functions) Order 2009 (SI 2009/3021) explains who may exercise the functions of a constable under ss 17 and 19.
60 The Criminal Procedure Rules 2013 also apply where the application is made in the Crown Court: specifically, persons entitled to appear and public hearing and record of proceedings to receive evidence before a nominated court.
61 The Act allows copies of banking ledgers and other account books to be used in evidence.
62 Now incorporated into the Crown Prosecution Service
63 PACE, ss 8 (search warrants for indictable offences), 9 (excluded and special procedure material),15 (search warrants safeguards),16 (execution of warrants), 17 (entry for purpose of arrest),18 (entry and search after arrest), 19 (general power of seizure), 21 (access and copying), 22 (retention), 24 (arrest without warrant), 32 (search upon arrest), 54 (searches of detained persons), 55 (intimate searches), 62 (intimate samples), 63 (other samples), 66 (codes of practice) and Sch 1 all apply to Customs investigators.
64 Which covers false accounting, forgery, conspiracy to defraud, perjury and false statements to income tax authorities.

4.51 The power to obtain a production order does not apply to items subject to legal professional privilege which is defined in para 5 of Sch 1AA as per the same definition in s 10 of PACE.

4.52 In relation to VAT investigations, Customs investigators have PACE powers of s 8 (search warrant) and ss 18 and 32 (entry and search after arrest) with a specified power to obtain a production order under the Value Added Tax Act 1994.

4.53 In relation to excise investigations into duty evasion, Customs can use general PACE powers and in addition have general powers of entry, search and seizure, both with and without warrant, as per s 118C of the Customs and Excise Management Act 1979, as added by the Finance Act 1991. Customs can also seize items for forfeiture by ss 161 and 161A of the Customs and Excise Management Act 1979.

DEPARTMENT OF BUSINESS, INNOVATIONS AND SKILLS

4.54 The Secretary of State for Trade and Industry has wide investigatory powers under the Companies Act 1985, as amended by the Companies Act 1989. Section 453A gives a broad power to enter premises without warrant in relation to investigation of a company's affairs where the Secretary of State thinks there is good reason to do so. Section 447 allows for the production of documents; failure to comply with s 447 allows a power of entry under warrant by s 448. Once on the premises a search may be carried out, documents may be seized and preserved. Copies of documents may be taken, to which s 50 of the Criminal Justice and Police Act 2001 applies.

FINANCIAL CONDUCT AUTHORITY

4.55 The Financial Services and Markets Act 2000 (FSMA) gave the Financial Services Authority (FSA) supervisory control over all aspects of the financial services industry; this has now been taken over by the Prudential Regulation Authority and Financial Conduct Authority (FCA), which replaced the FSA on 1 April 2013. FCA officials can carry out a general investigation of an authorised person or business under s 167, or investigate particular circumstances which suggest a breach of the financial regulations or commission of a criminal offence.

4.56 *Search, Seizure and Investigations*

4.56 Section 176 of FSMA provides a power to obtain a search warrant, execution of which must be by a constable; ss 15 and 16 of PACE apply. Documents can be seized, material preserved and copies taken. Section 50 of the Criminal Justice and Police Act 2001 applies.

Chapter 5

Alternatives to Prosecution

CAUTIONS[1]

Introduction

5.1 As with almost any type of criminal offending, there are levels of seriousness ranging from the trivial to that of utmost gravity in relation to fraud. Equally there are those of obvious simplicity and those of startling complexity. As a result of that and as a result of financial pressures on the prosecution agencies a number of alternatives to prosecution have arisen.

5.2 The question of whether there is any alternative to prosecution will lie in the hands of a number of agencies, the putative defendant and his advisors being at the end of the chain of those who can influence such decisions. We consider two of these below, namely the very common police cautions (both simple and conditional in relation to adults only) and the brand new deferred prosecution agreements. Civil proceedings in the First-tier Tribunal (Tax Chamber) are also considered below.

Simple police cautions

5.3 Simple police cautions are a non-statutory measure designed to provide the Police and the Crown Prosecution Service (CPS) with an alternative means for dealing with low level, mainly first-time offending, when specific criteria are met.[2] However, in dealing with fraud, where there has been a loss, if a caution is suitable the police may consider a conditional caution with a condition, for example, to pay compensation.

---

1 With thanks to Paul Hynes QC for his assistance.
2 See the Ministry of Justice Simple Caution Guidance, November 2013 at http://www.justice.gov.uk/downloads/oocd/adult-simple-caution-guidance-oocd.pdf (wording taken from para 6).

5.4 *Alternatives to Prosecution*

5.4 Annex A of the Ministry of Justice Simple Caution Guidance provides an overview of the factors when considering whether to offer a simple caution.[3]

5.5 Unless a Superintendent or above and the CPS agree, a simple caution will not be administered for an indictable only offence (although the CPS may instruct the police to issue a caution, in which case that instruction will be binding).[4] There must be exceptional circumstances for this to occur. Those exceptional circumstances (which include cases for non-specified either-way offences which would normally be dealt with in the Crown Court, namely banking and insurance fraud, confidence fraud and possessing, making or supplying articles for use in fraud, as well as theft, handling stolen goods, and offences under the Identity Act 2006, Identity Documents Act 2010 and Forgery Act 1861[5]) are stated to be that:

> 'the public interest does not required the immediate prosecution of the offender and that if the offender was prosecuted there would be reasons why the court would not impose a period of imprisonment or high level community order.'[6]

5.6 In determining the answer to that question the decision-maker will have regard to:

- the extent of culpability/and or harm caused;
- the degree of intention or the foreseeability of any resultant harm;
- any significant aggravating and mitigating factors;
- the lack of previous similar convictions or cautions; and
- any other factors likely to impact upon sentence and the overall justice of the case, including whether it would be appropriate for it to be dealt with in an open court.

5.7 They may be administered for either-way offences, including fraud based upon the evidential and public interest tests as set out in the guidance. However, unless the exceptional circumstances as outlined above apply, the seriousness of the offence in question may well take it out of the sphere of offending that might make a simple caution a proportionate disposal.

---

[3] Appendix 5.
[4] Ministry of Justice Simple Caution Guidance at para 39.
[5] Ibid at Annex B.
[6] Ibid at para 22.

5.8 The police will, in the first instance, have recourse to the National Decision Model[7] and College of Policing Gravity Factors Matrix. Cases 'routinely' dealt with in the Crown Court are usually unsuitable for a simple caution; so when considering an offence of fraud, deference should be given to the Sentencing Guidelines[8].

The evidential test

5.9 Put simply, the police must apply the evidential test as set out in the Code for Crown Prosecutors.[9] That is, there must be, before anything else, a realistic prospect of conviction. Whilst that can include a confession, it is entirely clear from the case law that the police must not use the offer of a simple caution to secure a confession which means that the evidential test is then met from as long ago as 1997 in *R (on the application of Thompson) v Metropolitan Police.*[10]

The public interest test

5.10 If there is a realistic prospect of conviction, then the police must consider whether it is in the public interest to offer a simple caution. Again, recourse must be had to the Code for Crown Prosecutors.[11] This will include, where possible, the consultation of any victim to the disposal, although any negative view is not dispositive as the decision is that of the police in consultation with the CPS.

The procedures

5.11 The law is that an admission of guilt must be made before the offer of a simple caution. Access to legal advice should be offered by the police before the offer of such. The reality is that representatives often 'sound out' the police about a simple caution and, if the requisite informal agreement is given, offer up their client's confession. Any defence raised to a charge (anything other than a full admission) should result in no caution being administered. Equally doubts about the mental health of the person making the confession should also rule out the offering of a simple caution.

---

7 Appendix 6
8 Appendix 1
9 http://www.cps.gov.uk/publications/code_for_crown_prosecutors/.
10 [1997] WLR 1519.
11 http://www.cps.gov.uk/publications/code_for_crown_prosecutors/.

5.12 *Alternatives to Prosecution*

5.12 If a caution is offered, then before it is accepted, the implications, meaning and consequences of accepting the caution must be explained. If it is not done then the administration of a caution may fall foul of judicial review.[12] People should be made aware that they do not need to take immediate decisions and, if they don't have legal advice (despite being offered it previously), they may take it. Again, given offences of fraud involve dishonesty, a caution for such is likely to have significant consequences upon, for example, future employment or foreign travel. The record of simple caution is kept on the Police National Computer (PNC), although they are considered 'spent' for the purposes of the Rehabilitation of Offenders Act 1974 at the point of administration.[13] If a simple caution is offered and accepted then the offender, as they will become, should sign the form, which also sets out the implications in writing. They should be provided with a copy of that which they have signed.

Conclusion

5.13 For a full history and analysis of the caution, and the challenges which can be made, then recourse should be made to *R (on the application of Stratton) v Chief Constable of Thames Valley Police*[14] which, amongst other things, specifically approved the procedures in the Ministry of Justice Simple Caution Guidance for drawing the consequences of accepting a caution to the offender's attention.

Conditional police cautions

5.14 The Director of Public Prosecutions (DPP) has issued guidance to the Police and Crown Prosecution Service, dated April 2013, under s 37A of the Police and Criminal Evidence Act 1984 (POCA 1984), together with a Code of Practice.[15] The Guidance states:

> 'A conditional caution may be appropriate where the decision maker believes that while the public interest requires a prosecution in the first instance the interests of the victim, community or offender are better served by the offender complying with suitable conditions aimed at reparation,

---

12 See, for example, *Chief Constable of Humberside Police v The Information Commissioner* [2010] WLR 1136.
13 As a result they do not need to be disclosed unless listed in the Exceptions Order as amended. Additionally they are also disclosed under Disclosure and Barring Service standard and enhanced checks, unless they are old or minor (see *T v Chief Constable of Greater Manchester Police* [2014] UKSC 35).
14 [2013] EWHC 1561 (Admin).
15 http://www.cps.gov.uk/publications/directors_guidance/adult_conditional_cautions.html .

rehabilitation, punishment or in the case of a foreign national offender removal from the jurisdiction'.[16]

5.15 A conditional caution may be offered for any summary or either-way offence. However, for a serious either-way offence (which are the same for those in relation to simple cautions, including fraud), it may only be offered if exceptional circumstances apply, which are akin to those considered for simple cautions. If, however, the offence is committed by a relevant foreign offender, it may facilitate the removal of and non-return of the same.[17]

5.16 An indictable only offence may be the subject of a conditional caution but must be approved by a Deputy Chief Crown Prosecutor..The relevant tests to be met are the evidential test and public interest test, again taken from the Code for Crown Prosecutors.

5.17 If a conditional caution is appropriate, then a financial penalty can be offered such as compensation or to make a payment to a charity or community fund, but only from the list of offences in the Order made under s 23A of the Criminal Justice Act 2003 (as amended).[18] Happily the list of offences is simply broken down into summary only, either-way or indictable albeit a different form is supplied.[19]

DEFERRED PROSECUTION AGREEMENTS

5.18 The deferred prosecution agreement (DPA) was created by Sch 17 to the Crime and Courts Act 2013. It came in February 2014. At the same time Pt 12 of the Criminal Procedure Rules 2013 (now Pt 12 of the Criminal Procedure Rules 2014)[20] came into force, as did the Code of Practice jointly issued by the Directors of Public Prosecutions and the Serious Fraud Office.[21] Whilst both are of profound importance, the Code provides guidance as to *when* a DPA is likely to be entered into. the sorts of factors the prosecution will take into account and the Rules will mandate *how* a DPA will be undertaken through once the decision has been taken by the prosecution to offer it.

---

16 http://www.cps.gov.uk/publications/directors_guidance/adult_conditional_cautions.html at para 15.1.
17 http://www.cps.gov.uk/publications/directors_guidance/adult_conditional_cautions.html at paras 4 and 5. See also para 15.2 for the detailed requirements.
18 The Criminal Justice Act 2003 (Conditional Cautions: Financial Penalties) Order 2013, SI 2013/615.
19 Appendix 5 – http://www.cps.gov.uk/publications/directors_guidance/adult_conditional_ cautions.html at Annex C.
20 Appendix 7
21 Appendix 8

5.19 *Alternatives to Prosecution*

5.19 Only a body corporate can, at this stage, be subject to a DPA. Such is their current novelty and complexity that when one is instituted a judge will be assigned by the President of the Queen's Bench Division to deal with an individual DPA from start to finish. It is then likely to be delegated to any permanent judge at the Southwark Crown Court in its capacity as the central fraud court for England. Whilst there are many issues, one of the more of them, addressed below, is that of disclosure to the body corporate before it enters the agreement.

Schedule 17 of the Crime and Courts Act 2013

5.20 Section 45 of the Crime and Courts Act 2013 encourages the reader to refer to Sch 17 of the same Act where the framework for DPAs is set out. DPAs may only be entered into by a body corporate, partnership or unincorporated association. They may *not* be entered into by individuals.[22] Schedule 17 is in three parts. The first part deals with DPAs and how they are to operate. The second part lists exhaustively (although with provision for the Secretary of State to add to them) the offences to which a DPA may be entered into and the third part sets out the consequential and transitional provisions.

The behaviour to which a DPA can relate

5.21 Dealing with them in reverse order, para 39 in Pt 3 provides that conduct 'which may be taken account of' to which a DPA can relate can be conduct prior to the implementation of the Schedule or the addition of an offence by the Secretary of State – in other words the conduct to which the DPA relates may have occurred at any time. It is therefore not entirely clear whether *all* the conduct can have occurred prior to the implementation of Sch 17, or whether *some* of the alleged offending must have occurred post-implementation of the Schedule (or the addition of further offences by the Secretary of State) so that the rest 'may be taken account of'.

The offences to which a DPA can relate

5.22 Paragraphs 15 to 30 in Pt 2 set out, exhaustively, the list of offences to which a DPA can relate. They are:

- conspiracy to defraud;

---

22 Schedule 17, para 4(1).

Deferred prosecution agreements **5.24**

- cheating the Public Revenue;

- fraud, possession of articles for use in fraud, making or supplying articles for use in fraud and obtaining serves dishonestly, under the Fraud Act 2006;

- bribery offences under ss 1, 2, 6 and 7 of the Bribery Act 2010;

- money laundering, failing to disclose and tipping off under the Proceeds of Crime Act 2002 and the offence under reg 45 of the Money Laundering Regulations 2007;

- theft, false accounting, suppression of information and dishonestly retaining a wrongful credit, under the Theft Act 1968;

- fraudulent evasion of duty, offences relating to the exporting of goods and untrue declarations, under the Customs and Excise Management Act 1979;

- forgery, copying, using or using a copy of a false instrument and offences relating to money orders, etc under the Forgery and Counterfeiting Act 1981;

- destroying company documents, under s 450 of the Companies Act 1985;

- fraudulent trading, and offences under ss 658 and 680 of the Companies Act 2006;

- fraudulent evasion of VAT, under s 72 of the Value Added Tax Act 1994; and

- contraventions of ss 23, 25, 85, 346, 397 and 398 of the Financial Services and Markets Act 2000.

5.23 Paragraph 31 gives the Secretary of State power to add to the list any 'financial or economic crime' or to remove an offence. Paragraphs 1 to 14 in Pt 1 provides the framework for the operation of DPAs. The position is as follows.

The operation of a DPA

5.24 As already stated, the offences to which a DPA may be made are exhaustively set out and apply to economic or financial crime. A DPA itself is simply an agreement between the designated prosecutors and the person – that

5.25 *Alternatives to Prosecution*

is, the body corporate, partnership or unincorporated association whom the prosecution is considering prosecuting.[23] The designated prosecutors are:

- the Director of Public Prosecutions;
- the Director of the Serious Fraud Office; and
- any other prosecutor designated by the Secretary of State.

5.25 These prosecutors must give their personal attention to a DPA and personally exercise the power to enter into it, unless they are unavailable, in which case they may delegate it, in writing, to another prosecutor.[24] Importantly, for example, the general delegation in the Prosecution of Offences Act 1985 does not apply.[25] If the DPA is entered into and the person has agreed to comply with the requirements, the consequences if the court approves the DPA are that:

- proceedings will be instituted by the prosecution, preferring a bill of indictment with the consent of a judge of the Crown Court against the person;
- the proceedings will automatically be suspended;
- the suspension may not be lifted, save upon application by the prosecutor to the Crown Court (and then not until the DPA is no longer in force); and
- during the period of suspension, no one may prosecute the person for the alleged offence.[26]

It is vital to note, in a case where there are international aspects, that the DPA does not appear to be any form of bar upon a prosecution in a different country for the same alleged offence.

5.26 The following table summarises the various steps involved:[27]

---

23 Schedule 17, para 1.
24 Ibid, para 3.
25 Ibid, para 3(2).
26 Ibid, para 2.
27 These tables were developed by the Ministry of Justice as an interpretation for a visual presentation, 'Deferred Prosecution Agreements: How will it work in Practice', given by Joanna Savage, Policy Manager, Ministry of Justice (with Nicola Howard of 25 Bedford Row and Stephenson Harwood) on 16 January 2014. The tables are gratefully reproduced by permission – they are not formal Ministry of Justice 'guidance' on DPAs.

Deferred prosecution agreements **5.26**

Model of Deferred Prosecution Agreement process (pre-agreement)

	Stages 1	Stages 2	Stages 3	Stages 4	Stages 5	Stages 6	Stages 7
Life of the case	Potential case identified either by self-reporting or by prosecutor	Preliminary investigation, based on but not limited to internal investigation. Includes liaison with overseas jurisdictions re: extent of criminality and available assets	Prosecutor decides: extent of criminality, geographical reach, potential charges, and use of DPA in principle etc	Organisation agrees to voluntarily enter into DPA process. Detailed discussions between the parties of facts and potential terms to put before a judge	Agreement reviewed and developed further to judicial indications	DPA approved and reasons given, agreement publicly outlined, indictment laid and suspended subject to the agreed terms	DPA published by prosecutor, details of declarations and reasons of the court made public

Judicial Involvement and court approval

Proceedings commenced in the Crown Court

Preliminary hearing in private
Judge applies 2 tests:
(1) whether in principle a DPA is in the interests of justice, and
(2) whether emerging terms & conditions would be fair, reasonable and proportionate

Hearing in private –
Judge applies same 2 tests and indicates approval of the proposed DPA package
Either short adjournment or moving straight into:

Hearing in open court:
- indictment formally laid
- Judge outlines and explains and formally approves the DPA
- the agreement is signed and becomes binding

Guidance

Stages 1-3:
Primary legislation
DPA Code of Practice for Prosecutors
Code for Crown Prosecutors

Stages 4-5:
Primary legislation
DPA Code of Practice for Prosecutors
Code for Crown Prosecutors
Sentencing Council guidelines
Criminal Procedure Rules

Stages 6-7:
Primary legislation
DPA Code of Practice for Prosecutors
Code for Crown Prosecutors
Sentencing Council guidelines
Criminal Procedure Rules

5.27 Alternatives to Prosecution

The content of a DPA

5.27 A DPA must contain a statement of facts relating to the alleged offence, which may include admissions by the person.[28] Those responsible for piloting the scheme have indicated that whilst admissions are not required, there 'must be an acceptance [that] wrongdoing occurred.'[29] Given that a DPA is a negotiated agreement that is to act (if all goes well) as a substitute for a prosecution, such an acceptance appears to be a likely outcome of events. However it is difficult to see the statutory requirement for it, albeit that it features squarely in the Code on DPAs.[30] The statement of facts however, must be agreed. The Court will not act as a dispute-solving mediator.

5.28 After the statement of facts, the DPA will have an expiry date. That is to say a date upon which, if there has been no breach, the agreement will cease.

5.29 The DPA will also impose requirements upon the person. Schedule 17 does not provide an exhaustive list in order to preserve flexibility and creativity when it comes to DPAs. However it does provide examples of terms. The Code requires that they are fair, reasonable and proportionate,[31] which can only be judged on a 'case-by-case' basis. Unsurprisingly, most of these requirements are financial in one way or another, namely:

- to pay the prosecutor a financial penalty;[32]
- to compensate victims of the alleged offence;
- to donate money to charity or another third party;
- To disgorge any profits made from the alleged offending;
- to pay any reasonable costs of the prosecutor in relation to the alleged offence or the DPA;
- to co-operate in any investigation related to the alleged offence;
- to implement a compliance programme or make changes to an existing compliance programme relating to the person's policies or training of employees or both;[33] and

---

28 Schedule 17 para 5(1).
29 'Deferred Prosecution Agreements: How will it work in Practice', given by Joanna Savage, Policy Manager, Ministry of Justice (with Nicola Howard of 25 Bedford Row and Stephenson Harwood), 16 January 2014. Ministry of Justice tables gratefully used by permission.
30 Code on DPAs, section 6.
31 Schedule 17 para 7(1)(b) and para 8(1)(b).
32 Ibid, para 14 states that such sums, as well as those relating to disgorged profits, are to be paid into the Consolidated Fund.
33 Ibid, para 5 3).

- a term setting out the consequences of a failure by the person to comply with any other term[34].

It can immediately be seen that DPAs may become money-making devices in terms of any financial penalty being paid to the prosecutor together with the costs, not just of entering the DPA, but of the investigation into the alleged offence itself, which may be huge. However any financial penalty agreed between the prosecutor and the person must be broadly comparable to the fine a court would have imposed upon conviction of the person for the alleged offence following a plea of guilty.[35]

5.30 For the sentences for various offences please see Chapter 9 on sentencing and the Sentencing Council's new guidelines.

Guidance and rules

5.31 There are three primary sources of guidance and rules:

- the Sentencing Council's guidelines;
- the Code on DPAs agreed between the Director of Public Prosecutions and the Serious Fraud Office; and
- Pt 12 of the Criminal Procedure Rules 2013.

The Code on DPAs

5.32 Paragraph 6 of Sch 17 requires the Directors to jointly issue the Code. This is to set down the general principles to be applied in determining whether a DPA is likely to be appropriate, and the disclosure of information to the person in the course of negotiations for a DPA and after a DPA has been agreed. It also may (and does) give guidance on any other relevant matter, including the use of material obtained in the DPA negotiation process, variations of a DPA, termination of a DPA and the steps a prosecutor can take and what may occur of the prosecutor suspects a breach of a DPA.

Disclosure

5.33 The latter is particular importance. It is likely that a number of DPAs will come about due to 'self reporting' by the person involved. However

---

34 Ibid, para 5(5).
35 Ibid, para 5(4).

5.34 *Alternatives to Prosecution*

even in that case, but especially where it has arisen out of an investigation, the economic, political and other pressures may be such that the person feels there is no option but to agree to the DPA and the terms suggested by the prosecutor. Given that the disclosure regime under the Criminal Procedure and Investigations Act 1996 does not to apply unless and until the suspension of proceedings is lifted under para 2(3) (at which point it does apply),[36] it is more important than ever that proper disclosure of material which might undermine the notional prosecution that could come if a DPA was not agreed is provided to the person, so that informed choices can be made. Otherwise the spectre of information which would have materially altered the person's decision-making process coming to light after the DPA has been entered into and fines paid, for example, cannot be discounted.

5.34 The Code does make provision for the service of 'unused material'. The prosecutor should:

> 'ensure that negotiations are fair and that [the suspect] is not misled as to the strength of the prosecution case. The prosecution must always be alive to the potential need to disclosure material, in the interests of justice and fairness in the particular circumstances of any case. For instance, disclosure ought to be made of information that might undermine the factual basis of conclusions drawn by the person from the material disclosed by them.'[37]

5.35 The disclosure responsibilities of the prosecution will be included in the Terms and Conditions letter sent to the person at the outset.

General principles

5.36 The Code on DPAs is a long document (see Appendix 8), comprising 16 sections.

5.37 Section 1 sets out the two-stage test to be considered by the prosecutor. It is familiar in that it begins with the evidential test as contained in the Code for Crown Prosecutors,[38] but, if the traditional evidential test is not met, it goes on to state:

> 'There is at least a reasonable suspicion that the commercial organization has committed the offence, and there are reasonable grounds for believing that a continued investigation would provided further evidence within a reasonable period of time, so that all the evidence together would be capable

---

36 Criminal Procedure and Investigations Act 1996, s 1(2)(g).
37 Code for DPAs, section 5.2.
38 https://www.cps.gov.uk/publications/code_for_crown_prosecutors/.

of establishing a realistic prospect of conviction in accordance with the Full Code Test'.

It is understandable that due to the early stages of the investigation the Full Code Test might not be met. However this principle seems to provide any answer the relevant prosecutor wants to arrive at, fueling the suspicion that DPAs will be used where, perhaps, a prosecution is properly merited. There is then a public interest test that simply provides that a DPA would be appropriate where the public interest is served in not prosecuting.

5.38 Section 2 then sets out in greater detail the balancing exercises that need to be undertaken, the various other external codes and guidance to be considered and the factors that will either support a prosecution or militate toward a DPA. Of the latter the first (and it would seem most important) factor is the 'genuinely proactive approach' by the organisation, including self-reporting and remedial actions already taken such as compensation.[39] However it is important to note that in weighing such a factor *towards* a DPA for the organisation, the Code itself recognises that it is likely individuals will be incriminated along the way and that '[I]t will ordinarily be appropriate that those individuals be investigated and where appropriate prosecuted.'[40] That position has the obvious potential to create enormous conflicts of interest and practical problems in self-reporting or taking other action, as the 'saving' of the company on the one hand may lead to the downfall of the individuals on the other.It remains to be seen in practice how this is going to work bearing in mind always the duty of full and frank disclosure that is imposed upon the person who is negotiating a DPA (as, for example, one of the terms of which, as we have seen, can be to assist in the investigation).

5.39 Section 3 of the Code provides the detailed procedure upon which a DPA may be offered, negotiations conducted and the process moved forward.

5.40 Section 4 of the Code provides guidance on the use of information obtained by the prosecution during the DPA negotiation period. Paragraph 13 of Sch 17 appears to set out, comprehensively, what use may be made of information, something the Code recognises.[41] All information and the DPA itself (if there is one) can be used subsequently in a prosecution against the person, albeit in different ways.

5.41 The DPA itself is treated by para 13 as an admission made under s 10 of the Criminal Justice Act 1967. That is to say, unless the court grants leave to withdraw the admission (and it is unclear at this stage whether the court is able

---

39 Code for DPAs, section 2.8.2(i).
40 Ibid, section 2.9.1.
41 Ibid, section 4.1.

5.42 *Alternatives to Prosecution*

to do that with a DPA treated as an admission), the DPA would go before a jury as agreed evidence of its content. If, as the Code requires, it contains at least an acknowledgement of wrongdoing, this is likely to be powerful evidence led by the prosecution. However, where no DPA has been entered into, material showing a person has entered into negotiations and material created solely for the purpose of preparing the DPA or the statement of facts may only be used in a limited way for the purposes of a prosecution against a person, namely the provision of inaccurate, misleading or incomplete information or on some other prosecution where in evidence the person makes a statement inconsistent with that material, provided that evidence is adduced or a question asked by or on behalf of the person.[42]

5.42 Section 5 deals with unused material and disclosure, which has been discussed above.

5.43 Section 6 provides guidance on the crucial statement of facts reflecting the mandatory requirement in para 5(1) of Sch 17. As already stated, it is this part of the Code that seems to require the 'acknowledgement of wrongdoing' rather than anything in Sch 17. However, as the DPA is the gift of the prosecution, if there is no such acknowledgment, then there will be no DPA. Thus, it becomes a question of how much the person is willing to risk that there will be no prosecution if the DPA is not entered into. Additionally, as we have seen, the DPA becomes an admission in any subsequent trial. Acknowledgments of wrongdoing are useful to the prosecution in trials.

5.44 Section 7 discusses the potential terms. These must be fair, reasonable and proportionate. They are required to be clear – clarity is critical to compliance and makes breach proceedings easier to bring if that is what occurs. Any term must record that the DPA relates only to the offences in the draft indictment that will be suspended upon the court's approval (and accordingly it is said prosecutors must not agree to a term which would prevent prosecution for anything else not contained in that draft, even if knowledge of it arose from the DPA negotiation process). In relation to the investigation, the DPA will contain a term requiring the person to provide information relevant to the offence including during the lifetime of the DPA.

5.45 Paragraph 5(5) of Sch 17 permits a term to be included setting out the consequences of a failure to adhere to a term. The Code is fairly clear that such a power can be used to set out a timetable for non-payments, with interest to accrue; this – implicitly at least – is not to be used to tie the prosecutors hands when it comes to serious breaches.

---

42 Schedule 17 para 13(4), (5) and (6); Code on DPAs, section 4.

5.46 The Code also discusses the use of monitors. Their primary duty is to assess and monitor the person's internal controls and advice on steps to improve compliance. The person, if a monitor is imposed as a term of the DPA, will be responsible for all steps including payments and, it seems, appointment. The person will provide, at the preliminary hearing, three potential monitors to the court together with relevant information on experience and costs but with a preferred option marked. The Code indicates the prosecutor should normally accept the preferred choice; but if there is a conflict of interest or a mark over experience, the court or the prosecution may veto the choice.[43] Whilst all of this provides the minimum of aggravation on the part of the prosecutor it is fairly easy to see how a person could manipulate the system. What the monitor does, as no two programmes are identical, is to a degree left to them; however, the Code does specify 11 examples of what might be in the programme at para 52.

5.47 Section 8 discusses financial penalties. Although this will be an agreed term, the prosecution must provide to the court all the information it needs – such as victim impact statements and any sentencing guidelines – so that the court can satisfy itself that the financial penalty is appropriate. Schedule 17 requires the penalty to be broadly comparable to a fine the person would expect to receive after a plea of guilty.

5.48 Section 9 discusses the preliminary hearing. Part 12 of the Criminal Procedure Rules 2014 provides the detailed requirements (see Appendix 7); Sch 17 requires such a hearing. After negotiations have begun, but before an agreement is reached, the prosecutor must apply to the court for a declaration that entering into a DPA with a person is likely to be in the interests of justice and the proposed terms, at that point, are fair reasonable and proportionate. The court must give reasons for making or not making the declaration. This hearing, the court's decision and any reasons given must be in private.

5.49 Sections 10 and 11 deal with the final hearing. Part 12 of the Criminal Procedure Rules 2014 provides the detailed requirements (see Appendix 7); again Sch 17 requires such a hearing. Once there is agreement between the prosecutor and the person, the prosecutor must apply to the Crown Court for a declaration that the DPA is in the interests of justice and the terms are fair, reasonable and proportionate. However this cannot take place unless the declaration sought at the preliminary hearing has been made.

5.50 The DPA will come into force upon the declaration at the final hearing being made when the court will give its reasons for making (or not making) the declaration. The hearing may be in private, but the decision and

---

43 Code on DPAs, section 8.3.

5.51 *Alternatives to Prosecution*

reasons must be in public. The Code envisages the hearings almost always being in private due to the uncertainty about what the judge will do; any application refused in open court might lead, it is said, to uncertainties and destabilisation.[44]

5.51 It is unclear whether judges will accede to this suggestion that final hearings 'will almost always' be in private. To get to a final hearing, a preliminary hearing will have taken place and the declaration will have been received that, provisionally, the court approves of the DPA process. The principles of open justice may trump whatever 'uncertainty' is created (which the Code doesn't particularise) so that a person might need to expect everything to be aired publicly. Section 14 of the Code discusses applications to be heard in private but simply starts with the uncontroversial proposition that hearings should be in public unless otherwise necessary. This is particularly so as Sch 17 requires the prosecutor to publish the DPA, the court's original and final declarations with reasons (and refusal with reasons if there is one). The Code indicates that will be on the CPS or SFO website.

5.52 There is the ability to postpone publication for as long as required by the court if it appears necessary for avoiding substantial risk of prejudice to the administration of justice in any legal proceedings.[45] These concepts are familiar, but the postponement is temporary, so the DPA will be published at some point.

5.53 Section 12 moves on to deal with guidance on breaches of the terms of the DPA. If the prosecution believes that the person is in breach of the term(s) she may apply to the Crown Court to decide whether, on the balance of probabilities, that is so. If she doesn't decide to bring proceedings, despite holding the belief, that decision and reasons must be published. If that finding is made then the court can invite the prosecutor and the person to agree proposals to remedy the problem or terminate the DPA. If proposals are agreed they must, again, be fair, reasonable and proportionate. The Code anticipates minor breaches being resolved in this way.[46]

5.54 If the DPA is terminated then the prosecutor may apply to have the suspension of the indictment lifted and, thereafter, proceed to trial. That would require the Full Code Test to be met, which would involve a reconsideration of the evidence and the public interest. Additionally if monies have been paid over in consequence of a DPA, no refund is available nor other relief from any term already satisfied.[47] This hearing must, according to rule 12.2(c) of the

---

44 Code on DPAs, section 10.4.
45 Schedule 17 para 12.
46 Code on DPAs, section 12.4.
47 Code on DPAs, section 11, paragraph 77

Deferred prosecution agreements **5.59**

Criminal Procedure Rules 2014 be in public. Whatever decision is made it, and the reasons for it must be published unless prohibited.

5.55 Paragraph 9 of Sch 17 doesn't provide for a burden of proof, but it seems unless there is a good reason to the contrary, it will be for the alleging party – the prosecutor – to prove its allegations. Additionally there appears little scope for an appeal. A DPA, or perhaps the decision to find a breach or terminate it, is not a conviction or sentence so as to engage the Criminal Appeal Act 1968 (for the purposes of the Court of Appeal (Criminal Division). Equally, given the DPA rests upon an indictment preferred and then suspended it might be something 'relating to a trial upon indictment' and therefore precludes judicial review under s 29(3) of the Senior Courts Act 1981. There also appears to be no mechanism for the Court of Appeal (Civil Division) to hear any form of appeal.

5.56 After breach proceedings costs may be claimed by the winning side.[48]

5.57 Section 13 provides guidance on variation of a DPA. Both the prosecution and the person may agree to vary the terms of the DPA. That will occur if the court has invited them to do so after finding a breach, or if it is required in order to avoid a failure by the person to meet its obligations due to circumstances that were not existing, and couldn't have been foreseen by the prosecutor as existing, at the time the DPA was agreed. The Code does not foresee such variations as regular; rather very much the exception to changing a DPA which is:

> 'a serious sanction for criminal conduct and will have been approved by the court on that basis. In the vast majority of cases the terms of a DPA that are approved at a final hearing should be strictly complied with in their entirety, failing which [the person] risks prosection'.[49]

5.58 If a variation is sought, the prosecutor must apply for a declaration that the variation is in the interests of justice and that the terms are fair, reasonable and proportionate. That may be done in private, but any decision and reasons must be made public. The prosecutor must then publish the same unless prohibited from doing so. Costs may be sought of the hearing.

5.59 Section 14 deals with discontinuance of a DPA, if a DPA gets that far. When the DPA has expired, the prosecution will give notice to the court to discontinue the suspended proceedings. A DPA is not deemed to have expired if there are outstanding breach proceedings, outstanding agreements

---

48 Criminal Procedure Rules 2013, r 76(1)(c).
49 Code on DPAs, section 13.2(ii).

5.60 *Alternatives to Prosecution*

required to agree proposals to remedy any proven failure or outstanding compliance with such agreed proposals. If, at breach proceedings after the DPA has expired, the court finds there was no breach, the DPA will be deemed to have expired upon the decision of the court. If the court terminates the DPA, the DPA will be deemed not to have expired at all. If proposals for remedy are required and complied with, the DPA will be deemed to expire upon compliance.

5.60 As a result of discontinuance there may be no fresh prosecution against the person, unless it is discovered that, after the DPA has expired, the person gave inaccurate, misleading or incomplete information to the prosecutor during the DPA negotiations and the person knew or ought to have known this was so. Again the prosecutor must publish the discontinuance of the DPA and the person's compliance with it, unless prohibited from doing so.

5.61 Section 14 deals with applications to be heard in private and section 16 provides for publication and postponement of publication of decisions and information.

5.62 The Code is an important and dynamic document that anyone considering entering into a DPA or advising upon them must be intimately familiar with. It doesn't so much as provide guidance in many areas, but stipulates courses of conduct that are unlikely to be departed from by the prosecution in whose sole gift a DPA is.

5.63 A model of the Deferred Prosecution Agreement process can be seen from the following table:[50]

---

50 These tables were developed by the Ministry of Justice as an interpretation for a visual presentation, 'Deferred Prosecution Agreements: How will it work in Practice', given by Joanna Savage, Policy Manager, Ministry of Justice (with Nicola Howard of 25 Bedford Row and Stephenson Harwood) on 16 January 2014. The tables are gratefully reproduced by permission – they are not formal Ministry of Justice 'guidance' on DPAs.

Deferred prosecution agreements 5.63

Model of Deferred Prosecution Agreement process (deferral period)

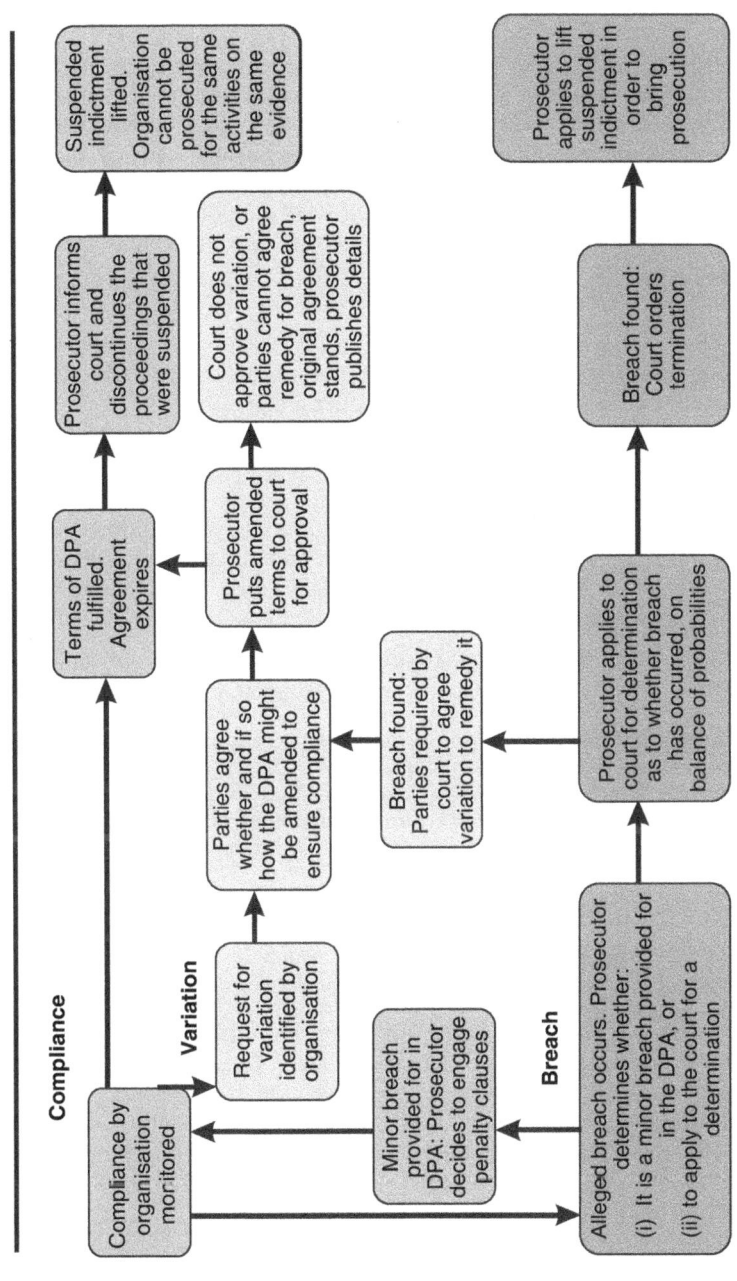

5.64 *Alternatives to Prosecution*

Part 12 of the Criminal Procedure Rules 2014

5.64 Part 12 of the Criminal Procedure Rules 2014 provides the detailed framework that both sides must adhere when presenting the DPA process to the court and following it through. The Part takes its definitions from Sch 17, together with the requirements for the various parts of the process. It also requires the reduction to writing of anything that is put before the court for a decision and mandates the content of such documents so as to provide the greatest assistance to the court and the maximum transparency to those observing.

5.65 Of particular note is r 12.2(3)(b) and (c), which requires that the court must not determine an application for approval for a DPA, its terms or a variation of the terms, unless both parties are present and:

'(b) the prosecutor provides the court with a written declaration that, for the purposes of the application:

  (i) the investigator enquiring into the alleged offence or offences has certified that no information has been supplied which the investigator knows to be inaccurate, misleading and incomplete and

  (ii) the prosecutor has complied with the prosecution obligation to disclose material to the defendant; and

(c) the defendant provides the court with a written declaration that, for the purposes of the application:

  (i) the defendant has not supplied any information which the defendant knows to be inaccurate, misleading or incomplete and

  (ii) the individual through whom the defendant makes the declaration has made reasonable enquiries and believes the defendants declaration to be true.'

This places within secondary legislation the aspiration set out in the Code that proper disclosure will be made on the footing of a duty to the court squarely on the shoulders of the prosecutor. It also places a duty on the investigator to certify what he knows. The concomitant duty upon the person or the individual make the declaration on behalf of the person is the same; save that the individual must make reasonable enquiries about that which the person has said.

5.66 These are to give comfort to a court being asked to take a very important step on poorer information than that which the parties exchanged in the course of a detailed and likely lengthy negotiation process, so that it can have maximum confidence it has not been misled and is doing its public duty. Any breach of this rule is likely to be viewed as a contempt of court and, if proven, dealt with extremely seriously. This sanction, applicable to both sides, brings personal responsibility to those involved to ensure that they get it right. It goes over and above that available for breach of the DPA and, in particular, puts the DPP and DSFO at the forefront of certification together with the senior individual from the body accepting the DPA.

THE FIRST-TIER TRIBUNAL

Introduction

5.67 As touched upon at the beginning of the section on MTIC fraud in Chapter 3, allegations often now end up being litigated within the context of VAT tribunal hearings. It should be noted that statements or evidence obtained or served in the course of Tribunal proceedings will be prima facie admissible in any subsequent criminal proceedings. A trader may end up being an appellant in the VAT tribunal where a VAT reclaim has been denied by the Revenue (Commissioners) in a number of situations.

Example 1: Denial of a claim for repayment of VAT. A trader is involved in a transaction deal in respect of which the trader is entitled to apply for a VAT repayment. Customs Assurance officers are suspicious of the transaction and refuse to make the repayment. The trader may apply to VAT tribunal for payment.

Example 2: S 726 Notice. A trader is involved in a transaction which turns out to be fraudulent. He deals in 'specified goods' within the meaning of Revenue regulations, eg computer parts or mobile telephones; as a consequence he is eligible to be served with a s 726 Notice.

5.68 The effect of s 726 is to make the trader jointly and severally liable for the unpaid VAT of a missing trader who is involved in the same transaction. S.726 only bites where the trader upon whom the notice is served 'knew or ought to have known' that the VAT in respect of the transaction would go unpaid. One can see, therefore, that in the context of both criminal and civil proceedings, 'due diligence' checks on trading partners are important to the prospects of a successful defence. Equally, from an investigator's perspective, the absence or poor quality nature of 'due diligence' checks give rise to the conclusion that the trader 'ought to have known' that the transaction involved fraud, for which the VAT would not be paid.

5.69 *Alternatives to Prosecution*

Practice and procedure at First-tier Tribunals[51]

5.69 The state is represented by the Commissioners (Revenue) as respondents and the trader appears as the appellant. First-tier Tribunal case law covers all aspects of VAT appeal work, from deregistration to disputed reclaims, including those with a disputed MTIC fraud background.

5.70 Although the appeal is brought on behalf of the trader, Commissioners tend to go first in opening their response (the respondent's case) and calling live evidence and reading statements, as it is for the Commissioners to demonstrate that the trader knew or should have known that they were involved in a MTIC deal. Immediately after the respondents open their case, and before any evidence is called, the appellant opens the trader's case. Both sides have to provide a written opening in advance of the appeal, cross-service of skeletons by both parties, serving copies on the Tribunal in advance. The time frame for such service will be determined at a pre-trial review earlier in proceedings. Witness statements similarly are cross-served in advance, with agreed trial bundles of documents served upon the tribunal in advance.

5.71 Examination in chief can be extremely short with both sides almost tendering their own witnesses for cross-examination. This is not a procedural requirement but a practice that has developed from other civil proceedings, primarily as statements of truth are signed by witnesses. It is assumed that a party calling a witness need not, in chief, go through the witness statement verbatim.

5.72 The Commissioners will often call visiting assurance officers, a 'refusing' officer, policy officers, quasi-generic Revenue expert officers on topics such as the nature of MTIC fraud, 'grey markets', contra trading, anti-fraud measures such as Notice 726 Joint and Several Liability notices, due diligence measures and bank practices (often involving FCIB).

5.73 Both sides close their case: Commissioner respondents first, appellants second. The tribunal expects written closings, which can be developed orally.

Background reading/knowledge

5.74 The issue and question to be answered in the tribunal is often: 'Can the Commissioners prove (the burden being on the respondent) on the civil balance of probabilities (ie more likely than not) that the trading company/

---

51 See Tribunal Procedure (First-tier Tribunal) (Tax Chamber) Rules 2009.

individual '"knew or should have known" that the deal involved MTIC fraud.' Hence a good working knowledge of how Commissioners can prove a MTIC fraud is essential.

Relevant case law

5.75 Cases relevant to this area are:

- *Optigen Ltd, Fulcrum Electronics Ltd and Bond House Systems Ltd v Commissioners of Customs & Excise*[52] – in January 2006, the ECJ held that a taxable person who did not know and had no means of knowing that his purchase was connected with VAT fraud had the right to deduct the input tax incurred on that purchase;

- *Axel Kittel v Belgium; Belgium v Recolta Recycling SPRL* (C-439/04) and (C-440/04)[53] – the ECJ held that the right to deduct input tax should be denied where the taxable person knew or should have known that his transaction was connected with VAT fraud;

- *Mobilx Ltd (in Administration), Calltell Telecom Ltd, Blue Sphere Global Ltd v HMRC*;[54]

- *HMRC v Livewire Telecom & Olympia Technology Ltd*;[55]

- *Dragon Futures Ltd v Revenue and Customs Commissioners*;[56] and

- *Meridian Global Funds Management Asia v Securities Commission*,[57] *In re Supply of Ready Mixed Concrete (No 2)*,[58] *McNicholas Construction Co Ltd v Customs and Excise Commissioners*,[59] *In re Hampshire Land*,[60] *Bank of India v Morris*,[61] and *Stone & Rolls v Moore Stephens*[62] for the law on attribution of knowledge to companies in particular circumstances, as applied in *Commissioner v Greener Solutions Limited*.[63]

5.76 The burden is on the respondent to prove that the only reasonable explanation for the circumstances in which the transactions in question were

---

52 [2006] ECR I-483.
53 [2006] ECR 1-6161.
54 [2010] EWCA Civ 517, [2010] STC 1436.
55 [2009] EWHC 15 (Ch), [2009] STC 643, [2010] UKFTT 45(TC).
56 [2007] STI 373.
57 [1995] 2 AC 500.
58 [1995] 1 AC 456.
59 [2000] STC 553.
60 [1896] 2 Ch 743.
61 [2005] EWCA (Civ) 693, [2005] 2 BCLC 328.
62 [2009] 1 AC 1391.
63 [2012] UKUT 18 TCC.

5.76 *Alternatives to Prosecution*

undertaken was that they were connected with fraud: see para 77 of *Mobilx*[64] in which LJ Moses said:

'The question was not whether Mobilx should have known that its transactions were more likely than not to be connected with fraud. The correct question *is whether it should have known that its transactions were connected with fraud.* That, as I have said, could be established by demonstrating that it ought to have known that the only reasonable explanation for the circumstances in which the transactions in question were undertaken was that they were connected with fraud.' [Emphasis added]

---

64 [2010] EWCA Civ 517.

Chapter 6

The Role of the Preparatory Hearing, Case Management and Interlocutory Appeals

PREPARATORY HEARINGS UNDER THE CRIMINAL JUSTICE ACT 1987 AND CASE MANAGEMENT

Introduction

6.1 The Roskill Commission Report[1] was published as long ago as 1986, and marked a sea change in the way fraud cases would be handled. The Criminal Justice Act 1987 was passed by Parliament, creating, amongst other things, the Serious Fraud Office.

6.2 So it was in 1988 that, as the Court of Appeal (Criminal Division) had held previously that it had no jurisdiction to consider issues prior to the conclusion of a case,[2] for the first time the availability of an interlocutory appeal was created under s 9(1) of the Criminal Justice Act 1987, by invention of the 'preparatory hearing'. Such an appeal vested in either side. Up until that point, the only avenues of appeal were post conviction[3] (and sentence[4]) for a defendant and on a point of law[5] for the prosecution, via the Attorney General. In relation to such appeals by the Attorney General, the acquitted defendant was not in peril.

6.3 As can be seen below, however, the landscape has changed beyond recognition since 1987 in terms of preparatory hearings and with the creation of the prosecution's right to apply to appeal against a 'terminating ruling',[6] that

---

1 Fraud Trials Committee Report 1986 (The 'Roskill Report').
2 *R v Jeffries* [1969] 1 QB 120.
3 Criminal Appeal Act 1968, s 1.
4 Criminal Appeal Act 1968, s 9.
5 Criminal Justice Act 1972, s 36.
6 Criminal Justice 2003, s 58.

6.4 *The Role of the Preparatory Hearing, Case Management etc*

is, a ruling by the judge in the Crown Court that brings proceedings to an end on one or more counts.

6.4 However the Court of Appeal (Criminal Division) has successfully sought to minimise the number of interlocutory appeals by reducing the proper scope for the ordering of a preparatory hearing. In effect only if there is a point of law that requires appellate determination prior to trial should one be ordered.[7] Particular regard should be given to the Crown Court's wider case management powers pursuant to s 40 of the Criminal Procedure and Investigations Act 1996 and the Criminal Procedure Rules 2013[8] that now significantly overlap with the Court's powers under the preparatory hearing regimes.[9]

6.5 In relation to preparatory hearings, when one commences the trial is deemed to have started. This can, unless care is taken, have unintended consequences, for example, a defendant's custody time limits will cease to apply.[10]

6.6 Finally the Court of Appeal (Criminal Division) has also provided clear guidance as to how it will consider an appeal against a terminating ruling and the effect of the prosecution not complying with the procedural requirements prior to any appeal or application for leave.[11]

Ordering a preparatory hearing

6.7 Before considering the criteria that need fulfilling under the statutes, it is important to note how the Court of Appeal (Criminal Division) has guided judges in the Crown Court about whether to exercise their discretion to order such a hearing.

6.8 In *R v I*,[12] Lord Justice Hughes V-P (as he then was) said:

'21. … It is emphatically not the case that most heavy fraud or similar cases will nowadays call for a preparatory hearing. Virtually the only reason

---

7 *R v I* [2010] 1 Cr App R 10.
8 SI 2013/1554.
9 This work is not concerned with either (i) terrorism cases or (ii) the possibility of a judge alone trial under s 44 of the Criminal Justice Act 2003. In each of these two scenarios, however, a preparatory hearing is mandatory. Equally, as s 43 of the Criminal Justice Act 2003 in relation to judge alone trials in cases of 'serious fraud' have been repealed (having never been brought into force) we do not consider them. In each of these two scenarios, however, a preparatory hearing is mandatory.
10 Criminal Justice Act 1987, s 8; *Kanaris v Governor of Pentenville Prison* [2003] 2 Cr App R 1 – the ability to undertaken statutory pre-trial hearings under s 40 of the Criminal Procedure and Investigations Act 1996 will also be affected.
11 *R v T (N)* [2010] 2 Cr App R 12.
12 [2010] 1 Cr App R 10.

Preparatory hearings under the Criminal Justice Act 1987 **6.10**

for directing such a hearing nowadays is if the judge is going to have to give a ruling which ought to be the subject of an interlocutory appeal. Such rulings are few and far between and do not extend to most rulings of law. An interlocutory appeal can be a most beneficial process in a few, very limited, circumstances. If a discrete point of law arises, its resolution in this court can if necessary be accomplished within a very short time-frame and this can avoid the risk of many weeks of waste trial time.'

There will therefore need to be a compelling case that an appeal at an interlocutory stage is something that will be of profound importance to the continuation or otherwise of the proceedings as opposed to a matter of interest or ruling upon the evidence. An example, it is submitted, might include a ruling that, if decided the other way, would halt a lengthy and expensive trial in its tracks.

6.9 Leaving aside the interlocutory appeal, the reality is that most if not all of the 'additional' case management powers that were given to judges of the Crown Court upon the commencement of a preparatory hearing are now a part of the judge's 'full time' powers pursuant, in the main, to the statutory pre-trial review created by s 40 of the Criminal Procedure and Investigations Act 1996 and the powers under Pt 3 of Criminal Procedure Rules (Appendix 3). It is to be noted however that if a preparatory hearing is validly ordered then there is no power to rescind that ruling and, as a result, appeals to the Court of Appeal (Criminal Division) will be available.[13]

Pre-trial rulings and case management

6.10 Section 40 of the Criminal Procedure and Investigations Act 1996 creates a power for the court to make pre-trial rulings at a pre-trial hearing.[14] That states:

'Power to make rulings.

(1) A judge may make at a pre-trial hearing a ruling as to—

    (a) any question as to the admissibility of evidence;

    (b) any other question of law relating to the case concerned.

(2) A ruling may be made under this section—

    (a) on an application by a party to the case, or

    (b) of the judge's own motion.

---

13 *R v Y; R v Z* [2013] 1 Cr App R 21; in relation to s 29 of the Criminal Procedure and Investigations Act 1996 preparatory hearings. 'Pre-trial hearing' defined in s 39.
14 Criminal Procedure and Investigations Act 1996, s 39 defines a 'pre-trial hearing' as, in effect, a matter relating to trial on indictment where the accused has been sent and is prior to the trial starting.

6.11 *The Role of the Preparatory Hearing, Case Management etc*

(3) Subject to subsection (4), a ruling made under this section has binding effect from the time it is made until the case against the accused or, if there is more than one, against each of them is disposed of; and the case against an accused is disposed of if—

  (a) he is acquitted or convicted, or

  (b) the prosecutor decides not to proceed with the case against him.

(4) A judge may discharge or vary (or further vary) a ruling made under this section if it appears to him that it is in the interests of justice to do so; and a judge may act under this subsection—

  (a) on an application by a party to the case, or

  (b) of the judge's own motion.

(5) No application may be made under subsection (4)(a) unless there has been a material change of circumstances since the ruling was made or, if a previous application has been made, since the application (or last application) was made.

(6) The judge referred to in subsection (4) need not be the judge who made the ruling or, if it has been varied, the judge (or any of the judges) who varied it.

(7) For the purposes of this section the prosecutor is any person acting as prosecutor, whether an individual or a body.'

As a result the court is able to consider, prior to trial, nearly any issue that might arise which affects the conduct of the case.

Part 3 of the Criminal Procedure Rules 2014

6.11 Part 1 of the Criminal Procedure Rules 2014 provides by secondary legislation the 'overriding objective' of dealing with cases 'justly' that it is the responsibility of all parties to the proceedings to further.

6.12 Part 3 of the Criminal Procedure Rules gives the criminal courts considerable case management powers (see Appendix 3). These include:

'3.2 (3) ... actively managing the case by giving any direction appropriate to the needs of that case as early as possible.'

As a result it can be seen why Hughes LJ, V-P (as he then was), in *R v I*[15] attempted to curtail the use of preparatory hearings to those cases requiring an important decision to be considered by the Court of Appeal (Criminal

---

15 [2010] 1 Cr App R 10.

Division) prior to trial. There is now, it would appear, very little by way of case management that requires a preparatory hearing.

Sections 7–10 of the Criminal Justice Act 1987

6.13 Notwithstanding the Crown Court's wide powers of case management, the Criminal Justice Act 1987 is, although marginalised, a relevant piece of legislation. It specifically applies only to cases of complex fraud (unlike the provisions of the Criminal Procedure and Investigations Act 1996 – see below – which appear to be of general application). Rules 3.14–3.18 in Pt 3 of the Criminal Procedure Rules 2014 applies to such applications (see Appendix 3) and requires the use of relevant forms.[16]

6.14 Sections 7–10 state:

'7 Power to order preparatory hearing.

(1) Where it appears to a judge of the Crown Court that the evidence on an indictment reveals a case of fraud of such seriousness or complexity that substantial benefits are likely to accrue from a hearing (in this Act referred to as a "preparatory hearing") before the jury are sworn, for the purpose of—

    (a) identifying issues which are likely to be material to the verdict of the jury;

    (b) assisting their comprehension of any such issues;

    (c) expediting the proceedings before the jury; or

    (d) assisting the judge's management of the trial,

he may order that such a hearing shall be held.

(2) A judge may make an order under subsection (1) above on the application either of the prosecution or of the person indicted or, if the indictment charges a number of persons, any of them, or of his own motion.

(3) If a judge orders a preparatory hearing, he may also order the prosecution to prepare and serve any documents that appear to him to be relevant and whose service could be ordered at the preparatory hearing by virtue of this Part of this Act or Crown Court Rules.

(4) Where—

    (a) a judge has made an order under subsection (3) above; and

    (b) the prosecution have complied with it,

---

16 http://www.justice.gov.uk/courts/procedure-rules/criminal/formspage.

6.14 *The Role of the Preparatory Hearing, Case Management etc*

>the judge may order the person indicted or, if the indictment charges a number of persons, any of them to prepare and serve any documents that appear to him to be relevant and whose service could be so ordered at the preparatory hearing.

(5) An order under this section may specify the time within which it is to be complied with, but Crown Court Rules may make provision as to the minimum or maximum time that may be specified for compliance.

8 Commencement of trial and arraignment.

(1) If a judge orders a preparatory hearing, the trial shall begin with that hearing.

(2) Arraignment shall accordingly take place at the start of the preparatory hearing.

9 The preparatory hearing.

(1) At the preparatory hearing the judge may exercise any of the powers specified in this section.

(2) The judge may adjourn a preparatory hearing from time to time.

(3) He may determine—

    (a) ...

    (aa) a question arising under section 6 of the Criminal Justice Act 1993 (relevance of external law to certain charges of conspiracy, attempt and incitement);

    (b) any question as to the admissibility of evidence; and

    (c) any other question of law relating to the case.

    (d) any question as to the severance or joinder of charges.

(4) He may order the prosecution—

    (a) to supply the court and the defendant or, if there is more than one, each of them with a statement (a 'case statement') of the following—

        (i) the principal facts of the prosecution case;

        (ii) the witnesses who will speak to those facts;

        (iii) any exhibits relevant to those facts;

        (iv) any proposition of law on which the prosecution proposes to rely; and

        (v) the consequences in relation to any of the counts in the indictment that appear to the prosecution to flow from the matters stated in pursuance of sub-paragraphs (i) to (iv) above;

Preparatory hearings under the Criminal Justice Act 1987 **6.14**

(b) to prepare their evidence and other explanatory material in such a form as appears to him to be likely to aid comprehension by the jury and to supply it in that form to the court and to the defendant or, if there is more than one, to each of them;

(c) to give the court and the defendant or, if there is more than one, each of them notice of documents the truth of the contents of which ought in the prosecution's view to be admitted and of any other matters which in their view ought to be agreed;

(d) to make any amendments of any case statement supplied in pursuance of an order under paragraph (a) above that appear to the court to be appropriate, having regard to objections made by the defendant or, if there is more than one, by any of them.

(5) Where—

(a) a judge has ordered the prosecution to supply a case statement; and

(b) the prosecution have complied with the order,

he may order the defendant or, if there is more than one, each of them—

(i) to give the court and the prosecution a statement in writing setting out in general terms the nature of his defence and indicating the principal matters on which he takes issue with the prosecution;

(ii) to give the court and the prosecution notice of any objections that he has to the case statement;

(iii) to inform the court and the prosecution of any point of law (including a point as to the admissibility of evidence) which he wishes to take, and any authority on which he intends to rely for that purpose;

(iv) to give the court and the prosecution a notice stating the extent to which he agrees with the prosecution as to documents and other matters to which a notice under subsection (4)(c) above relates and the reason for any disagreement.

(6) Crown Court Rules may provide that except to the extent that disclosure is required—

(a) by section 5(7) of the Criminal Procedure and Investigations Act 1996 (alibi); or

(b) by rules under section 81 of the Police and Criminal Evidence Act 1984 (expert evidence),

a summary required by virtue of subsection (5) above need not disclose who will give evidence.

6.14 *The Role of the Preparatory Hearing, Case Management etc*

(7) A judge making an order under subsection (5) above shall warn the defendant or, if there is more than one, all of them of the possible consequence under section 10 (1) below of not complying with it.

(8) If it appears to a judge that reasons given in pursuance of subsection (5)(iv) above are inadequate, he shall so inform the person giving them, and may require him to give further or better reasons.

(9) An order under this section may specify the time within which any specified requirement contained in it is to be complied with, but Crown Court Rules may make provision as to the minimum or maximum time that may be specified for compliance.

(10) An order or ruling made under this section shall have effect during the trial, unless it appears to the judge, on application made to him during the trial, that the interests of justice require him to vary or discharge it.

(11) An appeal shall lie to the Court of Appeal from any order or ruling of a judge under subsection (3)(b) or (c) above, but only with the leave of the judge or of the Court of Appeal.

(12) Subject to rules of court made under section 53(1) of the Supreme Court Act 1981 (power by rules to distribute business of Court of Appeal between its civil and criminal divisions), the jurisdiction of the Court of Appeal under subsection (11) above shall be exercised by the criminal division of the court; and the reference in that subsection to the Court of Appeal shall be construed as a reference to that division.

(13) The judge may continue a preparatory hearing notwithstanding that leave to appeal has been granted under subsection (11) above, but no jury shall be sworn until after the appeal has been determined or abandoned.

(14) On the termination of the hearing of an appeal, the Court of Appeal may confirm, reverse or vary the decision appealed against.

9A Orders before preparatory hearing.

(1) Subsection (2) below applies where—

    (a) a judge orders a preparatory hearing, and

    (b) he decides that any order which could be made under section 9(4) or (5) above at the hearing should be made before the hearing.

(2) In such a case—

    (a) he may make any such order before the hearing (or at the hearing), and

    (b) subsections (4) to (10) of section 9 above shall apply accordingly.]

10 Later stages of trial.

(1) Any party may depart from the case he disclosed in pursuance of a requirement imposed under section 9 above.

(2) Where—

(a) a party departs from the case he disclosed in pursuance of a requirement imposed under section 9 above, or

(b) a party fails to comply with such a requirement,

the judge or, with the leave of the judge, any other party may make such comment as appears to the judge or the other party (as the case may be) to be appropriate and the jury may draw such inference as appears proper.

(3) In deciding whether to give leave the judge shall have regard—

(a) to the extent of the departure or failure, and

(b) to whether there is any justification for it.

(4) Except as provided by this section no part—

(a) of a statement given under section 9(5) above, or

(b) of any other information relating to the case for the accused or, if there is more than one, the case for any of them, which was given in pursuance of a requirement imposed under section 9 above,

may be disclosed at a stage in the trial after the jury have been sworn without the consent of the accused concerned.'

Thus it must appear to the court that the *evidence* reveals a fraud of such seriousness or complexity *and* substantial benefits must accrue by reference to one of the purposes in s 7.

6.15 In *R v H*,[17] the House of Lords said, in the speech of Lord Mance at 91:

'In my view it is necessary to return to first principles, and take a fresh look at the legislation. I consider that courts have to date failed to recognize its full scope, and have in their caution introduced certain limitations which have deprived it much utility ... once a preparatory hearing has been validly ordered under s 7, the judge has powers under s 9 which are independent of s 7'.

---

17 [2007] 2 Cr App R 6.

6.16 *The Role of the Preparatory Hearing, Case Management etc*

Thus in order for a case to meet the relevant criteria the *purpose(s)* of a preparatory hearing must be one or more of:[18]

- identifying the issues relevant to the decisions that will need to be made in the trial;
- assisting the jury in their comprehension of those issues; and/or
- assisting the judge in managing the trial.

6.16 Once that has been done then the court must be *able* to determine:[19]

- a question of the relevance of external law in relation to conspiracy, attempt and incitement
- any question of admissibility of evidence
- any other question of law
- any question of severance or joinder of charges.

6.17 Applications for disclosure do not, ordinarily, raise questions of law and therefore do not fall to be appealed in a case where a preparatory hearing has been ordered.[20]

Criminal Procedure and Investigations Act 1996

6.18 In 1995, Parliament enacted the Criminal Procedure and Investigations Act 1996. One aspect of this legislation was to extend the preparatory hearing regime created by the Criminal Justice Act 1987 and reserved for complex fraud to any case that met the criteria. Rules 3.14–3.18 of the Criminal Procedure Rules 2014 also apply to such applications (see Appendix 3) and also require the use of the relevant forms.[21]

6.19 Its provisions are subtly different to its counterpart in s 7 of the Criminal Justice Act 1987. Here it must appear to the court that the *indictment* reveals a case of such complexity and seriousness or show such length that substantial benefits will accrue from holding a preparatory hearing. However, if it appears to the court that criteria under s 7 of the Criminal Justice Act 1987 are made out for the purposes of fraud, a judge can only order a preparatory hearing under the Criminal Procedure and Investigations Act 1996 if the matter involves terrorism. As a result the court should, it is suggested, proceed under the 1987 Criminal Justice Act regime. For completeness, however, we include

---

18 Criminal Justice Act 1987, s 7(1)(a)–(d).
19 Criminal Justice Act 1987, s 9(3)(aa)–(d).
20 *R v H* [2007] 2 Cr App R 6.
21 http://www.justice.gov.uk/courts/procedure-rules/criminal/formspage.

the text of ss 29–33 of the Criminal Procedure and Investigations Act 1996 (see Appendix 4).

Appeals

6.20 If a party wishes to appeal a decision to the Court of Appeal (Criminal Division) then, under either regime, it requires the leave of the trial court or the Court of Appeal (Criminal Division) directly.[22] The Court of Appeal (Criminal Division) has expressed itself willing to consider, as a preliminary issue, whether in the first instance the Crown Court has validly exercised its power to order a preparatory hearing based on the principles outlined above. If it concludes that this is not happened then the appeal will not be effective.[23] If leave is obtained and the appeal heard then the Court of Appeal (Criminal Division) can allow or dismiss the appeal in whole or in part in the traditional way.

6.21 There is an ability to appeal to the Supreme Court that will require the Court of Appeal (Criminal Division) to certify the case contains a point of general public importance. It will then usually refuse leave to appeal requiring the aggrieved party to seek leave direct from the Supreme Court.[24]

INTERLOCUTORY APPEALS AFTER TERMINATING RULINGS BY THE PROSECUTION UNDER THE CRIMINAL JUSTICE ACT 2003

Which rulings are included?

6.22 The prosecution's power to appeal a 'terminating ruling' is statutory and limited. The entire jurisdiction is contained with ss 58–61 of the Criminal Justice Act 2003 (informed by the interpretations in s 74). Sections 58–61 say:

58 General right of appeal in respect of rulings

(1) This section applies where a judge makes a ruling in relation to a trial on indictment at an applicable time and the ruling relates to one or more offences included in the indictment.

(2) The prosecution may appeal in respect of the ruling in accordance with this section.

---

22 Criminal Justice Act 1987, s 9(11).
23 *R v Ward* [2003] 2 Cr App R 20.
24 Criminal Appeal Act 1968, s 33(1).

6.22   *The Role of the Preparatory Hearing, Case Management etc*

(3) The ruling is to have no effect whilst the prosecution is able to take any steps under subsection (4).

(4) The prosecution may not appeal in respect of the ruling unless—

    (a) following the making of the ruling, it—

        (i) informs the court that it intends to appeal, or

        (ii) requests an adjournment to consider whether to appeal, and

    (b) if such an adjournment is granted, it informs the court following the adjournment that it intends to appeal.

(5) If the prosecution requests an adjournment under subsection (4)(a)(ii), the judge may grant such an adjournment.

(6) Where the ruling relates to two or more offences—

    (a) any one or more of those offences may be the subject of the appeal, and

    (b) if the prosecution informs the court in accordance with subsection (4) that it intends to appeal, it must at the same time inform the court of the offence or offences which are the subject of the appeal.

(7) Where—

    (a) the ruling is a ruling that there is no case to answer, and

    (b) the prosecution, at the same time that it informs the court in accordance with subsection (4) that it intends to appeal, nominates one or more other rulings which have been made by a judge in relation to the trial on indictment at an applicable time and which relate to the offence or offences which are the subject of the appeal,

that other ruling, or those other rulings, are also to be treated as the subject of the appeal.

(8) The prosecution may not inform the court in accordance with subsection (4) that it intends to appeal, unless, at or before that time, it informs the court that it agrees that, in respect of the offence or each offence which is the subject of the appeal, the defendant in relation to that offence should be acquitted of that offence if either of the conditions mentioned in subsection (9) is fulfilled.

(9) Those conditions are—

    (a) that leave to appeal to the Court of Appeal is not obtained, and

    (b) that the appeal is abandoned before it is determined by the Court of Appeal.

Interlocutory appeals after terminating rulings by the prosecution etc **6.22**

(10) If the prosecution informs the court in accordance with subsection (4) that it intends to appeal, the ruling mentioned in subsection (1) is to continue to have no effect in relation to the offence or offences which are the subject of the appeal whilst the appeal is pursued.

(11) If and to the extent that a ruling has no effect in accordance with this section—

  (a) any consequences of the ruling are also to have no effect,

  (b) the judge may not take any steps in consequence of the ruling, and

  (c) if he does so, any such steps are also to have no effect.

(12) Where the prosecution has informed the court of its agreement under subsection (8) and either of the conditions mentioned in subsection (9) is fulfilled, the judge or the Court of Appeal must order that the defendant in relation to the offence or each offence concerned be acquitted of that offence.

(13) In this section 'applicable time', in relation to a trial on indictment, means any time (whether before or after the commencement of the trial) before the time when the judge starts his summing-up to the jury.

(14) The reference in subsection (13) to the time when the judge starts his summing-up to the jury includes the time when the judge would start his summing-up to the jury but for the making of an order under Part 7.

59 Expedited and non-expedited appeals

(1) Where the prosecution informs the court in accordance with section 58(4) that it intends to appeal, the judge must decide whether or not the appeal should be expedited.

(2) If the judge decides that the appeal should be expedited, he may order an adjournment.

(3) If the judge decides that the appeal should not be expedited, he may—

  (a) order an adjournment, or

  (b) discharge the jury (if one has been sworn).

(4) If he decides that the appeal should be expedited, he or the Court of Appeal may subsequently reverse that decision and, if it is reversed, the judge may act as mentioned in subsection (3)(a) or (b).

60 Continuation of proceedings for offences not affected by ruling

(1) This section applies where the prosecution informs the court in accordance with section 58(4) that it intends to appeal.

6.23 *The Role of the Preparatory Hearing, Case Management etc*

(2) Proceedings may be continued in respect of any offence which is not the subject of the appeal.

61 Determination of appeal by Court of Appeal

(1) On an appeal under section 58, the Court of Appeal may confirm, reverse or vary any ruling to which the appeal relates.

(2) Subsections (3) to (5) apply where the appeal relates to a single ruling.

(3) Where the Court of Appeal confirms the ruling, it must, in respect of the offence or each offence which is the subject of the appeal, order that the defendant in relation to that offence be acquitted of that offence.

(4) Where the Court of Appeal reverses or varies the ruling, it must, in respect of the offence or each offence which is the subject of the appeal, do any of the following—

   (a) order that proceedings for that offence may be resumed in the Crown Court,

   (b) order that a fresh trial may take place in the Crown Court for that offence,

   (c) order that the defendant in relation to that offence be acquitted of that offence.

(5) But the Court of Appeal may not make an order under subsection (4)(c) in respect of an offence unless it considers that the defendant could not receive a fair trial if an order were made under subsection (4)(a) or (b).

(6) Subsections (7) and (8) apply where the appeal relates to a ruling that there is no case to answer and one or more other rulings.

(7) Where the Court of Appeal confirms the ruling that there is no case to answer, it must, in respect of the offence or each offence which is the subject of the appeal, order that the defendant in relation to that offence be acquitted of that offence.

(8) Where the Court of Appeal reverses or varies the ruling that there is no case to answer, it must in respect of the offence or each offence which is the subject of the appeal, make any of the orders mentioned in subsection (4)(a) to (c) (but subject to subsection (5)).

6.23 A ruling is defined by s 74(1) of the Criminal Justice Act 2003 as including:

'a decision, determination, direction, finding, notice, order, refusal rejection or requirement'.

Interlocutory appeals after terminating rulings by the prosecution etc **6.26**

In short only those rulings that bring the case to an end, eg a stay for an abuse of process or an allowance of a submission at the close of the prosecution case that there is no case to answer, or effectively bring the case to an end, eg a decision not to adjourn a trial when the prosecution has no witnesses available causing them to have to offer no evidence, will permit the prosecution to seek leave to appeal against that ruling.[25] It must be a terminating ruling before the jurisdiction arises to seek leave to appeal.[26]

6.24 In *Clarke*,[27] the Court of Appeal (Criminal Division) said by way of guidance to prosecutors:

> 'Is the court entitled to interfere with it [the ruling]? The limitation in the statute is clear. We may not do so unless it was not reasonable for the judge to have made the ruling. Time and time again in this court emphasis has been laid on the simple proposition that case management decisions are made by trial judges not this court.'

That limitation applies to any type of ruling.

Prosecutor's responsibilities

6.25 Given the fundamental change that the Criminal Justice Act 2003 brought in relation to the prosecution appealing against Crown Court rulings that, if successful, have the consequence of a defendant being put back into peril, the Court of Appeal (Criminal Division) has interpreted the procedural requirements as being absolute; that is to say a failure on the part of the prosecution to adhere to the statutory requirements will prove fatal to any application for leave to appeal, irrespective of the merits of the case.

6.26 The most important is the 'acquittal agreement.' In *R v T*,[28] Lord Judge CJ, heading a five-judge Court of Appeal (Criminal Division), said:

> '12. It is a feature of this legislation that the court has no inherent jurisdiction to hear an appeal by the prosecution against a terminating ruling. Jurisdiction does not arise unless the prosecution has complied with the pre-conditions that enable the appeal to be brought. In effect s 58(8) requires the prosecution to undertake that if they conditions in ss 9 are fulfilled, the defendant will be acquitted.
>
> [...]

---

25 *R v Clarke* [2008] 1 Cr App R 33 at 28.
26 Section 62 of the Criminal Justice Act 2003 contains provision for appeals against 'evidential rulings' but these have not been brought into force and there appears to be no suggestion that this is imminent. As a result these are not considered.
27 [2008] 1 Cr App R 33.
28 [2010] 2 Cr App R 12.

6.27 *The Role of the Preparatory Hearing, Case Management etc*

19. The requirement that the statutory undertaking in relation to the acquittal agreement should be given, and the latest time for giving it, are pre-conditions to this particular appeal process. Unless these mandatory pre-conditions are established, the court is unable to vest itself with a jurisdiction which it does not have, or permit the prosecution to exercise a power which it has failed to exercise in accordance with the statutory provisions.

20. ... This court cannot cure or ignore non-compliance by the prosecution with the pre-conditions in s 58(4) and 58(8). The prosecution must itself ensure compliance.'

Appeals

6.27 If the prosecution do seek leave to appeal against a terminating ruling, then either the Court of Appeal (Criminal Division) will grant leave to appeal and allow it, (in which case the matter is usually remitted back to the Crown Court) or refuse the appeal (if it grants leave). In reality there is a 'rolled up' hearing. Some hearings are more urgent than others. As a result the statute contemplates an 'expedited hearing', where the jury in the Crown Court case is kept until the Court of Appeal (Criminal Division) has delivered its ruling.[29] Alternatively, where the matter is not under pressure of time, the case will proceed at the normal pace and the jury discharged.[30]

6.28 Like non-adherence to the 'acquittal agreement', a requirement of the statute is that if the prosecution lose their application for leave to appeal or the appeal itself, then the consequence is that the defendant is acquitted of the charges against him.[31] That is the statutory 'price the prosecution pay' for the ability to bring an appeal in the first place and it applies whether or not the defendant was acquitted in the Crown Court. In other words, if the Crown Court, for example, stays the proceedings as an abuse of the court's process but does not acquit the defendant, and if the prosecution then lose in the Court of Appeal (Criminal Division), the defendant will be acquitted.

6.29 As with interlocutory appeals brought by virtue of a preparatory hearing, there is, with terminating rulings, a facility to appeal to the Supreme Court. Again this requires the Court of Appeal (Criminal Division) to certify a point of public importance as well as the requirement for leave, usually directly from the Supreme Court.[32]

---

29 Criminal Justice Act 2003, s 59(2).
30 Criminal Justice Act 2003, s 59(3)(b).
31 Criminal Justice Act 2003, s 61(3) and (7).
32 Criminal Appeal Act 1968, s 33(1).

Chapter 7

Disclosure

INTRODUCTION

7.1 Disclosure of material in the possession of the prosecution to the defence is of central theoretical and practical importance to criminal litigation and proceedings. The prosecution bear an important duty and responsibility in considering and putting in place a proper system of effective, timely disclosure. Disclosure is closely linked to public interest immunity, in which the prosecution might seek not to disclose sensitive material. The importance of full and timely disclosure in ensuring the right to a fair trial cannot be overstated. Clear recognition of the need for proper disclosure can be found in various sources:

- The Attorney-General's Guidelines 2005 state:

    'Disclosure is one of the most important issues in the criminal justice system and the application of proper and fair disclosure is a vital component of a fair criminal justice system. The "golden rule" is that fairness requires full disclosure should be made of all material held by the prosecution that weakens its case or strengthens that of the defence.'[1]

- The Disclosure Protocol 2006 states:

    'disclosure is one of the most important – as well as one of the most abused – procedures relating to criminal trials.'[2]

- The Attorney-General's Guidelines on Disclosure 2013[3] state:

---

1   See Foreword by Lord Goldsmith the Attorney-General in 'Attorney General's Guidelines on Disclosure' (April 2005) available at https://www.gov.uk/attorney-generals-guidelines-on-disclosure-2005-and-2011.
2   See http://webarchive.nationalarchives.gov.uk/+/http:/www.justice.gov.uk/criminal/procrules_fin/contents/pd_protocol/pd_protocol_disclosure.htm.
3   Which replaces the Attorney Generals Guidelines of 2005 as of December 2013. See www.gov.uk/government/publications/attorney-generals-guidelines-on-disclosure-2013.

7.2 *Disclosure*

'Proper disclosure of unused material, made through a rigorous and carefully considered application of the law, remains a crucial part of a fair trial, and essential to avoiding miscarriages of justice.[4]

7.2 Recognition of the importance of disclosure is also made clear in domestic case law. The House of Lords stated in *R v H and C*:[5]

'Fairness ordinarily requires that any material held by the prosecution which weakens its case or strengthens that of the defendant, if not relied on as part of its formal case against the defendant, should be disclosed to the defence. Bitter experience has shown that miscarriages of justice may occur where such material is withheld from disclosure. The golden rule is that full disclosure of such material should be made'.[6]

7.3 There should be fair disclosure of information to an accused by the prosecution as 'an inseparable part of a fair trial',[7] under common law, the Criminal Procedure and Investigations Act 1996 (as amended by the Criminal Justice Act 2003), Art 6 of the ECHR and relevant disclosure guidelines.

COMMON LAW

7.4 For investigations which began prior to 1 April 1997, common law governs disclosure as opposed to statutory provision. The high point of the common law regime was a duty to disclose any evidence which tended to weaken the prosecution or strengthen the defence case, and to require judicial sanction where it was proposed that such material be withheld on the basis of public interest immunity.[8] The prosecution had the primary task of deciding what was relevant, and the appropriate test emerged in *R v Keane*,[9] namely material that could be seen:

- to be relevant or possibly relevant to an issue in the case;
- to raise or possibly raise a new issue which was not apparent from the used evidence, or
- to hold out a real prospect of providing a lead to evidence falling within either of the first two categories.

---

4   See Foreword (at p 3 of the Guidelines) by the Attorney General Dominic Grieve QC MP and The Lord Chief Justice Lord Thomas, available at https://www.gov.uk/government/publications/attorney-generals-guidelines-on-disclosure-2013.
5   [2004] 2 AC 134 at 147.
6   Per Lord Bingham at para 14 of the judgment.
7   See para 1 of AG Guidelines 2005 at https://www.gov.uk/attorney-generals-guidelines-on-disclosure-2005-and-2011. www.gov.uk/government/uploads/system/uploads/ _2005.pdf.
8   *R v Ward* [1993] 2 All ER 577, [1993] 96 Cr App R 1.
9   [1994] 2 All ER 478, [1994] 99 Cr App R 1.

STATUTORY BASIS: CRIMINAL PROCEDURE AND INVESTIGATIONS ACT 1996

7.5 Based largely on the Royal Commission on Criminal Justice recommendations,[10] the Criminal Procedure and Investigations Act 1996 (CPIA 1996) imposed a statutory regime on criminal trials at all levels in cases where the investigation has commenced on or after 1 April 1997, with amendments introduced by the Criminal Justice Act 2003 (CJA 2003) being operative for investigations commencing after 4 April 2005.

7.6 The scheme set out in the CPIA 1996 (as amended by the CJA 2003) is designed to ensure that there is fair disclosure of material which may be relevant to an investigation and which does not form part of the prosecution case. CPIA disclosure should assist the defence in the timely preparation and presentation of the defence case and assist the court in focusing upon relevant trial issues.

7.7 The CPIA disclosure regime is based upon the duty to record and retain all relevant material obtained in the course of an investigation.[11] Thereafter, the prosecution must disclose anything which might undermine the prosecution case or assist the defence case by way of primary disclosure.[12] The defence may then provide a defence statement document which is the basis upon which the prosecutor decides whether there is any material which might reasonably be expected to assist the defence in a process of secondary disclosure, which is now a continuing duty of disclosure.[13]

7.8 If the defence complain that the disclosure provided by the prosecution is inadequate and deficient, the defence may apply, under CPIA 1996, s 8, for a court order for further disclosure. Such applications are difficult to mount successfully. First, the defence must have served a defence statement before a s 8 application can be made, and judges are discouraged from ordering the service of material which is not directly referable to an issue identified therein. Secondly, the defence will almost inevitably be asking for material that by the nature of the procedure the defence is unable to specify with any particularity, the defence knowledge being heavily reliant upon the accuracy and detail of the prosecution description on unused material disclosure schedules. The prosecutor may be allowed, at trial, to comment on the failure of the defence to provide any adequate and timely defence statement,[14] the judge deciding upon any inference arguments.

---

10 1993, Cm 2263.
11 CPIA 1996, s 23.
12 CPIA 1996, s 3.
13 CPIA 1996, s 5. Secondary disclosure no longer exists, as the prosecution are now under a duty of continuing disclosure as per the amending provisions –CJA 2003, Sch 37(3), para 1.
14 CPIA 1996, s 11.

7.9 *Disclosure*

7.9 The prosecution has a continuing duty, throughout proceedings, to keep the question of disclosure under review.[15] The prosecution may apply to the court to withhold information from the defence, on grounds of public interest immunity.[16]

Post-CPIA guidance and amendments

7.10 Since the introduction of the CPIA 1996, the disclosure regime has been amended by statute and guidelines issued to assist in the disclosure process. In November 2000, revised Attorney General's Guidelines[17] stressed that material that overburdens the participants in the trial process, diverts attention from the relevant issues and leads to unjustifiable delay should not be disclosed. The Criminal Justice Act 2003, Control and Management of Heavy Fraud (and other complex criminal cases) Protocol 2005, Attorney General's Guidelines on Disclosure 2005 and the Disclosure Protocol relating to the Management of Unused Material 2006[18] provided further disclosure checks and balances.

7.11 The main reforms of the CPIA system[19] saw the introduction of a single disclosure test for the prosecution, an increase in defence duties and extended penalties for non-compliance. Section 32 of the Criminal Justice Act 2003[20] amends the CPIA 1996 by imposing a new single disclosure test applicable to all stages of proceedings, namely that material should be disclosed, 'which might reasonably be considered capable of undermining the case for the prosecution against the accused or of assisting the case for the accused.' This test is applicable at the primary disclosure stage and thereafter as a continuing duty, replacing secondary disclosure. Defence statements should set out the nature of the defence, matters of fact in dispute, any points of law (including admissibility issues and abuse of process),[21] notice of an intention to

---

15 CPIA 1996, s 9, as amended by CJA 2003.
16 CPIA 1996, s 15.
17 29 November 2000 – now see the Attorney General's Revised Guidelines on Disclosure (issued April 2005), with Supplementary Attorney General's Guidelines on Disclosure of Digitally Stored Material (issued 14 July 2011).
18 Drafted by Mr Justice Fulford, Mr Justice Oppenshaw and representatives from the CPS, SFO and CEPO – operative and published 20 February 2006: see http://webarchive.nationalarchives.gov.uk/+/http:/www.justice.gov.uk/criminal/procrules_fin/contents/pd_protocol/pd_protocol_disclosure.htm.
19 Applicable to investigations commenced on or after the 4 April 2005.
20 Applicable to investigations started on or after 4 April 2005.
21 As per CPIA 1996, s 6A.

call witnesses should be provided, experts instructed need to be disclosed and adverse inferences are more enthusiastically encouraged.[22]

7.12 It is the clear intent of the Criminal Justice Act 2003, the Disclosure Protocol 2006 and the Attorney General's Guidelines on Disclosoure 2013, that defence statements should be sufficiently detailed to make the disclosure and case management process meaningful; a mere reiteration, in the defence statement, of a not guilty plea is a practice which is discouraged by statute, guidance and the judiciary.[23] The Disclosure Protocol makes the point that following initial disclosure by the prosecution the next critical step in the preparation for trial is the service of the defence statement, referring to it as a 'mandatory requirement'. The Disclosure Protocol fails to make any accommodation for a defendant who refuses for tactical reasons to serve a Defence Statement. The Disclosure Protocol stipulates that the defence statement must be served by the due date, whereupon the judge should then examine it and, should it not be fit for purpose, 'make a full investigation of the reasons for this failure to comply with the mandatory obligation of the accused'. A failure to serve a defence statement can be met with a judicial inquisition, with possible judicial warnings pursuant to CPIA 1996, s 6E(2).

7.13 Where the disclosure fault lies with the prosecution, judges are restricted to posing 'searching questions' and, 'having done this and explored the reasons for default', giving clear directions to ensure that the failings are addressed and remedied well in advance of the trial date. Unfortunately, whilst the ultimate sanction for a recalcitrant defendant is the drawing of an inference under CPIA 1996, s 11, it is difficult to see what the court can do to a prosecutor without exercising a disciplinary function. Exclusion of evidence, for example, would not ordinarily seem appropriate absent the demonstration of some otherwise incurable prejudice linked to disclosure failings.

7.14 The Disclosure Protocol acknowledges that 'it is vital to a fair trial that the prosecution are mindful of their continuing duty of disclosure', but then goes on to suggest that the defence be required to specify items in which they are interested and why, before embarking upon an application pursuant to s 8. This is contingent upon the disclosure schedule being complete and reliable, and the Disclosure Protocol then encourages the prosecution and ultimately the court to reject requests which do not relate to a matter raised in a defence statement. The Disclosure Protocol also recognises the need for

---

22 However, in *R v Rochford (Gavin)* [2010] EWCA Crim 1928, a judicial attempt to punish a failure to serve a Defence Statement as a contempt found little favour with the Court of Appeal on the basis that the sanctions for non-compliance were explicit in the statute, and it was not open to the court to add its own extra-statutory punishment.

23 See *R v Patrick Bryant* [2005] EWCA Crim 2079.

7.15 *Disclosure*

the prosecution to assign sufficient resources to disclosure questions, stating that the larger and more complex the case, the more important it is for the prosecution to fulfil their disclosure responsibilities and assign sufficient prosecution resources to the task.[24]

7.15 The Disclosure Protocol concludes by emphasising the duty of every judge to actively manage disclosure issues in every case. 'The judge must seize the initiative and drive the case along towards an efficient effective and timely resolution having regard to the overriding objective of the Criminal Procedure Rules (Part 1)'.[25]

E-DISCLOSURE

7.16 In July 2011, the Attorney General issued Supplementary Attorney-General's Guidelines[26] on digitally stored material[27] to assist prosecutors, investigators and defence practitioners in the conduct of e-disclosure. The detailed guidance was felt necessary as the number of cases involving digitally stored material and the scale of the digital material has increased in recent years. The 2011 Guidelines are not detailed operational guidelines but set out a common approach to disclosure of digitally stored material; the Attorney-General's Guidelines on Disclosure 2013 specifically preserved the 2011 Guidelines by annexing them in full to the 2013 Guidelines and make reference to digital material.[28]

7.17 Paragraph 27 of the 2011 Guidelines explains that the disclosure officer's obligation to inspect retained material may be fulfilled in relation to digitally stored material by using search terms or dip sampling methods, so long as the material is described on the schedules as clearly as possible and the manner and extent of the inspection is recorded along with the justification for adopting that approach.

---

24 Disclosure Protocol 2006, para 30.
25 The Protocol, para 63 at p 20.
26 The Guidelines apply to all searches whether under PACE 1984, s 2(4) of the Criminal Justice Act 1987, the Criminal Procedure and Investigations Act 1996, or the Criminal Justice and Police Act 2001 (CJPA 2001).
27 The Guidelines apply to all material which is (a) created natively such as e-mails, office files, system files, digital photographs, audio, and (b) digitised from an analogue form such as faxed and scanned documents and photographs. Such material being stored on (a) optical media (eg CD, DVD, Blu-ray) (b) solid state media (eg removable memory cards, solid state music players or mobile devices) or (c) magnetic media (eg disk drives and back up tapes).
28 See the 2013 Guidelines, para 48.

E-disclosure **7.19**

7.18 The 2011 Guidelines[29] in line with existing best practice recognises:

'(i) Investigating and prosecuting agencies, especially in large and complex cases, will apply their respective case management and disclosure strategies and policies and be transparent with the defence and the courts about how the prosecution has approached complying with its disclosure obligations in the context of the individual case; and,

(ii) The defence will be expected to play their part in defining the real issues in the case. In this context, the defence will be invited to participate in defining the scope of the reasonable searches that may be made of digitally stored material by the investigator to identify material that might reasonably be expected to undermine the prosecution case or assist the defence.'

7.19 The Guidelines highlight the active role that the defence team is expected to play in identifying relevant trial issues and assisting in case management by defining relevant search terms for electronic disclosure searches of unused material to identify material that might reasonably be expected to undermine the prosecution case or assist the defence case. The general principles[30] to be followed by investigators in handling and examining digital material are:

'(i) No action taken by investigators or their agents should change data held on a computer or storage media which may subsequently be relied upon in court;

(ii) In circumstances where a person finds it necessary to access original data held on computer or storage media, that person must be competent to do so and be able to give evidence explaining the relevance and implications of their actions;

(iii) An audit trail or other record of all processes applied to computer-based electronic evidence should be created and preserved. An independent third party should be able to examine those processes; and,

(iv) The person in charge of the investigation has overall responsibility for ensuring that the law and these principles are followed.'

---

29 The 2011 Guidelines, para 3.
30 See para 8 of the 2011 Guidelines, based on Good Practice Guide for Computer Based Electronic Evidence (Version 0.1.4) published by the Association of Chief Police Officers.

7.20 *Disclosure*

7.20 The Guidelines[31] consider the practicalities of:

- viewing, copying and seizing digital evidence both at the location of a search and elsewhere (such as cloud computing hosted by a third party)
- the effect seizure of such material (including computers) may have on an individual and business
- imaging specific folders, files or categories of data without seizing the hard drive or other media; and
- where it is not feasible to obtain an image of digital material, the likely timescale for returning seized items.

7.21 Digital material must not be seized if an investigator has reasonable grounds for believing it is subject to legal professional privilege, other than where ss 50 or 51 of the Criminal Justice and Police Act 2001 (CJPA 2001) apply.[32] If such material is seized it must be isolated from other seized material and any other investigation material in the possession of the investigating authority. The material must be examined as soon as reasonably practicable to determine which elements may be retained and which should be returned.[33] Retention of material is limited to evidence and relevant material (as defined in the Code of Practice issued under the CPIA 1996). Where either evidence or relevant material cannot be separated (without prejudging the investigation or proceedings) from non-relevant material, that material can also be retained. However, inextricably linked (non-relevant) material must not be examined, imaged, copied or used for any purpose other than for providing the source of or the integrity of the linked material.[34]

7.22 There are four categories of material that may be retained:[35]

(1) evidence or potential evidence in the case;

(2) inextricably linked non-relevant material;

(3) scheduled unused material; and

(4) non-relevant material that is inextricably linked to relevant unused material.

7.23 The balance of any digital material should be returned in accordance with ss 53–55 of CJPA 2001.[36]

---

31 See paras 12, 14, 17 and 18 of the 2011 Guidelines.
32 See para 15 and paras 28–35 inclusive of the 2011 Guidelines for specific guidance on legal professional privilege.
33 2011 Guidelines, para 22.
34 Ibid, para 25.
35 Ibid, para 26.
36 See para 27 of the 2011 Guidelines.

7.24 Specific guidance in relation to legal professional privilege is contained in paras 28–35 inclusive of the 2011 Guidelines.

7.25 To sum up:

- The CJPA 2001 must be complied with.
- Potential LPP material must be separated from other material usually by 'bagging up'.
- Examination of such material may be undertaken by a person independent of the investigation, to determine whether material may attract LPP.
- Where material has been identified as potentially containing LPP it must be reviewed by an independent lawyer. No member of the investigative or prosecution team involved in either the current investigation or, if the LPP material relates to other criminal proceedings, in those proceedings should have sight of or access to the LPP material.
- If the material is voluminous, search terms or other filters may have to be used to identify the LPP material. If so this will also have to be done by someone independent and not connected with the investigation.

ENCRYPTION

7.26 Part III of the Regulation of Investigatory Powers Act 2000 (RIPA 2000) and the Investigation of Protected Electronic Information Code of Practice govern encryption.[37] RIPA 2000 enables specified law enforcement agencies to compel individuals or companies to provide passwords or encryption keys for the purpose of rendering protected material readable. Failure to comply with RIPA Pt III orders is a criminal offence. The Code of Practice provides guidance when exercising powers under RIPA 2000, to require disclosure of protected electronic data in an intelligible form or to acquire the means by which protected electronic data may be accessed or put in an intelligible form.

SIFTING/EXAMINATION, KEEPING OF RECORDS AND SCHEDULING

7.27 When examining digital material, investigators and prosecutors have to comply with the PACE Code of Practice and pursue all reasonable lines of enquiry including those that point away from the suspect. However, the context of the case has to be considered and:

---

37 See further the CPS's Guidance RIPA Part III.

7.28 *Disclosure*

'It is not the duty of the prosecution to comb through all the material – eg every word or byte of computer material – in its possession on the lookout for anything which might conceivably or speculatively assist the defence'[38]

A sift by an investigator/disclosure officer manually assessing the content of the computer or other digital material from its directory and determining which files are relevant may be appropriate.[39]

7.28 Where there is an enormous volume of material it is perfectly proper[40] for the investigator/disclosure officer to search it by sample, key words, or other appropriate search tools or analytical techniques to locate relevant passages, phrases and identifiers.

7.29 Where search tools are used by the prosecution to examine digital material, it will usually be appropriate to provide the accused and the defence lawyers with a copy of reasonable search terms used, or to be used, and invite them to suggest any further reasonable search terms to ensure that reasonable and proportionate searches can be carried out.[41]

7.30 As there is a continuing duty to review disclosure, the sampling and searches may take place on a number of different occasions – possibly coinciding with different steps in the disclosure procedure:

- when further evidence or unused material is obtained;
- when a defence statement is served and/or amended;
- when a s 8 CPIA defence disclosure request is made; or
- when the defence reasonably request a further sampling or search.[42]

7.31 A record or log must be made of:

- all digital material seized or imaged and subsequently retained as relevant to the investigation;
- any strategy adopted for considering the e-material (including why certain categories have been searched for);
- details of the person who has carried out the process;
- the date and time it was carried out; and
- a record of the terms of the searches or processing that has been carried out.[43]

---

38 See para 41 of the Attorney General's Guidelines on Disclosure: Supplementary Guidelines on Digitally Stored Material (2011).
39 As per para 42.
40 As per para 43.
41 As per para 44.
42 See para 45.
43 See paras 46–48.

7.32 The material and product of the e-disclosure must be scheduled in accordance with PACE principles and the 1996 PACE Code of Practice.[44] In some enquiries it may not be practicable to list each item of material separately. If so, these may be listed in a block and described by quantity and generic title. Even if the material is listed in a block, the search terms used and any items of material which might satisfy the disclosure test are listed and described separately. In practical terms this will mean, where appropriate, cross-referencing the schedules to the disclosure management document. The remainder of any computer hard drive/media containing material which is not responsive to search terms or other analytical technique or not identified by any 'hits', and material identified by 'hits' but not examined, is unused material and should be recorded (if appropriate by a generic description) and retained.

DISCLOSURE IN PRACTICE

7.33 For some years after the implementation of the CPIA there has been amongst prosecutors at all levels an abrogation of their CPIA disclosure responsibility. This took a number of forms:

(1) The disclosure of what the investigators had, or claimed to have, by way of unused material, was largely rubber stamped on schedules with 'not disclosable'. Often the supervising lawyer had not inspected the material, had little or no understanding of the case as a whole and took no further part in the trial.

(2) A schedule with a blanket invitation to inspect was provided. This had two perceived advantages for the prosecution: first, the prosecution need not further concern themselves with what was, or was not, relevant or material, and secondly, the defence could not complain if something subsequently came to light as they had been given 'the keys to the warehouse'.

(3) the prosecution failure to take responsibility for the proper application of the materiality test themselves, but rather – in sensitive areas under the guise of public interest immunity – to seek judicial sanction for the withholding of information, which can hardly be said to be relevant at all.

7.34 The Disclosure Protocol[45] aimed to tackle such problems, by emphasising that the prosecution, defence and judges should scrupulously

---

44 See paras 50–53.
45 See paras 4 and 5 at p 2 of the 2006 Protocol. A new judicial disclosure protocol and a new AG's disclosure guidance are currently being drafted in response to the recommendations of Lord Justice Gross's review of disclosure in criminal proceedings of September 2011.

7.35 *Disclosure*

apply the CPIA principles, a point made by the Court of Appeal in *R v K (Note)*.[46] This point was emphasised in the Heavy Fraud Protocol 2005:

> 'The Prosecution should only disclose those documents which are relevant (ie likely to assist the defence or undermine the prosecution) … it is almost always undesirable to give the "warehouse key" to the defence'.

CPIA compliant disclosure is the approach to be adopted.

7.35 A CPIA compliant approach is important, as it will avoid any abrogation by the prosecution of their disclosure responsibility, and defence solicitors spending a disproportionate amount of time and resources on a 'morass' of documents. Moreover, judges are encouraged, by the Heavy Fraud Protocol 2005, to actively case manage disclosure, including setting out at the outset of proceedings a timetable for dealing with disclosure issues, notably defence disclosure requests which are detailed (as opposed to a general 'shopping list') in nature and which should be specific, manageable and realistic.

7.36 However, there remain inherent difficulties and problems with the amended CPIA disclosure regime. First, the prosecution are still required to make a value judgment in relation to every item which appears on the unused material schedules, to determine whether it might assist the defence case or undermine the prosecution case; this against a background of defence statements which are often brief and sometimes lacking in detail. Secondly, in large cases the unused material schedules contain thousands of items, with large quantities of documents, measured not in terms of lever arch files but tonnage, which are vaguely described. Thirdly, the disclosure process can be complicated further in cases in which investigations are inter-linked with other operations and multi-agency in nature. Criminals often operate within a spider's web of inter-related individuals and companies, involving cross-border criminality. Fourthly, before trial it is common for the defence to seek from the prosecution disclosure of particular categories of documents. Well aware of their CPIA obligations, the prosecution seek from the defence justification and a reason for the disclosure requested. This process sometimes becomes protracted and attritional in nature. The prosecution may regard the defence disclosure requests as a 'fishing' expedition with no sensible justification, which would stand up to strict CPIA scrutiny. On the other hand the defence may regard the prosecution stance as obstructive and unhelpful, the process culminating in voluminous correspondence.

7.37 The disclosure problems commonly arising in criminal proceedings have been the subject of a number of judicial reports, with the Butterfield Report[47] identifying a number of problems:

---

46 [2006] 2 All ER LR 552 (CA), as applied in *R v L* [2007] EWCA Crim 764.
47 See paras 12.28 to 12.29 at pp 256 to 259.

Effective disclosure **7.38**

(1) Judges are often faced with a defence disclosure request, under CPIA 1996, s 8, from the non-sensitive unused material schedule, which the prosecution claim is not CPIA disclosable. The judge then has to embark upon an enquiry which often involves a lengthy and sometimes complex defence explanation as to why the documents requested are disclosable.

(2) The judge before whom the disclosure request is made may:

(a) not be the allocated trial judge;

(b) have only a basic understanding of the facts of the case; and

(c) hear the application amongst many other directions hearing in a busy court list;

(3) In large complex cases, a strict compliance with the CPIA disclosure regime will involve the use of many resources in terms of personnel and hours spent considering disclosure issues.

(4) Creeping disclosure can be a problem as the prosecution are under a mandatory duty to continually review disclosure throughout criminal proceedings.

(5) The prosecution's non-sensitive unused material schedule needs to accurately describe and give sufficient detail to allow those (both prosecution and defence) who read it, to assess the potential evidential relevance and importance of the material. Descriptions of documents must be detailed, clear and accurate. The prosecution do not, save to the extent that they are informed by the defence statement, have sufficient information to know what may assist the defence case. The defence are in the best position to decide what documents are relevant to their case, the areas where there is no challenge to the prosecution case and areas where the defendant is not involved. If the unused material schedule is reliable in terms of accurate and sufficient detail, the defence should be able to disregard most of the unused material.

EFFECTIVE DISCLOSURE

7.38 There are two essentials in effecting proper statutory disclosure. First, all prosecution material (as per s 3(2) of the CPIA 1996) must be recorded, retained and indexed in such a way that it is accessible to the prosecution with an effective document handling system, which is properly operated. Secondly, the material set out on the prosecution non-sensitive disclosure schedule must be disclosed to the defence if it falls within the CPIA 1996. Increasingly, documents recovered in the course of fraud investigations are scanned and available for dissemination on a compact disc or transferred electronically by PDF. Such a process avoids time-consuming and wasteful photocopying and

7.39 *Disclosure*

provides a useful facility to search a database of documentation quickly and efficiently.

7.39 To comply with their continuing duty of disclosure, the prosecution will need clear policies and systems for collating and analysing unused material. It is in this area that well focused defence requests are most likely to provide either the necessary disclosure or a demonstrable audit trail from which judicial inferences adverse to the prosecution can be drawn. Having said that, the Disclosure Protocol makes it clear that 'shopping list' requests for disclosure are 'wholly improper'.

7.40 There must be a rigorous application of CPIA principles at all levels within the criminal justice system, by all participants, with the consequence that defendants will be required to justify requests for additional material by reference to their stated Defence Statement. However, the disclosure balance is often difficult to strike and an overly restrictive view of the stated defence may cause problems, as the House of Lords recognised in *R v H and C*:[48]

> 'If material does not weaken the prosecution case or strengthen that of the defendant, there is no requirement to disclose it. For this purpose the parties' respective cases should not be restrictively analysed. But they must be carefully analysed, to ascertain the specific facts the prosecution seek to establish and the specific grounds on which the charges are resisted. The trial process is not well served if the defence are permitted to make general and unspecified allegations and then seek far-reaching disclosure in the hope that material may turn up to make them good. Neutral material or material damaging to the defendant need not be disclosed and should not be brought to the attention of the court.'

If disclosure is deemed appropriate, it is for the prosecutor to decide the form in which disclosure is made. Disclosure need not be in the same form as that in which the information was recorded. Guidance on case management issues relating to this point is given by Rose LJ in *R v CPS (Interlocutory application under sections 35/36 CPIA)*.[49]

ATTORNEY GENERAL'S GUIDELINES ON DISCLOSURE 2013[50]

7.41 Mindful of disclosure problems, revised Attorney General's Guidelines on Disclosure of Unused Material were published in December 2013 and became operative immediately. The 2013 Guidelines:

---

48 [2004] 2 AC 134, [2004] 2 Cr App R 10 per Lord Bingham at para 35.
49 [2005] EWCA Crim 2342.
50 See www.gov.uk/government/publications/attorney-generals-guidelines-on-disclosure-2013.

Attorney General's Guidelines on Disclosure 2013 **7.43**

'are intended to clarify the procedures to be followed and to encourage the active participation of all parties ... There are important roles for the prosecution, the defence and the court in ensuring that disclosure is conducted properly, including on the part of the investigating, case progression and disclosure officers, as well as the lawyers and advocates'[51]

It is envisaged by the 2013 Guidelines that the disclosure process is to be led by the Prosecution, which in turn triggers comprehensive Defence engagement, supervised and overseen by robust Judicial case management.

7.42 The 2013 Guidelines make this clear by emphasising:

- the importance of prosecution-led disclosure and the need to apply the CPIA regime in a 'thinking manner', not a box-ticking exercise,[52] but tailored, where appropriate, to the type of investigation or prosecution in question including digital material and large and complex cases;[53]

- that the CPIA requires a timely dialogue between the prosecution,[54] defence and the court to enable the prosecution properly to identify disclosable material;[55] and

- that a fair trial should not (i) require consideration of irrelevant material, (ii) involve spurious applications or arguments which serve to divert the trial process from examining the real issues before the court, (iii) be overburdened by disclosed material, (iv) lead to unjustifiable delays, and (v) waste resources.[56]

7.43 The general principles and practices of disclosure were adopted as:

(a) Disclosure refers to providing the defence with copies of or access to any prosecution material which might reasonably be considered capable of undermining the case for the prosecution against the accused or assisting the case for the accused, and which has not previously been disclosed.[57]

(b) In undertaking task (a), prosecutors will only be expected to anticipate such material in light of the information available at the time of the

---

51 See the Foreword (at p 3) by the Attorney General Dominic Grieve QC and the Lord Chief Justice Lord Thomas.
52 See para 10 of the 2013 Guidelines and *R v Olu, Wilson and Brooks* [2010] EWCA Crim 2975 at para 42.
53 See paras 48 and 50–51 of the 2013 Guidelines.
54 Which includes internal communications within the prosecution team of lawyers and investigating/disclosure officers as per para 11 of the 2013 Guidelines, keeping a full log of disclosure decisions with reasons kept on file.
55 See para 1 of the 2013 Guidelines.
56 See paras 2–3 of the 2013 Guidelines.
57 See para 4 of the 2013 Guidelines.

7.43 *Disclosure*

          disclosure decision and may take into account information revealed during questioning.[58]

(c)   In deciding whether material satisfies the disclosure, consideration should be given to (i) the use that might be made of it in cross-examination, (ii) its capacity to support submissions that could lead to exclusion of evidence, a stay of proceedings and ECHR breaches being proved, (iii) its capacity to explain, in full or part, the accused's action, (iv) the capacity to have bearing on scientific or medical evidence in the case, including material relating to the accused's mental or physical health, intellectual capacity or ill-treatment in custody.[59]

(d)   Disclosure must not be an open-ended trawl of unused material. The defence should direct the prosecution to material to ensure prosecutors make informed determinations about disclosure of unused material and state in a defence statement why the disclosure test is satisfied.[60]

(e)   The prosecution reviewing lawyer is central to ensuring all members of the prosecution team are aware of, and carry out, their disclosure duties.[61]

(f)   Investigators and disclosure officers must be fair and objective and work together with prosecutors to ensure that disclosure obligations are met in particular to retain and record relevant material, to review it and to reveal it to the prosecutor.[62]

(g)   Unused material schedules must be completed in a form (i) which not only reveals sufficient information to the prosecutor, but is (ii) transparent and thoughtful to command the confidence of the defence and the court ,and (iii) contains clear and accurate descriptions with sufficient detail to enable the prosecutor to make an informed disclosure decision.[63]

(h)   The duty of disclosure is a continuing one, which should be kept under review, including consideration of the defence statement which may (i) prompt/highlight other reasonable lines of enquiry, (ii) court directions for an adequate Defence Statement (iii) lead to cross-examination, prosecutor's comment and/or inferences at trial.[64]

(i)   Prosecution advocates must place themselves in a fully informed position to enable them to make decisions on disclosure and ensure

---

58   See para 5 of the 2013 Guidelines.
59   See paras 6 and 8 of the 2013 Guidelines.
60   See para 9 of the 2013 Guidelines.
61   See para 12 of the 2013 Guidelines.
62   See paras 15 and 17–22 of the 2013 Guidelines.
63   See para 23 of the 2013 Guidelines.
64   See paras 28–33 of the 2013 Guidelines.

proper disclosure from the moment of receiving instructions until the conclusion of the trial, reviewing disclosure throughout.[65]

(j) Defence engagement must be early and meaningful, with defence statements integral to focusing all parties attention on the relevant issues to identify exculpatory unused material and defence requests for disclosure to be relevant and of assistance in identifying material which satisfies the disclosure test.[66]

(k) Disclosure management documents should be used by the prosecution in large and complex cases, which should be served on the defence and court at an early stage.[67]

THIRD PARTY DISCLOSURE

7.44 One particular problem area involves material in the possession of third parties,[68] which causes practical and legal difficulties because the Prosecution are unaware and sometimes unable to access the same and there is no specific procedure for third party material disclosure in criminal proceedings, although the witness summons procedure under s 2 of the Criminal Procedure (Attendance of Witnesses) Act 1965 or s 97 of the Magistrates Court Act 1980 is often used by the defence to effect such disclosure from third party sources.

7.45 The CPIA Code and the Attorney General's Guidelines 2013[69] makes clear the obligation on the prosecution to pursue all reasonable lines of enquiry, which covers material held by third parties within and beyond the UK. If as a result of the duty to pursue all reasonable lines of enquiry, the investigator or prosecutor obtains or receives the material from the third party, then it must be dealt with in accordance with CPIA 1996, ie the prosecutor must disclose material if it meets the disclosure tests, subject to any public interest immunity claim. The person who has an interest in the material (the third party) may make representations to the court concerning public interest immunity (see s 16 of the CPIA 1996).

7.46 Material not in the possession of an investigator or prosecutor falls outside the CPIA 1996. In such cases the Attorney General Guidelines 2013[70]

---

65 See paras 35–37 of the 2013 Guidelines. In addition para 72 which states that: 'Where, after the conclusion of the proceedings, material comes to light, that might cast doubt upon the safety of the conviction, the prosecutor must consider disclosure of such material'.
66 See paras 39–42 of the 2013 Guidelines.
67 See para 51 of the 2013 Guidelines.
68 Such as local authorities, social services departments, hospitals, doctors, schools, businesses, professional bodies, providers of forensic services.
69 See paras 17, 20 , 31, 51(d)(v) and 59 of the 2013 Guidelines.
70 See paras 53–58 of the 2013 Guidelines.

7.47 *Disclosure*

prescribes the approach to be taken to disclosure of material held by third parties and other Government departments.

7.47 Any defence application for third party disclosure must identify what documents are sought and why they are said to be material evidence. In reply the third party may contest disclosure, asserting confidentiality or the right to privacy under Art 8 ECHR as grounds for refusing disclosure. For third party disclosure to take place, the material sought must be admissible evidence in criminal proceedings (see *R v Reading JJ, ex p Berkshire County Council*,[71] *R v Derby Magistrates'Court, ex p B*,[72] and *R v Alibhai*.)[73]

7.48 The Court of Appeal considered the issue of third party disclosure in *R v Alibhai*. The appellant was convicted of a conspiracy involving dishonest dealing in counterfeit Microsoft products. On appeal, it was argued that the convictions were unsafe in the light of significant difficulties with, and delays in securing disclosure of material held by third parties (principally Microsoft, and the FBI and an FBI participating informant who was the principal prosecution witness). The appeals were dismissed.

7.49 Where a complaint is made of non-disclosure of documents, it is not always necessary for an appellant to demonstrate that the disclosure of the material would have affected the outcome of the proceedings (it will often be difficult to assess, even with hindsight, the effect of a failure to disclose on the outcome: see *R v Ward*[74]).

7.50 In many cases, it would suffice for an appellant to show a prosecutor disclosure failure and suggest that it is reasonable to suppose such failure might have affected the outcome of the trial.

7.51 The Court of Appeal will not regard a conviction as unsafe unless the non-disclosure is significant 'in regard to any real issue' (see *R v Maguire*).[75] There may be cases in which the prosecution conduct might be so disgraceful as to warrant a stay in proceedings as an abuse of process.

7.52 In *Alibhai*, it could not be fairly said that the prosecution themselves behaved dishonorably or abused their power. The real problem was with potentially relevant documents and information in the hands of the third parties.

7.53 Before it can be said that there has been a breach of disclosure obligation, it must be shown that there was a suspicion that the third parties,

---

71 [1996] 1 Cr App R 239.
72 [1996] AC 487.
73 [2004] EWCA Crim 681.
74 (1993) 96 Cr App R 1 at p 22.
75 (1992) 94 Cr App R 133 at p 148. As applied in *Berry (Linton) v The Queen* [1992] 2 AC 364.

not only had potentially relevant material but that the material was not neutral or damaging to the defendants but damaging to the prosecution or of assistance to the defendant. Even if there is a necessary suspicion, the prosecutor is not under an absolute obligation to secure the disclosure of the material or information. There is a 'margin of consideration' as to what steps he regards as appropriate to the particular case.

OVERSEAS THIRD PARTY DISCLOSURE

7.54 The obligation on the investigator and prosecutor under the CPIA Code and the Attorney General's Guidelines 2013[76] to pursue all reasonable lines of enquiry also applies to material held overseas. Where it appears that there is relevant material, the prosecution must take reasonable steps to obtain it, either informally or making use of the powers contained in the Crime (International Co-operation) Act 2003 and any EU and international conventions. See the CPS Guidance Obtaining Evidence and Information from Abroad,[77] which considers mutual legal assistance and letters of request.

7.55 There may be cases where a foreign state or a foreign court refuses to make the material available to the investigator or prosecutor. There may be other cases where the foreign state, though willing to show the material to investigators, will not allow the material to be copied or otherwise made available and the courts of the foreign state will not order its provision.[78] It is for these reasons that there is no absolute duty on the prosecutor to disclose relevant material held overseas by entities not subject to the English and Welsh jurisdiction.[79]

7.56 The obligation on the investigator and prosecutor under the CPIA 1996 is to take reasonable steps. Where investigators are allowed to examine files of a foreign state but are not allowed to take copies or notes or list the documents held, there is no breach by the prosecution in its duty of disclosure by reason of its failure to obtain such material, provided reasonable steps have been taken to try and obtain the material. Whether the prosecution has complied with its duty is for the court to judge in each case allowing the prosecution a margin of consideration.[80]

7.57 In these circumstances it is important that the position is clearly set out in writing so that the court and the defence know what the position is.

---

76 See para 59 of the 2013 Guidelines.
77 See para 60 of the 2013 Guidelines and www.cps.gov.uk/legal/l_to_o/obtaining_evidence_and_information_from_abroad.
78 See para 61 of the 2013 Guidelines.
79 See para 62 of the 2013 Guidelines.
80 See para 63 of the 2013 Guidelines.

7.58 *Disclosure*

Investigators and prosecutors must record and explain the situation and set out, insofar as they are permitted by the foreign state, such information as they can and the steps they have taken.[81]

7.58 The Court of Appeal in *R v Flook*,[82] considered the extent of the prosecution's duty to disclose material held by individuals, companies and governments in foreign countries. The CPIA makes no specific provision for material held or inspected overseas. However, para 3.5 of the CPIA Code provides that 'the investigator should pursue all reasonable lines of enquiry, whether these point towards or away from the suspect', including enquiry in the European Union and beyond. The Court of Appeal noted that there was no absolute obligation on the prosecution to disclose relevant material held overseas outside of the European Union by entities not subject to the jurisdiction of the English courts. However, the prosecution must still record in writing and explain the position, disclose such information, as the foreign state permits, and set out for the court, the steps they had taken to obtain disclosure.

PUBLIC INTEREST IMMUNITY

7.59 Closely linked to the issue of disclosure is the topic of public interest immunity (PII). The PII doctrine as applicable to criminal proceedings is summarised by the House of Lords in *R v H and C*[83] in the following terms:

> 'Circumstances may arise in which material held by the prosecution and tending to undermine the prosecution or assist the defence cannot be disclosed to the defence, fully or even at all, without the risk of serious prejudice to an important public interest. The public interest most regularly engaged is that in the effective investigation and prosecution of serious crime, which may involve resort to informers and undercover agents, or the use of scientific or operational techniques (such as surveillance) which cannot be disclosed without exposing individuals to the risk of personal injury or jeopardising the success of future operations. In such circumstances some derogation from the golden rule of full disclosure may be justified but such derogation must always be the minimum derogation necessary to protect the public interest in question and must never imperil the overall fairness of the trial.'[84]

7.60 The proper approach to PII is provided in *R v H and C* at para 36, listing a series of questions:

---

81 See para 64 of the 2013 Guidelines.
82 [2010] Crim LR 148.
83 [2004] 2 AC 134.
84 *R v H and C* [2004] 2 AC 134 at [18], [2004] UKHL 3. This approach has been followed in a number of cases including *R v Lewis* [2005] Crim 859 and *Chemists (A Firm) v Revenue and Customs Commissioners* [2009] UKFTT 66 (TC).

Public interest immunity **7.61**

'(1) What is the material which the prosecution seek to withhold?

(2) Is the material such as may weaken the prosecution case or strengthen that of the defence? If No, disclosure should not be ordered. If Yes, full disclosure should (subject to (3), (4) and (5) below) be ordered.

(3) Is there a real risk of serious prejudice to an important public interest (and, if so, what) if full disclosure of the material is ordered? If No, full disclosure should be ordered.

(4) If the answer to (2) and (3) is Yes, can the defendant's interest be protected without disclosure or at least partial disclosure ? This question requires consideration of the material to be withheld, the facts and defence case, whether the prosecution should formally admit what the defence seek to establish, possibly in an edited or anonymised form. In appropriate cases the appointment of special counsel may be necessary to ensure a correct answer to (2) and (3) above.

(5) Do the measures proposed in answer to (4) represent the minimum derogation necessary to protect the public interest in question? If No, the court should order such greater disclosure as will represent the minimum derogation from the golden rule of full disclosure.

(6) If limited disclosure is ordered pursuant to (4) and (5) may the effect be to render the trial process unfair to the defendant? If yes, then fuller disclosure should be ordered even if this leads or may lead the prosecution to discontinue the proceedings so as to avoid having to make disclosure.

(7) If the answer to (6) when first given is No, does that remain the correct answer as the trial unfolds, evidence is adduced and the defence advanced?

It is important that the answer to (6) should not be treated as a final, once-and-for-all, answer but as a provisional answer which the court must keep under review.'

7.61 The Attorney General's Guidelines on Disclosure 2013 consider prosecution applications for non-disclosure in the public interest.[85] Before making such an application, prosecutors should aim to disclose as much of the material as they properly can, possibly in a redacted, edited or summary form.[86] The principles set out in *R v H and C* should be applied rigorously by the prosecutor and then by the court considering the material in the absence of the defendant to comply with ECHR, Art 6.[87] If prosecutors conclude that a

---

85 See paras 65–69 of the 2013 Guidelines.
86 See para 65 of the 2013 Guidelines.
87 See para 68 of the 2013 Guidelines.

7.62 *Disclosure*

fair trial cannot take place because material which satisfies the disclosure test cannot be disclosed, and this cannot be remedied by other means they should not continue with the case.[88]

7.62 When considering a prosecution application to withhold material, subject to PII, judges face a difficult balancing exercise between the protecting of sensitive material and the administration of justice in ensuring the defendant's right to a fair trial. The assertion by the prosecution of PII does not automatically lead to material being withheld. Formal procedures should be followed by the prosecution under Pt 22 of the Criminal Procedure Rules 2013 (SI 2013/1554), including:

- informing the court of compliance with the initial duty to disclose (r 22.2);
- providing the judge with a written description of the material upon which PII attaches (r 22.3(3));
- serving a written application upon anyone who is directly affected by the disclosure.

7.63 Further, the general rule is that the defence will have notice of the PII application (but not necessarily the category of material relied upon), and an opportunity to make representations before the prosecution make their ex parte oral representations (see *R v Davis, Johnson and Rowe*,[89] *Jasper v UK*,[90] *Fitt v UK*,[91] *PG v UK*[92] and *R v H*[93]).

7.64 Assistance is also given by the CPIA 1996 Code of Practice, which states that material of a sensitive nature, disclosure of which would, in the prosecution's view, give rise to a real risk of serious prejudice to the public interest, must be listed on a sensitive material schedule. In exceptional circumstances such material should be revealed to the prosecutor separately. Paragraph 6.12 of the CPIA Code lists 13 examples of sensitive material, covering a range of diverse topics and subjects: national security, domestic and foreign intelligence and security agencies, confidential, informants and undercover officers, surveillance premises, investigative techniques including covert surveillance methods, crime prevention, search warrants, identification parades, regulatory/supervisory financial investigations, social services investigations, private life of a witness. The list is not exhaustive

---

88 See para 69 of the 2013 Guidelines.
89 (1993) 97 Cr App R 110 at 114.
90 (2000) 30 EHRR 441.
91 (2000) 30 EHRR 480.
92 (2008) 46 EHRR 51.
93 [2004] 2 AC 134.

and the categories of PII are not closed, altering over time according to social conditions and legislation.[94]

7.65 Fraud prosecutions of an intelligence-led nature based on informant trade sources may well result in an informant-based PII application by the prosecution. In protecting informant sources, prosecution policy is neither to confirm nor deny the existence of an informant, a practice approved by the Court of Appeal in *R v Rossouw*.[95]

7.66 Where a participating informant is involved in the crime and/or called as a prosecution witness, the judge in deciding any disclosure issue has to take a robust approach and order disclosure if the defence being advanced (often 'set-up') justifies revelation of the informant background (see *R v Turner*,[96] *R v Patel*,[97] and *R v Early*[98]). Prosecution failures during PII applications can lead to cases being stayed as an abuse of process, a point highlighted in the judgment of Lord Justice Rose in *R v Early*:[99]

> '... in our judgment, if, in the course of a public interest immunity hearing or an abuse argument, whether on the voir dire or otherwise, prosecution witnesses lie in evidence to the judge, it is to be expected that, if the judges knows of this, or this Court of Appeal subsequently learns of it, an extremely serious view will be taken. It is likely that the prosecution case will be regarded as tainted beyond redemption, however strong the evidence against the defendant may otherwise be'.

7.67 Material generated by fraud related regulatory investigations may also attract a PII application. One such example arises from the Secretary of State's Companies Act 1985, s 431 power to appoint an inspector to investigate and report upon the affairs of a company if fraud, prejudice or mismanagement is alleged. Such an investigation has allied powers to order production of documents and evidence to the inspectors (as per CA 1985, s 434) and the inspector's report is admissible in any legal proceedings as expert opinion evidence (see CA 1985, s 441). The Secretary of State has a discretion under CA 1985, s 451A to disclose information obtained by inspectors to prosecuting authorities. Material generated by the inspector's investigation attracts PII (see *R v Cheltenham JJ ex p Secretary of State for Trade*[100]).

---

94 See *D v NSPCC* [1978] AC 171 at 230 and *R v Chief Constable of the West Midlands Police, ex p Wiley* [1995] 1 AC 274 at 290–291.
95 [2006] EWCA Crim 2980.
96 1995] 2 Cr App R 94.
97 [2002] Crim L R 304.
98 [2003] 1 Cr App R 19.
99 [2003] 1 Cr App R 19 at para 10.
100 [1977] 1 WLR 95.

7.68 *Disclosure*

7.68 Likewise, materials obtained by liquidators at voluntarily attended interviews during insolvency proceedings is subject to PII (see *Re Barlow Clowes Gilt Managers Ltd*,[101] and *R v Clowes*[102]).

SENTENCING MATERIAL DISCLOSURE

7.69 In all cases the prosecutor must disclose in the interests of justice any material which is relevant to sentence, including information which might mitigate the seriousness of the offence or which lays blame in part upon a co-accused or another person.[103]

---

101 [1992] Ch 208.
102 (1992) 95 Cr App R 440.
103 See para 71 of the 2013 Guidelines.

Chapter 8

Abuse of Process

INTRODUCTION

8.1 As part of a defendant's common law and ECHR right to a fair trial in fraud proceedings, they are entitled to a speedy trial, with proper disclosure of relevant material. In order to secure the right to a fair trial, defence lawyers have to consider and pursue the prosecution for full and timely disclosure and consider any State misconduct which may lead to unfairness. The criminal justice system has developed a number of judicial control mechanism safeguards and remedies to ensure a fair trial. This chapter aims to examine the use made of the abuse of process principle in fraud proceedings.

COMMON LAW DISCRETION

8.2 This common law power was recognised in *Connelly v DPP*,[1] where Lord Reid stated that the court had 'a residual discretion to prevent anything which savours of abuse of process',[2] and Lord Devlin stated that the courts have 'an inescapable duty to secure fair treatment for those who come or are brought before them'.[3] In more recent times, Lord Justice Neil, in *R v Beckford*,[4] stated that:

'the constitutional principle which underlies the jurisdiction to stay proceedings is that the courts have the power and the duty to protect the law by protecting its own purposes and functions'.

8.3 Since the implementation[5] of the Human Rights Act 1998 (HRA 1998),[6] direct regard should also be had to the European Convention for the Protection of Human Rights (ECHR) and the related Strasbourg jurisprudence.

---

1 [1964] AC 1254.
2 [1964] AC 1254 at 1296.
3 [1964] AC 1254 at 1354.
4 [1996] 1 Cr App R 94 at 100F.
5 2 October 2000.
6 Section 1(2) of HRA 1998 gives effect to Arts 2 to 12 and 14 of the ECHR. Schedule 1 to the HRA 1998 sets out the ECHR article rights.

8.4 *Abuse of Process*

Recognition of the importance of the European jurisprudence was highlighted in *R v Stratford Justices, ex p Imbert*.[7] Mr Justice Collins said that he was:

> 'prepared to accept that, since the question whether a prosecution should be stayed as an abuse of process arises because it is suggested that the accused cannot have a fair trial or that it would be unfair to try him, the court in deciding the issue can have regard to article 6 and to the jurisprudence on it.'[8]

DEFINITION

8.4 The most often cited definition of the abuse of process principle can be found in *R v Derby Crown Court ex p Brooks*,[9] where Lord Chief Justice Roger Ormrod stated:

> 'The power to stop a prosecution arises only when it is an abuse of the process of the court. It may be an abuse of process if either (a) the prosecution have manipulated or misused the process of the court so as to deprive the defendant of a protection provided by law or to take unfair advantage of a technicality, or (b) on the balance of probability the defendant has been, or will be, prejudiced in the preparation or conduct of his defence by delay on the part of the prosecution which is unjustifiable ... The ultimate objective of this discretionary power is to ensure that there should be a fair trial according to law, which involves fairness both to the defendant and the prosecution.'

8.5 Fairness is the defining principle, a point emphasised by Lord Clyde in *R v Martin*:[10]

> 'No single formulation will readily cover all cases, but there must be something so gravely wrong as to make it unconscionable that a trial should go forward, such as some fundamental disregard for basic human rights or some gross neglect of the elementary principles of fairness.'

8.6 In line with the above observations, proceedings are only stayed, in the words of Viscount Dilhorne in *DPP v Humphrys*,[11] in 'exceptional circumstances'. This approach has been consistently approved in recent cases such as *DPP v Alexander*,[12] where the court held that the doctrine of abuse of process was to be narrowly confined.

---

7 [1999] 2 Cr App R 276.
8 [1999] 2 Cr App R 276 at 281. See also *Edwards v UK* [1993] 15 EHRR 417 at 431.
9 [1985] 80 Cr App R 164, at pp 168–9.
10 [1998] AC 917, at pp 946–7.
11 [1977] AC 1.
12 [2011] WLR 653.

8.7 Basic issues of fairness, prejudice and the overall integrity of the criminal law process need to be considered.

THE TEST

8.8 When a court considers the exercise of its discretionary power to stay proceedings for an abuse, the test to be applied is that of fairness. Lord Justice Neill in *R v Beckford*,[13] observed that:

> 'The jurisdiction to stay can be exercised in many different circumstances. Nevertheless two main strands can be detected in the authorities:
>
> (a) cases where the court concludes that the defendant cannot receive a fair trial;
>
> (b) cases where the court concludes that it would be unfair for the defendant to be tried.'

In some cases the two categories may overlap. What is unfair and wrong will be for the court to determine on the individual facts of each case.

ABUSE OF PROCESS ISSUES

8.9 When an application is made by the defence for proceedings to be stayed, as an abuse of process, consideration should be given to the process by which the defendant was brought to court, including, inter alia,[14] the time delay involved, the disclosure and preservation of evidence, the rule of law, the methods used by state officials to investigate and prosecute the offence, any surrounding publicity and the ability of a defendant to participate in the proceedings.

Delay

8.10 The common law provides that a fair hearing must be timely: see *Connelly v DPP*.[15] The speedy trial right is also recognised in the ECHR, in broad terms, with Art 5(3) providing:

> 'Everyone arrested or detained...shall be brought promptly before a judge or other officer authorised by law to exercise judicial power and shall be entitled to trial within a reasonable time or to release pending trial.'

---

13 [1996] 1 Cr App R 94, at p 100G.
14 These factors are not exhaustive, a point recognised in *R v Martin (Alan)* [1998] 2 WLR 1 by Lord Lloyd who observed: 'the categories of abuse of process like the categories of negligence are never closed'.
15 [1964] AC 1254.

8.11 *Abuse of Process*

8.11 Article 6(1) states;

'In the determination of his civil rights and obligations or of any criminal charge against him, everyone is entitled to a fair and public hearing within a reasonable time by an independent and impartial tribunal.'

These provisions are designed to protect all parties from excessive procedural delay, so as to prevent a person charged from remaining 'too long in a state of uncertainty about his fate'[16] and 'underlines the importance of rendering justice without delays which might jeopardise its effectiveness and credibility',[17] bearing in mind that delay may result in the loss of exculpatory evidence or in a deterioration in the quality of evidence generally.[18]

8.12 The right is measured from date of charge, defined as the 'official notification given to an individual by the competent authority of an allegation that he committed a criminal offence' and not when the initial complaint is made or a preliminary investigation begun. The court in *Attorney General's Reference (No 2 of 2001)*[19] considered the Strasbourg *Eckle*[20] notification test: 'As a general rule, the relevant period will begin at the earliest time at which a person is officially alerted to the likelihood of criminal proceedings against him'.[21] Time will normally begin to run from the time of formal charge or service of a summons, and may start when an official indicates that a person will be reported with a view to a prosecution.[22] The burden is on the prosecution to explain and justify any excessive lapse of time.[23]

8.13 In the event of a breach of the art 6(1) reasonable time provision, a court is not compelled to stay proceedings.[24]

Common law prejudice

8.14 When considering common law delay, the decision in *Attorney-General's Reference (No 1 of 1990)*[25] cites a number of factors that need to be considered:

- the right of the prosecution to have serious allegations tried;
- the complexity of the proceedings;

---

16 *Stögmüller v Austria* (1979-80) 1 EHRR 155 at para 5 of the judgment.
17 *H v France* (1990) 12 EHRR 74, at para 58.
18 As per Lord Steyn in *Mills v HM Advocate* [2002] 3 WLR 1597.
19 [2004] 2 AC 72, [2004] 1 Cr App R 25.
20 *Eckle v Germany* (1983) 5 EHRR 1.
21 [2004] 1 Cr App R 25, at para 27.
22 *R v Gibbons* [1997] 2 NZLR 585.
23 *Dyer v Watson* [2002] UKPC D 1, [2004] 1 AC 379.
24 See *Attorney General's Reference (No 2 of 2001)* [2004] 1 Cr App R 25, *HM Advocate v R* [2004] 1 AC 462 and *Spiers v Ruddy* [2007] UKPC D2; [2008] 1 AC 873.
25 [1992] QB 630, [1992] 95 Cr App R 296.

- whether fault occurred and by whom;
- defendant delay;
- the defendant needs to show on a balance of probabilities that owing to the delay he will suffer serious prejudice to the extent that no fair trial can be held.

Common law factors

8.15 The factors considered by the courts in deciding whether a defendant's right to a fair trial had been infringed by delay are set out in Lord Templeman's judgment in *Bell v DPP of Jamaica*[26] and *Barker v Wingo*:[27]

- The length of delay – this is dependent upon the peculiar circumstances of the case. The delay that can be tolerated for an ordinary street crime is considerably less than that for a serious complex conspiracy charge.
- The justification put forward by the prosecution – a deliberate attempt to delay the trial in order to hamper the defence is to be weighed heavily against the prosecution. A more neutral reason such as negligence or overcrowded courts should be weighed less heavily but nevertheless should be considered since the ultimate responsibility for such circumstances rests with the state rather than the defendant. A valid reason such as a missing witness, should serve to justify the appropriate delay.
- The responsibility of the accused for asserting her/his rights.
- The prejudice to the accused, including the right to a speedy trial, which includes interests such as the avoidance of oppressive pre-trial incarceration, keeping anxiety and concern of the accused to a minimum and limiting the possibility of defence impairment (including loss of evidence and witness memory recall).

Delay issues

8.16 The issue of delay in criminal proceedings was considered by the House of Lords in the *Attorney General's Reference (No 2 of 2001)* [2003] UKHL 68, and stated a number of principles in relation to abuse of process applications:

- Delay per se is insufficient for a stay.
- What is required is delay plus consequential unfairness or serious prejudice to an accused, which could not be cured by exercise of a trial judge's discretion within the trial itself.

---

26 [1985] AC 937 at 951–952D–F.
27 (1972) 407 US 514.

8.17 *Abuse of Process*

- It will not be appropriate to stay the proceedings unless there can no longer be a fair trial or it would be unfair to try the defendant.
- It is the responsibility of the trial judge in a situation where unreasonable delay has been established to find a just and reasonable remedy. This can range from a public acknowledgement of the breach, action to expedite to the trial, directions to the jury or, in the case of a convicted defendant, reduction in the imposed sentence or penalty. Only in cases of serious prejudice leading to ineradicable unfairness or prosecution bad faith should a stay be imposed.
- The start point for the reasonable time period is the earliest time at which a person is officially alerted to the likelihood of criminal proceedings against him (possibly from date of arrest or charged

Guidance on delay

8.17 The correct approach when considering an application for a stay of proceedings, based upon delay, was examined by the Court of Appeal in *R v S (Stephen Paul)*.[28] Lord Justice Rose set out five principles which need to be considered:

'(1) even where delay was unjustifiable, a permanent stay should be the exception rather than the rule;

(2) where there was no fault on the part of the complainant or the prosecution, it would be very rare for a stay to be granted;

(3) no stay should be granted in the absence of serious prejudice to the defence so that no fair trial could be held;

(4) when assessing possible serious prejudice, the judge should bear in mind his or her power to regulate the admissibility of evidence and that the trial process itself should ensure that all relevant factual issues arising from delay would be placed before the jury for their consideration in accordance with appropriate directions from the judge;

(5) if, having considered all those factors, a judge's assessment was that a fair trial would be possible, a stay should not be granted.'

In their Lordships' judgment the discretionary decision whether to grant a stay as an abuse of process, because of delay, was an exercise in judicial assessment dependent on judgment rather than on any conclusion as to fact based on evidence. It was, therefore, potentially misleading to apply to the exercise of that discretion the language of burden and standard of proof, which was more apt to an evidence-based fact-finding process. The Court of Appeal dismissed the appeal against conviction.

---

28 *R v S* [2006] 2 Cr App R 23.

Trial process

8.18 The trial process itself is able, in many situations, to deal with the prejudice caused by long delays. Trial judges can use their discretion to exclude evidence, under s 78 of PACE 1984 and/or give an appropriate direction to the jury in the summing-up to remedy any prejudice to the defence caused by delay, as an alternative to staying proceedings. Such alternative remedies were recognised by Lord Justice Latham in *R v Maybery*,[29] when he said that the techniques (or 'control mechanisms') which the law had developed to deal with the problems of historic allegations were familiar 'over the years'. Trial judges should be made aware of their ability to regulate the admissibility of evidence and to warn the jury, in summing-up directions, about the dangers the defendant might encounter in answering certain historic allegations.[30]

Documents

8.19 In *R v Buzalek and Schiffer*,[31] the defendants were charged with fraudulent trading. The trial judge held that a six-year delay did not prevent the defendants having a fair trial. The Court of Appeal dismissed the appeals against conviction because the case turned largely on documents and accordingly it was possible for witnesses to refresh their memories from documents.

Complexity

8.20 The complexity of a case, both factual and legally, may lead to a justifiable delay, not amounting to an abuse of delay. The Privy Council, in *Mungroo v R*,[32] dismissed an appeal based on unconscionable delay of four years between arrest and trial. The delay resulted from (a) the complexity of the complainant authority body, which required investigation of 20 cases of suspected false claims, payments and forgeries, (b) the factual complexity of the case, (c) legal complexity and (d) the complexity of the manner of proof.

Disclosure issues

8.21 Where the defence base their abuse of process complaint on prosecution failure to make full, proper and timely disclosure, a number of issues need to be considered:[33]

---

29 [2003] EWCA Crim 782.
30 As applied in *R v JW* [2013] NICA 6, where the appeal court stated that the trial judge should direct the jury on how the defendant might be prejudiced by the delay.
31 [1991] Crim LR 115.
32 [1991] 1 WLR 1351, [1992] 95 Cr App R 334.
33 See Mr Justice Randerson's list in *Attorney-General v District Court at Hamilton* [2004] 3 NZLR 777 at para 791.

8.22 *Abuse of Process*

- whether the failure to disclose was due to inadvertence, inefficiency or deliberate conduct;
- whether the prosecutor had acted in good faith;
- whether the non-disclosure could damage the prosecution case or advance that of the defence;
- the extent of any prejudice to the accused in the conduct of his or her defence as a result of the non-disclosure;
- whether the accused could nevertheless receive a fair trial without undue delay;
- whether remedies short of a stay could achieve a fair trial (such as an adjournment to allow disclosure and instructions to be taken on the new disclosure, and the exclusion of evidence); and
- at appeal level, whether taking all the circumstances of the trial into account, there was a real possibility that the jury would have arrived at a different verdict.[34]

JUDICIAL TRIAL CONTROL MECHANISMS

8.22 There are a number of alternative remedies to staying proceedings as an abuse, including exclusion of evidence under s 78 of PACE 1984 and judicial direction during the trial judge's summing-up to the jury. It is clear from case law that the abuse of process principle is not applicable to proceedings, evidentially, in a number of ways, the application of s 78 being more appropriate:

- the abuse of process remedy does not operate in relation to rulings as to evidential admissibility (see *R v Maguire and Heffenan*[35]);
- an abuse of process application cannot be used to exclude evidence under s 78 of PACE 1984 (see *R v Aujla*[36]);
- in relation to bad character, there is no reason in principle why evidence relating to stayed allegations should not be admissible in any subsequent trial (see *R v Edwards, Rowland, McLean, Smith, Enright and Gray*,[37] *R v Ngyuen*,[38] and *DPP v Agyemang*[39]); and
- information supplied by a person/company (under statutory compulsion) to one government agency, can be used to form the basis of a subsequent prosecution by another law enforcement agency (see *R v Brady*[40]).

---

34 *McInnes v HM Advocate* [2010] UKSC 7, applying *Spiers v Ruddy* [2008] 1 AC 873; [2007] UKPC D2.
35 [2009] EWCA Crim 462.
36 [1998] 2 Cr App R 16, followed in *R v P (Telephone Intercepts: Admissibility of Evidence)*, the Times, 23 May 2000.
37 [2006] 2 Cr App R 4.
38 [2008] 2 Cr App R 9.
39 [2009] EWCA 1542 (Admin).
40 [2005] 1 Cr App R 5.

Chapter 9

Sentencing

INTRODUCTION

9.1 The sentencing hearing is one of the most important hearings to take place; for the person about to be sentenced, the victims of any offending and the state. In fraud cases the disposal of a defendant's case can be broken into three elements namely:

- Sentence
- Ancillary Orders
- Confiscation

In all cases the first will occur. In many cases the second and third will also be present. We deal below with three of the more prevalent ancillary orders. Confiscation dealings are dealt with in Chapter 3 in the section entitled 'Missing trader intra-community fraud'.[1]

9.2 From 1 October 2014, the Sentencing Council's definitive guideline on fraud, bribery and money laundering[2] issued under s 120 of the Coroners and Justice Act 2009 and applying to all offenders who are 18 or over and to organisations will apply to all cases to be sentenced on or after that date. The offences it applies to are:

- fraud (in terms of the offences under the Fraud Act 2006), conspiracy to defraud and False Accounting (s 17 of the Theft Act 1968);
- possessing, making or supplying articles for use in fraud;
- revenue fraud (including the fraudulent evasion of VAT under s 72 of the Value Added Tax Act 1994, income tax evasion under s 106A of the Taxes Management Act 1970, the fraudulent evasion of excise duty and

---

[1] See also A Eissa and R Barber, *Confiscation Law Handbook* (Bloomsbury Professional, 2011). Additionally, if there is confiscation, then compensation and any other financial order may only be considered at the time of the confiscation proceedings (s 13 of the Proceeds of Crime Act 2002).
[2] Appendix 1.

9.3 *Sentencing*

the improper importation of goods (under ss 50, 170 and 170B of the Customs and Excise Management Act 1979 and cheating the public revenue). It is worth noting that the sums in the guideline are truly 'eye watering'. The starting point in a case involving loss or intended loss to HMRC is based upon £80 million;

- benefit fraud (including dishonest representations for obtaining benefit under s111A of the Social Security Administration Act 1992)
- money laundering; and
- bribery.

If the guideline does not apply to an offence, then, although on occasion it may be useful for reference, then any guideline case from the Court of Appeal (Criminal Division) will continue to bind the lower courts.

SENTENCING GUIDELINES

9.3 These broaden significantly the sorts of offences that guidelines apply to, moving away from those primarily under the Fraud Act 2006 as covered by the predecessor guidelines. We have included as an appendix the sentencing guidelines. As a result we do not take each of these in turn below – rather we explain how the guidelines work.

9.4 In particular, these guidelines now cover conspiracy to defraud, cheating the revenue, money laundering and bribery as well as those under the Fraud Act 2006. Most (although not all) of the offences considered in detail in this book will therefore fall to be sentenced by reference to these guidelines.

9.5 The guidelines are split into offences (and themselves annex fine and community service 'bands'). Thereafter eight discreet steps are identified. As an example, the first part of the guidelines deal with offences under the Fraud Act 2006 and conspiracy to defraud (as well as false accounting).

9.6 **Step one** is to determine, by reference to the now well-known concepts of 'culpability' and 'harm' the offence category using the tables in the guidelines. 'Culpability' is determined by weighing up all the factors of the case to determine the offender's role and the extent to which the offending was planned and the sophistication with which it was carried out. 'Harm' is initially assessed by the actual or intended or risked loss that may arise from the offence. A loss is 'intended' if circumstances prevent an actual loss occurring. It would appear that no distinction is drawn between actual or intended loss. Risk of loss is however said to be less serious. Such a risk, for example in relation to mortgage fraud, involves a consideration of the likelihood of harm occurring and the amount of it if it were to occur. If no (or no significant) loss has occurred then an offender should find himself moved down a category in relation to harm. However each case will depend on its circumstances. 'Harm' is not limited to the financial harm. There is also the impact upon the victim to consider. Once the category has been determined by reference to loss an offender may find himself moved up a category, moved up within a category or not moved at all depending upon the impact to the victim.

9.7 **Step two** is to fix the starting point for the offence. It is important to note that here the starting point applies to all offenders irrespective of plea or previous convictions. Any larger or smaller values than those the starting point is based upon should lead to adjustments in the appropriate way. Additionally if the value 'greatly exceeds' the highest amount in the highest category it 'may' be appropriate to move outside the identified range. There are then a series of aggravating and mitigating factors to consider. These are non-exhaustive but it is worth noting that the lack of any previous convictions or relevant or recent previous convictions is a mitigating factor that should reduce the seriousness of the offence or reflect personal mitigation. A consideration of these (and any other identified and relevant) factors should lead to adjustments either up or down from the starting point.

9.8 Explicit in the guideline is reference to consecutive sentencing for multiple offences which might be appropriate where large sums are involved. Such sentences had been predicted prior to the publication of the guidelines. In *Attorney General's References (Nos 7 and 8 of 2013) (R v Kallakis and Williams); R v Levene)*,[3] the Court of Appeal said:

> '77. We turn, secondly, to the question whether a consecutive sentence should have been imposed for the count 21 fraud. We do not accept that a consecutive sentence would have indicated a view that the maximum sentence for conspiracy to defraud was inadequate. On the contrary, the effect of the concurrent sentence is, in our view, to give the impression that the offenders have entirely escaped the consequences of a serious fraud in which substantial loss has resulted. It is true that the nature of the fraud was similar and that it overlapped in time with the count 1 conspiracy but Bank of Scotland was a separate victim, separately targeted, and, unlike the count 1 offence, a substantial loss was realised. We have no doubt that a consecutive sentence for the offence was required, subject to the principle of totality.'

9.9 **Step 3** requires the court to take account of any assistance given or offered to a prosecutor that may discount the sentence. This is principally pursuant to ss 73 and 74 of the Serious Organised Crime and Police Act 2005. This is something that may not arise with frequency. However, for the principles to be applied, consideration should be given to *R v P*.[4]

---

3   [2014] 1 Cr App R (S) 26.
4   [2008] 2 Cr App R (S) 5.

9.10 *Sentencing*

9.10 **Step 4** requires the court to take account of any potential reduction for a guilty plea. This is in accordance with s 144 of the Criminal Justice Act 2003 and the guilty plea guideline. The guilty plea is usually the most important mitigation available to a defendant and can reduce any sentence (normally) by up to one-third. The plea of guilty does not diminish the seriousness of the offence with which someone has been charged. Rather, the reduction in sentence is a pragmatic recognition that guilty pleas save the tax-payer a considerable sum of money in terms of resources, (both financial and time) and can spare the victims the trauma of the need to give evidence. The reduction therefore encourages guilty pleas.

9.11 There are a number of things that ought to always be considered in relation to guilty pleas. First, and most importantly, as the Fraud Guidelines state, the court must have regard to the Sentencing Guidelines Council guidance on guilty pleas from 2007. We have included these short guidelines at Appendix 2 so that they may be considered. Secondly, these were considered, it seems almost exhaustively, in *R v Caley*.[5] There, Lord Justice Hughes V-P (as he then was) said:

'2. The starting point is in statute. Section 144(1) of the Criminal Justice Act 2003 is mandatory:

'(1) In determining what sentence to pass on an offender who has pleaded guilty to an offence....a court must take into account:

(a) the stage in the proceedings...at which the offender indicated his intention to plead guilty, and

(b) the circumstances in which this indication was given.'

Section 174 requires the court which moderates the sentence on this basis to say that it is doing so.

3. We draw attention to the wording. The statute refers to the defendant 'indicating his intention' to plead guilty, not to his being arraigned and actually entering such a plea. By definition, the latter will often be at a later convenient opportunity in the court timetable.

4. Section 144 reflects the practice which the criminal courts had developed over many years. The SGC Guideline identifies the purpose of the practice at para.2.2:

'A reduction in sentence is appropriate because a guilty plea avoids the need for a trial (thus enabling other cases to be disposed of more expeditiously), shortens the gap between charge and sentence, saves considerable cost, and, in the case of an early plea, saves victims and witnesses from the concern about having to give evidence. The reduction principle derives from the need for the effective administration of justice and not as an aspect of mitigation.'

---

5 [2013] 2 Cr App R (S) 47.

5. In order of importance, plainly the first is the benefit for victims and witnesses. The impact of crime on its victims can be enormous or slight, but whether it is large or small the knowledge that a defendant has accepted his guilt and that punishment will follow normally reduces that impact substantially and thus brings significant benefit to the victim. It is generally worse for the victim when the offender, although guilty, is defiant. The same applies to the impact on those who may have to give evidence; they include, but are not confined to, the victim. A few may relish it, or think that they will, but for most the process is normally stressful and often unavoidably uncomfortable. Moreover the anticipation may often be painful, sometimes even more than the actuality. For both victims and witnesses the benefit from a plea of guilty remains even when it comes late, but generally speaking the later it is the less the benefit.

6. The second major reason for the practice is a more pragmatic one but it is nevertheless vital in the public interest. The expenditure in public time and money on trials and on preparation for trials is considerable. The case must be thoroughly prepared so that the exacting standard of proof rightly required in a criminal case can be met. Further investigation is likely to be necessary, as may the assembly of a good deal more evidence, lay and expert. Such steps are necessary, but expensive. They are avoided or much reduced by an admission of guilt. The public's limited resources can then be concentrated on those cases where a trial will really be necessary, and such cases will not be delayed, often with accused persons in custody. At present something of the order of 75 per cent of all Crown Court cases result in pleas of guilty; if in all those cases the defendants were out of defiance or otherwise to insist on each detail of the case being proved to the hilt the administration of criminal justice would be in danger of collapse.

7. As the SGC's statement of purpose makes clear, a plea of guilty may of course be an indication of remorse for the offence, but it may not be and the two things are not the same. A defendant may indeed regret his offence, and, beyond that, it may be clear that he wishes to avoid doing it again. Equally, however, he may plead guilty not because he regrets committing the crime but simply because he does not see a way of avoiding the consequences. The benefits which we have described which come from a defendant who is guilty admitting that he is so remain present if it is a case of the latter type. Moreover, it accords with elementary instincts of justice to recognise the difference between two defendants, one of whom is defiant and requires the public to prove every dot and comma of the case against him and the other of whom accepts his guilt.

8. The well established mechanism by which this is done is by reducing the sentence which would have been imposed after a trial by a proportion, on a sliding scale depending on when the plea of guilty was indicated. The largest reduction is of about one third, and is to be accorded, under the well established practice and the SGC Guideline, to defendants who

9.12 *Sentencing*

indicate their plea of guilty at the 'first reasonable opportunity'. Thereafter the proportionate reduction diminishes. A plea of guilty at the door of the trial court will still attract some reduction, but it is likely to be of the order of one tenth.'

9.12 One matter, explicitly related to large frauds, was not ventilated in *Caley*. That is whether a *larger* discount should be preserved in cases where very considerable amounts of court time and public expense are saved and where, as it is put, a defendant in a multi-handed case 'breaks ranks' to plead guilty, but closer to trial.

9.13 In *R v Buffrey*[6] (as approved in *Attorney General's References (Nos 7 and 8 of 2013) (R v Kallakis and Williams); R v Levene*[7]) it was held:

'But some reduction, clearly, must be made and because frauds of this kind are complex and do take a long time to unravel, it is well known that they have become a burden on the criminal justice system. They are very costly, both in time and in money. They cause stress to jurors who have to try them, to judges who have to try them, to those who have to conduct them and, not least of course, to the witnesses and to the defendants themselves who have to endure long periods of investigation in Court.

All those matters, in our judgment, justify the Court in applying a considerable discount where somebody does, albeit late in the day, face up to what he has done and plead guilty. It would be quite wrong for us to suggest that there was any absolute rule as to what the discount should be. Each case must be assessed by the trial judge on its own facts and there will be considerable variance as between one case and another.'

Nothing it would seem in the guidelines or *Caley* detracts from the application of this principle in an appropriate case.

9.14 Thirdly, courts now operate an 'early guilty plea scheme'. From a defendant's perspective, for maximum credit for a plea of guilty a court will normally expect adherence to the scheme. This also has case management implications that are vital for the smooth running of a court. That will mean that for a maximum one-third discount a plea should be tendered in the Magistrates' Court if possible or indicated at a preliminary hearing or a hearing fixed for the purpose of entering an 'early guilty plea'. Thereafter the traditional sliding scale will follow.

9.15 **Step 5** requires the court to ensure that the total sentence is just and proportionate to the overall offending. This reflects the 'totality' principle and includes the situation where an offender is serving a sentence for something else.

---

6 (1993) 14 Cr App R (S) 511.
7 [2014] 1 Cr App R (S) 26.

Corporate offending **9.23**

9.16 **Step 6** requires the court to consider confiscation if the prosecutor requires it or the court thinks it is just to do so. Additionally the court must consider compensation. The court will also consider ancillary orders such as a financial reporting order or a serious crime prevention order.

9.17 **Step 7** requires the court to give reasons for and explain the effect of the sentence.

9.18 **Step 8** requires the court to consider whether to credit time spent on bail on a qualifying electronic tag in accordance with s 240A of the Criminal Justice Act 2003.

CORPORATE OFFENDING

9.19 The guidelines also include a section on sentencing corporate offenders on or after 1 October 2014. They indicate that nearly all cases will need to be allocated to the Crown Court and remind us that this is mandatory if confiscation is to be considered. The offences covered are:

- conspiracy to defraud;
- cheating the public revenue;
- offences under ss 1, 6 and 7 of the Fraud Act 2006;
- false accounting (s 17 of the Theft Act 1968);
- offences under s 70 of the Value Added Tax Act 1994 and s 170 of the Customs and Excise Management Act 1979;
- bribery; and
- money laundering.

The maximum sentence is, in the Crown Court, an unlimited fine. As with individual offences there are a number of steps (although in this case ten and not eight).

9.20 **Step 1** is to consider compensation. Reasons should be given if an order is not made and, if means are limited, compensation should take priority.

9.21 **Step 2** involves considering confiscation. As no financial penalty can be made if a confiscation inquiry is embarked upon until the end of that inquiry, the two will need to go together.

9.22 **Step 3** is to determine the offence category with regard to culpability and harm in the normal way.

9.23 **Step 4** is to determine the starting point. As there can only realistically be a financial penalty there is a 'harm figure' that is multiplied by a relevant

9.24 *Sentencing*

percentage drawn from a band to represent the culpability level. Once the starting point is identified, the court will then balance any aggravating or mitigating features beginning with the non-exhaustive list set out in the guidelines. Here, however, s 164 of the Criminal Justice Act 2003 requires the court, whilst reflecting the seriousness of the offence within the fine, to take account of the means of the offender. In order to do that, depending on the nature of the body corporate, a certain level of information is required:

- companies – annual accounts with the focus upon turnover, profit before tax, director's remuneration and so on. A failure to present accounts may lead to the inference that the company can pay any appropriate fine;

- partnerships – as above;

- local authorities, fire authorities and similar public bodies – the Annual Revenue Budget ('ARB') is the best indication of the size of the body;

- Health trusts – MONITOR is the independent regulator that publishes quarterly reports and annual figures which should show the relative financial strength of the organisation; and

- charities – audited annual accounts should provide the information the court requires.

9.24 **Step 5** is the adjustment of the fine if there are any other factors the court can take into account. This involves the court 'stepping back' and considering the financial impact of all the orders it may make – compensation and confiscation as well as a fine. A fine is looking to achieve the removal of all gain, additional punishment and deterrence. It should be substantial enough to have a real economic impact to ensure that those responsible for the company are properly aware of the seriousness of what has occurred. However the court must bear in mind whether any unacceptable harm to third parties might be caused by a fine that otherwise meets the objectives.

9.25 **Step 6** involves considering any reduction due to assistance rendered to the authorities in the normal way.

9.26 **Step 7** involves a consideration of the discount for a plea of guilty in consideration of the guilty plea guidelines in the normal way.

9.27 **Step 8** involves considering whether to make any ancillary orders in the normal way.

9.24 **Step 9** involves ensuring the 'totality' principle is not offended in the normal way.

9.28 **Step 10** involves the giving of reasons in the normal way.

Previous Court of Appeal authority

9.29 Where an offence is included within the Sentencing Guidelines, previous Court of Appeal authority is likely now to be of limited assistance as, it would appear, the guidelines are generally accepted to lead to an increase in sentencing for such offences.

Specific frauds

9.30 We have in this book dealt with a number of specific types of fraud. Most will be covered by these guidelines; some will not. For ease of reference we have, in the bodies of the relevant chapters, set out relevant sentencing authority. We repeat what is said above: where the guidelines apply any previous authority will be of limited value.

ANCILLARY ORDERS

9.31 There is a plethora of ancillary orders available to the courts. Most will depend on the type of case before the court and, as ever, the individual facts of the case. In relation to fraud cases there are three which appear to have become the most prevalent and should, therefore, be considered.

Financial reporting order

9.32 A financial reporting order (FRO) is made under s 76(1) of the Serious Organised Crime and Police Act 2005. An FRO comes into force on the day it is made and may be made for a period of up to 15 years (or 20 if the sentence is life imprisonment) if the Crown Court is sentencing for a listed offence (or five years if the matter is in the Magistrates' Court) if the court is satisfied:

'that the risk of the person's committing another offence mentioned in subsection (3) is sufficiently high to justify the making of a financial reporting order'.

9.33 For our purposes the listed offences include:

- conspiracy to defraud;
- offences under ss 1 and 11 of the Fraud Act 2006;
- false accounting;
- any offence in Sch 2 to the Proceeds of Crime Act 2002 ('lifestyle offences');
- offences under ss 1, 2 and 6 of the Bribery Act 2010;

9.34 *Sentencing*

- section 329 of the Proceeds of Crime Act 2002; and
- cheating the public revenue.

9.34 In *R v Wright*[8] the Court of Appeal said:

'13. We should say that whilst this form of order is newly created it ought not to be thought that it is routinely to be made without proper thought. We do not seek to set out any general rules for when it will be appropriate or not. This is not the right place in which to do that. No doubt the paradigm case for such an order is the defendant with a history of unsatisfactory business or financial dealing who at some stage at least is likely to be at large and engaged in business, commercial or financial activity which would otherwise be unsupervised or unmonitored. But it is perfectly clear that the section embraces also the appellant who is going to be a prisoner and, at least in the case of the very exceptional facts of this prisoner, we have no doubt that an order can be appropriate.

14. We are quite sure that judges who are asked to make financial reporting orders should give careful consideration to whether it would actually achieve anything. They should certainly look at alternative powers which are available to financial investigators if they would have much the same effect. We have applied our minds to precisely that question in this case.'

Serious crime prevention order

9.35 Applications for serious crime prevention orders (SCPOs) are governed by Pt 50 of the Criminal Procedure Rules 2014. These applications are made under s 19 of the Serious Crime Act 2007 but recourse must be had to the entirety of Pt 1 to ensure no errors occur and in particular ss 6 to 15 which is headed 'Safeguards'.

9.36 More and more frequently these applications are being made as against defendants convicted of fraud. The jurisdiction is shared between the High Court and the Crown Court, but it is the Crown Court, upon conviction for 'serious offences', that include conspiracy to defraud, false accounting and offences under ss 1, 6 and 7 of the Fraud Act 2006, which may make such an order if, and only if, the prosecutor applies for it. In this instance, due to the intrusive nature of the SCPO, the application must be made by the DPP (or DSFO) or someone he has personally delegated the function to. The general delegation within the Prosecution of Offences Act 1985 is not sufficient in this instance.

9.37 Section 19(2) provides:

'The Crown Court may, in addition to dealing with the person in relation to the offence, make an order if it has reasonable grounds to believe that

---

8 [2009] 2 Cr App R (S) 45.

Ancillary orders **9.38**

the order would protect the public by preventing, restricting or disrupting involvement by the person in serious crime in England and Wales'.

The maximum an SCPO may be made for is five years (although any individual term may be for less – it cannot be for more). It is renewable in the High Court. Unless ordered otherwise, an SCPO runs from the date of the offender's release from custody.

9.38 In *R v Hancox and Duffy*,[9] the Court of Appeal gave detailed guidance as to how such orders should be applied for and made. The headnote provides a proper summary. It says:

> 'Serious crime prevention orders were preventive orders, designed according to the statute to "prevent, restrict or disrupt" defendants in the commission of serious crime. Orders could be made by the High Court on application or by the Crown Court following conviction.
>
> The necessary preconditions for making such an order were first that the defendant had been convicted of a "serious offence" listed in the 2007 Act Sch 1 Pt 1. They included drugs, arms and people trafficking, armed robbery, money laundering, fraud, various revenue offences, corruption and bribery, counterfeiting, blackmail and certain intellectual property offences; and also certain prostitution and sexual offences involving organisation. There was a residual power to treat a particular case involving an unscheduled offence as "serious" if the court considered that it ought to be so treated. Counterfeiting was an offence listed in the Schedule.
>
> Secondly, an application for an order must be made by the Director of Public Prosecutions, the Director of the Revenue and Customs Prosecution Office or the Director of the Serious Fraud Office. The general delegation of the authority of the Director of Public Prosecutions by the Prosecution of Offences Act 1985 to all Crown prosecutors did not apply, although delegation to specified individual Crown prosecutors was authorised.
>
> Thirdly, the court must have reasonable grounds for believing that an order would protect the public by preventing, restricting or disrupting involvement by the defendant in serious crime. Proceedings relating to a serious crime prevention order were civil proceedings, and the court was not limited to evidence which would have been admissible in the criminal prosecution. The standard of proof was the civil standard. Breach of an order was a criminal offence punishable with up to five years' imprisonment.
>
> Section 19(2) of the Act provided that a serious crime prevention order might be made only if the court had reasonable grounds to believe that an order would protect the public by preventing, restricting or disrupting

---

9   [2010] 2 Cr App R (S) 74.

9.38 *Sentencing*

involvement by the defendant in serious crime, as defined in Sch 1, in England and Wales. It followed that the court in making an order was concerned with future risk. There must be a real or significant risk (not a bare possibility) that the defendant would commit further serious offences.

If an order was made, it might contain such provisions as the court considered appropriate for the purpose of protecting the public by preventing, restricting or disrupting involvement by the defendant in serious crime. The power was not expressly couched in terms of necessity, but the court doubted that the different form of words made a significant difference in practice. It was accepted that the principles set out in *Mee [2004] EWCA Crim 629; [2004] 2 Cr App R (S) 8* (p 434), in the context of travel restriction orders under the Criminal Justice and Police Act 2001 s 33, applied equally to serious crime prevention orders. Such orders could be made only for the purpose for which the powers were given by statute and must be proportionate. The necessity for an order to be proportionate also followed from the fact that they would almost inevitably engage the European Convention on Human Rights art 8. It was not enough that the order might have some public benefit in preventing, restricting, or disrupting involvement by the defendant in serious crime. The interference which it would create with the defendant's freedom of action must be justified by the benefit.

The provisions of the order must be commensurate with the risk. Much of what was said in *Boness [2005] EWCA Crim 2395; [2006] 1 Cr App R (S) 120* (p 690) on the topic of an anti-social behaviour order would apply equally to serious crime prevention orders. That decision emphasised the importance of the order being practicable and enforceable, and satisfying a test of precision and certainty. Preventive orders of this kind created for the defendant a new criminal offence punishable with imprisonment for up to five years. They must be expressed in terms from which the offender or any police officer contemplating enforcement, could readily know what he might and might not do. Like other forms of preventive order, a serious crime prevention order was not an additional alternative form of sentence. It was not designed to punish. It was not to be imposed because it was thought that the defendant deserved it.

The appellants were involved in counterfeiting operations on a commercial scale, which involved the investment of substantial sums in equipment and materials. Notes with a face value of almost £2 million were recovered. The first appellant was 84 years old and the second 57 years old. The orders prohibited the appellants from buying various equipment or materials and required them to notify the police or serious organised crime authority of any premises owned or occupied, any vehicle to which the defendant had access or any change of name or address. Further detailed provisions were included in the orders affecting each appellant. For the first appellant it was submitted that the making of any order was wrong in principle because his age and ill health were such that there was no risk that he might commit any further serious offences. It was accepted that the first appellant had a number of potentially serious health conditions and that they were not likely to improve. However, neither age nor his medical conditions had prevented the first appellant from taking an active part in the offence or from travelling. The assessment of the risk was for the judge. The Court agreed that the first appellant's medical condition was relevant but did not agree that it demonstrated that the risk that he would commit further serious offences of counterfeiting was negligible. The sentencing judge was entitled to come to the conclusion that he did. The Court considered that the specific restrictions placed on the first appellant were proportionate. They were tailored to what he had done and might do again. They were designed in the terms of the statute to disrupt any future commission of a serious offence; to make it clear to the first appellant that he was being monitored in his relevant activities was a legitimate aim of the order. In the case of the second appellant the Court had reached the conclusion that the order was justified and proportionate. A provision of the order relating to the notification of mobile telephones and other similar devices was proportionate to their demonstrated role in the offences.'

Disqualification as a company director

9.39 Many offences involve the use (or abuse) of a company as a vehicle for fraud. Where a person is convicted of an indictable offence (either summarily or upon indictment) in connection with promotion, formation, management, liquidation or striking off of a company, with the receivership of a company's property or with his being the administrative receiver of a company, then the court can consider a disqualification. As a result the Crown Court and the Magistrates' Court have, pursuant to ss 1 and 2 of the Company Directors Disqualification Act 1986, the discretion to disqualify a person as being a director of a company, acting as a receiver of a company's property in any way, or whether directly or indirectly taking part in the promotion, formation or management of the company without leave of the court and not acting as an insolvency practitioner. There is a single order which has the consequence of forbidding all of the above behaviour.

9.40 A court may take into account behaviour that is not the subject of a conviction even if a person would be criminally liable for such behaviour.

9.41 The maximum period is 15 years in the Crown Court and five years in the Magistrates' Court, and begins, unless any direction is made by the court to the contrary, 21 days after the order. If a person is already disqualified then any additional disqualification must be concurrent.

9.42 *Sentencing*

9.42 In *R v Cadman*,[10] the Court of Appeal conducted an extensive review of the relevant case law on the issue. They said:

'24. We turn now to a digest of the authorities. *Sevenoaks Stationers (Retail) Ltd [1991] Ch 164*, dealt with an accountant who over five years with five separate companies which had all become insolvent had accrued total indebtedness of approximately £560,000. There were no audited accounts and he had traded whilst insolvent in relation to at least one company. This amounted to incompetence or negligence in a very marked degree falling short of dishonesty. His disqualification period was reduced to five years. This case is memorable for the trio of brackets it established, later to be adopted with approval in *Millard (1994) 15 Cr App R (S) 445*. (1) The top bracket, periods of over 10 years, should be reserved for particularly serious cases. These may include cases where a director who has already one period of disqualification imposed upon him falls to be disqualified yet again. (2) The minimum bracket of two to five years' disqualification should be applied where, though disqualification is mandatory, the case is, relatively, not very serious. (3) The middle bracket of disqualification, from six to 10 years, should apply to serious cases which do not merit the top bracket'.

---

10   [2012] 2 Cr App R (S) 88.

Appendix 1

Fraud, Bribery and Money Laundering Offences: Definitive Guideline

[Pages 1 to 3 of this document are not reproduced here. All page references in the document are to the document itself and not to this book; for ease of reference the original document page numbers are reproduced at the top of each page of the document.]

Appendix 1 *Fraud, Bribery and Money Laundering Offences etc*

Applicability of guideline

In accordance with section 120 of the Coroners and Justice Act 2009, the Sentencing Council issues this definitive guideline. It applies to all individual offenders aged 18 and older and to organisations who are sentenced on or after 1 October 2014, regardless of the date of the offence.

Section 125(1) of the Coroners and Justice Act 2009 provides that when sentencing offences committed after 6 April 2010:

"Every court –

(a) must, in sentencing an offender, follow any sentencing guideline which is relevant to the offender's case, and

(b) must, in exercising any other function relating to the sentencing of offenders, follow any sentencing guidelines which are relevant to the exercise of the function,

unless the court is satisfied that it would be contrary to the interests of justice to do so."

This guideline applies only to individual offenders aged 18 and older or organisations. General principles to be considered in the sentencing of youths are in the Sentencing Guidelines Council's definitive guideline, *Overarching Principles – Sentencing Youths*.

Structure, ranges and starting points
For the purposes of section 125(3)–(4) Coroners and Justice Act 2009, the guideline specifies *offence ranges* – the range of sentences appropriate for each type of offence. Within each offence, the Council has specified a number of *categories* which reflect varying degrees of seriousness. The offence range is split into *category ranges* – sentences appropriate for each level of seriousness. The Council has also identified a starting point within each category.

Starting points define the position within a category range from which to start calculating the provisional sentence. The court should consider further features of the offence or the offender that warrant adjustment of the sentence within the range, including the aggravating and mitigating factors set out at step two.[1] Starting points and ranges apply to all offenders, whether they have pleaded guilty or been convicted after trial. Credit for a guilty plea is taken into consideration only after the appropriate sentence has been identified.[2]

Information on community orders and fine bands is set out in the annex at page 54.

---
1 Aggravating and mitigating factors are at step four in the guideline for organisations. In the guideline for organisations, having identified a provisional sentence within the range at step four, the court is required to consider a further set of factors that may require a final adjustment to the sentence at step five
2 In the guideline for organisations, guilty pleas are considered at step seven; in the guidelines for individuals, guilty pleas are considered at step four

Fraud

Fraud by false representation, fraud by failing to disclose information, fraud by abuse of position
Fraud Act 2006 (section 1)
Triable either way

Conspiracy to defraud
Common law
Triable on indictment only

Maximum: 10 years' custody
Offence range: Discharge – 8 years' custody

False accounting
Theft Act 1968 (section 17)
Triable either way

Maximum: 7 years' custody
Offence range: Discharge – 6 years and 6 months' custody

Effective from 1 October 2014

Appendix 1 *Fraud, Bribery and Money Laundering Offences etc*

STEP ONE
Determining the offence category

The court should determine the offence category with reference to the tables below. In order to determine the category the court should assess **culpability** and **harm**.

The level of **culpability** is determined by weighing up all the factors of the case to determine the offender's role and the extent to which the offending was planned and the sophistication with which it was carried out.

Culpability demonstrated by one or more of the following:

A – High culpability

A leading role where offending is part of a group activity

Involvement of others through pressure, influence

Abuse of position of power or trust or responsibility

Sophisticated nature of offence/significant planning

Fraudulent activity conducted over sustained period of time

Large number of victims

Deliberately targeting victim on basis of vulnerability

B – Medium culpability

Other cases where characteristics for categories A or C are not present

A significant role where offending is part of a group activity

C – Lesser culpability

Involved through coercion, intimidation or exploitation

Not motivated by personal gain

Peripheral role in organised fraud

Opportunistic 'one-off' offence; very little or no planning

Limited awareness or understanding of the extent of fraudulent activity

Where there are characteristics present which fall under different levels of culpability, the court should balance these characteristics to reach a fair assessment of the offender's culpability.

Fraud, Bribery and Money Laundering Offences etc

Harm is initially assessed by the actual, intended or risked loss as may arise from the offence.

The values in the table below are to be used for **actual** or **intended** loss only.

Intended loss relates to offences where circumstances prevent the actual loss that is intended to be caused by the fraudulent activity.

> **Risk of loss** (for instance in mortgage frauds) involves consideration of both the likelihood of harm occurring and the extent of it if it does. Risk of loss is less serious than actual or intended loss. Where the offence has caused risk of loss but no (or much less) actual loss the normal approach is to move down to the corresponding point in the next category. This may not be appropriate if either the likelihood or extent of risked loss is particularly high.

Harm A – Loss caused or intended

Category	Loss	Starting point
Category 1	£500,000 or more	Starting point based on £1 million
Category 2	£100,000 – £500,000 **or** Risk or category 1 harm	Starting point based on £300,000
Category 3	£20,000 – £100,000 **or** Risk of category 2 harm	Starting point based on £50,000
Category 4	£5,000 – £20,000 **or** Risk of category 3 harm	Starting point based on £12,500
Category 5	Less than £5,000 **or** Risk of category 4 harm	Starting point based on £2,500

Risk of category 5 harm, move down the range within the category

Harm B – Victim impact demonstrated by one or more of the following:

The court should then take into account the level of harm caused to the victim(s) or others to determine whether it warrants the sentence being moved up to the corresponding point in the next category or further up the range of the initial category.

High impact – move up a category; if in category 1 move up the range

Serious detrimental effect on the victim whether financial or otherwise, for example substantial damage to credit rating

Victim particularly vulnerable (due to factors including but not limited to their age, financial circumstances, mental capacity)

Medium impact – move upwards within the category range

Considerable detrimental effect on the victim whether financial or otherwise

Lesser impact – no adjustment

Some detrimental impact on victim, whether financial or otherwise

Effective from 1 October 2014

Appendix 1   *Fraud, Bribery and Money Laundering Offences etc*

STEP TWO
Starting point and category range

Having determined the category at step one, the court should use the appropriate starting point (as adjusted in accordance with step one above) to reach a sentence within the category range in the table below. The starting point applies to all offenders irrespective of plea or previous convictions.

Where the value is larger or smaller than the amount on which the starting point is based, this should lead to upward or downward adjustment as appropriate.

Where the value greatly exceeds the amount of the starting point in category 1, it may be appropriate to move outside the identified range.

TABLE 1
Section 1 Fraud Act 2006
conspiracy to defraud
Maximum: 10 years' custody

Harm	Culpability A	Culpability B	Culpability C
Category 1 £500,000 or more	**Starting point** 7 years' custody	**Starting point** 5 years' custody	**Starting point** 3 years' custody
Starting point based on £1 million	**Category range** 5 – 8 years' custody	**Category range** 3 – 6 years' custody	**Category range** 18 months' – 4 years' custody
Category 2 £100,000–£500,000	**Starting point** 5 years' custody	**Starting point** 3 years' custody	**Starting point** 18 months' custody
Starting point based on £300,000	**Category range** 3 – 6 years' custody	**Category range** 18 months' – 4 years' custody	**Category range** 26 weeks' – 3 years' custody
Category 3 £20,000 - £100,000	**Starting point** 3 years' custody	**Starting point** 18 months' custody	**Starting point** 26 weeks' custody
Starting point based on £50,000	**Category range** 18 months' – 4 years' custody	**Category range** 26 weeks' – 3 years' custody	**Category range** Medium level community order – 1 year's custody
Category 4 £5,000- £20,000	**Starting point** 18 months' custody	**Starting point** 26 weeks' custody	**Starting point** Medium level community order
Starting point based on £12,500	**Category range** 26 weeks' – 3 years' custody	**Category range** Medium level community order – 1 year's custody	**Category range** Band B fine – High level community order
Category 5 Less than £5,000	**Starting point** 36 weeks' custody	**Starting point** Medium level community order	**Starting point** Band B fine
Starting point based on £2,500	**Category range** High level community order – 1 year's custody	**Category range** Band B fine – 26 weeks' custody	**Category range** Discharge – Medium level community order

Effective from 1 October 2014

Fraud, Bribery and Money Laundering Offences etc

TABLE 2
Section 17 Theft Act 1968: false accounting
Maximum: 7 years' custody

Harm	Culpability A	Culpability B	Culpability C
Category 1 £500,000 or more	**Starting point** 5 years 6 months' custody	**Starting point** 4 years' custody	**Starting point** 2 years 6 months' custody
Starting point based on £1 million	**Category range** 4 years' – 6 years 6 months' custody	**Category range** 2 years 6 months' – 5 years' custody	**Category range** 15 months' – 3 years 6 months' custody
Category 2 £100,000–£500,000	**Starting point** 4 years' custody	**Starting point** 2 years 6 months' custody	**Starting point** 15 months' custody
Starting point based on £300,000	**Category range** 2 years 6 months' – 5 years' custody	**Category range** 15 months' – 3 years 6 months' custody	**Category range** 26 weeks' – 2 years 6 months' custody
Category 3 £20,000–£100,000	**Starting point** 2 years 6 months' custody	**Starting point** 15 months' custody	**Starting point** High level community order
Starting point based on £50,000	**Category range** 15 months' – 3 years 6 months' custody	**Category range** High level community order – 2 years 6 months' custody	**Category range** Low level community order – 36 weeks' custody
Category 4 £5,000–£20,000	**Starting point** 15 months' custody	**Starting point** High level community order	**Starting point** Low level community order
Starting point based on £12,500	**Category range** High level community order – 2 years 6 months' custody	**Category range** Low level community order – 36 weeks' custody	**Category range** Band B fine – Medium level community order
Category 5 Less than £5,000	**Starting point** 26 weeks' custody	**Starting point** Low level community order	**Starting point** Band B fine
Starting point based on £2,500	**Category range** Medium level community order – 36 weeks' custody	**Category range** Band B fine – Medium level community order	**Category range** Discharge – Low level community order

See page 10.

Appendix 1   *Fraud, Bribery and Money Laundering Offences etc*

FRAUD

The table below contains a non-exhaustive list of additional factual elements providing the context of the offence and factors relating to the offender.

Identify whether any combination of these or other relevant factors should result in an upward or downward adjustment from the sentence arrived at so far.

Consecutive sentences for multiple offences may be appropriate where large sums are involved.

Factors increasing seriousness	Factors reducing seriousness or reflecting personal mitigation
Statutory aggravating factors:	No previous convictions **or** no relevant/recent convictions
Previous convictions, having regard to a) the nature of the offence to which the conviction relates and its relevance to the current offence; and b) the time that has elapsed since the conviction	Remorse
	Good character and/or exemplary conduct
Offence committed whilst on bail	Little or no prospect of success
Other aggravating factors:	Serious medical conditions requiring urgent, intensive or long-term treatment
Steps taken to prevent the victim reporting or obtaining assistance and/or from assisting or supporting the prosecution	Age and/or lack of maturity where it affects the responsibility of the offender
Attempts to conceal/dispose of evidence	Lapse of time since apprehension where this does not arise from the conduct of the offender
Established evidence of community/wider impact	Mental disorder or learning disability
Failure to comply with current court orders	Sole or primary carer for dependent relatives
Offence committed on licence	Offender co-operated with investigation, made early admissions and/or voluntarily reported offending
Offences taken into consideration	
Failure to respond to warnings about behaviour	Determination and/or demonstration of steps having been taken to address addiction or offending behaviour
Offences committed across borders	Activity originally legitimate
Blame wrongly placed on others	

See page 11.

Fraud, Bribery and Money Laundering Offences etc

STEP THREE
Consider any factors which indicate a reduction, such as assistance to the prosecution
The court should take into account sections 73 and 74 of the Serious Organised Crime and Police Act 2005 (assistance by defendants: reduction or review of sentence) and any other rule of law by virtue of which an offender may receive a discounted sentence in consequence of assistance given (or offered) to the prosecutor or investigator.

STEP FOUR
Reduction for guilty pleas
The court should take account of any potential reduction for a guilty plea in accordance with section 144 of the Criminal Justice Act 2003 and the *Guilty Plea* guideline.

STEP FIVE
Totality principle
If sentencing an offender for more than one offence, or where the offender is already serving a sentence, consider whether the total sentence is just and proportionate to the overall offending behaviour.

STEP SIX
Confiscation, compensation and ancillary orders
The court must proceed with a view to making a confiscation order if it is asked to do so by the prosecutor or if the court believes it is appropriate for it to do so.

Where the offence has resulted in loss or damage the court must consider whether to make a compensation order.

If the court makes both a confiscation order and an order for compensation and the court believes the offender will not have sufficient means to satisfy both orders in full, the court must direct that the compensation be paid out of sums recovered under the confiscation order (section 13 of the Proceeds of Crime Act 2002).

The court may also consider whether to make ancillary orders. These may include a deprivation order, a financial reporting order, a serious crime prevention order and disqualification from acting as a company director.

STEP SEVEN
Reasons
Section 174 of the Criminal Justice Act 2003 imposes a duty to give reasons for, and explain the effect of, the sentence.

STEP EIGHT
Consideration for time spent on bail
The court must consider whether to give credit for time spent on bail in accordance with section 240A of the Criminal Justice Act 2003.

Effective from 1 October 2014

Appendix 1 *Fraud, Bribery and Money Laundering Offences etc*

Blank page

Possessing, making or supplying articles for use in fraud

Possession of articles for use in frauds
Fraud Act 2006 (section 6)

Triable either way
Maximum: 5 years' custody
Offence range: Band A fine – 3 years' custody

Making or supplying articles for use in frauds
Fraud Act 2006 (section 7)

Triable either way
Maximum: 10 years' custody
Offence range: Band C fine – 7 years' custody

Effective from 1 October 2014

Appendix 1   *Fraud, Bribery and Money Laundering Offences etc*

POSSESSING, MAKING OR SUPPLYING ARTICLES FOR USE IN FRAUD

STEP ONE
Determining the offence category

The court should determine the offence category with reference to the tables below. In order to determine the category the court should assess **culpability** and **harm**.

The level of **culpability** is determined by weighing up all the factors of the case to determine the offender's role and the extent to which the offending was planned and the sophistication with which it was carried out.

Culpability demonstrated by one or more of the following:

A – High culpability

A leading role where offending is part of a group activity

Involvement of others through pressure, influence

Abuse of position of power or trust or responsibility

Sophisticated nature of offence/significant planning

Fraudulent activity conducted over sustained period of time

Articles deliberately designed to target victims on basis of vulnerability

B – Medium culpability

Other cases where characteristics for categories A or C are not present

A significant role where offending is part of a group activity

C – Lesser culpability

Performed limited function under direction

Involved through coercion, intimidation or exploitation

Not motivated by personal gain

Opportunistic 'one-off' offence; very little or no planning

Limited awareness or understanding of extent of fraudulent activity

Where there are characteristics present which fall under different levels of culpability, the court should balance these characteristics to reach a fair assessment of the offender's culpability.

Harm

This guideline refers to preparatory offences where no substantive fraud has been committed. The level of **harm** is determined by weighing up all the factors of the case to determine the harm that would be caused if the article(s) were used to commit a substantive offence.

Greater harm

Large number of articles created/supplied/in possession

Article(s) have potential to facilitate fraudulent acts affecting large number of victims

Article(s) have potential to facilitate fraudulent acts involving significant sums

Use of third party identities

Offender making considerable gain as result of the offence

Lesser harm

All other offences

Fraud, Bribery and Money Laundering Offences etc

STEP TWO
Starting point and category range

Having determined the category at step one, the court should use the appropriate starting point to reach a sentence within the category range in the table below. The starting point applies to all offenders irrespective of plea or previous convictions.

Section 6 Fraud Act 2006: Possessing articles for use in fraud
Maximum: 5 years' custody

Harm	Culpability		
	A	B	C
Greater	**Starting point** 18 months' custody	**Starting point** 36 weeks' custody	**Starting point** High level community order
	Category range 36 weeks' custody – 3 years' custody	**Category range** High level community order – 2 years' custody	**Category range** Medium level community order – 26 weeks' custody
Lesser	**Starting point** 26 weeks' custody	**Starting point** Medium level community order	**Starting point** Band B fine
	Category range High level community order – 18 months' custody	**Category range** Low level community order – 26 weeks' custody	**Category range** Band A fine – Medium level community order

Section 7 Fraud Act 2006: Making or adapting or supplying articles for use in fraud
Maximum: 10 years' custody

Harm	Culpability		
	A	B	C
Greater	**Starting point** 4 years 6 months' custody	**Starting point** 2 years 6 months' custody	**Starting point** 1 year's custody
	Category range 3 – 7 years' custody	**Category range** 18 months' – 5 years' custody	**Category range** High level community order – 3 years' custody
Lesser	**Starting point** 2 years' custody	**Starting point** 36 weeks' custody	**Starting point** Medium level community order
	Category range 26 weeks' – 4 years' custody	**Category range** Low level community order – 2 years' custody	**Category range** Band C fine – 26 weeks' custody

Effective from 1 October 2014

Appendix 1 *Fraud, Bribery and Money Laundering Offences etc*

POSSESSING, MAKING OR SUPPLYING ARTICLES FOR USE IN FRAUD

The table below contains a non-exhaustive list of additional factual elements providing the context of the offence and factors relating to the offender.

Identify whether any combination of these or other relevant factors should result in an upward or downward adjustment from the starting point

Consecutive sentences for multiple offences may be appropriate where large sums are involved.

Factors increasing seriousness	Factors reducing seriousness or reflecting personal mitigation
Statutory aggravating factors:	
Previous convictions, having regard to a) the nature of the offence to which the conviction relates and its relevance to the current offence; and b) the time that has elapsed since the conviction	No previous convictions **or** no relevant/recent convictions
	Remorse
	Good character and/or exemplary conduct
Offence committed whilst on bail	Little or no prospect of success
Other aggravating factors:	Serious medical conditions requiring urgent, intensive or long-term treatment
Steps taken to prevent the victim reporting or obtaining assistance and/or from assisting or supporting the prosecution	Age and/or lack of maturity where it affects the responsibility of the offender
Attempts to conceal/dispose of evidence	Lapse of time since apprehension where this does not arise from the conduct of the offender
Established evidence of community/wider impact	Mental disorder or learning disability
Failure to comply with current court orders	Sole or primary carer for dependent relatives
Offence committed on licence	Offender co-operated with investigation, made early admissions and/or voluntarily reported offending
Offences taken into consideration	
Failure to respond to warnings about behaviour	Determination and/or demonstration of steps having been taken to address addiction or offending behaviour
Offences committed across borders	Activity originally legitimate
Blame wrongly placed on others	

See page 17.

Fraud, Bribery and Money Laundering Offences etc

STEP THREE
Consider any factors which indicate a reduction, such as assistance to the prosecution
The court should take into account sections 73 and 74 of the Serious Organised Crime and Police Act 2005 (assistance by defendants: reduction or review of sentence) and any other rule of law by virtue of which an offender may receive a discounted sentence in consequence of assistance given (or offered) to the prosecutor or investigator.

STEP FOUR
Reduction for guilty pleas
The court should take account of any potential reduction for a guilty plea in accordance with section 144 of the Criminal Justice Act 2003 and the *Guilty Plea* guideline.

STEP FIVE
Totality principle
If sentencing an offender for more than one offence, or where the offender is already serving a sentence, consider whether the total sentence is just and proportionate to the overall offending behaviour.

STEP SIX
Confiscation, compensation and ancillary orders
The court must proceed with a view to making a confiscation order if it is asked to do so by the prosecutor or if the court believes it is appropriate for it to do so.

Where the offence has resulted in loss or damage the court must consider whether to make a compensation order.

If the court makes both a confiscation order and an order for compensation and the court believes the offender will not have sufficient means to satisfy both orders in full, the court must direct that the compensation be paid out of sums recovered under the confiscation order (section 13 of the Proceeds of Crime Act 2002).

The court may also consider whether to make any ancillary orders.

STEP SEVEN
Reasons
Section 174 of the Criminal Justice Act 2003 imposes a duty to give reasons for, and explain the effect of, the sentence.

STEP EIGHT
Consideration for time spent on bail
The court must consider whether to give credit for time spent on bail in accordance with section 240A of the Criminal Justice Act 2003.

Effective from 1 October 2014

Appendix 1 *Fraud, Bribery and Money Laundering Offences etc*

POSSESSING, MAKING OR SUPPLYING ARTICLES FOR USE IN FRAUD

Blank page

Revenue fraud

Fraud
Conspiracy to defraud (common law)
Triable on indictment only
Fraud Act 2006 (section 1)
Triable either way

Maximum: 10 years' custody
Offence range: Low level community order – 8 years' custody

False accounting
Theft Act 1968 (section 17)

Fraudulent evasion of VAT; False statement for VAT purposes; Conduct amounting to an offence
Value Added Tax Act 1994 (section 72)

Fraudulent evasion of income tax
Taxes Management Act 1970 (section 106A)

Fraudulent evasion of excise duty; Improper importation of goods
Customs and Excise Management Act 1979 (sections 50, 170 and 170B)

Triable either way
Maximum: 7 years' custody
Offence range: Band C fine – 6 years and 6 months' custody

Fraud
Cheat the public revenue (common law)
Triable on indictment only
Maximum: Life imprisonment
Offence range: 3 – 17 years' custody

Effective from 1 October 2014

Appendix 1   *Fraud, Bribery and Money Laundering Offences etc*

REVENUE FRAUD

STEP ONE
Determining the offence category

The court should determine the offence category with reference to the tables below. In order to determine the category the court should assess **culpability** and **harm**.

The level of **culpability** is determined by weighing up all the factors of the case to determine the offender's role and the extent to which the offending was planned and the sophistication with which it was carried out.

Culpability demonstrated by one or more of the following:

A – High culpability

A leading role where offending is part of a group activity

Involvement of others through pressure/influence

Abuse of position of power or trust or responsibility

Sophisticated nature of offence/significant planning

Fraudulent activity conducted over sustained period of time

B – Medium culpability

Other cases where characteristics for categories A or C are not present

A significant role where offending is part of a group activity

C – Lesser culpability

Involved through coercion, intimidation or exploitation

Not motivated by personal gain

Opportunistic 'one-off' offence; very little or no planning

Performed limited function under direction

Limited awareness or understanding of extent of fraudulent activity

Harm – Gain/intended gain to offender or loss/intended loss to HMRC

Category 1
£50 million or more
Starting point based on £80 million

Category 2
£10 million–£50 million
Starting point based on £30 million

Category 3
£2 million–£10 million
Starting point based on £5 million

Category 4
£500,000–£2 million
Starting point based on £1 million

Category 5
£100,000–£500,000
Starting point based on £300,000

Category 6
£20,000–£100,000
Starting point based on £50,000

Category 7
Less than £20,000
Starting point based on £12,500

Where there are characteristics present which fall under different levels of culpability, the court should balance these characteristics to reach a fair assessment of the offender's culpability.

Effective from 1 October 2014

Fraud, Bribery and Money Laundering Offences etc

STEP TWO
Starting point and category range

Having determined the category at step one, the court should use the appropriate starting point to reach a sentence within the category range in the table below. The starting point applies to all offenders irrespective of plea or previous convictions.

Where the value is larger or smaller than the amount on which the starting point is based, this should lead to upward or downward adjustment as appropriate.

Where the value greatly exceeds the amount of the starting point in category 1, it may be appropriate to move outside the identified range.

TABLE 1
Section 1 Fraud Act 2006
Conspiracy to defraud (common law)
Maximum: 10 years' custody

For offences where the value of the fraud is over £2 million refer to the corresponding category in Table 3 subject to the maximum sentence of 10 years for this offence.

Harm	Culpability		
	A	B	C
Category 4 £500,000–£2 million	**Starting point** 7 years' custody	**Starting point** 5 years' custody	**Starting point** 3 years' custody
Starting point based on £1 million	**Category range** 5 – 8 years' custody	**Category range** 3 – 6 years' custody	**Category range** 18 months' – 4 years' custody
Category 5 £100,000–£500,000	**Starting point** 5 years' custody	**Starting point** 3 years' custody	**Starting point** 18 months' custody
Starting point based on £300,000	**Category range** 3 – 6 years' custody	**Category range** 18 months' – 4 years' custody	**Category range** 26 weeks' – 3 years' custody
Category 6 £20,000–£100,000	**Starting point** 3 years' custody	**Starting point** 18 months' custody	**Starting point** 26 weeks' custody
Starting point based on £50,000	**Category range** 18 months' – 4 years' custody	**Category range** 26 weeks' – 3 years' custody	**Category range** Medium level community order – 1 year's custody
Category 7 Less than £20,000	**Starting point** 18 months' custody	**Starting point** 36 weeks' custody	**Starting point** Medium level community order
Starting point based on £12,500	**Category range** 36 weeks' – 3 years' custody	**Category range** Medium level community order – 18 months' custody	**Category range** Low level community order – High level community order

Appendix 1 *Fraud, Bribery and Money Laundering Offences etc*

REVENUE FRAUD

TABLE 2
Section 17 Theft Act 1968: False Accounting
Section 72(1) Value Added Tax Act 1994: Fraudulent evasion of VAT
Section 72(3) Valued Added Tax Act 1994: False statement for VAT purposes
Section 72(8) Value Added Tax Act 1994: Conduct amounting to an offence
Section 106(a) Taxes Management Act 1970: Fraudulent evasion of income tax
Section 170(1)(a)(i), (ii), (b), 170(2)(a), 170B Customs and Excise Management Act 1979: Fraudulent evasion of excise duty
Section 50(1)(a), (2) Customs and Excise Management Act 1979: Improper importation of goods
Maximum: 7 years' custody

Harm	Culpability A	Culpability B	Culpability C
Category 4 £500,000–£2 million	**Starting point** 5 years 6 months' custody	**Starting point** 4 years' custody	**Starting point** 2 years 6 months' custody
Starting point based on £1 million	**Category range** 4 years' – 6 years 6 months' custody	**Category range** 2 years 6 months' – 5 years' custody	**Category range** 15 months' – 3 years 6 months' custody
Category 5 £100,000–£500,000	**Starting point** 4 years' custody	**Starting point** 2 years 6 months' custody	**Starting point** 15 months' custody
Starting point based on £300,000	**Category range** 2 years 6 months' – 5 years' custody	**Category range** 15 months' – 3 years 6 months' custody	**Category range** 26 weeks' – 2 years 6 months' custody
Category 6 £20,000–£100,000	**Starting point** 2 years 6 months' custody	**Starting point** 15 months' custody	**Starting point** High level community order
Starting point based on £50,000	**Category range** 15 months' – 3 years 6 months' custody	**Category range** High level community order – 2 years 6 months' custody	**Category range** Low level community order – 36 weeks' custody
Category 7 Less than £20,000	**Starting point** 15 months' custody	**Starting point** 26 weeks' custody	**Starting point** Medium level community order
Starting point based on £12,500	**Category range** 26 weeks' – 2 years 6 months' custody	**Category range** Medium level community order – 15 months' custody	**Category range** Band C fine – High level community order

See page 23.

Effective from 1 October 2014

Fraud, Bribery and Money Laundering Offences etc

TABLE 3
Cheat the Revenue (common law)
Maximum: Life imprisonment

Where the offending is on the most serious scale, involving sums significantly higher than the starting point in category 1, sentences of 15 years and above may be appropriate depending on the role of the offender. In cases involving sums below £2 million the court should refer to Table 1.

Harm	Culpability		
	A	B	C
Category 1 £50 million or more	**Starting point** 12 years' custody	**Starting point** 8 years' custody	**Starting point** 6 years' custody
Starting point based on £80 million	**Category range** 10 – 17 years' custody	**Category range** 7 – 12 years' custody	**Category range** 4 – 8 years' custody
Category 2 £10 million–£50 million	**Starting point** 10 years' custody	**Starting point** 7 years' custody	**Starting point** 5 years' custody
Starting point based on £30 million	**Category range** 8 – 13 years' custody	**Category range** 5 – 9 years' custody	**Category range** 3 – 6 years' custody
Category 3 £2 million–£10 million	**Starting point** 8 years' custody	**Starting point** 6 years' custody	**Starting point** 4 years' custody
Starting point based on £5 million	**Category range** 6 – 10 years' custody	**Category range** 4 – 7 years' custody	**Category range** 3 – 5 years' custody

See page 24.

Effective from 1 October 2014

Appendix 1   *Fraud, Bribery and Money Laundering Offences etc*

REVENUE FRAUD

The table below contains a non-exhaustive list of additional factual elements providing the context of the offence and factors relating to the offender.

Identify whether any combination of these or other relevant factors should result in any further upward or downward adjustment from the starting point.

Consecutive sentences for multiple offences may be appropriate where large sums are involved.

Factors increasing seriousness	Factors reducing seriousness or reflecting personal mitigation
Statutory aggravating factors:	No previous convictions **or** no relevant/recent convictions
Previous convictions, having regard to a) the nature of the offence to which the conviction relates and its relevance to the current offence; and b) the time that has elapsed since the conviction	Remorse
	Good character and/or exemplary conduct
Offence committed whilst on bail	Little or no prospect of success
Other aggravating factors:	Serious medical condition requiring urgent, intensive or long term treatment
Involves multiple frauds	Age and/or lack of maturity where it affects the responsibility of the offender
Number of false declarations	
Attempts to conceal/dispose of evidence	Lapse of time since apprehension where this does not arise from the conduct of the offender
Failure to comply with current court orders	
Offence committed on licence	Mental disorder or learning disability
Offences taken into consideration	Sole or primary carer for dependent relatives
Failure to respond to warnings about behaviour	Offender co-operated with investigation, made early admissions and/or voluntarily reported offending
Blame wrongly placed on others	Determination and/or demonstration of steps having been taken to address addiction or offending behaviour
Damage to third party (for example as a result of identity theft)	Activity originally legitimate
Dealing with goods with an additional health risk	
Disposing of goods to under age purchasers	

See page 25.

Effective from 1 October 2014

Fraud, Bribery and Money Laundering Offences etc

STEP THREE
Consider any factors which indicate a reduction, such as assistance to the prosecution
The court should take into account sections 73 and 74 of the Serious Organised Crime and Police Act 2005 (assistance by defendants: reduction or review of sentence) and any other rule of law by virtue of which an offender may receive a discounted sentence in consequence of assistance given (or offered) to the prosecutor or investigator.

STEP FOUR
Reduction for guilty pleas
The court should take account of any potential reduction for a guilty plea in accordance with section 144 of the Criminal Justice Act 2003 and the *Guilty Plea* guideline.

STEP FIVE
Totality principle
If sentencing an offender for more than one offence, or where the offender is already serving a sentence, consider whether the total sentence is just and proportionate to the overall offending behaviour.

STEP SIX
Confiscation, compensation and ancillary orders
The court must proceed with a view to making a confiscation order if it is asked to do so by the prosecutor or if the court believes it is appropriate for it to do so.

Where the offence has resulted in loss or damage the court must consider whether to make a compensation order.

If the court makes both a confiscation order and an order for compensation and the court believes the offender will not have sufficient means to satisfy both orders in full, the court must direct that the compensation be paid out of sums recovered under the confiscation order (section 13 of the Proceeds of Crime Act 2002).

The court may also consider whether to make ancillary orders. These may include a deprivation order, a financial reporting order, a serious crime prevention order and disqualification from acting as a company director.

STEP SEVEN
Reasons
Section 174 of the Criminal Justice Act 2003 imposes a duty to give reasons for, and explain the effect of, the sentence.

STEP EIGHT
Consideration for time spent on bail
The court must consider whether to give credit for time spent on bail in accordance with section 240A of the Criminal Justice Act 2003.

Effective from 1 October 2014

Appendix 1 *Fraud, Bribery and Money Laundering Offences etc*

REVENUE FRAUD

Blank page

Benefit fraud

Dishonest representations for obtaining benefit etc
Social Security Administration Act 1992 (section 111A)

Tax Credit fraud
Tax Credits Act 2002 (section 35)

False accounting
Theft Act 1968 (section 17)

Triable either way
Maximum: 7 years' custody
Offence range: Discharge – 6 years 6 months' custody

False representations for obtaining benefit etc
Social Security Administration Act 1992 (section 112)

Triable summarily only
Maximum: Level 5 fine and/or 3 months' custody
Offence range: Discharge – 12 weeks' custody

Fraud by false representation, fraud by failing to disclose information, fraud by abuse of position
Fraud Act 2006 (section 1)
Triable either way

Conspiracy to defraud
Common law
Triable on indictment only

Maximum: 10 years' custody
Offence range: Discharge – 8 years' custody

Effective from 1 October 2014

Appendix 1 Fraud, Bribery and Money Laundering Offences etc

BENEFIT FRAUD

STEP ONE
Determining the offence category

The court should determine the offence category with reference to the tables below. In order to determine the category the court should assess **culpability** and **harm**.

The level of **culpability** is determined by weighing up all the factors of the case to determine the offender's role and the extent to which the offending was planned and the sophistication with which it was carried out.

Culpability demonstrated by one or more of the following:

A – High culpability

A leading role where offending is part of a group activity

Involvement of others through pressure/influence

Abuse of position of power or trust or responsibility

Sophisticated nature of offence/significant planning

B – Medium culpability

Other cases where characteristics for categories A or C are not present

Claim not fraudulent from the outset

A significant role where offending is part of a group activity

C – Lesser culpability

Involved through coercion, intimidation or exploitation

Performed limited function under direction

Harm – Amount obtained or intended to be obtained

Category 1
£500,000–£2 million
Starting point based on £1 million

Category 2
£100,000–£500,000
Starting point based on £300,000

Category 3
£50,000–£100,000
Starting point based on £75,000

Category 4
£10,000–£50,000
Starting point based on £30,000

Category 5
£2,500–£10,000
Starting point based on £5,000

Category 6
Less than £2,500
Starting point based on £1,000

Where there are characteristics present which fall under different levels of culpability, the court should balance these characteristics to reach a fair assessment of the offender's culpability.

Fraud, Bribery and Money Laundering Offences etc

STEP TWO
Starting point and category range

Having determined the category at step one, the court should use the appropriate starting point to reach a sentence within the category range in the table below. The starting point applies to all offenders irrespective of plea or previous convictions.

Where the value is larger or smaller than the amount on which the starting point is based, this should lead to upward or downward adjustment as appropriate.

Where the value greatly exceeds the amount of the starting point in category 1, it may be appropriate to move outside the identified range.

BENEFIT FRAUD

TABLE 1
Section 111A Social Security Administration Act 1992: Dishonest representations to obtain benefit etc
Section 35 Tax Credits Act 2002: Tax Credit fraud
Section 17 Theft Act 1968: False accounting
Maximum: 7 years' custody

Harm	Culpability		
	A	B	C
Category 1 £500,000 or more	**Starting point** 5 years 6 months' custody	**Starting point** 4 years' custody	**Starting point** 2 years 6 months' custody
Starting point based on £1 million	Category range 4 years' – 6 years 6 months' custody	Category range 2 years 6 months' – 5 years' custody	Category range 15 months' – 3 years 6 months' custody
Category 2 £100,000–£500,000	**Starting point** 4 years' custody	**Starting point** 2 years 6 months' custody	**Starting point** 1 year's custody
Starting point based on £300,000	Category range 2 years 6 months' – 5 years' custody	Category range 15 months' – 3 years 6 months' custody	Category range 26 weeks' – 2 years 6 months' custody
Category 3 £50,000–£100,000	**Starting point** 2 years 6 months' custody	**Starting point** 1 year's custody	**Starting point** 26 weeks' custody
Starting point based on £75,000	Category range 2 years' – 3 years 6 months' custody	Category range 26 weeks' – 2 years 6 months' custody	Category range High level community order – 36 weeks' custody
Category 4 £10,000–£50,000	**Starting point** 18 months' custody	**Starting point** 36 weeks' custody	**Starting point** Medium level community order
Starting point based on £30,000	Category range 36 weeks' – 2 years 6 months' custody	Category range Medium level community order – 21 months' custody	Category range Low level community order – 26 weeks' custody
Category 5 £2,500–£10,000	**Starting point** 36 weeks' custody	**Starting point** Medium level community order	**Starting point** Low level community order
Starting point based on £5,000	Category range Medium level community order – 18 months' custody	Category range Low level community order – 26 weeks' custody	Category range Band B fine – Medium level community order
Category 6 Less than £2,500	**Starting point** Medium level community order	**Starting point** Low level community order	**Starting point** Band A fine
Starting point based on £1,000	Category range Low level community order – 26 weeks' custody	Category range Band A fine – Medium level community order	Category range Discharge – Band B fine

Effective from 1 October 2014

Appendix 1 *Fraud, Bribery and Money Laundering Offences etc*

TABLE 2
Section 112 Social Security Administration Act 1992: False representations for obtaining benefit etc
Maximum: Level 5 fine and/or 3 months' custody

BENEFIT FRAUD

Harm	Culpability		
	A	**B**	**C**
Category 5 Above £2,500	**Starting point** High level community order	**Starting point** Medium level community order	**Starting point** Low level community order
Starting point based on £5,000	**Category range** Medium level community order – 12 weeks' custody	**Category range** Band B fine – High level community order	**Category range** Band A fine – Medium level community order
Category 6 Less than £2,500	**Starting point** Medium level community order	**Starting point** Band B fine	**Starting point** Band A fine
Starting point based on £1,000	**Category range** Low level community order – High level community order	**Category range** Band A fine – Band C fine	**Category range** Discharge – Band B fine

See page 31.

Effective from 1 October 2014

TABLE 3
Section 1 Fraud Act 2006
Conspiracy to defraud (common law)
Maximum: 10 years' custody

Harm	Culpability		
	A	**B**	**C**
Category 1 £500,000 or more	**Starting point** 7 years' custody	**Starting point** 5 years' custody	**Starting point** 3 years' custody
Starting point based on £1 million	**Category range** 5 – 8 years' custody	**Category range** 3 – 6 years' custody	**Category range** 18 months' – 4 years' custody
Category 2 £100,000–£500,000	**Starting point** 5 years' custody	**Starting point** 3 years' custody	**Starting point** 15 months' custody
Starting point based on £300,000	**Category range** 3 – 6 years' custody	**Category range** 18 months' – 4 years' custody	**Category range** 26 weeks' – 3 years' custody
Category 3 £50,000–£100,000	**Starting point** 3 years' custody	**Starting point** 15 months' custody	**Starting point** 36 weeks' custody
Starting point based on £75,000	**Category range** 2 years 6 months' – 4 years' custody	**Category range** 36 weeks' – 3 years' custody	**Category range** 26 weeks' – 1 year's custody
Category 4 £10,000–£50,000	**Starting point** 21 months' custody	**Starting point** 1 year's custody	**Starting point** High level community order
Starting point based on £30,000	**Category range** 1 year's – 3 years' custody	**Category range** High level community order – 2 years' custody	**Category range** Low level community order – 26 weeks' custody
Category 5 £2,500–£10,000	**Starting point** 1 year's custody	**Starting point** High level community order	**Starting point** Medium level community order
Starting point based on £5,000	**Category range** High level community order – 2 years' custody	**Category range** Low level community order – 26 weeks' custody	**Category range** Band C fine – High level community order
Category 6 Less than £2,500	**Starting point** High level community order	**Starting point** Low level community order	**Starting point** Band B fine
Starting point based on £1,000	**Category range** Low level community order – 26 weeks' custody	**Category range** Band B fine – Medium level community order	**Category range** Discharge – Band C fine

BENEFIT FRAUD

Effective from 1 October 2014

Appendix 1 *Fraud, Bribery and Money Laundering Offences etc*

32 Fraud, Bribery and Money Laundering Offences Definitive Guideline

The table below contains a non-exhaustive list of additional factual elements providing the context of the offence and factors relating to the offender.

Identify whether any combination of these or other relevant factors should result in any further upward or downward adjustment from the starting point.

Consecutive sentences for multiple offences may be appropriate where large sums are involved.

BENEFIT FRAUD

Factors increasing seriousness	Factors reducing seriousness or reflecting personal mitigation
Statutory aggravating factors:	No previous convictions **or** no relevant/recent convictions
Previous convictions, having regard to a) the nature of the offence to which the conviction relates and its relevance to the current offence; and b) the time that has elapsed since the conviction	Remorse
	Good character and/or exemplary conduct
Offence committed whilst on bail	Serious medical condition requiring urgent, intensive or long term treatment
Other aggravating factors:	Legitimate entitlement to benefits not claimed
Claim fraudulent from the outset	Little or no prospect of success
Proceeds of fraud funded lavish lifestyle	Age and/or lack of maturity where it affects the responsibility of the offender
Length of time over which the offending was committed	
Number of false declarations	Lapse of time since apprehension where this does not arise from the conduct of the offender
Attempts to conceal/dispose of evidence	
Failure to comply with current court orders	Mental disorder or learning disability
Offence committed on licence	Sole or primary carer for dependent relatives
Offences taken into consideration	Offender co-operated with investigation, made early admissions and/or voluntarily reported offending
Failure to respond to warnings about behaviour	Determination and/or demonstration of steps having been taken to address addiction or offending behaviour
Blame wrongly placed on others	
Damage to third party (for example as a result of identity theft)	Offender experiencing significant financial hardship or pressure at time fraud was committed due to **exceptional** circumstances

See page 33.

Effective from 1 October 2014

Fraud, Bribery and Money Laundering Offences etc

STEP THREE
Consider any factors which indicate a reduction, such as assistance to the prosecution
The court should take into account sections 73 and 74 of the Serious Organised Crime and Police Act 2005 (assistance by defendants: reduction or review of sentence) and any other rule of law by virtue of which an offender may receive a discounted sentence in consequence of assistance given (or offered) to the prosecutor or investigator.

STEP FOUR
Reduction for guilty pleas
The court should take account of any potential reduction for a guilty plea in accordance with section 144 of the Criminal Justice Act 2003 and the *Guilty Plea* guideline.

STEP FIVE
Totality principle
If sentencing an offender for more than one offence, or where the offender is already serving a sentence, consider whether the total sentence is just and proportionate to the overall offending behaviour.

STEP SIX
Confiscation, compensation and ancillary orders
The court must proceed with a view to making a confiscation order if it is asked to do so by the prosecutor or if the court believes it is appropriate for it to do so.

Where the offence has resulted in loss or damage the court must consider whether to make a compensation order.

If the court makes both a confiscation order and an order for compensation and the court believes the offender will not have sufficient means to satisfy both orders in full, the court must direct that the compensation be paid out of sums recovered under the confiscation order (section 13 of the Proceeds of Crime Act 2002).

The court may also consider whether to make any ancillary orders.

STEP SEVEN
Reasons
Section 174 of the Criminal Justice Act 2003 imposes a duty to give reasons for, and explain the effect of, the sentence.

STEP EIGHT
Consideration for time spent on bail
The court must consider whether to give credit for time spent on bail in accordance with section 240A of the Criminal Justice Act 2003.

Appendix 1 *Fraud, Bribery and Money Laundering Offences etc*

Blank page

Money laundering

Concealing/disguising/converting/transferring/removing criminal property from England & Wales
Proceeds of Crime Act 2002 (section 327)

Entering into arrangements concerning criminal property
Proceeds of Crime Act 2002 (section 328)

Acquisition, use and possession of criminal property
Proceeds of Crime Act 2002 (section 329)

Triable either way
Maximum: 14 years' custody
Offence range: Band B fine – 13 years' imprisonment

Effective from 1 October 2014

Appendix 1 *Fraud, Bribery and Money Laundering Offences etc*

STEP ONE
Determining the offence category

The court should determine the offence category with reference to the tables below. In order to determine the category the court should assess **culpability** and **harm**.

The level of **culpability** is determined by weighing up all the factors of the case to determine the offender's role and the extent to which the offending was planned and the sophistication with which it was carried out.

Culpability demonstrated by one or more of the following:

A – High culpability

A leading role where offending is part of a group activity

Involvement of others through pressure, influence

Abuse of position of power or trust or responsibility

Sophisticated nature of offence/significant planning

Criminal activity conducted over sustained period of time

B – Medium culpability

Other cases where characteristics for categories A or C are not present

A significant role where offending is part of a group activity

C – Lesser culpability

Performed limited function under direction

Involved through coercion, intimidation or exploitation

Not motivated by personal gain

Opportunistic 'one-off' offence; very little or no planning

Limited awareness or understanding of extent of criminal activity

Where there are characteristics present which fall under different levels of culpability, the court should balance these characteristics to reach a fair assessment of the offender's culpability.

Harm A

Harm is initially assessed by the value of the money laundered.

Category 1
£10 million or more
Starting point based on £30 million

Category 2
£2 million–£10 million
Starting point based on £5 million

Category 3
£500,000–£2 million
Starting point based on £1 million

Category 4
£100,000–£500,000
Starting point based on £300,000

Category 5
£10,000–£100,000
Starting point based on £50,000

Category 6
Less than £10,000
Starting point based on £5,000

Harm B

Money laundering is an integral component of much serious criminality. **To complete the assessment of harm, the court should take into account the level of harm associated with the underlying offence to determine whether it warrants upward adjustment of the starting point within the range, or in appropriate cases, outside the range.**

Where it is possible to identify the underlying offence, regard should be given to the relevant sentencing levels for that offence.

Effective from 1 October 2014

Fraud, Bribery and Money Laundering Offences etc

STEP TWO
Starting point and category range

Having determined the category at step one, the court should use the appropriate starting point (as adjusted in accordance with step one above) to reach a sentence within the category range in the table below. The starting point applies to all offenders irrespective of plea or previous convictions.

Where the value is larger or smaller than the amount on which the starting point is based, this should lead to upward or downward adjustment as appropriate.

Where the value greatly exceeds the amount of the starting point in category 1, it may be appropriate to move outside the identified range.

Section 327 Proceeds of Crime Act 2002: Concealing/disguising/converting/transferring/removing criminal property from England & Wales
Section 328 Proceeds of Crime Act 2002: Entering into arrangements concerning criminal property
Section 329 Proceeds of Crime Act 2002: Acquisition, use and possession of criminal property
Maximum: 14 years' custody

Harm	Culpability A	Culpability B	Culpability C
Category 1 £10 million or more	**Starting point** 10 years' custody	**Starting point** 7 years' custody	**Starting point** 4 years' custody
Starting point based on £30 million	**Category range** 8 – 13 years' custody	**Category range** 5 – 10 years' custody	**Category range** 3 – 6 years' custody
Category 2 £2 million–£10 million	**Starting point** 8 years' custody	**Starting point** 5 years' custody	**Starting point** 3 years 6 months' custody
Starting point based on £5 million	**Category range** 6 – 9 years' custody	**Category range** 3 years 6 months' – 7 years' custody	**Category range** 2 – 5 years' custody
Category 3 £500,000–£2 million	**Starting point** 7 years' custody	**Starting point** 5 years' custody	**Starting point** 3 years' custody
Starting point based on £1 million	**Category range** 5 – 8 years' custody	**Category range** 3 – 6 years' custody	**Category range** 18 months' – 4 years' custody
Category 4 £100,000–£500,000	**Starting point** 5 years' custody	**Starting point** 3 years' custody	**Starting point** 18 months' custody
Starting point based on £300,000	**Category range** 3 – 6 years' custody	**Category range** 18 months' – 4 years' custody	**Category range** 26 weeks' – 3 years' custody
Category 5 £10,000–£100,000	**Starting point** 3 years' custody	**Starting point** 18 months' custody	**Starting point** 26 weeks' custody
Starting point based on £50,000	**Category range** 18 months' – 4 years' custody	**Category range** 26 weeks' – 3 years' custody	**Category range** Medium level community order – 1 year's custody
Category 6 Less than £10,000	**Starting point** 1 year's custody	**Starting point** High level community order	**Starting point** Low level community order
Starting point based on £5,000	**Category range** 26 weeks' – 2 years' custody	**Category range** Low level community order – 1 year's custody	**Category range** Band B fine – Medium level community order

Effective from 1 October 2014

Appendix 1   *Fraud, Bribery and Money Laundering Offences etc*

The table below contains a non-exhaustive list of additional factual elements providing the context of the offence and factors relating to the offender.

Identify whether any combination of these or other relevant factors should result in an upward or downward adjustment of the sentence arrived at thus far.

Consecutive sentences for multiple offences may be appropriate where large sums are involved.

Factors increasing seriousness	Factors reducing seriousness or reflecting personal mitigation
Statutory aggravating factors:	No previous convictions **or** no relevant/recent convictions
Previous convictions, having regard to a) the nature of the offence to which the conviction relates and its relevance to the current offence; and b) the time that has elapsed since the conviction	Remorse
	Little or no prospect of success
Offence committed whilst on bail	Good character and/or exemplary conduct
Other aggravating factors:	Serious medical conditions requiring urgent, intensive or long-term treatment
Attempts to conceal/dispose of evidence	Age and/or lack of maturity where it affects the responsibility of the offender
Established evidence of community/wider impact	
Failure to comply with current court orders	Lapse of time since apprehension where this does not arise from the conduct of the offender
Offence committed on licence	Mental disorder or learning disability
Offences taken into consideration	Sole or primary carer for dependent relatives
Failure to respond to warnings about behaviour	Offender co-operated with investigation, made early admissions and/or voluntarily reported offending
Offences committed across borders	
Blame wrongly placed on others	Determination and/or demonstration of steps having been taken to address addiction or offending behaviour
Damage to third party for example loss of employment to legitimate employees	Activity originally legitimate

See page 39.

Fraud, Bribery and Money Laundering Offences etc

STEP THREE
Consider any factors which indicate a reduction, such as assistance to the prosecution
The court should take into account sections 73 and 74 of the Serious Organised Crime and Police Act 2005 (assistance by defendants: reduction or review of sentence) and any other rule of law by virtue of which an offender may receive a discounted sentence in consequence of assistance given (or offered) to the prosecutor or investigator.

STEP FOUR
Reduction for guilty pleas
The court should take account of any potential reduction for a guilty plea in accordance with section 144 of the Criminal Justice Act 2003 and the *Guilty Plea* guideline.

STEP FIVE
Totality principle
If sentencing an offender for more than one offence, or where the offender is already serving a sentence, consider whether the total sentence is just and proportionate to the overall offending behaviour.

STEP SIX
Confiscation, compensation and ancillary orders
The court must proceed with a view to making a confiscation order if it is asked to do so by the prosecutor or if the court believes it is appropriate for it to do so.

Where the offence has resulted in loss or damage the court must consider whether to make a compensation order.

If the court makes both a confiscation order and an order for compensation and the court believes the offender will not have sufficient means to satisfy both orders in full, the court must direct that the compensation be paid out of sums recovered under the confiscation order (section 13 of the Proceeds of Crime Act 2002).

The court may also consider whether to make ancillary orders. These may include a deprivation order, a financial reporting order, a serious crime prevention order and disqualification from acting as a company director.

STEP SEVEN
Reasons
Section 174 of the Criminal Justice Act 2003 imposes a duty to give reasons for, and explain the effect of, the sentence.

STEP EIGHT
Consideration for time spent on bail
The court must consider whether to give credit for time spent on bail in accordance with section 240A of the Criminal Justice Act 2003.

Effective from 1 October 2014

Appendix 1 *Fraud, Bribery and Money Laundering Offences etc*

Blank page

Bribery

Bribing another person
Bribery Act 2010 (section 1)

Being bribed
Bribery Act 2010 (section 2)

Bribery of foreign public officials
Bribery Act 2010 (section 6)

Triable either way
Maximum: 10 years' custody
Offence range: Discharge – 8 years' custody

Appendix 1 Fraud, Bribery and Money Laundering Offences etc

BRIBERY

STEP ONE
Determining the offence category

The court should determine the offence category with reference to the tables below. In order to determine the category the court should assess **culpability** and **harm**.

The level of **culpability** is determined by weighing up all the factors of the case to determine the offender's role and the extent to which the offending was planned and the sophistication with which it was carried out.

Harm is assessed in relation to any impact caused by the offending (whether to identifiable victims or in a wider context) and the actual or intended gain to the offender.

Culpability demonstrated by one or more of the following:

A – High culpability

A leading role where offending is part of a group activity

Involvement of others through pressure, influence

Abuse of position of significant power or trust or responsibility

Intended corruption (directly or indirectly) of a senior official performing a public function

Intended corruption (directly or indirectly) of a law enforcement officer

Sophisticated nature of offence/significant planning

Offending conducted over sustained period of time

Motivated by expectation of substantial financial, commercial or political gain

B – Medium culpability

All other cases where characteristics for categories A or C are not present

A significant role where offending is part of a group activity

C – Lesser culpability

Involved through coercion, intimidation or exploitation

Not motivated by personal gain

Peripheral role in organised activity

Opportunistic 'one-off' offence; very little or no planning

Limited awareness or understanding of extent of corrupt activity

Where there are characteristics present which fall under different levels of culpability, the court should balance these characteristics to reach a fair assessment of the offender's culpability.

Harm demonstrated by one or more of the following factors:

Category 1	• Serious detrimental effect on individuals (for example by provision of substandard goods or services resulting from the corrupt behaviour) • Serious environmental impact • Serious undermining of the proper function of local or national government, business or public services • Substantial actual or intended financial gain to offender or another or loss caused to others
Category 2	• Significant detrimental effect on individuals • Significant environmental impact • Significant undermining of the proper function of local or national government, business or public services • Significant actual or intended financial gain to offender or another or loss caused to others • Risk of category 1 harm
Category 3	• Limited detrimental impact on individuals, the environment, government, business or public services • Risk of category 2 harm
Category 4	• Risk of category 3 harm

Risk of harm involves consideration of both the likelihood of harm occurring and the extent of it if it does. Risk of harm is less serious than the same actual harm. Where the offence has caused risk of harm but no (or much less) actual harm, the normal approach is to move to the next category of harm down. This may not be appropriate if either the likelihood or extent of potential harm is particularly high.

Fraud, Bribery and Money Laundering Offences etc

STEP TWO
Starting point and category range

Having determined the category at step one, the court should use the corresponding starting point to reach a sentence within the category range below. The starting point applies to all offenders irrespective of plea or previous convictions.

Section 1 Bribery Act 2010: Bribing another person
Section 2 Bribery Act 2010: Being bribed
Section 6 Bribery Act 2010: Bribery of foreign public officials
Maximum: 10 years' custody

Harm	Culpability		
	A	B	C
Category 1	**Starting point** 7 years' custody	**Starting point** 5 years' custody	**Starting point** 3 years' custody
	Category range 5 – 8 years' custody	**Category range** 3 – 6 years' custody	**Category range** 18 months' – 4 years' custody
Category 2	**Starting point** 5 years' custody	**Starting point** 3 years' custody	**Starting point** 18 months' custody
	Category range 3 – 6 years' custody	**Category range** 18 months' – 4 years' custody	**Category range** 26 weeks' – 3 years' custody
Category 3	**Starting point** 3 years' custody	**Starting point** 18 months' custody	**Starting point** 26 weeks' custody
	Category range 18 months' – 4 years' custody	**Category range** 26 weeks' – 3 years' custody	**Category range** Medium level community order – 1 year's custody
Category 4	**Starting point** 18 months' custody	**Starting point** 26 weeks' custody	**Starting point** Medium level community order
	Category range 26 weeks' – 3 years' custody	**Category range** Medium level community order – 1 year's custody	**Category range** Band B fine – High level community order

See page 44.

Effective from 1 October 2014

Appendix 1 *Fraud, Bribery and Money Laundering Offences etc*

BRIBERY

The table below contains a non-exhaustive list of additional factual elements providing the context of the offence and factors relating to the offender.

Identify whether any combination of these or other relevant factors should result in an upward or downward adjustment from the starting point.

Consecutive sentences for multiple offences may be appropriate where large sums are involved.

Factors increasing seriousness	Factors reducing seriousness or reflecting personal mitigation
Statutory aggravating factors:	No previous convictions **or** no relevant/recent convictions
Previous convictions, having regard to a) the nature of the offence to which the conviction relates and its relevance to the current offence; and b) the time that has elapsed since the conviction	Remorse
	Good character and/or exemplary conduct
Offence committed whilst on bail	Little or no prospect of success
Other aggravating factors:	Serious medical conditions requiring urgent, intensive or long-term treatment
Steps taken to prevent victims reporting or obtaining assistance and/or from assisting or supporting the prosecution	Age and/or lack of maturity where it affects the responsibility of the offender
Attempts to conceal/dispose of evidence	Lapse of time since apprehension where this does not arise from the conduct of the offender
Established evidence of community/wider impact	Mental disorder or learning disability
Failure to comply with current court orders	Sole or primary carer for dependent relatives
Offence committed on licence	Offender co-operated with investigation, made early admissions and/or voluntarily reported offending
Offences taken into consideration	
Failure to respond to warnings about behaviour	
Offences committed across borders	
Blame wrongly placed on others	
Pressure exerted on another party	
Offence committed to facilitate other criminal activity	

See page 45.

Fraud, Bribery and Money Laundering Offences etc

STEP THREE
Consider any factors which indicate a reduction, such as assistance to the prosecution
The court should take into account sections 73 and 74 of the Serious Organised Crime and Police Act 2005 (assistance by defendants: reduction or review of sentence) and any other rule of law by virtue of which an offender may receive a discounted sentence in consequence of assistance given (or offered) to the prosecutor or investigator.

STEP FOUR
Reduction for guilty pleas
The court should take account of any potential reduction for a guilty plea in accordance with section 144 of the Criminal Justice Act 2003 and the *Guilty Plea* guideline.

STEP FIVE
Totality principle
If sentencing an offender for more than one offence, or where the offender is already serving a sentence, consider whether the total sentence is just and proportionate to the overall offending behaviour.

STEP SIX
Confiscation, compensation and ancillary orders
The court must proceed with a view to making a confiscation order if it is asked to do so by the prosecutor or if the court believes it is appropriate for it to do so.

Where the offence has resulted in loss or damage the court must consider whether to make a compensation order.

If the court makes both a confiscation order and an order for compensation and the court believes the offender will not have sufficient means to satisfy both orders in full, the court must direct that the compensation be paid out of sums recovered under the confiscation order (section 13 of the Proceeds of Crime Act 2002).

The court may also consider whether to make ancillary orders. These may include a deprivation order, a financial reporting order, a serious crime prevention order and disqualification from acting as a company director.

STEP SEVEN
Reasons
Section 174 of the Criminal Justice Act 2003 imposes a duty to give reasons for, and explain the effect of, the sentence.

STEP EIGHT
Consideration for time spent on bail
The court must consider whether to give credit for time spent on bail in accordance with section 240A of the Criminal Justice Act 2003.

Appendix 1 *Fraud, Bribery and Money Laundering Offences etc*

BRIBERY

Blank page

Corporate Offenders:
Fraud, Bribery and Money Laundering

Fraud
Conspiracy to defraud (common law)
Cheat the public revenue (common law)
Triable only on indictment

Fraud Act 2006 (sections 1, 6 and 7)
Theft Act 1968 (section 17)
Value Added Tax Act 1994 (section 72)
Customs and Excise Management Act 1979 (section 170)
Triable either way

Bribery
Bribery Act 2010 (sections 1, 2, 6 and 7)
Triable either way

Money laundering
Proceeds of Crime Act 2002 (sections 327, 328 and 329)
Triable either way

Maximum: Unlimited fine

Most cases of corporate offending in this area are likely to merit allocation for trial to the Crown Court.

Committal for sentence is mandatory if confiscation (see step two) is to be considered. (Proceeds of Crime Act 2002 section 70).

Effective from 1 October 2014

Appendix 1 *Fraud, Bribery and Money Laundering Offences etc*

STEP ONE
Compensation

The court must consider making a compensation order requiring the offender to pay compensation for any personal injury, loss or damage resulting from the offence in such an amount as the court considers appropriate, having regard to the evidence and to the means of the offender.

Where the means of the offender are limited, priority should be given to the payment of compensation over payment of any other financial penalty.

Reasons should be given if a compensation order is not made.

(See section 130 Powers of Criminal Courts (Sentencing) Act 2000)

STEP TWO
Confiscation

Confiscation must be considered if either the Crown asks for it or the court thinks that it may be appropriate.

Confiscation must be dealt with before, and taken into account when assessing, any other fine or financial order (except compensation).

(See Proceeds of Crime Act 2002 sections 6 and 13)

See page 49.

STEP THREE
Determining the offence category

The court should determine the offence category with reference to **culpability** and **harm**.

Culpability		Harm	
The sentencer should weigh up all the factors of the case to determine **culpability**. **Where there are characteristics present which fall under different categories, the court should balance these characteristics to reach a fair assessment of the offender's culpability.**		Harm is represented by a financial sum calculated by reference to the table below	
Culpability demonstrated by the offending corporation's role and motivation. May be demonstrated by one or more of the following **non-exhaustive** characteristics.		**Amount obtained or intended to be obtained (or loss avoided or intended to be avoided)**	
A – High culpability		Fraud	For offences of fraud, conspiracy to defraud, cheating the Revenue and fraudulent evasion of duty or VAT, harm will normally be the actual or intended gross gain to the offender.
Corporation plays a leading role in organised, planned unlawful activity (whether acting alone or with others)		Bribery	For offences under the Bribery Act the appropriate figure will normally be the gross profit from the contract obtained, retained or sought as a result of the offending. An alternative measure for offences under section 7 may be the likely cost avoided by failing to put in place appropriate measures to prevent bribery.
Wilful obstruction of detection (for example destruction of evidence, misleading investigators, suborning employees)			
Involving others through pressure or coercion (for example employees or suppliers)			
Targeting of vulnerable victims or a large number of victims		Money laundering	For offences of money laundering the appropriate figure will normally be the amount laundered or, alternatively, the likely cost avoided by failing to put in place an effective anti-money laundering programme if this is higher.
Corruption of local or national government officials or ministers			
Corruption of officials performing a law enforcement role			
Abuse of dominant market position or position of trust or responsibility		General	Where the actual or intended gain cannot be established, the appropriate measure will be the amount that the court considers was likely to be achieved in all the circumstances.
Offending committed over a sustained period of time			
Culture of wilful disregard of commission of offences by employees or agents with no effort to put effective systems in place (section 7 Bribery Act only)			In the absence of sufficient evidence of the amount that was likely to be obtained, 10–20 per cent of the relevant revenue (for instance between 10 and 20 per cent of the worldwide revenue derived from the product or business area to which the offence relates for the period of the offending) **may** be an appropriate measure.
B – Medium culpability			
Corporation plays a significant role in unlawful activity organised by others			
Activity not unlawful from the outset			
Corporation reckless in making false statement (section 72 VAT Act 1994)			
All other cases where characteristics for categories A or C are not present			There may be large cases of fraud or bribery in which the true harm is to commerce or markets generally. That may justify adopting a harm figure beyond the normal measures here set out.
C – Lesser culpability			
Corporation plays a minor, peripheral role in unlawful activity organised by others			
Some effort made to put bribery prevention measures in place but insufficient to amount to a defence (section 7 Bribery Act only)			
Involvement through coercion, intimidation or exploitation			

Effective from 1 October 2014

Appendix 1 *Fraud, Bribery and Money Laundering Offences etc*

STEP FOUR
Starting point and category range

Having determined the culpability level at step three, the court should use the table below to determine the starting point within the category range below. The starting point applies to all offenders irrespective of plea or previous convictions.

The harm figure at step three is multiplied by the relevant percentage figure representing culpability.

	Culpability Level		
	A	B	C
Harm figure multiplier	**Starting point** 300%	**Starting point** 200%	**Starting point** 100%
	Category range 250% to 400%	**Category range** 100% to 300%	**Category range** 20% to 150%

Having determined the appropriate starting point, the court should then consider adjustment within the category range for aggravating or mitigating features. In some cases, having considered these factors, it may be appropriate to move outside the identified category range. (See below for a **non-exhaustive** list of aggravating and mitigating factors.)

Factors increasing seriousness	Factors reducing seriousness or reflecting mitigation
Previous relevant convictions or subject to previous relevant civil or regulatory enforcement action	No previous relevant convictions or previous relevant civil or regulatory enforcement action
Corporation or subsidiary set up to commit fraudulent activity	Victims voluntarily reimbursed/compensated
Fraudulent activity endemic within corporation	No actual loss to victims
Attempts made to conceal misconduct	Corporation co-operated with investigation, made early admissions and/or voluntarily reported offending
Substantial harm (whether financial or otherwise) suffered by victims of offending or by third parties affected by offending	Offending committed under previous director(s)/manager(s)
Risk of harm greater than actual or intended harm (for example in banking/credit fraud)	Little or no actual gain to corporation from offending
Substantial harm caused to integrity or confidence of markets	
Substantial harm caused to integrity of local or national governments	
Serious nature of underlying criminal activity (money laundering offences)	
Offence committed across borders or jurisdictions	

Effective from 1 October 2014

Fraud, Bribery and Money Laundering Offences etc

General principles to follow in setting a fine
The court should determine the appropriate level of fine in accordance with section 164 of the Criminal Justice Act 2003, which requires that the fine must reflect the seriousness of the offence and requires the court to take into account the financial circumstances of the offender.

Obtaining financial information
Companies and bodies delivering public or charitable services
Where the offender is a company or a body which delivers a public or charitable service, it is expected to provide comprehensive accounts for the last three years, to enable the court to make an accurate assessment of its financial status. In the absence of such disclosure, or where the court is not satisfied that it has been given sufficient reliable information, the court will be entitled to draw reasonable inferences as to the offender's means from evidence it has heard and from all the circumstances of the case.

1. *For companies*: annual accounts. Particular attention should be paid to turnover; profit before tax; directors' remuneration, loan accounts and pension provision; and assets as disclosed by the balance sheet. Most companies are required to file audited accounts at Companies House. Failure to produce relevant recent accounts on request may properly lead to the conclusion that the company can pay any appropriate fine.

2. *For partnerships*: annual accounts. Particular attention should be paid to turnover; profit before tax; partners' drawings, loan accounts and pension provision; assets as above. Limited liability partnerships (LLPs) may be required to file audited accounts with Companies House. If adequate accounts are not produced on request, see paragraph 1.

3. *For local authorities, fire authorities and similar public bodies*: the Annual Revenue Budget ("ARB") is the equivalent of turnover and the best indication of the size of the defendant organisation. It is unlikely to be necessary to analyse specific expenditure or reserves unless inappropriate expenditure is suggested.

4. *For health trusts*: the independent regulator of NHS Foundation Trusts is Monitor. It publishes quarterly reports and annual figures for the financial strength and stability of trusts from which the annual income can be seen, available via www.monitor-nhsft.gov.uk. Detailed analysis of expenditure or reserves is unlikely to be called for.

5. *For charities*: it will be appropriate to inspect annual audited accounts. Detailed analysis of expenditure or reserves is unlikely to be called for unless there is a suggestion of unusual or unnecessary expenditure.

Effective from 1 October 2014

Appendix 1 *Fraud, Bribery and Money Laundering Offences etc*

STEP FIVE
Adjustment of fine

Having arrived at a fine level, the court should consider whether there are any further factors which indicate an adjustment in the level of the fine. The court should 'step back' and consider the overall effect of its orders. The combination of orders made, compensation, confiscation and fine ought to achieve:
- the removal of all gain
- appropriate additional punishment, and
- deterrence

The fine may be adjusted to ensure that these objectives are met in a fair way. The court should consider any further factors relevant to the setting of the level of the fine to ensure that the fine is proportionate, having regard to the size and financial position of the offending organisation and the seriousness of the offence.

The fine must be substantial enough to have a real economic impact which will bring home to both management and shareholders the need to operate within the law. Whether the fine will have the effect of putting the offender out of business will be relevant; in some bad cases this may be an acceptable consequence.

In considering the ability of the offending organisation to pay any financial penalty the court can take into account the power to allow time for payment or to order that the amount be paid in instalments.

The court should consider whether the level of fine would otherwise cause unacceptable harm to third parties. In doing so the court should bear in mind that the payment of any compensation determined at step one should take priority over the payment of any fine.

The table below contains a **non-exhaustive** list of additional factual elements for the court to consider. The Court should identify whether any combination of these, or other relevant factors, should result in a proportionate increase or reduction in the level of fine.

Factors to consider in adjusting the level of fine
Fine fulfils the objectives of punishment, deterrence and removal of gain
The value, worth or available means of the offender
Fine impairs offender's ability to make restitution to victims
Impact of fine on offender's ability to implement effective compliance programmes
Impact of fine on employment of staff, service users, customers and local economy (but not shareholders)
Impact of fine on performance of public or charitable function

Effective from 1 October 2014

Fraud, Bribery and Money Laundering Offences etc

STEP SIX
Consider any factors which would indicate a reduction, such as assistance to the prosecution
The court should take into account sections 73 and 74 of the Serious Organised Crime and Police Act 2005 (assistance by defendants: reduction or review of sentence) and any other rule of law by virtue of which an offender may receive a discounted sentence in consequence of assistance given (or offered) to the prosecutor or investigator.

STEP SEVEN
Reduction for guilty pleas
The court should take into account any potential reduction for a guilty plea in accordance with section 144 of the Criminal Justice Act 2003 and the *Guilty Plea* guideline.

STEP EIGHT
Ancillary Orders
In all cases the court must consider whether to make any ancillary orders.

STEP NINE
Totality principle
If sentencing an offender for more than one offence, consider whether the total sentence is just and proportionate to the offending behaviour.

STEP TEN
Reasons
Section 174 of the Criminal Justice Act 2003 imposes a duty to give reasons for, and explain the effect of, the sentence.

Effective from 1 October 2014

Appendix 1 *Fraud, Bribery and Money Laundering Offences etc*

Annex

Fine bands and community orders

FINE BANDS

In this guideline, fines are expressed as one of three fine bands (A, B or C).

Fine Band	Starting point (applicable to all offenders)	Category range (applicable to all offenders)
Band A	50% of relevant weekly income	25 – 75% of relevant weekly income
Band B	100% of relevant weekly income	75 – 125% of relevant weekly income
Band C	150% of relevant weekly income	125 – 175% of relevant weekly income

COMMUNITY ORDERS

In this guideline, community sentences are expressed as one of three levels (low, medium and high).

An illustrative description of examples of requirements that might be appropriate for each level is provided below. Where two or more requirements are ordered, they must be compatible with each other.

Low	Medium	High
In general, only one requirement will be appropriate and the length may be curtailed if additional requirements are necessary		More intensive sentences which combine two or more requirements may be appropriate
Suitable requirements might include one or more of: • 40 – 80 hours unpaid work; • prohibited activity requirement; • curfew requirement within the lowest range (for example, up to 12 hours per day for a few weeks)	Suitable requirements might include one or more of: • greater number of hours of unpaid work (for example, 80 – 150 hours); • prohibited activity requirement; • an activity requirement in the middle range (20 – 30 days); • curfew requirement within the middle range (for example, up to 12 hours for two to three months)	Suitable requirements might include one or more of: • 150 – 300 hours of unpaid work; • activity requirement up to the maximum of 60 days; • curfew requirement up to 12 hours per day for 4 – 6 months; • exclusion order lasting in the region of 12 months.

The tables are also set out in the *Magistrates' Court Sentencing Guidelines* which includes further guidance on fines and community orders.

Effective from 1 October 2014

Appendix 2

Reduction in Sentence for a Guilty Plea: Definitive Guideline*

FOREWORD

One of the first guidelines to be issued by the Sentencing Guidelines Council related to the statutory obligation to take account of any guilty plea when determining sentence. As set out in the Foreword to that guideline,[1] the intention was 'to promote consistency in sentencing by providing clarity for courts, court users and victims so that everyone knows exactly what to expect'. Prior to that guideline there had been different understandings of the purpose of the reduction and the extent of any reduction given.

Since the guideline was issued, there has been much greater clarity but there still remain concerns about some of the content of the guideline and about the extent to which the guideline has been consistently applied. Accordingly the Council has undertaken a review of the guideline (in accordance with the statutory obligation placed upon it to do so from time to time[2]); it has also requested that the Judicial Studies Board consider further ways in which judicial training can incorporate the guideline.

The Council is extremely grateful to the Sentencing Advisory Panel for the speed and thoroughness with which it has prepared its Advice following extensive consultation. The Council has accepted almost all the recommendations of the Panel; the issues and arguments are set out fully in the Panel's advice (see www.sentencing-guidelines.gov.uk). This revised guideline applies to all cases sentenced on or after 23 July 2007.

The Council has agreed with the Panel that the general approach of the guideline is correct in setting out clearly the purpose of the reduction for a guilty plea, in settling for a reduction no greater than one third (with lower levels of reduction where a plea is entered other than at the first reasonable opportunity) and in continuing to provide for a special approach when fixing the minimum term for a life sentence imposed following conviction for murder.

---

*   Published by the Sentencing Guidelines Secretariat, July 2007.
1   Published December 2004.
2   Criminal Justice Act 2003, s 170(4).

Appendix 2 *Reduction in Sentence for a Guilty Plea: Definitive Guideline*

The Council has agreed with the Panel that some discretion should be introduced to the approach where the prosecution case is 'overwhelming'.

The Council has not accepted the Panel's recommendation in relation to circumstances where a magistrates' court is sentencing an offender for a number of offences where the overall maximum imprisonment is 6 months. The Council continues to consider that there must be some incentive to plead guilty in such circumstances; this is consistent with other aspects of the guideline.

The Council has not accepted the Panel's recommendation in relation to the 'capping' of the effect of reduction on very large fines. The number of such fines is very low and the Council was not convinced that the arguments were strong enough to justify a departure from the general approach in the guideline not to 'cap' the effect of the reduction.

In addition, the revised guideline provides guidance as to when the 'first reasonable opportunity' is likely to occur in relation to indictable only offences; emphasises that remorse and material assistance provided to prosecuting authorities are separate issues from those to which the guideline applies and makes clear that the approach to calculation of the reduction where an indeterminate sentence is imposed (other than that following conviction for murder) should be the same as that for determinate sentences.

Since the guideline was issued in 2004, there have been changes in the statutory provisions governing the reduction for guilty plea and in those relating to sentences for public protection. The review has provided an opportunity to bring the guideline up to date and those changes have been incorporated.

The Council published a draft guideline in accordance with section 170(8) of the Criminal Justice Act 2003 inviting responses by 14 March 2007. A response has been received from the Home Affairs Committee, a response has been received from the Attorney General and 7 other responses have been received. A summary of the responses and the decisions of the Council has been published separately.

Chairman of the Council

July 2007

REDUCTION IN SENTENCE FOR A GUILTY PLEA

A. *Statutory Provisions*

Section 144 Criminal Justice Act 2003 provides:

(1) In determining what sentence to pass on an offender who has pleaded guilty to an offence in proceedings before that or another court, a court must take into account:

   (a) the stage in the proceedings for the offence at which the offender indicated his intention to plead guilty, and

   (b) the circumstances in which this indication was given.

Reduction in Sentence for a Guilty Plea

(2) In the case of an offence the sentence for which falls to be imposed under subsection (2) of section 110 or 111 of the Sentencing Act,[3] nothing in that subsection prevents the court, after taking into account any matter referred to in subsection (1) of this section, from imposing any sentence which is not less than 80 per cent of that specified in that subsection.

Section 174(2) Criminal Justice Act 2003 provides:

(2) In complying with subsection (1)(a), the court must:
    (a) ……..,
    (b) ……..,
    (c) ……..,
    (d) where as a result of taking into account any matter referred to in section 144(1), the court imposes a punishment on the offender which is less severe than the punishment it would otherwise have imposed, state that fact, …
    (e) ……..

1.1 This guideline applies whether a case is dealt with in a magistrates' court or in the Crown Court and whenever practicable in the youth court (taking into account legislative restrictions such as those relevant to the length of Detention and Training orders).

1.2 The application of this guideline to sentencers when arriving at the appropriate minimum term for the offence of murder is set out in Section F.

1.3 This guideline can also be found at www.sentencing-guidelines.gov.uk or can be obtained from the Council's Secretariat at 4th Floor, 8-10 Great George Street, London SW1P 3AE.

B. *Statement of Purpose*

2.1 When imposing a custodial sentence, statute requires that a court must impose the shortest term that is commensurate with the seriousness of the offence(s).[4] Similarly, when imposing a community order, the restrictions on liberty must be commensurate with the seriousness of the offence(s).[5] Once that decision is made, a court is required to give consideration to the reduction for any guilty plea. As a result, the final sentence after the reduction for a guilty plea will be less than the seriousness of the offence requires.

2.2 A reduction in sentence is appropriate because a guilty plea avoids the need for a trial (thus enabling other cases to be disposed of more expeditiously), shortens the gap between charge and sentence, saves considerable cost, and, in the case of an early plea, saves victims and witnesses from the concern about

---

[3] These provisions prescribe minimum mandatory sentences in certain circumstances.
[4] Criminal Justice Act 2003, s.153(2)
[5] Criminal Justice Act 2003, s.148(2)

Appendix 2 *Reduction in Sentence for a Guilty Plea: Definitive Guideline*

having to give evidence. The reduction principle derives from the need for the effective administration of justice and not as an aspect of mitigation.

2.3   Where a sentencer is in doubt as to whether a custodial sentence is appropriate, the reduction attributable to a guilty plea will be a relevant consideration. Where this is amongst the factors leading to the imposition of a non-custodial sentence, there will be no need to apply a further reduction on account of the guilty plea. A similar approach is appropriate where the reduction for a guilty plea is amongst the factors leading to the imposition of a financial penalty or discharge instead of a community order.

2.4   When deciding the most appropriate length of sentence, the sentencer should address separately the issue of remorse, together with any other mitigating features, before calculating the reduction for the guilty plea. Similarly, assistance to the prosecuting or enforcement authorities is a separate issue which may attract a reduction in sentence under other procedures; care will need to be taken to ensure that there is no 'double counting'.

2.5   The implications of other offences that an offender has asked to be taken into consideration should be reflected in the sentence before the reduction for guilty plea has been applied.

2.6   A reduction in sentence should only be applied to the punitive elements of a penalty.[6] The guilty plea reduction has no impact on sentencing decisions in relation to ancillary orders, including orders of disqualification from driving.

C. Application of the Reduction Principle

3.1 Recommended Approach

The court decides sentence for the offence(s) taking into account aggravating and mitigating factors and any other offences that have been formally admitted (TICs)
↓
The court selects the amount of the reduction by reference to the sliding scale
↓
The court applies the reduction
↓
When pronouncing sentence the court should usually state what the sentence would have been if there had been no reduction as a result of the guilty plea.

---

6   Where a court imposes an indeterminate sentence for public protection, the reduction principle applies in the normal way to the determination of the minimum term (see para. 5.1, footnote and para. 7 below) but release from custody requires the authorisation of the Parole Board once that minimum term has been served.

Reduction in Sentence for a Guilty Plea

D. *Determining the Level of Reduction*

4.1   The level of reduction should be a proportion of the total sentence imposed, with the proportion calculated by reference to the circumstances in which the guilty plea was indicated, in particular the stage in the proceedings. The greatest reduction will be given where the plea was indicated at the 'first reasonable opportunity'.

4.2   Save where section 144(2) of the 2003 Act applies,[7] the level of the reduction will be gauged on a sliding scale ranging from a recommended one third (where the guilty plea was entered at the first reasonable opportunity in relation to the offence for which sentence is being imposed), reducing to a recommended one quarter (where a trial date has been set) and to a recommended one tenth (for a guilty plea entered at the 'door of the court' or after the trial has begun). See diagram below.

4.3   The level of reduction should reflect the stage at which the offender indicated a willingness to admit guilt to the offence for which he is eventually sentenced:

(i)   the largest recommended reduction will not normally be given unless the offender indicated willingness to admit guilt at the first reasonable opportunity; when this occurs will vary from case to case (see Annex 1 for illustrative examples);

(ii) where the admission of guilt comes later than the first reasonable opportunity, the reduction for guilty plea will normally be less than one third;

(iii) where the plea of guilty comes very late, it is still appropriate to give some reduction;

(iv) if after pleading guilty there is a Newton hearing and the offender's version of the circumstances of the offence is rejected, this should be taken into account in determining the level of reduction;

(v)   if the not guilty plea was entered and maintained for tactical reasons (such as to retain privileges whilst on remand), a late guilty plea should attract very little, if any, discount.

In each category, there is a presumption that the recommended reduction will be given unless there are good reasons for a lower amount.		
First reasonable opportunity	After a trial date is set	Door of the court after trial has begun
========	============	============
recommended 1/3	**recommended 1/4**	**recommended 1/10**

---

7   See section A above.

Appendix 2 *Reduction in Sentence for a Guilty Plea: Definitive Guideline*

E. Withholding a Reduction

On the basis of dangerousness

5.1 Where a sentence for a 'dangerous offender' is imposed under the provisions in the Criminal Justice Act 2003, whether the sentence requires the calculation of a minimum term or is an extended sentence, the approach will be the same as for any other determinate sentence (see also section G below).[8]

Where the prosecution case is overwhelming

5.2 The purpose of giving credit is to encourage those who are guilty to plead at the earliest opportunity. Any defendant is entitled to put the prosecution to proof and so every defendant who is guilty should be encouraged to indicate that guilt at the first reasonable opportunity.

5.3 Where the prosecution case is overwhelming, it may not be appropriate to give the full reduction that would otherwise be given. Whilst there is a presumption in favour of the full reduction being given where a plea has been indicated at the first reasonable opportunity, the fact that the prosecution case is overwhelming without relying on admissions from the defendant may be a reason justifying departure from the guideline.

5.4 Where a court is satisfied that a lower reduction should be given for this reason, a recommended reduction of 20% is likely to be appropriate where the guilty plea was indicated at the first reasonable opportunity.

5.5 A Court departing from a guideline must state the reasons for doing so.[9]

Where the maximum penalty for the offence is thought to be too low

5.6 The sentencer is bound to sentence for the offence with which the offender has been charged, and to which he has pleaded guilty. The sentencer cannot remedy perceived defects (for example an inadequate charge or maximum penalty) by refusal of the appropriate discount.

---

[8] There will be some cases arising from offences committed before the commencement of the relevant provisions of the Criminal Justice Act 2003 in which a court will determine that a longer than commensurate, extended, or indeterminate sentence is required for the protection of the public. In such a case, the minimum custodial term (but not the protection of public element of the sentence) should be reduced to reflect the plea.

[9] Criminal Justice Act 2003, s. 174(2)(a).

Where jurisdictional issues arise

(i) Where sentencing powers are limited to 6 months imprisonment despite multiple offences

5.7 When the total sentence for both or all of the offences is 6 months imprisonment, a court may determine to impose consecutive sentences which, even allowing for a reduction for a guilty plea where appropriate on each offence, would still result in the imposition of the maximum sentence available. In such circumstances, in order to achieve the purpose for which the reduction principle has been established,[10] some modest allowance should normally be given against the total sentence for the entry of a guilty plea.

(ii) Where a maximum sentence might still be imposed

5.8 Despite a guilty plea being entered which would normally attract a reduction in sentence, a magistrates' court may impose a sentence of imprisonment of 6 months for a single either-way offence where, but for the plea, that offence would have been committed to the Crown Court for sentence.

5.9 Similarly, a detention and training order of 24 months may be imposed on an offender aged under 18 if the offence is one which would but for the plea have attracted a sentence of long-term detention in excess of 24 months under the Powers of Criminal Courts (Sentencing) Act 2000, section 91.

F. *Application to Sentencing for Murder*

6.1 Murder has always been regarded as the most serious criminal offence and the sentence prescribed is different from other sentences. By law, the sentence for murder is imprisonment (detention) for life and an offender will remain subject to the sentence for the rest of his/her life.

6.2 The decision whether to release the offender from custody during this sentence will be taken by the Parole Board which will consider whether it is safe to release the offender on licence. The Court that imposes the sentence is required by law to set a minimum term that has to be served before the Parole Board may start to consider whether to authorise release on licence. If an offender is released, the licence continues for the rest of the offender's life and recall to prison is possible at any time.

6.3 Uniquely, Parliament has set starting points[11] (based on the circumstances of the killing) which a Court will apply when it fixes the minimum term. Parliament has further prescribed that, having identified the appropriate starting point, the Court must then consider whether to increase or reduce it in the light of aggravating or mitigating factors, some of which are

---

10 see section B above.
11 Criminal Justice Act 2003, schedule 21.

Appendix 2 *Reduction in Sentence for a Guilty Plea: Definitive Guideline*

listed in statute. Finally, Parliament specifically provides[12] that the obligation to have regard to any guilty plea applies to the fixing of the minimum term, by making the same statutory provisions that apply to other offences apply to murder without limiting the courts discretion (as it did with other sentences under the Powers of Criminal Courts (Sentencing) Act 2000).

6.4 There are important differences between the usual fixed term sentence and the minimum term set following the imposition of the mandatory life sentence for murder. The most significant of these, from the sentencer's point of view, is that a reduction for a plea of guilty in the case of murder will have double the effect on time served in custody when compared with a determinate sentence. This is because a determinate sentence will provide (in most circumstances) for the release of the offender[13] on licence half way through the total sentence whereas in the case of murder a minimum term is the period in custody before consideration is given by the Parole Board to whether release is appropriate.

6.5 Given this difference, the special characteristic of the offence of murder and the unique statutory provision of starting points, careful consideration will need to be given to the extent of any reduction and to the need to ensure that the minimum term properly reflects the seriousness of the offence. Whilst the general principles continue to apply (both that a guilty plea should be encouraged and that the extent of any reduction should reduce if the indication of plea is later than the first reasonable opportunity), the process of determining the level of reduction will be different.

6.6 APPROACH

1. Where a Court determines that there should be a whole life minimum term, there will be no reduction for a guilty plea.

2. In other circumstances,

    (a) the Court will weigh carefully the overall length of the minimum term taking into account other reductions for which the offender may be eligible so as to avoid a combination leading to an inappropriately short sentence;

    (b) where it is appropriate to reduce the minimum term having regard to a plea of guilty, the reduction will not exceed one sixth and will never exceed 5 years;

    (c) the sliding scale will apply so that, where it is appropriate to reduce the minimum term on account of a guilty plea, the recommended reduction (one sixth or five years whichever is the less) is only available where there has been an indication of willingness to plead

---

12 Criminal Justice Act 2003, schedule 1 para 12(c).
13 In accordance with the provisions of the Criminal Justice Act 2003.

guilty at the first reasonable opportunity, with a recommended 5% for a late guilty plea;

(d) the Court should then review the sentence to ensure that the minimum term accurately reflects the seriousness of the offence taking account of the statutory starting point, all aggravating and mitigating factors and any guilty plea entered.

G. *Application to other Indeterminate Sentences*

7.1   There are other circumstances in which an indeterminate sentence will be imposed. This may be a discretionary life sentence or imprisonment for public protection.

7.2   As with the mandatory life sentence imposed following conviction for murder, the Court will be obliged to fix a minimum term to be served before the Parole Board is able to consider whether the offender can be safely released.

7.3   However, the process by which that minimum term is fixed is different from that followed in relation to the mandatory life sentence and requires the Court first to determine what the equivalent determinate sentence would have been. Accordingly, the approach to the calculation of the reduction for any guilty plea should follow the process and scale adopted in relation to determinate sentences, as set out in section D above.

ANNEX 1

FIRST REASONABLE OPPORTUNITY

1. The critical time for determining the reduction for a guilty plea is the first reasonable opportunity for the defendant to have indicated a willingness to plead guilty. This opportunity will vary with a wide range of factors and the Court will need to make a judgement on the particular facts of the case before it.

2. The key principle is that the purpose of giving a reduction is to recognise the benefits that come from a guilty plea not only for those directly involved in the case in question but also in enabling Courts more quickly to deal with other outstanding cases.

3. This Annex seeks to help Courts to adopt a consistent approach by giving examples of circumstances where a determination will have to be made:

(a) the first reasonable opportunity may be the first time that a defendant appears before the court and has the opportunity to plead guilty;

Appendix 2 *Reduction in Sentence for a Guilty Plea: Definitive Guideline*

(b) but the court may consider that it would be reasonable to have expected an indication of willingness even earlier, perhaps whilst under interview;

Note: For a) and b) to apply, the Court will need to be satisfied that the defendant (and any legal adviser) would have had sufficient information about the allegations

(c) where an offence triable either way is committed to the Crown Court for trial and the defendant pleads guilty at the first hearing in that Court, the reduction will be less than if there had been an indication of a guilty plea given to the magistrates' court (recommended reduction of one third) but more than if the plea had been entered after a trial date had been set (recommended reduction of one quarter), and is likely to be in the region of 30%;

(d) where an offence is triable only on indictment, it may well be that the first reasonable opportunity would have been during the police station stage; where that is not the case, the first reasonable opportunity is likely to be at the first hearing in the Crown Court;

(e) where a defendant is convicted after pleading guilty to an alternative (lesser) charge to that to which he/she had originally pleaded not guilty, the extent of any reduction will be determined by the stage at which the defendant first formally indicated to the court willingness to plead guilty to the lesser charge, and the reason why that lesser charge was proceeded with in preference to the original charge.

Appendix 3

The Criminal Procedure Rules 2014 (SI 2014/1610)

PART 3

CASE MANAGEMENT

GENERAL RULES

When this Part applies

3.1.

(1) Rules 3.1 to 3.12 apply to the management of each case in a magistrates' court and in the Crown Court (including an appeal to the Crown Court) until the conclusion of that case.

(2) Rules 3.13 to 3.26 apply where—

    (a) the defendant is sent to the Crown Court for trial;

    (b) a High Court or Crown Court judge gives permission to serve a draft indictment; or

    (c) the Court of Appeal orders a retrial.

[Note. Rules that apply to procedure in the Court of Appeal are in Parts 65 to 73 of these Rules.

A magistrates' court may send a defendant for trial in the Crown Court under section 51 or 51A of the Crime and Disorder Act 1998. See Part 9 for the procedure on allocation and sending for trial.

Under paragraph 2(1) of Schedule 17 to the Crime and Courts Act 2013 and section 2 of the Administration of Justice (Miscellaneous Provisions) Act 1933, the Crown Court may give permission to serve a draft indictment where it approves a deferred prosecution agreement. See Part 12 for the rules about that procedure and Part 14 for the rules about indictments.

Appendix 3 *The Criminal Procedure Rules 2014 (SI 2014/1610)*

The procedure for applying for the permission of a High Court judge to serve a draft indictment is in rules 6 to 10 of the Indictments (Procedure) Rules 1971. See also the Practice Direction.

The Court of Appeal may order a retrial under section 8 of the Criminal Appeal Act 1968 (on a defendant's appeal against conviction) or under section 77 of the Criminal Justice Act 2003 (on a prosecutor's application for the retrial of a serious offence after acquittal). Section 8 of the 1968 Act, and rules 41.14 and 41.15, require the arraignment of a defendant within 2 months.]

The duty of the court

3.2.

(1) The court must further the overriding objective by actively managing the case.

(2) Active case management includes—

    (a) the early identification of the real issues;

    (b) the early identification of the needs of witnesses;

    (c) achieving certainty as to what must be done, by whom, and when, in particular by the early setting of a timetable for the progress of the case;

    (d) monitoring the progress of the case and compliance with directions;

    (e) ensuring that evidence, whether disputed or not, is presented in the shortest and clearest way;

    (f) discouraging delay, dealing with as many aspects of the case as possible on the same occasion, and avoiding unnecessary hearings;

    (g) encouraging the participants to co-operate in the progression of the case; and

    (h) making use of technology.

(3) The court must actively manage the case by giving any direction appropriate to the needs of that case as early as possible.

The duty of the parties

3.3.

Each party must—

    (a) actively assist the court in fulfilling its duty under rule 3.2, without or if necessary with a direction; and

    (b) apply for a direction if needed to further the overriding objective.

General Rules

Case progression officers and their duties

3.4.

(1) At the beginning of the case each party must, unless the court otherwise directs—

    (a) nominate someone responsible for progressing that case; and

    (b) tell other parties and the court who that is and how to contact that person.

(2) In fulfilling its duty under rule 3.2, the court must where appropriate—

    (a) nominate a court officer responsible for progressing the case; and

    (b) make sure the parties know who that is and how to contact that court officer.

(3) In this Part a person nominated under this rule is called a case progression officer.

(4) A case progression officer must—

    (a) monitor compliance with directions;

    (b) make sure that the court is kept informed of events that may affect the progress of that case;

    (c) make sure that he or she can be contacted promptly about the case during ordinary business hours;

    (d) act promptly and reasonably in response to communications about the case; and

    (e) if he or she will be unavailable, appoint a substitute to fulfil his or her duties and inform the other case progression officers.

The court's case management powers

3.5.

(1) In fulfilling its duty under rule 3.2 the court may give any direction and take any step actively to manage a case unless that direction or step would be inconsistent with legislation, including these Rules.

(2) In particular, the court may—

    (a) nominate a judge, magistrate or justices' legal adviser to manage the case;

    (b) give a direction on its own initiative or on application by a party;

    (c) ask or allow a party to propose a direction;

Appendix 3 *The Criminal Procedure Rules 2014 (SI 2014/1610)*

    (d)   for the purpose of giving directions, receive applications and representations by letter, by telephone or by any other means of electronic communication, and conduct a hearing by such means;

    (e)   give a direction—

        (i)   at a hearing, in public or in private, or

        (ii)   without a hearing;

    (f)   fix, postpone, bring forward, extend, cancel or adjourn a hearing;

    (g)   shorten or extend (even after it has expired) a time limit fixed by a direction;

    (h)   require that issues in the case should be—

        (i)   identified in writing,

        (ii)   determined separately, and decide in what order they will be determined; and

    (i)   specify the consequences of failing to comply with a direction.

(3)   A magistrates' court may give a direction that will apply in the Crown Court if the case is to continue there.

(4)   The Crown Court may give a direction that will apply in a magistrates' court if the case is to continue there.

(5)   Any power to give a direction under this Part includes a power to vary or revoke that direction.

(6)   If a party fails to comply with a rule or a direction, the court may—

    (a)   fix, postpone, bring forward, extend, cancel or adjourn a hearing;

    (b)   exercise its powers to make a costs order; and

    (c)   impose such other sanction as may be appropriate.

[Note. Depending upon the nature of a case and the stage that it has reached, its progress may be affected by other Criminal Procedure Rules and by other legislation. The note at the end of this Part lists other rules and legislation that may apply.

See also rule 3.9 (Case preparation and progression).

The court may make a costs order under—

    (a)   section 19 of the Prosecution of Offences Act 1985, where the court decides that one party to criminal proceedings has incurred costs as a result of an unnecessary or improper act or omission by, or on behalf of, another party;

General Rules

(b) section 19A of that Act, where the court decides that a party has incurred costs as a result of an improper, unreasonable or negligent act or omission on the part of a legal representative;

(b) section 19B of that Act, where the court decides that there has been serious misconduct by a person who is not a party.

Under some other legislation, including Parts 33, 34 and 35 of these Rules, if a party fails to comply with a rule or a direction then in some circumstances—

(a) the court may refuse to allow that party to introduce evidence;

(b) evidence that that party wants to introduce may not be admissible;

(c) the court may draw adverse inferences from the late introduction of an issue or evidence.

See also—

(a) section 81(1) of the Police and Criminal Evidence Act 1984 and section 20(3) of the Criminal Procedure and Investigations Act 1996 (advance disclosure of expert evidence);

(b) section 11(5) of the Criminal Procedure and Investigations Act 1996 (faults in disclosure by accused);

(c) section 132(5) of the Criminal Justice Act 2003 (failure to give notice of hearsay evidence).]

Application to vary a direction

3.6.

(1) A party may apply to vary a direction if—

    (a) the court gave it without a hearing;

    (b) the court gave it at a hearing in that party's absence; or

    (c) circumstances have changed.

(2) A party who applies to vary a direction must—

    (a) apply as soon as practicable after becoming aware of the grounds for doing so; and

    (b) give as much notice to the other parties as the nature and urgency of the application permits.

Agreement to vary a time limit fixed by a direction

3.7.

(1) The parties may agree to vary a time limit fixed by a direction, but only if—

Appendix 3 *The Criminal Procedure Rules 2014 (SI 2014/1610)*

    (a)   the variation will not—

        (i)   affect the date of any hearing that has been fixed, or

        (ii) significantly affect the progress of the case in any other way;

    (b)   the court has not prohibited variation by agreement; and

    (c)   the court's case progression officer is promptly informed.

(2)   The court's case progression officer must refer the agreement to the court if in doubt that the condition in paragraph (1)(a) is satisfied.

Court's power to vary requirements under this Part

3.8.

(1)   The court may—

    (a)   shorten or extend (even after it has expired) a time limit set by this Part; and

    (b)   allow an application or representations to be made orally.

(2)   A person who wants an extension of time must—

    (a)   apply when serving the application or representations for which it is needed; and

    (b)   explain the delay.

Case preparation and progression

3.9.

(1)   At every hearing, if a case cannot be concluded there and then the court must give directions so that it can be concluded at the next hearing or as soon as possible after that.

(2)   At every hearing the court must, where relevant—

    (a)   if the defendant is absent, decide whether to proceed nonetheless;

    (b)   take the defendant's plea (unless already done) or if no plea can be taken then find out whether the defendant is likely to plead guilty or not guilty;

    (c)   set, follow or revise a timetable for the progress of the case, which may include a timetable for any hearing including the trial or (in the Crown Court) the appeal;

    (d)   in giving directions, ensure continuity in relation to the court and to the parties' representatives where that is appropriate and practicable; and

General Rules

      (e)   where a direction has not been complied with, find out why, identify who was responsible, and take appropriate action.

(3)   In order to prepare for the trial, the court must take every reasonable step—

      (a)   to encourage and to facilitate the attendance of witnesses when they are needed; and

      (b)   to facilitate the participation of any person, including the defendant.

(4)   Facilitating the participation of the defendant includes finding out whether the defendant needs interpretation because—

      (a)   the defendant does not speak or understand English; or

      (b)   the defendant has a hearing or speech impediment.

(5)   Where the defendant needs interpretation—

      (a)   the court officer must arrange for interpretation to be provided at every hearing which the defendant is due to attend;

      (b)   interpretation may be by an intermediary where the defendant has a speech impediment, without the need for a defendant's evidence direction;

      (c)   on application or on its own initiative, the court may require a written translation to be provided for the defendant of any document or part of a document, unless—

           (i)   translation of that document, or part, is not needed to explain the case against the defendant, or

          (ii)   the defendant agrees to do without and the court is satisfied that the agreement is clear and voluntary and that the defendant has had legal advice or otherwise understands the consequences;

      (d)   on application by the defendant, the court must give any direction which the court thinks appropriate, including a direction for interpretation by a different interpreter, where—

           (i)   no interpretation is provided,

          (ii)   no translation is ordered or provided in response to a previous application by the defendant, or

          (iii)   the defendant complains about the quality of interpretation or of any translation.

(6)   Facilitating the participation of any person includes giving directions for the appropriate treatment and questioning of a witness or the defendant,

Appendix 3 *The Criminal Procedure Rules 2014 (SI 2014/1610)*

especially where the court directs that such questioning is to be conducted through an intermediary.

[Note. Part 29 (Measures to assist a witness or defendant to give evidence) contains rules about an application for a defendant's evidence direction under (among other provisions) sections 33BA and 33BB of the Youth Justice and Criminal Evidence Act 1999.

See also Directive 2010/64/EU of the European Parliament and of the Council of 20th October, 2010, on the right to interpretation and translation in criminal proceedings.

Where a trial in the Crown Court will take place in Wales and a participant wishes to use the Welsh language, see rule 3.26.

Where a trial in a magistrates' court will take place in Wales, a participant may use the Welsh language: see rule 37.13.]

Readiness for trial or appeal

3.10.

(1) This rule applies to a party's preparation for trial or appeal, and in this rule and rule 3.11 'trial' includes any hearing at which evidence will be introduced.

(2) In fulfilling the duty under rule 3.3, each party must—

    (a) comply with directions given by the court;

    (b) take every reasonable step to make sure that party's witnesses will attend when they are needed;

    (c) make appropriate arrangements to present any written or other material; and

    (d) promptly inform the court and the other parties of anything that may—

        (i) affect the date or duration of the trial or appeal, or

        (ii) significantly affect the progress of the case in any other way.

(3) The court may require a party to give a certificate of readiness.

Conduct of a trial or an appeal

3.11.

In order to manage a trial or an appeal, the court—

    (a) must establish, with the active assistance of the parties, what are the disputed issues;

General Rules

- (b) must consider setting a timetable that—
  - (i) takes account of those issues and of any timetable proposed by a party, and
  - (ii) may limit the duration of any stage of the hearing;
- (c) may require a party to identify—
- (i) which witnesses that party wants to give evidence in person,
  - (ii) the order in which that party wants those witnesses to give their evidence,
  - (iii) whether that party requires an order compelling the attendance of a witness,
  - (iv) what arrangements are desirable to facilitate the giving of evidence by a witness,
- (v) what arrangements are desirable to facilitate the participation of any other person, including the defendant,
  - (vi) what written evidence that party intends to introduce,
  - (vii) what other material, if any, that person intends to make available to the court in the presentation of the case, and
  - (viii) whether that party intends to raise any point of law that could affect the conduct of the trial or appeal; and
- (d) may limit—
  - (i) the examination, cross-examination or re-examination of a witness, and
  - (ii) the duration of any stage of the hearing.

[Note. See also rules 3.5 (The court's case management powers) and 3.9 (Case preparation and progression).]

Case management forms and records

3.12.

(1) The case management forms set out in the Practice Direction must be used, and where there is no form then no specific formality is required.

(2) The court must make available to the parties a record of directions given.

(3) Where a person is entitled or required to attend a hearing, the court officer must give as much notice as reasonably practicable to—

- (a) that person; and
- (b) that person's custodian (if any).

Appendix 3 *The Criminal Procedure Rules 2014 (SI 2014/1610)*

PREPARATION FOR TRIAL IN THE CROWN COURT

Pre-trial hearings: general rules

3.13.

(1) The Crown Court—

    (a) may, and in some cases must, conduct a preparatory hearing where rule 3.14 applies;

    (b) must conduct a plea and case management hearing unless the circumstances make that unnecessary;

    (c) may conduct any other pre-trial hearing where—

        (i) the court anticipates a guilty plea, or

        (ii) it is necessary to conduct such a hearing in order to give directions for an effective trial.

(2) A pre-trial hearing—

    (a) must be in public, as a general rule, but all or part of the hearing may be in private if the court so directs; and

    (b) must be recorded, in accordance with rule 5.5 (Recording and transcription of proceedings in the Crown Court).

(3) Where the court determines a pre-trial application in private, it must announce its decision in public.

[Note. See also the general rules in the first section of this Part (rules 3.1 to 3.12) and the other rules in this section.

The Practice Direction lists the circumstances in which the Crown Court should conduct a plea and case management hearing.

There are rules relevant to applications which may be made at a pre-trial hearing in Part 16 (Reporting, etc. restrictions), Part 19 (Bail and custody time limits), Part 22 (Disclosure), Part 28 (Witness summonses, warrants and orders), Part 29 (Measures to assist a witness or defendant to give evidence), Part 33 (Expert evidence), Part 34 (Hearsay evidence), Part 35 (Evidence of bad character) and Part 36 (Evidence of a complainant's previous sexual behaviour).

On an application to which Part 19 (Bail and custody time limits) applies, rule 19.2 (exercise of court's powers under that Part) may require the defendant's presence, which may be by live link. Where rule 19.10 applies (Consideration of bail in a murder case), the court officer must arrange for the Crown Court to consider bail within 2 business days of the first hearing in the magistrates' court.

Under section 40 of the Criminal Procedure and Investigations Act 1996, a pre-trial ruling about the admissibility of evidence or any other question of law is binding unless it later appears to the court in the interests of justice to discharge or vary that ruling.]

Preparatory hearing

3.14.

(1) This rule applies where the Crown Court—

    (a) can order a preparatory hearing, under—

        (i) section 7 of the Criminal Justice Act 1987 (cases of serious or complex fraud), or

        (ii) section 29 of the Criminal Procedure and Investigations Act 1996 (other complex, serious or lengthy cases);

    (b) must order such a hearing, to determine an application for a trial without a jury, under—

        (i) section 44 of the Criminal Justice Act 2003 (danger of jury tampering), or

        (ii) section 17 of the Domestic Violence, Crime and Victims Act 2004 (trial of sample counts by jury, and others by judge alone);

    (c) must order such a hearing, under section 29 of the 1996 Act, where section 29(1B) or (1C) applies (cases in which a terrorism offence is charged, or other serious cases with a terrorist connection).

(2) The court may decide whether to order a preparatory hearing—

    (a) on an application or on its own initiative;

    (b) at a hearing (in public or in private), or without a hearing;

    (c) in a party's absence, if that party—

        (i) applied for the order, or

        (ii) has had at least 14 days in which to make representations.

[Note. See also section 45(2) of the Criminal Justice Act 2003 and section 18(1) of the Domestic Violence, Crime and Victims Act 2004.

At a preparatory hearing, the court may—

    (a) *require the prosecution to set out its case in a written statement, to arrange its evidence in a form that will be easiest for the jury (if there is one) to understand, to prepare a list of agreed facts, and to amend the case statement following representations from the*

Appendix 3 *The Criminal Procedure Rules 2014 (SI 2014/1610)*

>   *defence (section 9(4) of the 1987 Act, section 31(4) of the 1996 Act); and*
>
> (b) *require the defence to give notice of any objection to the prosecution case statement, and to give notice stating the extent of agreement with the prosecution as to documents and other matters and the reason for any disagreement (section 9(5) of the 1987 Act, section 31(6), (7), (9) of the 1996 Act).*
>
> *Under section 10 of the 1987 Act, and under section 34 of the 1996 Act, if either party later departs from the case or objections disclosed by that party, then the court, or another party, may comment on that, and the court may draw such inferences as appear proper.]*

Application for preparatory hearing

3.15.

(1) A party who wants the court to order a preparatory hearing must—

    (a) apply in writing—

        (i) as soon as reasonably practicable, and in any event

        (ii) not more than 14 days after the defendant pleads not guilty;

    (b) serve the application on—

        (i) the court officer, and

        (ii) each other party.

(2) The applicant must—

    (a) if relevant, explain what legislation requires the court to order a preparatory hearing;

    (b) otherwise, explain—

        (i) what makes the case complex or serious, or makes the trial likely to be long,

        (ii) why a substantial benefit will accrue from a preparatory hearing, and

        (iii) why the court's ordinary powers of case management are not adequate.

(3) A prosecutor who wants the court to order a trial without a jury must explain—

    (a) where the prosecutor alleges a danger of jury tampering—

        (i) what evidence there is of a real and present danger that jury tampering would take place,

Preparation for Trial in the Crown Court

   (ii) what steps, if any, reasonably might be taken to prevent jury tampering, and

   (iii) why, notwithstanding such steps, the likelihood of jury tampering is so substantial as to make it necessary in the interests of justice to order such a trial; or

(b) where the prosecutor proposes trial without a jury on some counts on the indictment—

   (i) why a trial by jury involving all the counts would be impracticable,

   (ii) how the counts proposed for jury trial can be regarded as samples of the others, and

   (iii) why it would be in the interests of justice to order such a trial.

Application for non-jury trial containing information withheld from a defendant

3.16.

(1) This rule applies where—

   (a) the prosecutor applies for an order for a trial without a jury because of a danger of jury tampering; and

   (b) the application includes information that the prosecutor thinks ought not be revealed to a defendant.

(2) The prosecutor must—

   (a) omit that information from the part of the application that is served on that defendant;

   (b) mark the other part to show that, unless the court otherwise directs, it is only for the court; and

   (c) in that other part, explain why the prosecutor has withheld that information from that defendant.

(3) The hearing of an application to which this rule applies—

   (a) must be in private, unless the court otherwise directs; and

   (b) if the court so directs, may be, wholly or in part, in the absence of a defendant from whom information has been withheld.

(4) At the hearing of an application to which this rule applies—

   (a) the general rule is that the court will receive, in the following sequence—

Appendix 3 *The Criminal Procedure Rules 2014 (SI 2014/1610)*

        (i) representations first by the prosecutor and then by each defendant, in all the parties' presence, and then

        (ii) further representations by the prosecutor, in the absence of a defendant from whom information has been withheld; but

    (b) the court may direct other arrangements for the hearing.

(5) Where, on an application to which this rule applies, the court orders a trial without a jury—

    (a) the general rule is that the trial will be before a judge other than the judge who made the order; but

    (b) the court may direct other arrangements.

Representations in response to application for preparatory hearing

3.17.

(1) This rule applies where a party wants to make representations about—

    (a) an application for a preparatory hearing;

    (b) an application for a trial without a jury.

(2) Such a party must—

    (a) serve the representations on—

        (i) the court officer, and

        (ii) each other party;

    (b) do so not more than 14 days after service of the application;

    (c) ask for a hearing, if that party wants one, and explain why it is needed.

(3) Where representations include information that the person making them thinks ought not be revealed to another party, that person must—

    (a) omit that information from the representations served on that other party;

    (b) mark the information to show that, unless the court otherwise directs, it is only for the court; and

    (c) with that information include an explanation of why it has been withheld from that other party.

(4) Representations against an application for an order must explain why the conditions for making it are not met.

Preparation for Trial in the Crown Court

Commencement of preparatory hearing

3.18.

At the beginning of a preparatory hearing, the court must—

    (a) announce that it is such a hearing; and

    (b) take the defendant's plea under rule 3.24 (Arraigning the defendant on the indictment), unless already done.

[Note. See section 8 of the Criminal Justice Act 1987 and section 30 of the Criminal Procedure and Investigations Act 1996.]

Defence trial advocate

3.19.

(1) The defendant must notify the court officer of the identity of the intended defence trial advocate—

    (a) as soon as practicable, and in any event no later than the day of the plea and case management hearing;

    (b) in writing, or orally at the plea and case management hearing.

(2) The defendant must notify the court officer in writing of any change in the identity of the intended defence trial advocate as soon as practicable, and in any event not more than 5 business days after that change.

Application to stay case for abuse of process

3.20.

(1) This rule applies where a defendant wants the Crown Court to stay the case on the grounds that the proceedings are an abuse of the court, or otherwise unfair.

(2) Such a defendant must—

    (a) apply in writing—

        (i) as soon as practicable after becoming aware of the grounds for doing so,

        (ii) at a pre-trial hearing, unless the grounds for the application do not arise until trial, and

        (iii) in any event, before the defendant pleads guilty or the jury (if there is one) retires to consider its verdict at trial;

Appendix 3 *The Criminal Procedure Rules 2014 (SI 2014/1610)*

    (b)   serve the application on—
        (i)   the court officer, and
        (ii) each other party; and
    (c)   in the application—
        (i)   explain the grounds on which it is made,
        (ii)   include, attach or identify all supporting material,
        (iii) specify relevant events, dates and propositions of law, and
        (iv) identify any witness the applicant wants to call to give evidence in person.

(3) A party who wants to make representations in response to the application must serve the representations on—
    (a)   the court officer; and
    (b)   each other party,

not more than 14 days after service of the application.

Application for joint or separate trials, etc.

3.21.

(1) This rule applies where a party wants the Crown Court to order—
    (a)   the joint trial of—
        (i)   offences charged by separate indictments, or
        (ii) defendants charged in separate indictments;
    (b)   separate trials of offences charged by the same indictment;
    (c)   separate trials of defendants charged in the same indictment; or
    (d)   the deletion of a count from an indictment.

(2) Such a party must—
    (a)   apply in writing—
        (i)   as soon as practicable after becoming aware of the grounds for doing so, and
        (ii) before the trial begins, unless the grounds for the application do not arise until trial;
    (b)   serve the application on—
        (i)   the court officer, and
        (ii) each other party; and

(c) in the application—

    (i) specify the order proposed, and

    (ii) explain why it should be made.

(3) A party who wants to make representations in response to the application must serve the representations on—

    (a) the court officer; and

    (b) each other party,

not more than 14 days after service of the application.

[Note. See section 5 of the Indictments Act 1915. Rule 14.2 governs the form and content of an indictment.]

Order for joint or separate trials, or amendment of the indictment

3.22.

(1) This rule applies where the Crown Court makes an order—

    (a) on an application under rule 3.21 applies (Application for joint or separate trials, etc.); or

    (b) amending an indictment in any other respect.

(2) Unless the court otherwise directs, the court officer must endorse any paper copy of each affected indictment made for the court with—

    (a) a note of the court's order; and

    (b) the date of that order.

Application for indication of sentence

3.23.

(1) This rule applies where a defendant wants the Crown Court to give an indication of the maximum sentence that would be passed if a guilty plea were entered when the indication is sought.

(2) Such a defendant must—

    (a) apply in writing as soon as practicable; and

    (b) serve the application on—

        (i) the court officer, and

        (ii) the prosecutor.

Appendix 3 *The Criminal Procedure Rules 2014 (SI 2014/1610)*

(3) The application must—
- (a) specify—
    - (i) the offence or offences to which it would be a guilty plea, and
    - (ii) the facts on the basis of which that plea would be entered; and
- (b) include the prosecutor's agreement to, or representations on, that proposed basis of plea.

(4) The prosecutor must—
- (a) provide information relevant to sentence, including—
    - (i) any previous conviction of the defendant, and the circumstances where relevant,
    - (ii) any statement of the effect of the offence on the victim, the victim's family or others; and
- (b) identify any other matter relevant to sentence, including—
    - (i) the legislation applicable,
    - (ii) any sentencing guidelines, or guideline cases, and
    - (iii) aggravating and mitigating factors.

(5) The hearing of the application—
- (a) may take place in the absence of any other defendant;
- (b) must be attended by—
    - (i) the applicant defendant's legal representatives (if any), and
    - (ii) the prosecution advocate.

Arraigning the defendant on the indictment

3.24.

(1) In order to take the defendant's plea, the Crown Court must—
- (a) ensure that the defendant is correctly identified by the indictment;
- (b) in respect of each count in the indictment—
    - (i) read the count aloud to the defendant, or arrange for it to be read aloud or placed before the defendant in writing,
    - (ii) ask whether the defendant pleads guilty or not guilty to the offence charged by that count, and
    - (iii) take the defendant's plea.

(2) Where a count is read which is substantially the same as one already read aloud, then only the materially different details need be read aloud.

(3) Where a count is placed before the defendant in writing, the court must summarise its gist aloud.

(4) In respect of each count in the indictment—

  (a) if the defendant declines to enter a plea, the court must treat that as a not guilty plea unless rule 38.11 applies (defendant unfit to plead);

  (b) if the defendant pleads not guilty to the offence charged by that count but guilty to another offence of which the court could convict on that count—

    (i) if the prosecutor and the court accept that plea, the court must treat the plea as one of guilty of that other offence, but

    (ii) otherwise, the court must treat the plea as one of not guilty;

  (c) if the defendant pleads a previous acquittal or conviction of the offence charged by that count—

    (i) the defendant must identify that acquittal or conviction in writing, explaining the basis of that plea, and

    (ii) the court must exercise its power to decide whether that plea disposes of that count.

[Note. See section 6 of the Criminal Law Act 1967 and section 122 of the Criminal Justice Act 1988.

Under section 6(2) of the 1967 Act, on an indictment for murder a defendant may instead be convicted of manslaughter or another offence specified by that provision. Under section 6(3) of that Act, on an indictment for an offence other than murder or treason a defendant may instead be convicted of another offence if—

  (a) *the allegation in the indictment amounts to or includes an allegation of that other offence; and*

  (b) *the Crown Court has power to convict and sentence for that other offence.]*

Place of trial

3.25.

(1) Unless the court otherwise directs, the court officer must arrange for the trial to take place in a courtroom provided by the Lord Chancellor.

(2) The court officer must arrange for the court and the jury (if there is one) to view any place required by the court.

[Note. See section 3 of the Courts Act 2003 and section 14 of the Juries Act 1974.

In some circumstances the court may conduct all or part of the hearing outside a courtroom.]

Use of Welsh language at trial

3.26.

Where the trial will take place in Wales and a participant wishes to use the Welsh language—

    (a) that participant must serve notice on the court officer, or arrange for such a notice to be served on that participant's behalf—

        (i) at or before the plea and case management hearing (if there is one), or

        (ii) if there is no such hearing, then in accordance with any direction given by the court; and

    (b) if such a notice is served, the court officer must arrange for an interpreter to attend the hearing.

[Note. See section 22 of the Welsh Language Act 1993.]

Other provisions affecting case management

Case management may be affected by the following other rules and legislation:

Criminal Procedure Rules

Part 9: allocation and sending for trial

Part 10: initial details of the prosecution case

Part 14: the indictment

Part 22: disclosure

Parts 27 – 36: the rules that deal with evidence

Part 37: trial and sentence in a magistrates' court

Part 38: trial and sentence in the Crown Court

Regulations

The Prosecution of Offences (Custody Time Limits) Regulations 1987

The Crime and Disorder Act 1998 (Service of Prosecution Evidence) Regulations 2005

The Criminal Procedure and Investigations Act 1996 (Defence Disclosure Time Limits) Regulations 2011

Acts of Parliament

Sections 10 and 18, Magistrates' Courts Act 1980: powers to adjourn hearings

Sections 128 and 129, Magistrates' Courts Act 1980: remand in custody by magistrates' courts

Sections 19 and 24A, Magistrates' Courts Act 1980 and sections 51 and 51A, Crime and Disorder Act 1998: allocation and sending for trial

Section 2, Administration of Justice (Miscellaneous Provisions) Act 1933: procedural conditions for trial in the Crown Court

Sections 8A and 8B, Magistrates' Courts Act 1980: pre-trial hearings in magistrates' courts

Section 7, Criminal Justice Act 1987; Parts III and IV, Criminal Procedure and Investigations Act 1996: pre-trial and preparatory hearings in the Crown Court

Section 9, Criminal Justice Act 1967: proof by written witness statement

Part 1, Criminal Procedure and Investigations Act 1996: disclosure.]

Appendix 4

Criminal Procedure and Investigations Act 1996

PART III

PREPARATORY HEARINGS

Introduction

28 Introduction

(1) This Part applies in relation to an offence if—

    (a) on or after the appointed day the accused is sent for trial for the offence concerned,

    (b) proceedings for the trial on the charge concerned are transferred to the Crown Court on or after the appointed day, or

    (c) a bill of indictment relating to the offence is preferred on or after the appointed day under the authority of section 2(2)(b) of the Administration of Justice (Miscellaneous Provisions) Act 1933 (bill preferred by direction of Court of Appeal, or by direction or with consent of a judge).

(2) References in subsection (1) to the appointed day are to such day as is appointed for the purposes of this section by the Secretary of State by order.

(3) If an order under this section so provides, this Part applies only in relation to the Crown Court sitting at a place or places specified in the order.

(4) References in this Part to the prosecutor are to any person acting as prosecutor, whether an individual or a body.

Preparatory hearings

29 Power to order preparatory hearing

(1) Where it appears to a judge of the Crown Court that an indictment reveals a case of such complexity, a case of such seriousness or a case whose

Appendix 4 *Criminal Procedure and Investigations Act 1996*

trial is likely to be of such length, that substantial benefits are likely to accrue from a hearing—

(a) before the time when the jury are sworn, and

(b) for any of the purposes mentioned in subsection (2),

he may order that such a hearing (in this Part referred to as a preparatory hearing) shall be held.

(1A) A judge of the Crown Court may also order that a preparatory hearing shall be held if an application to which section 45 of the Criminal Justice Act 2003 applies (application for trial without jury) is made.

(1B) An order that a preparatory hearing shall be held must be made by a judge of the Crown Court in every case which (whether or not it falls within subsection (1) or (1A)) is a case in which at least one of the offences charged by the indictment against at least one of the persons charged is a terrorism offence.

(1C) An order that a preparatory hearing shall be held must also be made by a judge of the Crown court in every case which (whether or not it falls within subsection (1) or (1A)) is a case in which—

(a) at least one of the offences charged by the indictment against at least one of the persons charged is an offence carrying a maximum of at least 10 years' imprisonment; and

(b) it appears to the judge that evidence on the indictment reveals that conduct in respect of which that offence is charged had a terrorist connection.

(2) The purposes are those of—

(a) identifying issues which are likely to be material to the determinations and findings which are likely to be required during the trial,

(b) if there is to be a jury, assisting their comprehension of those issues and expediting the proceedings before them,

(c) determining an application to which section 45 of the Criminal Justice Act 2003 applies,

(d) assisting the judge's management of the trial.

(e) considering questions as to the severance or joinder of charges,

(3) In a case in which it appears to a judge of the Crown Court that evidence on an indictment reveals a case of fraud of such seriousness or complexity as is mentioned in section 7 of the Criminal Justice Act 1987 (preparatory hearings in cases of serious or complex fraud)—

(a) the judge may make an order for a preparatory hearing under this section only if he is required to do so by subsection (1B) or (1C);

- (b) before making an order in pursuance of either of those subsections, he must determine whether to make an order for a preparatory hearing under that section; and
- (c) he is not required by either of those subsections to make an order for a preparatory hearing under this section if he determines that an order should be made for a preparatory hearing under that section;

and, in a case in which an order is made for a preparatory hearing under that section, requirements imposed by those subsections apply only if that order ceases to have effect.

(4) An order that a preparatory hearing shall be held may be made—
- (a) on the application of the prosecutor,
- (b) on the application of the accused or, if there is more than one, any of them, or
- (c) of the judge's own motion.

(5) The reference in subsection (1)(a) to the time when the jury are sworn includes the time when the jury would be sworn but for the making of an order under Part 7 of the Criminal Justice Act 2003.

(6) In this section 'terrorism offence' means—
- (a) an offence under section 11 or 12 of the Terrorism Act 2000 (c. 11) (offences relating to proscribed organisations);
- (b) an offence under any of sections 15 to 18 of that Act (offences relating to terrorist property);
- (c) an offence under section 38B of that Act (failure to disclose information about acts of terrorism);
- (d) an offence under section 54 of that Act (weapons training);
- (e) an offence under any of sections 56 to 59 of that Act (directing terrorism, possessing things and collecting information for the purposes of terrorism and inciting terrorism outside the United Kingdom);
- (f) an offence in respect of which there is jurisdiction by virtue of section 62 of that Act (extra-territorial jurisdiction in respect of certain offences committed outside the United Kingdom for the purposes of terrorism etc.);
- (g) an offence under Part 1 of the Terrorism Act 2006 (miscellaneous terrorist related offences);
- (h) conspiring or attempting to commit a terrorism offence;
- (i) incitement to commit a terrorism offence.

Appendix 4 *Criminal Procedure and Investigations Act 1996*

(7) For the purposes of this section an offence carries a maximum of at least 10 years' imprisonment if—

    (a) it is punishable, on conviction on indictment, with imprisonment; and

    (b) the maximum term of imprisonment that may be imposed on conviction on indictment of that offence is 10 years or more or is imprisonment for life.

(8) For the purposes of this section conduct has a terrorist connection if it is or takes place in the course of an act of terrorism or is for the purposes of terrorism.

(9) In subsection (8) 'terrorism' has the same meaning as in the Terrorism Act 2000 (see section 1 of that Act).

30 Start of trial and arraignment

If a judge orders a preparatory hearing—

(a) the trial shall start with that hearing, and

(b) arraignment shall take place at the start of that hearing, unless it has taken place before then.

31 The preparatory hearing

(1) At the preparatory hearing the judge may exercise any of the powers specified in this section.

(2) The judge may adjourn a preparatory hearing from time to time.

(3) He may make a ruling as to—

    (a) any question as to the admissibility of evidence;

    (b) any other question of law relating to the case

    (c) any question as to the severance or joinder of charges.

(4) He may order the prosecutor—

    (a) to give the court and the accused or, if there is more than one, each of them a written statement (a case statement) of the matters falling within subsection (5);

    (b) to prepare the prosecution evidence and any explanatory material in such a form as appears to the judge to be likely to aid comprehension by a jury and to give it in that form to the court and to the accused or, if there is more than one, to each of them;

    (c) to give the court and the accused or, if there is more than one, each of them written notice of documents the truth of the contents of which ought in the prosecutor's view to be admitted and of any other matters which in his view ought to be agreed;

(d) to make any amendments of any case statement given in pursuance of an order under paragraph (a) that appear to the judge to be appropriate, having regard to objections made by the accused or, if there is more than one, by any of them.

(5) The matters referred to in subsection (4)(a) are—

(a) the principal facts of the case for the prosecution;

(b) the witnesses who will speak to those facts;

(c) any exhibits relevant to those facts;

(d) any proposition of law on which the prosecutor proposes to rely;

(e) the consequences in relation to any of the counts in the indictment that appear to the prosecutor to flow from the matters falling within paragraphs (a) to (d).

(6) Where a judge has ordered the prosecutor to give a case statement and the prosecutor has complied with the order, the judge may order the accused or, if there is more than one, each of them—

(a) [...]

(b) to give the court and the prosecutor written notice of any objections that he has to the case statement;

(c) [...]

(7) Where a judge has ordered the prosecutor to give notice under subsection (4)(c) and the prosecutor has complied with the order, the judge may order the accused or, if there is more than one, each of them to give the court and the prosecutor a written notice stating—

(a) the extent to which he agrees with the prosecutor as to documents and other matters to which the notice under subsection (4)(c) relates, and

(b) the reason for any disagreement.

(8) A judge making an order under subsection (6) or (7) shall warn the accused or, if there is more than one, each of them of the possible consequence under section 34 of not complying with it.

(9) If it appears to a judge that reasons given in pursuance of subsection (7) are inadequate, he shall so inform the person giving them and may require him to give further or better reasons.

(10) An order under this section may specify the time within which any specified requirement contained in it is to be complied with.

(11) An order or ruling made under this section shall have effect throughout the trial, unless it appears to the judge on application made to him that the interests of justice require him to vary or discharge it.

Appendix 4 *Criminal Procedure and Investigations Act 1996*

32 Orders before preparatory hearing

(1) This section applies where—

  (a) a judge orders a preparatory hearing, and

  (b) he decides that any order which could be made under section 31(4) to (7) at the hearing should be made before the hearing.

(2) In such a case—

  (a) he may make any such order before the hearing (or at the hearing), and

  (b) section 31(4) to (11) shall apply accordingly.

33 Criminal Procedure Rules

(1) Criminal Procedure Rules may provide that except to the extent that disclosure is required—

  (a) by rules under section 81 of the Police and Criminal Evidence Act 1984 (expert evidence), or

  (b) by section 5(7) of this Act,

anything required to be given by an accused in pursuance of a requirement imposed under section 31 need not disclose who will give evidence.

(2) Criminal Procedure Rules may make provision as to the minimum or maximum time that may be specified under section 31(10).

34 Later stages of trial

(1) Any party may depart from the case he disclosed in pursuance of a requirement imposed under section 31.

(2) Where—

  (a) a party departs from the case he disclosed in pursuance of a requirement imposed under section 31, or

  (b) a party fails to comply with such a requirement,

the judge or, with the leave of the judge, any other party may make such comment as appears to the judge or the other party (as the case may be) to be appropriate and the jury or, in the case of a trial without a jury, the judge may draw such inference as appears proper.

(3) In doing anything under subsection (2) or in deciding whether to do anything under it the judge shall have regard—

  (a) to the extent of the departure or failure, and

  (b) to whether there is any justification for it.

Preparatory Hearings

(4) Except as provided by this section, in the case of a trial with a jury no part—

(a) of a statement given under section 31(6)(a), or

(b) of any other information relating to the case for the accused or, if there is more than one, the case for any of them, which was given in pursuance of a requirement imposed under section 31,

may be disclosed at a stage in the trial after the jury have been sworn without the consent of the accused concerned.

Appeals

35 Appeals to Court of Appeal

(1) An appeal shall lie to the Court of Appeal from any ruling of a judge under section 31(3), from the refusal by a judge of an application to which section 45 of the Criminal Justice Act 2003 applies or from an order of a judge under section 43 or 44 of that Act which is made on the determination of such an application, but only with the leave of the judge or of the Court of Appeal.

(2) The judge may continue a preparatory hearing notwithstanding that leave to appeal has been granted under subsection (1), but the preparatory hearing shall not be concluded until after the appeal has been determined or abandoned.

(3) On the termination of the hearing of an appeal, the Court of Appeal may confirm, reverse or vary the decision appealed against.

(4) Subject to rules of court made under section 53(1) of the Supreme Court Act 1981 (power by rules to distribute business of Court of Appeal between its civil and criminal divisions)—

(a) the jurisdiction of the Court of Appeal under subsection (1) above shall be exercised by the criminal division of the court;

(b) references in this Part to the Court of Appeal shall be construed as references to that division.

36 Appeals to House of Lords.

(1) In the Criminal Appeal Act 1968, in—

(a) section 33(1) (right of appeal to House of Lords), and

(b) section 36 (bail),

after '1987' there shall be inserted 'or section 35 of the Criminal Procedure and Investigations Act 1996'.

Appendix 4 *Criminal Procedure and Investigations Act 1996*

(2) The judge may continue a preparatory hearing notwithstanding that leave to appeal has been granted under Part II of the Criminal Appeal Act 1968, but the preparatory hearing shall not be concluded until after the appeal has been determined or abandoned.

Reporting restrictions

37 Restrictions on reporting

(1) Except as provided by this section—

 (a) no written report of proceedings falling within subsection (2) shall be published in the United Kingdom;

 (b) no report of proceedings falling within subsection (2) shall be included in a relevant programme for reception in the United Kingdom.

(2) The following proceedings fall within this subsection—

 (a) a preparatory hearing;

 (b) an application for leave to appeal in relation to such a hearing;

 (c) an appeal in relation to such a hearing.

(3) The judge dealing with a preparatory hearing may order that subsection (1) shall not apply, or shall not apply to a specified extent, to a report of—

 (a) the preparatory hearing, or

 (b) an application to the judge for leave to appeal to the Court of Appeal under section 35(1) in relation to the preparatory hearing.

(4) The Court of Appeal may order that subsection (1) shall not apply, or shall not apply to a specified extent, to a report of —

 (a) an appeal to the Court of Appeal under section 35(1) in relation to a preparatory hearing,

 (b) an application to that Court for leave to appeal to it under section 35(1) in relation to a preparatory hearing, or

 (c) an application to that Court for leave to appeal to the House of Lords under Part II of the Criminal Appeal Act 1968 in relation to a preparatory hearing.

(5) The House of Lords may order that subsection (1) shall not apply, or shall not apply to a specified extent, to a report of—

 (a) an appeal to that House under Part II of the Criminal Appeal Act 1968 in relation to a preparatory hearing, or

(b) an application to that House for leave to appeal to it under Part II of the Criminal Appeal Act 1968 in relation to a preparatory hearing.

(6) Where there is only one accused and he objects to the making of an order under subsection (3), (4) or (5) the judge or the Court of Appeal or the House of Lords shall make the order if (and only if) satisfied after hearing the representations of the accused that it is in the interests of justice to do so; and if the order is made it shall not apply to the extent that a report deals with any such objection or representations.

(7) Where there are two or more accused and one or more of them objects to the making of an order under subsection (3), (4) or (5) the judge or the Court of Appeal or the House of Lords shall make the order if (and only if) satisfied after hearing the representations of each of the accused that it is in the interests of justice to do so; and if the order is made it shall not apply to the extent that a report deals with any such objection or representations.

(8) Subsection (1) does not apply to—

(a) the publication of a report of a preparatory hearing,

(b) the publication of a report of an appeal in relation to a preparatory hearing or of an application for leave to appeal in relation to such a hearing,

(c) the inclusion in a relevant programme of a report of a preparatory hearing, or

(d) the inclusion in a relevant programme of a report of an appeal in relation to a preparatory hearing or of an application for leave to appeal in relation to such a hearing,

at the conclusion of the trial of the accused or of the last of the accused to be tried.

(9) Subsection (1) does not apply to a report which contains only one or more of the following matters—

(a) the identity of the court and the name of the judge;

(b) the names, ages, home addresses and occupations of the accused and witnesses;

(c) the offence or offences, or a summary of them, with which the accused is or are charged;

(d) the names of counsel and solicitors in the proceedings;

(e) where the proceedings are adjourned, the date and place to which they are adjourned;

(f) any arrangements as to bail;

Appendix 4 *Criminal Procedure and Investigations Act 1996*

(g) whether a right to representation funded by the Legal Services Commission as part of the Criminal Defence Service was granted to the accused or any of the accused.

(10) The addresses that may be published or included in a relevant programme under subsection (9) are addresses—

(a) at any relevant time, and

(b) at the time of their publication or inclusion in a relevant programme;

and 'relevant time' here means a time when events giving rise to the charges to which the proceedings relate occurred.

(11) Nothing in this section affects any prohibition or restriction imposed by virtue of any other enactment on a publication or on matter included in a programme.

(12) In this section—

(a) 'publish', in relation to a report, means publish the report, either by itself or as part of a newspaper or periodical, for distribution to the public;

(b) expressions cognate with 'publish' shall be construed accordingly;

(c) 'relevant programme' means a programme included in a programme service, within the meaning of the Broadcasting Act 1990.

38 Offences in connection with reporting

(1) If a report is published or included in a relevant programme in contravention of section 37 each of the following persons is guilty of an offence—

(a) in the case of a publication of a written report as part of a newspaper or periodical, any proprietor, editor or publisher of the newspaper or periodical;

(b) in the case of a publication of a written report otherwise than as part of a newspaper or periodical, the person who publishes it;

(c) in the case of the inclusion of a report in a relevant programme, any body corporate which is engaged in providing the service in which the programme is included and any person having functions in relation to the programme corresponding to those of an editor of a newspaper.

(2) A person guilty of an offence under this section is liable on summary conviction to a fine of an amount not exceeding level 5 on the standard scale.

(3) Proceedings for an offence under this section shall not be instituted in England and Wales otherwise than by or with the consent of the Attorney General.

(3A) Proceedings for an offence under this section shall not be instituted in Northern Ireland otherwise than by or with the consent of the Attorney General for Northern Ireland.

(4) Subsection (12) of section 37 applies for the purposes of this section as it applies for the purposes of that.

Appendix 5

Simple Cautions for Adult Offenders[*]

INTRODUCTION

1. This guidance is for police officers and Crown Prosecutors[1] in England and Wales for dealing with criminal offences. It also provides guidance to the public as to how cautions should be administered, and what factors should be taken into account by relevant authorities.

2. **This guidance replaces Guidance on Simple Cautions published by the Ministry of Justice ('MoJ') on 8 April 2013**. It should be applied to all decisions relating to simple cautions from the commencement date, regardless of when the offence was committed.

3. It should be used in conjunction with the Director's Guidance on Charging issued by the Director of Public Prosecutions under section 37A of the Police and Criminal Evidence Act 1984.[2]

4. There is a range of out of court disposals available to the police and CPS. A decision to administer a simple caution needs to be taken in the context of all the available out of court disposals. The national framework on out of court disposals should be used to assist police and prosecutors and can be found at www.justice.gov.uk/out-of-court-disposals

Aims and purpose of the simple caution for adult offenders scheme

5. The aims of the simple caution are:

    – to offer a proportionate response to low level offending where the offender has admitted the offence;

    – To deliver swift, simple and effective justice that carries a deterrent effect;

---

[*] Issued by the Ministry of Justice. Commencement date: 14 November 2013
[1] Other bodies, for example, local authorities who have separate caution schemes, are not bound by this guidance although they may adopt this guidance if they wish.
[2] The Director's Guidance is available on the Crown Prosecution Service (CPS) website at http://www.cps.gov.uk/publications/directors_guidance/index.html.

Appendix 5 *Simple Cautions for Adult Offenders*

- To record an individual's criminal conduct for possible reference in future criminal proceedings or in criminal record or other similar checks;
- To reduce the likelihood of re-offending;
- To increase the amount of time officers spend dealing with more serious crime and reduce the amount of time police officers spend completing paperwork and attending court, whilst simultaneously reducing the burden on the courts.

Overview of the scheme

6. The simple caution (once known as a formal or police caution) is a non statutory disposal for adult offenders aged 18 or over. The scheme is designed to provide the police and Crown Prosecution Service (CPS) with an alternative means for dealing with low-level, mainly first time offending when specified public interest and eligibility criteria are met. Only in exceptional circumstances should it be used to deal with more serious offences.

7. The simple caution should not be confused with a conditional caution (a caution with conditions attached) introduced by the Criminal Justice Act 2003. Separate guidance on this scheme is contained in The Code of Practice on Adult Conditional Cautions and the Directors Guidance on Adult Conditional Cautions.

8. Whether an offence or offender is suitable for a simple caution is an operational decision for the police and in some instances, the CPS, based on the specific circumstances of the individual case. Annex A provides an overview of factors to consider for whether a simple caution may be appropriate.

9. Simple cautions cannot be offered to an offender who has not admitted that they are guilty of the offence or who has raised a defence, and cannot be given to an offender who does not agree to accept the caution. Offenders retain the right to decline the offer of a simple caution – even where guilt has been admitted – and face being prosecuted.

10. In addition, simple cautions can only be given if the police officer is satisfied that there is sufficient evidence to provide a realistic prospect of conviction if the offender were to be prosecuted. They cannot be used unless this test is met. Similarly, cautions should not be given if it is in the public interest for the offender to be brought before the court. See paragraphs 39 – 43 for further guidance on applying the Code for Crown Prosecutors when taking decisions to offer a simple caution.

11. Simple cautions do form part of an offender's criminal record and may be used in future proceedings and in certain circumstances, may be made

available to an employer as part of a criminal record check. Offenders **must** be made aware of this **before** agreeing to accept a simple caution.

12. There is no right of appeal against the administration of a simple caution once it has been accepted by the offender and administered by the police. However, it may be challenged by way of a formal complaint to the police force that administered it and by a judicial review.

SECTION TWO: DECISION MAKING

Offences

13. Simple cautions are available for any offence but are primarily intended for low level, mainly first time offending.

Indictable only and specified either offences

14. **Simple cautions should not be given for indictable only offences**, unless a senior police officer of at least the rank of Superintendent believes there are exceptional circumstances and the CPS agrees.

15. **Simple cautions should not be given for** certain specified **either way offences** unless a senior police officer believes there are exceptional circumstances.

16. When deciding whether there are exceptional circumstances the relevant officer should take into account the factors set out in paragraph 23 below.

17. The specified either way offences are set out in Annex B and are summarised as follows:

    - Possession of a bladed article, offensive weapon or firearm in public; including threatening with a bladed article or offensive weapon in a public place or a school;
    - Child prostitution and pornography, cruelty to a child, indecent photographs of children; and
    - Supplying Class A drugs.

Decision making process for non-specified either way offence and summary only offences

18. An assessment of the seriousness of the offence is the starting point for considering whether a simple caution may be appropriate for non specified either way offence or a summary only offence. The more serious the offence, the less likely a simple caution will be appropriate. Wherever the circumstances of an offence indicate that an immediate custodial sentence or high level community order is the appropriate

Appendix 5 *Simple Cautions for Adult Offenders*

sentence, a simple caution should not be offered unless at least one of the exceptional circumstances set out at paragraph 21 below are met.

19. Any aggravating circumstances, including the methodology employed by the offender (for example, any breach of trust or advantage taken of the vulnerable or young) may all increase the seriousness of the offence to the point where the case should proceed to court. The National Decision Model and the College of Policing *Gravity Factors Matrix* should be used to assist officers in reaching this decision.

20. The Magistrates' Court Sentencing Guidelines provide a sentencing starting point for a range of offences dealt with by magistrates' courts at high level community order or period of imprisonment. The seriousness of the offence and the range of penalties likely to be considered must be carefully considered in every case taking into account the Magistrates' Court Sentencing Guidelines. Likewise cases routinely dealt with at the Crown Court (the Magistrates' Court Sentencing Guidelines indicate what type of cases these might be) should also generally proceed to court.

Exceptional circumstances test

21. A simple caution for an indictable only offence, a specified either way offence, an either way offence routinely dealt with at the Crown Court or any offence which the sentencing guidelines indicate that an immediate custodial sentence or high level community order is the appropriate sentence, may only be given in **exceptional circumstances**

22. The decision maker must conclude that the public interest does not require the immediate prosecution of the offender and that if the offender was prosecuted there would be reasons why the court would not impose a period of imprisonment or high level community order.

23. In assessing whether exceptional circumstances exist in a case, the following non exhaustive list of factors must be taken into account:

    – The extent of culpability and/or harm caused;

    – The degree of intention or the forseeability of any resultant harm;

    – Any significant aggravating factors;

    – Any significant mitigating factors;

    – The lack of any recent similar previous convictions or cautions;

    – Any other factors relating to the offender or commission of the offence likely to have a significant impact on sentence;

    – The overall justice of the case and whether the circumstances require it to be dealt with in open court;

Section Two: Decision Making

- The range of sentences appropriate to the circumstances of the case.

Specific Offence Types

Domestic Violence and Abuse

24. Positive action is recommended in cases of domestic violence and abuse to ensure the safety and protection of victims and children while allowing the Criminal Justice System to hold the offender to account. Domestic violence and abuse cases often involve a number of incidents prior to reporting to the police. A positive action approach considers the incident in its entirety and should focus investigative efforts on gathering sufficient evidence to be able to build a prosecution case that does not rely entirely on the victim's statement. Police and prosecutors should refer to the ACPO/CPS Charging checklist[3] to help secure evidence-based prosecutions which are not solely victim reliant.

25. Officers must follow the criteria for offering a simple caution as set out in this guidance, particularly where there is sufficient evidence in line with the Full Code Test and that the offender admits guilt and agrees to accept the simple caution. If the evidential stage of the Full Code test is satisfied then it will rarely be appropriate to deal with the case by way of a simple caution in cases of domestic violence and abuse. However, where a positive action policy has been adhered to but the victim does not support a prosecution and the available evidence (including any additional evidence adduced) would only support charging a very minor offence a simple caution can be considered in preference to a decision to take no further action.

Stalking and Harassment (racial or other)

26. In cases of stalking or harassment there are two additional considerations before a simple caution can be offered:

    a) administering a simple caution may render all conduct on which the caution is based inadmissible as evidence towards a course of conduct should this continue subsequently; and

    b) since a restraining order can only be issued by the court, the only way in which a victim would otherwise be protected against a future conduct would be by seeking, and self-funding, an anti-harassment injunction from a civil court (which is similar in effect to a restraining order and permits a victim to apply to the court for

---

3 www.cps.gov.uk/legal/assets/uploads/files/joint_cps_acpo_evidence_checklist_for_ domestic_violence_cases.doc

Appendix 5 *Simple Cautions for Adult Offenders*

a warrant of arrest in the event of a breach). In cases of stalking or aggravated harassment a prosecution should be pursued wherever possible to ensure an application for an order can be made.

27. For these reasons, the views of the victim should be fully considered and a simple caution only administered where the police are confident that the stalking or harassment will not continue subsequently and a harassment warning has not been previously issued.

Multiple Offences and Mixed Disposals

28. Where multiple related offences have been committed, in determining whether the case should proceed to court or is suitable for a simple caution, police and prosecutors should consider the totality of the offending.

29. It is possible to use different disposals where an offender has committed multiple but unrelated offences as part of the same incident. Depending on the nature of the offence, other disposal options than a simple caution are also available such as a cannabis warning, a Penalty Notice for Disorder (PND), a conditional caution or a charge. For example, if a person is arrested for being drunk and disorderly and when searched in custody is found to be carrying a selection of car keys and admits that their intention was to steal from cars, they may be simple cautioned for 'going equipped to steal' and issued with a PND for the drunk and disorderly offence.

30. Any decision on administering a simple caution as a disposal element when different disposals are used should be considered with regard to the Director's Guidance on Charging.[4]

Group offences

31. Where a number of individuals are involved in committing an offence the extent of their involvement and the experience and circumstances of each offender can vary greatly. While consistency is an important consideration in the decision of how to deal with such a case, it is important that each offender should be considered separately and consequently different disposals may be justified.

---

4   This is available on the CPS website http://www.cps.gov.uk/publications/directors_guidance/index.html.

Section Two: Decision Making

Other Serious Offences

32. Serious offences which would ordinarily attract a high end community order or immediate custody are generally not suitable for disposal through a simple caution.

33. As well as the specific offences noted in paragraph 17 which should not normally be disposed of by way of simple caution, care should be taken around administering a simple caution for sexual offences and serious violence against the person offences. ACPO charging guidance for particular offence types should be followed.

Offenders subject to police or court bail and/or court orders

34. It is also not generally appropriate to use a simple caution if the offender was on police bail, court bail or subject to a court order at the time of the commission of the offence. In general it would be more appropriate to prosecute in these cases, or for such offences to be taken into consideration in relation to any other on going prosecution of that offender. The CPS have published guidance on Offences to be Taken Into Consideration (TICs) which should be followed.

Circumstances when a simple caution should not be given

35. A simple caution is not an appropriate method of disposing of offences committed by serving prisoners or those subject to prison recall. This will include:

    o new offences committed by a prisoner whilst in custody;

    o new offences committed upon release from custody whilst subject to prison recall;

    o offences committed prior to an offender beginning a custodial sentence. This includes circumstances where the commission of the offences, or the offender's guilt, only becomes known whilst the offender is in custody or carrying out the court imposed sanction.

If any of the above applies the offender should not be given a simple caution.

The decision to offer a simple caution

Decision making powers

36. The police may make the decision to offer a simple caution for any summary only offence (an offence that it is always heard in a magistrates' court) or either way offences (an offence that may be heard in either

Appendix 5 *Simple Cautions for Adult Offenders*

a magistrates' court or the Crown Court). Paragraph 15 outlines those either way offences that must only be considered for a simple caution in exceptional circumstances where a senior police officer has made the decision that in all circumstances of the case a simple caution is the appropriate disposal.

37. Any cases involving indictable only offences (the most serious offences that must always be heard in the Crown Court) should always be referred to a senior officer who will take the decision to refer the case to the CPS for a decision on whether a simple caution is appropriate. **The police should not offer or administer a simple caution for an indictable only offence where it has not been agreed by the CPS**.

38. The CPS may also instruct a simple caution to be offered in any summary only or either way case where the criteria is met and this is considered the most appropriate and proportionate response to the offending behaviour and meets the justice of the case.

39. **If the CPS instructs that a simple caution should be offered in any case then this decision is binding upon the police**. If, however, a simple caution is deemed to be the appropriate disposal by the CPS and it then proves not possible to administer it to an offender for any reason (for example where he or she does not agree to accept it or fails to attend the police station) then the case should be referred back to the CPS for a decision on whether to pursue a prosecution. This applies to any type of offence where the CPS has instructed that a simple caution should be offered.

40. As set out in the Director's Guidance on Charging, police officers can seek advice from the CPS at any stage in an investigation on whether a simple caution may be an appropriate outcome. They are particularly encouraged to do so in serious either way offences such as those involving violence against the person and sexual offences which are serious in nature and in which it may be in the public interest to prosecute.

Evidential ground for giving a simple caution

41. In deciding whether to offer a simple caution the police or CPS must apply the Full Code Test as set out in the Code for Crown Prosecutors which can be found at:

    http://www.cps.gov.uk/publications/code_for_crown_prosecutors/

Full code test – evidential stage

42. The police or prosecutor must be satisfied that there is sufficient evidence to provide a realistic prospect of conviction in respect of each offence if the offender were to be prosecuted.

Section Two: Decision Making

43. Part of determining whether there is sufficient evidence to provide a realistic prospect of conviction may including assessing whether there has been a clear and reliable admission of the offence either verbally or in writing. **A simple caution must not be offered in order to secure an admission that could then provide sufficient evidence to meet the evidential limb of the Full Code test.** See also paragraphs 59-62 which give further guidance on the admission of guilt.

Full Code Test - public interest stage

44. Where there is sufficient evidence to provide a realistic prospect of conviction police officers and prosecutors must then go on to consider whether it is in the public interest to offer a simple caution as an alternative to prosecution in respect of the offence or offences.

45. The Public Interest stage is as set out in the Full Code Test and can be found on the CPS website.

    www.cps.gov.uk/publications/code_for_crown_prosecutors/

Offender

Previous Offending History

46. A simple caution should not be given where the person has been cautioned for or convicted of the same or similar offences within two years of the commission of current offence unless there are exceptional circumstances.

47. Decisions that exceptional circumstances exist which justify the repeated use of a simple caution must be made by an officer of at least the rank of Inspector unless a higher ranked officer is required by paragraphs 14 and 15 above. Guidance on exceptional circumstances is set out in paragraph 23 above.

48. In considering whether a simple caution is appropriate both national and locally held records must be checked before a simple caution is given.

49. A simple caution may be appropriate where:
    - There has been a sufficient lapse of time (at least 2 years) following a previous caution, other out-of-court disposal or conviction for the same or similar type of offence, to demonstrate that it had a deterrent effect;
    - The current offence is low level;
    - – for example, an offender with a previous caution for violence against the person offences should not normally be cautioned again for other offences involving violence;

Appendix 5 *Simple Cautions for Adult Offenders*

- The offender has previously complied with another form of out-of-court disposal;
- Giving a simple caution is likely to be the best outcome for the victim and the offender.

50. A simple caution will not be appropriate where the offence forms part of a pattern of offending. Police officers and prosecutors may consider that a different form of resolution, such as a prosecution, would be a more appropriate alternative for dealing with the offence.

Consent to simple caution

51. The offender must consent to the simple caution as an alternative to prosecution. The offender always has the right to decline the offer of a simple caution and opt instead to be prosecuted. Further details on consent is at paragraph 65.

Victim

52. Before a simple caution can be offered it is important to establish where appropriate and possible;
    - The views of any victim about the offence and the proposed method of disposal;
    - The nature of any harm or loss and its significance to the victim. These factors should be taken into account in considering whether a simple caution is appropriate.

53. Where there has been financial loss or loss of private property to an individual, although simple cautions are available, police officers should consider whether a conditional caution with conditions to repair damage or pay compensation is more suitable.

54. The views of the victim are important but are not conclusive. The decision to offer a simple caution lies with the police and/or the CPS who will take account of the views of the victim alongside wider public interest factors. Care must be taken not to raise the expectations of a victim whilst seeking their views.

55. If a victim declines to support a simple caution because they do not want any action to be taken, this should not automatically result in no further action being taken. Officers will need to consider wider evidential and public interest factors before dealing with the offence in this manner.

Section Three: Processes to Follow

Recording the decision to offer a simple caution

56. When considering the suitability of an offence for disposal by simple caution, the decision should be referred to an officer of at least Sergeant rank for approval who is not linked to the investigation into the offence, unless otherwise stated in this guidance that decisions need to be made by higher ranking officers. They should apply the criteria set out in this guidance to determine if a simple caution is appropriate. When the police officer has reached a decision in favour of administering a simple caution they should sign the custody record, or other suitable documentation, to say that they have approved this as the appropriate method of disposal. The rationale for the decision to offer a simple caution must be fully documented as well as the gravity factors matrix score to ensure the record can be retrieved if required during subsequent proceedings or as part of an audit.

57. If the case has been referred to the CPS, the Prosecutor should record their decision to charge, simple caution, offer another out-of-court disposal such as a conditional caution, or take no further action and their reasons why. Where the decision is to administer a simple caution for an indictable only offence the full reasons for that decision should be recorded.

SECTION THREE: PROCESSES TO FOLLOW

Administration of a Simple Caution

Overview

58. Before the simple caution is administered officers should ensure the offender has made an admission of guilt, understands the implications of accepting a simple caution and consents to accept it.

Admission of Guilt

59. An admission of guilt to committing the offence or offences must be made **before** the simple caution can be offered to the offender. **A simple caution must not be offered in order to secure an admission that could then provide sufficient evidence to meet the evidential stage of the Full Code test.**

60. A simple caution cannot be given to an offender who does not make a clear and reliable admission to committing the offence or offences for which the simple caution is being given. This is particularly important where there is any doubt at all about the mental state or capacity of the offender. In these circumstances a police officer should be particularly

Appendix 5 *Simple Cautions for Adult Offenders*

careful about accepting an admission of guilt. Police officers should refer to separate Police and Criminal Evidence Act 1984 (PACE) guidance on identifying and dealing with such offenders.

61. If an offender does admit guilt but also raises a defence the simple caution cannot be given. This includes where intent is denied or where a defence is offered; examples could include where the offender claims the offence was committed in self defence, or where the offender claims he or she has a good reason or lawful authority for having a bladed article in a public place.[5] An admission which may be qualified – where for example an offender commits an offence whilst under the influence of alcohol and cannot remember the full circumstances but evidence of involvement is agreed either through supporting witness evidence or other evidence (such as CCTV evidence) – may be considered a full and frank admission if all evidence is accepted by the offender.

62. The admission of guilt does not need to be made within a formal interview under PACE. However, the method for obtaining and recording the admission must be PACE compliant. PACE provides the following options:

    - An admission made in response to questions asked in a formal interview which is conducted and recorded in accordance with the relevant provisions of the PACE Codes whether within the police station or elsewhere.[6]

    - An unsolicited admission made without inducement or invitation to comment at any time outside the context of an interview.[7] A written record must be made and the offender invited to sign the record to confirm it's accuracy in accordance with the PACE Codes.[8] Depending on whether the offender has been arrested, the record must be made in the officer's notebook or by the custody officer or review officer in the offender's custody record. If a formal interview takes place after an unsolicited admission the admission must be put to the suspect at the start of the interview and the suspect asked to confirm or deny what they said.[9]

    - A formal written statement under caution made and recorded in accordance with the PACE Codes.[10]

---

5 Section 139 of the Criminal Justice Act 1988.
6 For the conduct & recording of interviews see PACE Code C sections 11 & 12 & Code E. C11.7 deals with written records, Code E with audio recording and C3.21 deals with voluntary interviews of suspects who are not under arrest.
7 See PACE Code C3.4, C15.5, C11.5.
8 See PACE Code C11.13 & 11.14.
9 See PACE Code C11.4 & E 4.6.
10 See PACE Code C Annex D.

Section Three: Processes to Follow

Explaining the Implications of Accepting a Simple Caution

63. Accepting a simple caution has potentially significant implications for an offender all of which **must** be explained to the offender **before** he or she is invited to accept it and the simple caution is administered. These are set out below.

A) *Significance of the admission of guilt*

64. A simple caution is an admission of guilt to committing an offence and forms part of an offender's criminal record.

B) *Criminal Record: Retention and Disclosure of the Simple Caution*

65. The simple caution forms part of an offender's criminal record and a record will be retained by the police for future use. It may also be disclosed in a court in any future proceedings.

66. A simple caution may be disclosed to a current or prospective employer in certain circumstances. Separate guidance governs the disclosure of criminal record information.

67. All information relating to simple cautions (as well as convictions) for a recordable offence is retained on the Police National Computer (PNC). ACPO guidelines set out how long this information will be retained for. The information is kept for police operational reasons and in the interest of prevention and detection of crime.

68. Legislation which came into effect in December 2008 brought simple cautions within the ambit of the Rehabilitation of Offenders Act 1974 (ROA). This means that simple cautions become spent immediately they are administered.[11] This means that an individual does not need to disclose a simple caution when asked unless they are seeking work in an occupation that is listed in the Exceptions Order to the ROA such as working with children and vulnerable adults or for other excepted purposes such as seeking to obtain certain licences. Cautions will also be disclosed under Disclosure and Barring Service (DBS) standard and enhanced checks. Further information can be obtained from the DBS.[12]

69. As well as the retention of the record of the simple caution, the offender's DNA profile and fingerprints, if taken, whether before or after the simple caution has been administered, may be retained by the police.

---

[11] The provisions in the ROA apply retrospectively to a simple caution that was administered prior to 19th December 2008 and therefore such a caution will also considered to be spent in the same way as one administered after that date.

[12] http://www.homeoffice.gov.uk/agencies-public-bodies/dbs/.

Appendix 5 *Simple Cautions for Adult Offenders*

C) Sexual Offences Act 2003 implications

70. Accepting a simple caution for an offence in Schedule 3 of the Sexual Offences Act 2003 will result in the offender becoming a 'relevant offender' for the purposes of the notification and registration requirements of Part 2 of that Act. This means that the offender will be put on the 'sex offender's register' for two years from the date of the simple caution.

D) Working with Children and Vulnerable Adults

71. The Disclosure and Barring Service (DBS) maintains the lists of those barred from working with children and vulnerable groups, including adults. A simple caution may be taken into account by the DBS when reaching a decision about the suitability of persons to work with children and adults. Accepting a simple caution for certain offences may lead to the offender's inclusion on such a list which will prevent them from working in a regulated post with children and vulnerable groups. Further information should be obtained from the DBS.

E) The potential for prosecution or civil action

72. If after the simple caution has been administered, new evidence comes to light suggesting that the offence(s) committed are more serious, a prosecution may still be brought. Additionally, if the offence(s) involve a victim or victims they might still take civil action or bring a private prosecution against the offender. The police may provide the offender's name and address to the victims if this is necessary for legal action to take place. Further details are at paragraphs 77 – 78 of this guidance.

73. It is very rare that these situations will occur, however, the possibility should still be explained to the offender.

F) Travel and Immigration

74. Countries requiring foreign nationals to obtain entry visas may require applicants to declare simple cautions on their application forms or at interview. Other country's immigration rules may mean that a person who has received a simple caution is refused entry as though they have a criminal conviction. The ROA only applies within the UK which means simple cautions, even if spent, may still need to be disclosed to some countries in some circumstances. This will vary from country to country and may apply to people who want to emigrate permanently or those who simply want to visit for short term purposes, such as on business, for a holiday or to study. For specific information on what an individual may be required to disclose, the relevant embassy of the country of travel should be contacted.

Section Three: Processes to Follow

Consent to Receiving a Simple Caution

75. A simple caution can only be given when the offender agrees to accept it. He or she should not be induced to accept a simple caution in any way and must not be pressed to make an instant decision on whether to accept a simple caution. They should be allowed to consider the matter and if need be, take independent legal advice.

Legal Advice

76. **Before** administering the simple caution the police officer should ensure that the offender has had the opportunity to receive free and independent legal advice in relation to the criminal offence. The offender's right to legal advice is set out under PACE and must be adhered to. The police officer must inform the offender of the evidence against them and the decision to offer a simple caution. Offenders and their legal representatives are entitled to seek and have disclosure of the evidence before the offender agrees to accept a simple caution.

Administering the Simple Caution

77. A simple caution should be administered by a Custody officer or other suitability trained person to whom this responsibility has been delegated. A simple caution may be administered in a police station, court building, the offices of any prosecutor or any other suitable location consistent with achieving the appropriate impact on the offender. It will not generally be appropriate to administer a simple caution in public (for example on the street) or in the offender's home. However, in exceptional circumstances such as an elderly or vulnerable offender, the simple caution may be administered in the offender's home or similar place, providing the correct procedure for administering the simple caution is adhered to.

78. At the point the simple caution is administered police officers must:
    - Ensure that the offender understands that he or she does not have to make an immediate decision on whether to accept the simple caution but can consider the matter and if need be take independent legal advice;
    - Ensure the offender understands he or she has the right to legal advice at any time during the process;
    - Ensure that the offender understands the effect of the simple cautions and the implications of accepting it as set out in paragraphs 53-64 above;
    - Ensure that the offender has made a clear and reliable admission of guilt in respect of the offence or offences for which the simple caution is being administered;
    - Confirm that the offender consents to accept a simple caution;

Appendix 5 *Simple Cautions for Adult Offenders*

- Ask the offender to sign a form setting out the implications of the simple caution 'the simple caution form';
- Sign the simple caution form themselves and provide the offender with a copy to take away.

79. When complying with paragraph 68 of this guidance, police officers must have regard to the provisions of PACE Code C concerning mentally disordered or mentally vulnerable offenders and the use of an appropriate adult. Police officers must also ensure that paragraph 68 is explained in a language that the offender can understand.

80. A simple caution is only deemed to be administered when the offender has signed the simple caution form which sets out that he or she has made an admission of guilt in respect of the offence or offences, his or her consent to accept the simple caution and makes clear the implications for accepting the simple caution as set out at paragraphs 53-64. The offender should be given a copy of the simple caution form to take away. The simple caution form should also include the offender's personal details including occupation and should provide full and clear details of the offence. This document must also be signed by the officer administering the simple caution.

POST ISSUE

81. Once the simple caution has been administered and the simple cautions form completed as at paragraph 70 police officers must update PNC to record that a simple caution has been given; the offence that was ultimately the subject of the simple caution must be recorded on the PNC. For example, if the offence was originally reported as Assault Occasioning Actual Bodily Harm, but upon considering the evidence the offence was reclassified as common assault, the PNC must be updated to record that the simple caution was administered for common assault.

82. In regard to simple cautions given by the police, records must be kept in accordance with relevant guidance.[13] Other relevant prosecutors and authorised persons may issue similar guidance to ensure that records are kept in accordance with any relevant legal responsibilities.

83. After the simple caution has been administered, police officers must also comply with any relevant requirements to notify other agencies of the simple caution; for example where the simple caution is administered for a sexual offence under Schedule 3 of the Sexual Offences Act 2003, the appropriate notification requirements must be carried out.

---

13 For example, see ACPO Retention Guidelines for Nominal Records on the Police National Computer.

Post Issue

Challenging a Simple Caution

84. There is no formal right of appeal against a simple caution once it has been administered as an offender must agree to accept a simple caution as the means of disposing of the offence. However, this does not prevent a person (for example an offender or a victim) who claims that it was not administered in accordance with this guidance from challenging the simple caution by way of a formal complaint against the police force or in court by way of judicial review.

85. To make a formal complaint to the police force a person can:

    - Make a complaint in writing to the Chief Constable of the police force that administered the simple caution or by visiting a police station;
    - Make a complaint to the Independent Police Complaints Commission (IPCC) to pass to the police force;
    - Authorise a third person (such as a solicitor or Citizens Advice Bureau) to submit the complaint on their behalf.

86. If the simple caution is set aside for any reason, whether following a challenge or for any other reason then the case should be reviewed again within the provisions of this guidance to consider whether a simple caution or other outcome is appropriate.

Civil Proceedings

87. If a simple caution has been given and the victim requests the offender's name and address in order to institute civil proceedings (for example, to claim compensation or seek an injunction) the information may be disclosed. Under the Data Protection Act 1998, personal data are exempt from the non-disclosure provisions where the disclosure is necessary for the purpose of, or in connection with, any legal proceedings or future legal proceedings. This includes circumstances where the data are required in order to obtain legal advice.

Subsequent Prosecutions (including private prosecution)

88. Usually, a person will only be prosecuted for an offence they have already been simple cautioned for if there is a substantial change in the material circumstances, or new evidence comes to light which suggests that the original offence is more serious than previously thought or if the decision to administer a simple caution was wrong. Even where a simple caution has been administered this may not preclude a private prosecution.[14] In addition, the decision to administer a simple caution may be judicially reviewed, either because the proper procedures and relevant guidance have not been followed or because it is claimed that

---

14 *Hayter v L* [1998] 1 WLR 654.

Appendix 5 *Simple Cautions for Adult Offenders*

the decision is unlawful, irrational or unreasonable on *Wednesbury* principles[15] the decision to authorise and administer a caution may be quashed and set aside. If this happens the slate is in effect wiped clean and the case must be reviewed again to decide the appropriate disposal. If the subsequent decision is to prosecute it does not follow that a prosecution for the alleged offence would inevitably amount to an abuse of process. This will be made on a case by case basis. It is unlikely that such action would occur, however in order to minimise the risk of an abuse of process argument, local arrangements should be put in place to ensure that when a simple caution is administered, the person being cautioned is informed in writing that the simple caution *may* not preclude a subsequent prosecution and that it *will* not preclude a civil action by an aggrieved party.[16]

Best Practice

89. Supervisory quality checks should be undertaken to ensure that simple cautions are used appropriately and in accordance with this guidance.

Enquiries about This Guidance

90. Enquiries about this guidance should be addressed to the Ministry of Justice.

ANNEX A

Overview of factors for considering whether a simple caution is appropriate	
Simple caution may be appropriate	For low level offending.
	For first time offenders.
Simple caution may not be appropriate	Where the offence is very minor. In these cases consideration should be given to a community resolution or other action short of a formal sanction.
	Where the offence is serious, for example an indictable only offence more serious either way offence where if prosecuted and convicted the likely sentence would be more than a high level community order or a period of imprisonment.
	Where the offender was on police or court bail or subject to a court order at the time of the commission of the offence.

---

15 *Associated Provincial Picture Houses Ltd v Wednesbury Corporation* [1948] 1 KB 223.
16 *Jones v Whalley* [2006] UKHL 41 (26 July 2006); *Hayter v L* [1998] 1 WLR 854; *Guest v Director of Public Prosecutions* [2009] EWHC 594.

Annex A

Overview of factors for considering whether a simple caution is appropriate	
Simple caution may not be appropriate – *continued*	For offences involving stalking, harassment or domestic violence.
	Where the offender has a previous criminal history.
	Where a conditional caution may be more appropriate; for example where has been financial loss or loss of private property to an individual or where rehabilitation may be appropriate.
	Where the offender is a foreign offender with no permission to be in the UK. For such cases police officers should consider whether a conditional caution with foreign offender conditions should be offered.
Simple caution should not be given	Where the offender does not admit the offence.
	Where the offender does not agree to accept the simple caution.
	Where the offender already has a previous caution/conviction for the same or similar type of offence in the past 2 years (unless there are exceptional circumstances).
	For indictable only offences, unless there are exceptional circumstances and the use of the simple caution has been approved by a senior police officer before being approved by the CPS.
	For certain either way offences except in exceptional circumstances where a senior police officer has made the decision that in all circumstances of the case a simple caution is the appropriate disposal, namely
	– Possession of a bladed article, offensive weapon or firearm in public
	– Child prostitution and pornography, cruelty to a child, indecent photographs of children and
	– Supplying Class A drugs
	Where there is not sufficient evidence to provide a realistic
	prospect of conviction. When the public interest requires the offender is prosecuted.
	Where the offence is committed by a serving prisoner or those subject to prison recall.

Appendix 5 *Simple Cautions for Adult Offenders*

ANNEX B – LEVELS OF AUTHORISATION

INDICTABLE ONLY OFFENCES

The decision to refer an indictable only case to the CPS to authorise the use of a simple caution must be made, in all cases, by a senior police officer of at least the rank of Superintendent.

SPECIFIC EITHER WAY OFFENCES

The decision to administer a simple caution for the following offences must be made, in all cases, by a senior police officer.

Possession of an offensive weapon – Section 1 Prevention of Crime Act 1953

Possession of a bladed article – Section 139 Criminal Justice Act 1988

Firearm, carrying in a public place – S 19 Firearms Act 1968

Cruelty to a child – Section 1 Children and Young Persons Act 1933

Child prostitution and pornography – Sexual Offences Act 2003

Indecent Photographs of children – Protection of Children Act 1978

Drugs – Class A Produce – Supply – Misuse of Drugs Act 1971

OTHER SERIOUS EITHER WAY OFFENCES

The decision to administer a simple caution for the following offences must be made, in all cases, by a senior police officer.

EITHER WAY OFFENCES HAVING A SENTENCING STARTING POINT IN MAGISTRATES' COURT SENTENCING GUIDELINES OF CUSTODY OR HIGH LEVEL COMMUNITY ORDER

Assault occasioning actual bodily harm – Section 47 Offences Against the Person Act (OAPA) 1863

Wounding or causing grievous bodily harm – Section 20 OAPA 1863

Harassment – putting people in fear of violence – Section 4 Protection from Harassment Act 1997

Stalking involving violence or serious alarm or distress – Section 4A Protection from Harassment Act 1997

Violent Disorder – Section 2 Public Order Act 1986 Affray – S3 Public Order Act 1986 Sexual Assault – Section 3 & Section 7 Sexual Offences Act 2003

Annex B – Levels of Authorisation

Witness Intimidation – Section 51 Criminal Justice and Public Order Act 1994 23

EITHER WAY OFFENCES ROUTINELY DEALT WITH AT THE CROWN COURT.

This is not a comprehensive list.

Arson – S 1 and S 4 Criminal Damage Act 1971

Assault occasioning actual bodily harm (including Racial or religiously aggravated) – S 47 OAPA 1863

Assault W/I to resist arrest – S38 Offences Against the Person Act 1861

Burglary (dwelling) – S 9 Theft Act 1968

Burglary (non dwelling) – S 9 Theft Act 1968

Criminal damage (including Racial or religiously aggravated) over £5,000 – Criminal Damage Act 1971

Cruelty to a child – S 1 Children and Young Persons Act 1933

Drugs – class A – possession – Misuse of Drugs Act 1971

Drugs – class B & C – supply possess w/I to supply Misuse of Drugs Act 1971

Drugs – Cultivation of cannabis – Misuse of Drugs Act 1971

Exploitation of prostitution – S 33A, S 52–53 Sexual Offences Act 2003

Fraud (banking & insurance) – Fraud Act 2006

Fraud (confidence) – Fraud Act 2006

Fraud (possessing, making or supplying articles for use) – Fraud Act 2006

Grievous bodily harm/unlawful wounding (including Racial or religiously aggravated) S 20 OAPA 1861

Handling Stolen Goods S 22 – Theft Act 1968

Harassment (including Racial or religiously aggravated) – Protection from Harassment Act 1997

Human Trafficking Offences – S 57–59 Sexual Offences Act 2003, S 4 Asylum and Immigration Act 2004, S 71 Coroners and Justice Act 2009

Identity documents – possess – Part 1 S 1–5 Forgery Act 1861, Identity Cards Act 2006, Identity Documents Act 2010

Keeping a brothel used for prostitution – Sexual Offences Act 1956

Protective Order – Breach of

Public order Act S 2 violent disorder

Appendix 5 *Simple Cautions for Adult Offenders*

Sexual Assault – S 3 & S 7 Sexual Offences Act 2003

Theft - Theft Act 1968

Threats to Kill – S 16 Offences Against the Person Act 1861

Voyeurism – S 67 Sexual Offences Act 2003

Witness intimidation – S 51 Criminal Justice and Public Order Act 1994

Cause death by Careless driving – S 2B Road Traffic Act 1988

Cause death by driving unlicensed/disqualified – S 3ZB Road Traffic Act 1988

Dangerous Driving – S 2A Road Traffic Act 1988

Appendix 6

National Decision Model: Cautions

OUT-OF-COURT DISPOSALS NATIONAL FRAMEWORK

Disposal Option	Offence type	Evidential standard	Admission of guilt required?	Consultation/ Agreement with agencies required?	Offender's explicit consent required?	Rehabilitation available?	Reparation/ restorative justice available?	Punitive available?	Forms part of a criminal record?
COMMUNITY RESOLUTION	May be less serious crime or incident	Reasonable suspicion, may deal with non-criminal matters	Acceptance of responsibility	✗	✓	✓	✓	✗	✗
CANNABIS WARNING	1st offence of cannabis possession for personal use.	Reasonable suspicion	✗	✗	✗	✗	✗	✗	✗ But may be disclosed on Enhanced DBS check
ADULT (18+) PND	Defined list of low-level disorder offences	Reason to believe a penalty offence has been committed	✗	✗	✗	Except if education scheme available locally ✗	✗	✓	✗ But may be disclosed on Enhanced DBS check
ADULT SIMPLE CAUTION	Any offence	Realistic prospect of conviction	✓	CPS should authorise if indictable only	✓	✓	✓	✗	✓
YOUTH CAUTION	Any offence	Realistic prospect of conviction	✓	CPS should authorise indictable only YOTS for any offence	✓	✓	✓	✗	✗ But may be disclosed on Enhanced DBS check
ADULT AND YOUTH CONDITIONAL CAUTION	Any offence in principle: but some exceptions for offence type in guidance	Realistic prospect of conviction	✓	YOTS for any offence if youth CPS must authorise indictable only	✓	✓	✓	✓	✓

Now you have considered which disposal may be appropriate, see the technical guidance on that disposal for more details and to comply with requirements for its use.

Appendix 7

Criminal Procedure Rules 2014

PART 12

DEFERRED PROSECUTION AGREEMENTS

When this Part applies

12.1.

(1) This Part applies to proceedings in the Crown Court under Schedule 17 to the Crime and Courts Act 2013.

(2) In this Part—

 (a) 'agreement' means a deferred prosecution agreement under paragraph 1 of that Schedule;

 (b) 'prosecutor' means a prosecutor designated by or under paragraph 3 of that Schedule; and

 (c) 'defendant' means the corporation, partnership or association with whom the prosecutor proposes to enter, or enters, an agreement.

[Note. Under Schedule 17 to the Crime and Courts Act 2013, a designated prosecutor may make a deferred prosecution agreement with a defendant, other than an individual, whom the prosecutor is considering prosecuting for an offences or offences listed in that Schedule. Under such an agreement, the defendant agrees to comply with its terms and the prosecutor agrees that, if the Crown Court approves those terms, then paragraph 2 of the Schedule will apply and —

 (a) the prosecutor will serve a draft indictment charging the defendant with the offence or offences the subject of the agreement;

 (b) the prosecution will be suspended under that paragraph, and the suspension may not be lifted while the agreement is in force; and

 (c) no-one may prosecute the defendant for the offence or offences charged while the agreement is in force, or after it expires if the defendant complies with it.

Appendix 7 *Criminal Procedure Rules 2014*

The Code for prosecutors issued under paragraph 6 of that Schedule contains guidance on the exercise of prosecution functions in relation to a deferred prosecution agreement.]

Exercise of court's powers

12.2.

(1) The court must determine an application to which this Part applies at a hearing, which—

    (a) must be in private, under rule 12.3 (Application to approve a proposal to enter an agreement);

    (b) may be in public or private, under rule 12.4 (Application to approve the terms of an agreement), rule 12.6 (Application to approve a variation of the terms of an agreement) or rule 12.9 (Application to postpone the publication of information by the prosecutor);

    (c) must be in public, under rule 12.5 (Application on breach of agreement) or rule 12.7 (Application to lift suspension of prosecution), unless the court otherwise directs.

(2) If at a hearing in private to which rule 12.4 or rule 12.6 applies the court approves the agreement or the variation proposed, the court must announce its decision and reasons at a hearing in public.

(3 The court must not determine an application under rule 12.3, rule 12.4 or rule 12.6 unless—

    (a) both parties are present;

    (b) the prosecutor provides the court with a written declaration that, for the purposes of the application—

        (i) the investigator enquiring into the alleged offence or offences has certified that no information has been supplied which the investigator knows to be inaccurate, misleading or incomplete, and

        (ii) the prosecutor has complied with the prosecution obligation to disclose material to the defendant; and

    (c) the defendant provides the court with a written declaration that, for the purposes of the application—

        (i) the defendant has not supplied any information which the defendant knows to be inaccurate, misleading or incomplete, and

        (ii) the individual through whom the defendant makes the declaration has made reasonable enquiries and believes the defendant's declaration to be true.

Deferred Prosecution Agreements

(4) The court must not determine an application under rule 12.5 or rule 12.7—
  (a) in the prosecutor's absence; or
  (b) in the absence of the defendant, unless the defendant has had at least 28 days in which to make representations.
(5) If the court approves a proposal to enter an agreement—
  (a) the general rule is that any further application to which this Part applies must be made to the same judge; but
  (b) the court may direct other arrangements.
(6) The court may adjourn a hearing—
  (a) if either party asks, or on its own initiative;
  (b) in particular, if the court requires more information about—
    (i) the facts of an alleged offence,
    (ii) the terms of a proposal to enter an agreement, or of a proposed agreement or variation of an agreement, or
    (iii) the circumstances in which the prosecutor wants the court to decide whether the defendant has failed to comply with the terms of an agreement.
(7) The court may—
  (a) hear an application under rule 12.4 immediately after an application under rule 12.3, if the court approves a proposal to enter an agreement;
  (b) hear an application under rule 12.7 immediately after an application under rule 12.5, if the court terminates an agreement.

[Note. See paragraphs 7(4), 8(5), (6) and 10(5), (6) of Schedule 17 to the Crime and Courts Act 2013.

The Code for prosecutors issued under paragraph 6 of that Schedule contains guidance on fulfilling the prosecution duty of disclosure.]

Application to approve a proposal to enter an agreement

12.3.

(1) This rule applies where a prosecutor wants the court to approve a proposal to enter an agreement.
(2) The prosecutor must—
  (a) apply in writing after the commencement of negotiations between the parties but before the terms of agreement have been settled; and

Appendix 7 *Criminal Procedure Rules 2014*

      (b)   serve the application on—

            (i)   the court officer, and

            (ii)   the defendant.

(3)   The application must—

      (a)   identify the parties to the proposed agreement;

      (b)   attach a proposed indictment setting out such of the offences listed in Part 2 of Schedule 17 to the Crime and Courts Act 2013 as the prosecutor is considering;

      (c)   include or attach a statement of facts proposed for inclusion in the agreement, which must give full particulars of each alleged offence, including details of any alleged financial gain or loss;

      (d)   include any information about the defendant that would be relevant to sentence in the event of conviction for the offence or offences;

      (e)   specify the proposed expiry date of the agreement;

      (f)   describe the proposed terms of the agreement, including details of any—

            (i)   monetary penalty to be paid by the defendant, and the time within which any such penalty is to be paid,

            (ii)   compensation, reparation or donation to be made by the defendant, the identity of the recipient of any such payment and the time within which any such payment is to be made,

            (iii) surrender of profits or other financial benefit by the defendant, and the time within which any such sum is to be surrendered,

            (iv) arrangement to be made in relation to the management or conduct of the defendant's business,

            (v)   co-operation required of the defendant in any investigation related to the offence or offences,

            (vi) other action required of the defendant,

            (vii) arrangement to monitor the defendant's compliance with a term,

            (viii) consequence of the defendant's failure to comply with a term, and

            (ix) prosecution costs to be paid by the defendant, and the time within which any such costs are to be paid;

Deferred Prosecution Agreements

- (g) in relation to those terms, explain how they comply with—
  - (i) the requirements of the code issued under paragraph 6 of Schedule 17 to the Crime and Courts Act 2013, and
  - (ii) any sentencing guidelines or guideline cases which apply;
- (h) contain or attach the defendant's written consent to the proposal; and
- (i) explain why—
  - (i) entering into an agreement is likely to be in the interests of justice, and
  - (ii) the proposed terms of the agreement are fair, reasonable and proportionate.

(4) If the proposed statement of facts includes assertions that the defendant does not admit, the application must—

(a) specify the facts that are not admitted; and

(b) explain why that is immaterial for the purposes of the proposal to enter an agreement.

[Note. See paragraphs 5 and 7 of Schedule 17 to the Crime and Courts Act 2013.]

Application to approve the terms of an agreement

12.4.

(1) This rule applies where—
  - (a) the court has approved a proposal to enter an agreement on an application under rule 12.3; and
  - (b) the prosecutor wants the court to approve the terms of the agreement.

(2) The prosecutor must—
  - (a) apply in writing as soon as practicable after the parties have settled the terms; and
  - (b) serve the application on—
    - (i) the court officer, and
    - (ii) the defendant.

(3) The application must—
  - (a) attach the agreement;

Appendix 7 *Criminal Procedure Rules 2014*

    (b)   indicate in what respect, if any, the terms of the agreement differ from those proposed in the application under rule 12.3;

    (c)   contain or attach the defendant's written consent to the agreement;

    (d)   explain why—

        (i)   the agreement is in the interests of justice, and

        (ii)   the terms of the agreement are fair, reasonable and proportionate;

    (e)   attach a draft indictment, charging the defendant with the offence or offences the subject of the agreement; and

    (f)   include any application for the hearing to be in private.

(4)   If the court approves the agreement and the draft indictment, the court officer must—

    (a)   endorse any paper copy of the indictment made for the court with—

        (i)   a note to identify it as the indictment approved by the court, and

        (ii)   the date of the court's approval; and

    (b)   treat the case as if it had been suspended by order of the court.

[Note. See paragraph 8 of Schedule 17 to the Crime and Courts Act 2013. See also rule 12.9 (Application to postpone the publication of information by the prosecutor).

Under paragraph 2(1) of Schedule 17 to the 2013 Act and section 2 of the Administration of Justice (Miscellaneous Provisions) Act 1933, the draft indictment to which this rule applies becomes an indictment when the court approves the agreement and consents to the service of that draft. Part 14 contains rules about indictments.

Under paragraph 2(2) of Schedule 17 to the 2013 Act, on approval of the draft indictment the proceedings are automatically suspended.

Under paragraph 13(2) of Schedule 17 to the 2013 Act, where the court approves an agreement the statement of facts contained in that agreement is to be treated as an admission by the defendant under section 10 of the Criminal Justice Act 1967 (proof by formal admission) in any criminal proceedings against the defendant for the alleged offence.]

Application on breach of agreement

12.5.

(1)   This rule applies where—

(a) the prosecutor believes that the defendant has failed to comply with the terms of an agreement; and

(b) the prosecutor wants the court to decide—

(i) whether the defendant has failed to comply, and

(ii) if so, whether to terminate the agreement, or to invite the parties to agree proposals to remedy that failure.

(2) The prosecutor must—

(a) apply in writing, as soon as practicable after becoming aware of the grounds for doing so; and

(b) serve the application on—

(i) the court officer, and

(ii) the defendant.

(3) The application must—

(a) specify each respect in which the prosecutor believes the defendant has failed to comply with the terms of the agreement, and explain the reasons for the prosecutor's belief; and

(b) attach a copy of any document containing evidence on which the prosecutor relies.

(4) A defendant who wants to make representations in response to the application must serve the representations on—

(a) the court officer; and

(b) the prosecutor,

not more than 28 days after service of the application.

[Note. See paragraph 9 of Schedule 17 to the Crime and Courts Act 2013. See also rule 12.9 (Application to postpone the publication of information by the prosecutor).]

Application to approve a variation of the terms of an agreement

12.6.

(1) This rule applies where the parties have agreed to vary the terms of an agreement because—

(a) on an application under rule 12.5 (Application on breach of agreement), the court has invited them to do so; or

(b) variation of the agreement is necessary to avoid a failure by the defendant to comply with its terms in circumstances that were not,

Appendix 7 *Criminal Procedure Rules 2014*

and could not have been, foreseen by either party at the time the agreement was made.

(2) The prosecutor must—

    (a) apply in writing, as soon as practicable after the parties have settled the terms of the variation; and

    (b) serve the application on—

        (i) the court officer, and

        (ii) the defendant.

(3) The application must—

    (a) specify each variation proposed;

    (b) contain or attach the defendant's written consent to the variation;

    (c) explain why—

        (i) the variation is in the interests of justice, and

        (ii) the terms of the agreement as varied are fair, reasonable and proportionate; and

    (d) include any application for the hearing to be in private.

[Note. See paragraph 10 of Schedule 17 to the Crime and Courts Act 2013. See also rule 12.9 (Application to postpone the publication of information by the prosecutor).]

Application to lift suspension of prosecution

12.7.

(1) This rule applies where—

    (a) the court terminates an agreement before its expiry date; and

    (b) the prosecutor wants the court to lift the suspension of the prosecution that applied when the court approved the terms of the agreement.

(2) The prosecutor must—

    (a) apply in writing, as soon as practicable after the termination of the agreement; and

    (b) serve the application on—

        (i) the court officer, and

        (ii) the defendant.

Deferred Prosecution Agreements

(3) A defendant who wants to make representations in response to the application must serve the representations on—

    (a) the court officer; and

    (b) the prosecutor,

not more than 28 days after service of the application.

[Note. See paragraphs 2(3) and 9 of Schedule 17 to the Crime and Courts Act 2013.]

Notice to discontinue prosecution

12.8.

(1) This rule applies where an agreement expires—

    (a) on its expiry date, or on a date treated as its expiry date; and

    (b) without having been terminated by the court.

(2) The prosecutor must—

    (a) as soon as practicable give notice in writing discontinuing the prosecution on the indictment approved by the court under rule 12.4 (Application to approve the terms of an agreement); and

    (b) serve the notice on—

        (i) the court officer, and

        (ii) the defendant.

[Note. See paragraph 11 of Schedule 17 to the Crime and Courts Act 2013.]

Application to postpone the publication of information by the prosecutor

12.9.

(1) This rule applies where the prosecutor—

    (a) makes an application under rule 12.4 (Application to approve the terms of an agreement), rule 12.5 (Application on breach of agreement) or rule 12.6 (Application to approve a variation of the terms of an agreement);

    (b) decides not to make an application under rule 12.5, despite believing that the defendant has failed to comply with the terms of the agreement; or

    (c) gives a notice under rule 12.8 (Notice to discontinue prosecution).

Appendix 7 *Criminal Procedure Rules 2014*

(2) A party who wants the court to order that the publication of information by the prosecutor about the court's or the prosecutor's decision should be postponed must—

    (a) apply in writing, as soon as practicable and in any event before such publication occurs;

    (b) serve the application on—

        (i) the court officer, and

        (ii) the other party; and

    (c) in the application—

        (i) specify the proposed terms of the order, and for how long it should last, and

        (ii) explain why an order in the terms proposed is necessary.

[Note. See paragraph 12 of Schedule 17 to the Crime and Courts Act 2013.

Part 16 of these Rules contains rules about applications for a restriction on reporting what takes place at a public hearing, or public access to what otherwise would be a public hearing.]

Duty of court officer, etc.

12.10.

(1) Unless the court otherwise directs, the court officer must—

    (a) arrange for the recording of proceedings on an application to which this Part applies;

    (b) arrange for the transcription of such a recording if—

        (i) a party wants such a transcript, or

        (ii) anyone else wants such a transcript (but that is subject to the restrictions in paragraph (2)).

(2) Unless the court otherwise directs, a person who transcribes a recording of proceedings under such arrangements—

    (a) must not supply anyone other than a party with a transcript of a recording of—

        (i) a hearing in private, or

        (ii) a hearing in public to which reporting restrictions apply;

Deferred Prosecution Agreements

(b) subject to that, must supply any person with any transcript for which that person asks—

(i) in accordance with the transcription arrangements made by the court officer, and

(ii) on payment by that person of any fee prescribed.

(3) The court officer must not identify either party to a hearing in private under rule 12.3 (Application to approve a proposal to enter an agreement) or rule 12.4 (Application to approve the terms of an agreement)—

(a) in any notice displayed in the vicinity of the courtroom; or

(b) in any other information published by the court officer.

Court's power to vary requirements under this Part

12.11.

(1) The court may—

(a) shorten or extend (even after it has expired) a time limit under this Part;

(b) allow there to be made orally—

(i) an application under rule 12.4 (Application to approve the terms of an agreement), or

(ii) an application under rule 12.7 (Application to lift suspension of prosecution)

where the court exercises its power under rule 12.2(7) to hear one application immediately after another.

(2) A party who wants an extension of time must—

(a) apply when serving the application or notice for which it is needed; and

(b) explain the delay.

Appendix 8

Deferred Prosecution Agreements Code of Practice

INTRODUCTION

This Deferred Prosecution Agreement Code of Practice ('DPA Code') is issued by the Director of Public Prosecutions and Director of the Serious Fraud Office pursuant to paragraph 6(1) of Schedule 17 to the Crime and Courts Act 2013 ('the Act').

Prosecutors should have regard to this DPA Code when:

i. Negotiating Deferred Prosecution Agreements ('DPAs') with an organisation ('P') whom the prosecutor is considering prosecuting for an offence specified in the Act;

ii. Applying to the court for the approval of a DPA;

and

iii. Overseeing DPAs after their approval by the court, in particular in relation to variation, breach, termination and completion.

1. WHETHER A DEFERRED PROSECUTION AGREEMENT IS A POSSIBLE DISPOSAL OF ALLEGED CRIMINAL CONDUCT

1.1. A DPA is a discretionary tool created by the Act to provide a way of responding to alleged criminal conduct. The prosecutor may invite P to enter into negotiations to agree a DPA as an alternative to prosecution.

1.2. In order to enter a DPA the prosecutor is to apply the following two stage test. Prosecutors must be satisfied and record that:

EVIDENTIAL STAGE

i. Either:

    a) the evidential stage of the Full Code Test in the Code for Crown Prosecutors is satisfied or, if this is not met, that

Appendix 8 *Deferred Prosecution Agreements Code of Practice*

b) there is at least a reasonable suspicion based upon some admissible evidence that P has committed the offence, and there are reasonable grounds for believing that a continued investigation would provide further admissible evidence within a reasonable period of time, so that all the evidence together would be capable of establishing a realistic prospect of conviction in accordance with the Full Code Test.

And

PUBLIC INTEREST STAGE

ii. The public interest would be properly served by the prosecutor not prosecuting but instead entering into a DPA with P in accordance with the criteria set out below.

1.3 The Prosecutor should first consider whether the test in paragraph 1.2 i a) is met. If it is not met consideration may be given to the test under paragraph 1.2 i b).

1.4 For the purposes of 1.2 i b) a reasonable time period will depend on all the facts and circumstances of the case, including its size, type and complexity.

1.5 If a DPA is considered appropriate by the relevant Director, having determined that either limb of the evidential stage is met, and that the public interest is best served by entering into a DPA, the prosecutor will (where the court approves the DPA) prefer an indictment. The indictment will however then immediately be suspended pending the satisfactory performance, or otherwise, of the DPA.

1.6 In cases where neither limb of the evidential stage can be met by the conclusion of any DPA negotiations and it is not considered appropriate to continue the criminal investigation, the prosecutor should consider whether a Civil Recovery Order is appropriate. Attention is drawn to the Attorney General's guidance to prosecuting bodies on their asset recovery powers under the Proceeds of Crime Act 2002, issued 5 November 2009.

2. FACTORS THAT THE PROSECUTOR MAY TAKE INTO ACCOUNT WHEN DECIDING WHETHER TO ENTER INTO A DPA

NEGOTIATIONS

2.1 An invitation to negotiate a DPA is a matter for the prosecutor's discretion. P has no right to be invited to negotiate a DPA. The SFO and

Factors that the Prosecution may take into account when deciding etc

the CPS are first and foremost prosecutors and it will only be in specific circumstances deemed by their Directors to be appropriate that they will decide to offer a DPA instead of pursuing the full prosecution of the alleged conduct. In many cases, criminal prosecution will continue to be the appropriate course of action. An invitation to enter DPA discussions is not a guarantee that a DPA will be offered at the conclusion of the discussions.

2.2 Where the prosecutor is satisfied that:
   i. either the evidential stage of the Full Code Test in the Code for Crown Prosecutors is met, or there is a reasonable suspicion based upon some admissible evidence that P has committed an offence;
   ii. the full extent of the alleged offending has been identified;

   and

   iii. the public interest would likely be met by a DPA,

   then the prosecutor may initiate DPA negotiations with any P who is being investigated with a view to prosecution in connection with an offence specified in the Act.

2.3 When considering whether a DPA may be appropriate the prosecutor will have regard to existing Codes of Practice and Guidance, in particular:
   i. The Code for Crown Prosecutors;
   ii. The Joint Prosecution Guidance on Corporate Prosecutions ('the Corporate Prosecution Guidance');
   iii. Bribery Act 2010: Joint Prosecution Guidance ('the Bribery Act Guidance');
   iv. The DPA Code.

2.4 Where either limb of the evidential stage is passed, the prosecutor must consider whether or not a prosecution is in the public interest. The more serious the offence, the more likely it is that prosecution will be required in the public interest. Indicators of seriousness include not just the value of any gain or loss, but also the risk of harm to the public, to unidentified victims, shareholders, employees and creditors and to the stability and integrity of financial markets and international trade. The impact of the offending in other countries, and not just the consequences in the UK, should be taken into account.

2.5 Prosecutors must balance factors for and against prosecution carefully and fairly. Public interest factors that can affect the decision to prosecute usually depend on the seriousness of the offence, which includes the culpability of P and the harm to the victim.

Appendix 8 *Deferred Prosecution Agreements Code of Practice*

A prosecution will usually take place unless there are public interest factors against prosecution which clearly outweigh those tending in favour of prosecution.

2.6 In applying the public interest factors when considering whether to charge, seek to enter a DPA or take no further criminal action the prosecutor undertakes a balancing exercise of the factors that tend to support prosecution and those that do not. This is an exercise of discretion. Which factors are considered relevant and what weight is given to each are matters for the individual prosecutor. It is quite possible that one public interest factor alone may outweigh a number of other factors which tend in the opposite direction. Decisions will be made on an individual case by case basis.

2.7 Prosecutors should have regard when considering the public interest stage to the UK's commitment to abide by the OECD Convention on 'Combating Bribery of Foreign Public Officials in International Business Transactions' in particular Article 5. Investigation and prosecution of the bribery of a foreign public official should not be influenced by considerations of national economic interest, the potential effect upon relations with another State or the identity of the natural or legal persons involved.

2.8 The prosecutor should have regard to the public interest factors set out in the Code for Crown Prosecutors. In addition the following non-exhaustive factors will be of relevance in deciding whether a prosecution is appropriate or not in order to satisfy the public interest:

2.8.1 Additional public interest factors in favour of prosecution

   i. A history of similar conduct (including prior criminal, civil and regulatory enforcement actions against P and/or its directors/partners and/or majority shareholders). Failing to prosecute in circumstances where there have been repeated or serious breaches of the law may not be a proportionate response and may not provide adequate deterrent effects.

   ii. The conduct alleged is part of the established business practices of P.

   iii. The offence was committed at a time when P had no or an ineffective corporate compliance programme and it has not been able to demonstrate a significant improvement in its compliance programme since then.

   iv. P has been previously subject to warning, sanctions or criminal charges and had nonetheless failed to take adequate action to prevent future unlawful conduct, or had continued to engage in the conduct.

Factors that the Prosecution may take into account when deciding etc

      v.   Failure to notify the wrongdoing within reasonable time of the offending conduct[1] coming to light.

      vi.   Reporting the wrongdoing but failing to verify it, or reporting it knowing or believing it to be inaccurate, misleading or incomplete.

      vii   Significant level of harm caused directly or indirectly to the victims of the wrongdoing or a substantial adverse impact to the integrity or confidence of markets, local or national governments.

2.8.2   Additional public interest factors against prosecution

      i.   Co-operation: Considerable weight may be given to a genuinely proactive approach adopted by P's management team when the offending is brought to their notice, involving within a reasonable time of the offending coming to light reporting P's offending otherwise unknown to the prosecutor and taking remedial actions including, where appropriate, compensating victims. In applying this factor the prosecutor needs to establish whether sufficient information about the operation and conduct of P has been supplied in order to assess whether P has been co-operative. Co-operation will include identifying relevant witnesses, disclosing their accounts and the documents shown to them. Where practicable it will involve making the witnesseA lack of a history of similar conduct involving prior criminal, civil and regulatory enforcement actions against P and/or its directors/partners and/or majority shareholders; The prosecutor should contact relevant regulatory departments (including where applicable those overseas) to ascertain whether there are existing investigations in relation to P and/or its directors/partners and/or majority shareholders;

      iii.   The existence of a proactive corporate compliance programme[2] both at the time of offending and at the time of reporting but which failed to be effective in this instance;

      iv.   The offending represents isolated actions by individuals, for example by a rogue director;

      v.   The offending is not recent and P in its current form is effectively a different entity from that which committed the offences – for example it has been taken over by another

---

1   For what is reasonable see paragraph 2.9 below.
2   The prosecutor may choose to bring in external resource to assist in the assessment of P's compliance culture and programme for example as described in any self-report.

Appendix 8 *Deferred Prosecution Agreements Code of Practice*

organisation, it no longer operates in the relevant industry or market, P's management team has completely changed, disciplinary action has been taken against all of the culpable individuals, including dismissal where appropriate, or corporate structures or processes have been changed to minimise the risk of a repetition of offending;

vi. A conviction is likely to have disproportionate consequences for P, under domestic law, the law of another jurisdiction including but not limited to that of the European Union, always bearing in mind the seriousness of the offence and any other relevant public interest factors;[3]

vii. A conviction is likely to have collateral effects on the public, P's employees and shareholders or P's and/or institutional pension holders.

2.9 With respect to the 'Additional public interest factors against prosecution', at paragraph 2.8.2 i. above:

2.9.1 The prosecutor in giving weight to P's self- report will consider the totality of information that P provides to the prosecutor. It must be remembered that when P self-reports it will have been incriminated by the actions of individuals. It will ordinarily be appropriate that those individuals be investigated and where appropriate prosecuted. P must ensure in its provision of material as part of the self-report that it does not withhold material that would jeopardise an effective investigation and where appropriate prosecution of those individuals. To do so would be a strong factor in favour of prosecution.

2.9.2 The prosecutor will also consider how early P self-reports, the extent that P involves the prosecutor in the early stages of an investigation (for example, in order to discuss work plans, timetabling, or to provide the opportunity to the prosecutor to give direction and where appropriate commence an early criminal investigation where it can use statutory powers in particular against individuals).

2.9.3 The prosecutor will consider whether any actions taken by P by not self-reporting earlier may have prejudiced the investigation into P or the individuals that incriminate P. In particular the prosecutor will critically assess the manner of any internal investigation to

---

[3] Any candidate or tenderer (including company directors and any person having powers of representation, decision or control) who has been convicted of fraud relating to the protection of the financial interests of the European Communities, corruption, or a money laundering offence is mandatorily excluded from participation in public contracts within the EU. Discretionary exclusion may follow in respect of a conviction for a criminal offence.

determine whether its conduct could have led to material being destroyed or the gathering of first accounts from suspects being delayed to the extent that the opportunity for fabrication has been afforded. Internal investigations which lead to such adverse consequences may militate against the use of DPAs.

2.10 The Bribery Act Guidance provides factors tending in favour of or against prosecution in respect of each offence under the Bribery Act 2010. In doing so it refers to the Code for Crown Prosecutors, the Corporate Prosecution Guidance and unique considerations appropriate to the particular bribery offence being considered. A prosecutor in considering the public interest under the Code for Crown Prosecutors in respect of a bribery offence must therefore also consider the current Bribery Act Guidance offered in respect of the particular offence under consideration.

3. PROCESS FOR INVITATION TO ENTER INTO NEGOTIATIONS

3.1 If the prosecutor decides to offer P the opportunity to enter into DPA negotiations, it will do so by way of a formal letter of invitation outlining the basis on which any negotiations will proceed.

3.2 That letter will constitute the beginning of the DPA negotiation period, which period will end on either the withdrawal of one or both parties from the process, or the approval/ refusal by the court of a DPA at a final hearing. Neither party will be obliged to give reasons for withdrawal from negotiations. However in the event of withdrawal from negotiations by the prosecutor it will ordinarily be appropriate to provide P with the gist of the reasons for doing so. In some instances this may not be possible without prejudicing the investigation.

3.3 All parties should keep in mind that DPAs are entirely voluntary agreements. The prosecutor is under no obligation to invite P to negotiate a DPA and P is under no obligation to accept that invitation should it be made. The terms of a DPA are similarly voluntary, and neither party is obliged to agree any particular term therein. The Act does not, and this DPA Code cannot, alter the law on legal professional privilege.

3.4 DPA negotiations must be transparent. The prosecutor must:

  i. Ensure that a full and accurate record of negotiations is prepared and retained. It is essential that a full written record is kept of every key action and event in the discussion process, including details of every offer or concession made by each party, and the reasons for every decision taken by the prosecutor. Meetings between the parties should be minuted and the minutes agreed and signed;

ii. Ensure that the prosecution and P have obtained sufficient information from each other so each can play an informed part in the negotiations;

iii. Ensure that documentation and any other material relevant to the matters the prosecutor is considering prosecuting is retained by P for any future prosecution;

iv. Ensure that the proposed DPA placed before the court fully and fairly reflects P's alleged offending; and

v. The prosecutor must not agree additional matters with P which are not recorded in the DPA and not made known to the court.

THE LETTER OF INVITATION

3.5 In order to initiate the DPA negotiations, the prosecutor will first send P a letter containing:

i. Confirmation of the prosecutor's decision to offer P the opportunity to enter into DPA negotiations;

ii. A request for confirmation of whether P wishes to enter into negotiations in accordance with the Act and this DPA Code; and

iii. A timeframe within which P must notify the prosecutor whether it accepts the invitation to enter into DPA negotiations.

UNDERTAKINGS

3.6 Where P agrees to engage in DPA negotiations, the prosecutor should send P a letter setting out the way in which the discussions will be conducted. This letter should make undertakings in respect of:

i. the confidentiality of the fact that DPA negotiations are taking place;

ii. the confidentiality of information provided by the prosecutor and P in the course of the DPA negotiations.3. Process for invitation to enter into negotiations

3.7 In doing so the undertaking will make clear:

i. the use which may be made by the prosecutor of information provided by P pursuant to paragraph 13 of Schedule 17 to the Act;

ii. that the law in relation to the disclosure of unused material may require the prosecutor to provide information received during the course of DPA negotiations to a defendant in criminal proceedings; and

iii. that the information may be disclosed as permitted by law.

3.8 The letter should also include:
   i. a statement of the prosecutor's responsibility for disclosure of material pursuant to this DPA Code;
   ii. a warning that the provision by P of inaccurate, misleading or incomplete information where P knew or ought to have known that the information was inaccurate, misleading or incomplete may lead to a prosecution of P: a. for an offence consisting of the provision of such inaccurate, misleading or incomplete information, and/or b. for an offence or offences which are the subject of an agreed DPA; and
   iii. the practical means by which the discussions will be conducted including appropriate time limits.
3.9 The prosecutor will require P to provide an undertaking:
   i. that information provided by the prosecutor in the course of DPA negotiations will be treated as confidential and will not be disclosed to any other party, other than for the purposes of the DPA negotiations or as required by law;

   and

   ii. all documentation or other material relevant to the matters the prosecutor is considering prosecuting is retained until P is released from the obligation to do so by the prosecutor.
3.10 In exceptional circumstances and where permitted by law the prosecutor may agree in writing to different terms regarding the confidentiality of information. Ordinarily the decision to vary confidentiality terms will be dealt with on a case by case basis at the point that the disclosure is considered. In deciding whether to make such an exceptional variation, for example in relation to a disclosure of information to third parties, the prosecutor will take into account that statutory and common law safeguards already exist in respect of disclosure of information to third parties.
3.11 Until the issues of confidentiality, use of and retention of information have been agreed to the satisfaction of both parties, and the agreement reflected in signed undertakings, the prosecutor must not continue with the substantive DPA negotiations.

4. SUBSEQUENT USE OF INFORMATION OBTAINED BY A PROSECUTOR DURING THE DPA NEGOTIATION PERIOD

4.1 The use to which information obtained by a prosecutor during the DPA negotiation period may subsequently be put is dealt with at paragraph

Appendix 8 *Deferred Prosecution Agreements Code of Practice*

13 of Schedule 17 to the Act. The use of any particular item is therefore governed by that legislation.

4.2 It is recognised that there is a balance to be struck between encouraging all parties to be able to negotiate freely, and the risk that P may seek knowingly (or when it should have known) to induce the prosecutor to enter into a DPA on an inaccurate, misleading or incomplete basis.

4.3 If P provides inaccurate, misleading or incomplete information where P knew or ought to have known that the information was inaccurate, misleading or incomplete, the prosecutor may instigate fresh proceedings against P for the same alleged offence in accordance with paragraph 11 of Schedule 17 to the Act notwithstanding any DPA that may have been approved.

4.4 There are two contexts within which information obtained by the prosecutor during the DPA negotiation period may subsequently be used.

　　i.　Where a DPA is approved by the court under paragraph 8 of Schedule 17 to the Act the legislation provides (at paragraph 13 (1) and (2) of Schedule 17) that the statement of facts contained in the DPA may be used in subsequent criminal proceedings as an admission in accordance with section 10 of the Criminal Justice Act 1967.

　　ii.　Where a DPA has not been concluded and the prosecutor chooses to pursue criminal proceedings against P, the material described in paragraph 13(6) of Schedule 17 to the Act may only be used in the limited circumstances described in paragraphs 13 (4) and (5) of Schedule 17 to the Act.

4.5 Apart from the material described at paragraph 13(6) of Schedule 17 to the Act, there is no limitation on the use to which other information obtained by a prosecutor during the DPA negotiation period may subsequently be put during criminal proceedings brought against P, or against anyone else (so far as the rules of evidence permit).

4.6 By way of non-exhaustive example, if the DPA negotiations fail the following types of document provided to a prosecutor in those negotiations would be available to be used by the prosecutor subject to the rules of evidence in a subsequent prosecution of P:

　　i.　pre-existing contemporary key documentation such as contracts, accountancy records including payments of any kind, any records evidencing the transfer of money, emailor other communications etc. provided to the prosecutor by P;

　　ii.　any internal or independent investigation report carried out by P and disclosed to the prosecutor prior to the DPA negotiation period commencing;

iii. any interview note or witness statement obtained from an employee of P and disclosed to the prosecutor prior to the DPA negotiation period commencing;

iv. any document obtained by the prosecutor at any time obtained from any source other than P; and

v. any information obtained by the prosecutor as a result of enquiries made as a result of information provided by P at any time.

5. UNUSED MATERIAL AND DISCLOSURE

5.1. Negotiations to enter into a DPA will necessarily take place prior to the institution of proceedings and the statutory disclosure rules will therefore not be engaged at this early stage.

5.2. P should have sufficient information to play an informed part in the negotiations. The purpose of disclosure here is to ensure that negotiations are fair and that P is not misled as to the strength of the prosecution case. The prosecutor must always be alive to the potential need to disclose material in the interests of justice and fairness in the particular circumstances of any case. For instance, disclosure ought to be made of information that might undermine the factual basis of conclusions drawn by P from material disclosed by P. A statement of the prosecutor's duty of disclosure will be included in the terms and conditions letter provided to P at the outset of the negotiations.

5.3. Consideration should be given to reasonable and specific requests for disclosure by P. Where the need for such disclosure is not apparent to the prosecutor, any disclosure may depend on what P chooses to reveal to the prosecutor about its case in order to justify the request.

5.4. The investigator's duty to pursue reasonable lines of inquiry in accordance with the CPIA 1996 Code of Practice is not affected by the introduction of DPAs or the application of this Code. What is reasonable in each case will depend upon the particular circumstances.

5.5. Before the final DPA hearing the prosecutor must obtain from the investigator enquiring into the alleged offence or offences information that will enable the prosecutor to make a written declaration to the court, as required by Criminal Procedure Rule 12.2 (3) (b), namely that:

i. the investigator enquiring into the offence or alleged offences has certified that no information has been supplied which the investigator knows to be inaccurate, misleading or incomplete; and

ii. the prosecutor has complied with the prosecution obligation to disclose material to the defendant.

Appendix 8 *Deferred Prosecution Agreements Code of Practice*

5.6. To satisfy (ii) above, the prosecutor should request that the investigator provide written certification to the prosecutor that any material retained by the investigator which may satisfy the test for prosecution disclosure as outlined in this DPA Code has been drawn to the attention of the prosecutor.

5.7. Where a DPA is approved by the court and a bill of indictment is preferred upon entering into a DPA, the CPIA will apply. However, the immediate suspension of the indictment will have the effect of immediately suspending with it the disclosure obligations imposed. The statutory disclosure obligations and standard directions providing time limits for compliance will only apply if the suspension is lifted in the event of termination of the DPA and the prosecution of P.

5.8. The disclosure duty of the prosecutor as outlined in this DPA Code is a continuing one and the prosecutor must disclose to P any material that comes to light after the DPA has been agreed which satisfies the test for disclosure above.

6. STATEMENT OF FACTS

6.1. The application must include a statement of facts which must:
   i. give particulars relating to each alleged offence;
   ii. include details where possible of any financial gain or loss, with reference to key documents that must be attached.

6.2. The parties should resolve any factual issues necessary to allow the court to agree terms of the DPA on a clear, fair and accurate basis. The court does not have the power to adjudicate upon factual differences in DPA proceedings.

6.3. There is no requirement for formal admissions of guilt in respect of the offences charged by the indictment though it will be necessary for P to admit the contents and meaning of key documents referred to in the statement of facts.

6.4. In the event that P is prosecuted for the alleged offence addressed by a court approved DPA, the statement of facts would be admissible against P in accordance with section 10 of the Criminal Justice Act 1967 in any subsequent criminal proceedings.

7. TERMS

7.1. A DPA may include a broad range of terms, some of which are detailed in a non- exhaustive list in paragraph 5(3) of Schedule 17 to the Act.

Terms

7.2. The prosecutor and P are required to agree the terms of a DPA[4] which are fair, reasonable and proportionate. What terms are fair, reasonable and proportionate, including the length of the DPA, will be determined on a case by case basis. The terms may consist of a combination of requirements and it will normally be fair, reasonable and proportionate for there to be a financial penalty. It is particularly desirable that measures should be included that achieve redress for victims, such as payment of compensation. Paragraph 5 of Schedule 17 to the Act suggests that a possible term of a DPA is the recovery of the reasonable costs of the prosecutor in relation to the alleged offence or the DPA. The prosecutor should ordinarily seek to recover these costs, including the costs of the investigation where they have been incurred by the prosecutor.

7.3. The basis of the DPA and its terms will be explained in an agreed written application to the court.

7.4. The terms must set out clearly the measures with which P must comply. Clarity is important so P understands what is required. Further, in the event of breach of a term drafting ambiguity will complicate breach proceedings.

7.5. The terms must be proportionate to the offence and tailored to the specific facts of the case.

7.6. The DPA must specify the end date.

7.7. The following will normally be requirements of the DPA:

   i. that the DPA relates only to the offences particularised in the counts of the draft indictment;[5]

   ii. a warranty provided by both P and with P's consent, its legal advisers[6] that the information provided to the prosecutor throughout the DPA negotiations and upon which the DPA is based does not knowingly, contain inaccurate, misleading or incomplete information relevant to the conduct P has disclosed to the prosecutor.

---

4   The length of a DPA will need to be sufficient to be capable of permitting compliance with other terms such as financial penalties paid in instalments, monitoring and co-operation with the investigations and trials into individuals.
5   Prosecutors should not agree to a term that would prevent P from being prosecuted for conduct not included in the indictment even where the conduct has been disclosed during the course of DPA negotiations but not charged.
6   The SRA Code of Conduct sets out in Chapter 5 the duties of a solicitor when conducting litigation or acting as an advocate. There are obligations on a solicitor:
   a. Not to attempt to deceive or knowingly or recklessly mislead the court [O5.1], b.Not to be complicit in any other person deceiving or misleading the court [O5.2], and c. Where relevant to inform their client of circumstances in which their duties to the court outweigh their obligations to their client [O5.4].

Appendix 8 *Deferred Prosecution Agreements Code of Practice*

       iii. a requirement on P to notify the prosecutor and to provide where requested any documentation or other material that it becomes aware of whilst the DPA is in force which P knows or suspects would have been relevant to the offences particularised in the draft indictment.

7.8. The following will normally be terms of a DPA:
       i. A financial order;
       ii. The payment of the reasonable costs of the prosecutor;
       iii. Co-operation with an investigation related to the alleged offence(s).[7]

7.9. The suggested financial terms may include but are not confined to: compensating victims; payment of a financial penalty; payment of the prosecutor's costs; donations to charities which support the victims of the offending; disgorgement of profits. There is no requirement to include all or any of these terms all of which are a matter of negotiation with P and subject to judicial oversight. The following should be noted:

       i. A late payment may constitute a breach of the DPA leading to breach and termination. It may however be appropriate to make provision for short delays pursuant to paragraph 5 (5) of Schedule 17 to the Act requiring the payment of interest on any payment(s) not paid by the date agreed and specify the rate that applies.[8]

       ii. Where payment of a donation, compensation, financial penalty and/or costs is an agreed term of the DPA, the starting point should be that monies are ordered to be paid within seven days of the final hearing and this should be a standard term unless not fair, reasonable or proportionate.

       iii. Where a financial penalty is to be imposed, the figure agreed must approximate to what would have been imposed had P pleaded guilty (see section 8).

       iv. There should be a transparent and consistent approach to the setting of a financial penalty that is analogous to the sentencing framework for setting fines so the parties and the court will know before they enter into the process what the appropriate starting point is.

       v. Financial penalties and disgorgements of profits will be paid to the prosecutor and then passed to the Consolidated Fund. Charitable donations and compensation will be paid by P directly or through an intermediary agreed by the parties and approved by the court

---

7 For example in respect of individuals. The obligation would include the provision of material to be used in evidence and for the purposes of disclosure.

8 The rate should ordinarily be not less than the rate of interest payable on post judgment debts at the date when the DPA is approved

Terms

as part of the DPA. P will provide confirmation and supporting evidence to the prosecutor of this as required.

7.10 Other terms that may be agreed might include:
 i. prohibiting P from engaging in certain activities.
 ii. financial reporting obligations.
 iii. putting in place a robust compliance and/or monitoring programme.
 iv. co-operation with sector wide investigations.

MONITORS

7.11 An important consideration for entering into a DPA is whether P already has a genuinely proactive and effective corporate compliance programme. The use of monitors should therefore be approached with care. The appointment of a monitor will depend upon the factual circumstances of each case and must always be fair, reasonable and proportionate.

7.12 A monitor's primary responsibility is to assess and monitor P's internal controls, advise of necessary compliance improvements that will reduce the risk of future recurrence of the conduct subject to the DPA and report specified misconduct to the prosecutor.

7.13 Where the terms require a monitor to be appointed it is the responsibility of P to pay all the costs of the selection, appointment, remuneration of the monitor, and reasonable costs of the prosecutor associated with the monitorship during the monitoring period. In assessing whether a term of monitoring may satisfy the statutory test the prosecutor should give consideration to the costs of such a term as these may be relevant.

7.14 P shall afford to the monitor complete access to all relevant aspects of its business during the course of the monitoring period as requested by the monitor. Any legal professional privilege that may exist in respect of investigating compliance issues that arise during the monitorship is unaffected by the Act, this DPA Code or a DPA.

7.15 As part of the DPA negotiations P should provide the prosecutor and the court with details of three potential monitors, including relevant qualifications, specialist knowledge and experience; any associations the monitor has or has had with P and/or associated companies and/or person(s) or any named companies or person(s) that feature in the DPA to avoid any conflict of interest; and an estimate of costs of the monitorship.

7.16 P should indicate their preferred monitor with reasons for the preference.

7.17 The prosecutor should ordinarily accept P's preferred monitor. However where the prosecutor considers there to be a conflict of interest or that the monitor is inappropriate, or does not have the requisite experience and authority, they may reject the proposed appointment. Similarly the court

Appendix 8 *Deferred Prosecution Agreements Code of Practice*

may register its dissatisfaction with the selection by not approving the proposed term.

7.18 Where monitorship is proposed to be a term of a DPA, before the DPA is approved the monitor will be selected, provisionally appointed, the terms of the monitorship agreed by the parties to the DPA, a detailed work plan for the first year (to include the method of review and frequency of reporting to the prosecutor) and an outline work plan for the remainder of the monitoring period agreed with the monitor including provisions or limits as to costs. The monitor's report should include a breakdown of his proposed costs, and on what matters costs are incurred.

7.19 Terms of the DPA should include the length of time the monitors should be appointed. Provision should however be made in the DPA that if the monitor is satisfied that P's policies are functioning properly such that there is no need for further monitoring, the monitor may inform the prosecutor who will, subject to being satisfied through discussion with the monitor that the monitor's views are reasonable, agree to the termination or suspension of the monitor's appointment. Conversely the DPA should provide that, if the monitor and the prosecutor agree that P has not, or it appears will not by the end of the monitoring period have successfully satisfied its obligations with respect to the monitor's mandate, the term of the monitorship will be extended provided that no extension exceeds the length of the DPA.

7.20 Monitors' reports and associated correspondence shall be designated confidential with disclosure restricted to the prosecutor, P and the court, save as otherwise permitted by law.

7.21 No two monitoring programmes will be the same, given the varying facts and circumstances of each case including the nature and size of P. Terms included in the monitor's agreement may include, but are not limited to, ensuring that P has in place:[9]

   i. a code of conduct;

   ii. an appropriate training and education programme;

   iii. internal procedures for reporting conduct issues which enable officers and employees to report issues in a safe and confidential manner;

   iv. processes for identifying key strategic risk areas;

   v. reasonable safeguards to approve the appointment of representatives and payment of commissions;

   vi. a gifts and hospitality policy;

---

9 These policies and procedures are not intended to provide an indication of what can amount to adequate procedures under s. 7 Bribery Act 2010.

vii. reasonable procedures for undertaking due diligence on potential projects, acquisitions, business partners, agents, representatives, distributors, sub-contractors and suppliers;

viii. procurement procedures which minimise the opportunity of misconduct;

ix. contract terms between P and its business partners, subcontractors, distributors, and suppliers include express contractual obligations and remedies in relation to misconduct;

x. internal management and audit processes which include reasonable controls against misconduct where appropriate;

xi. policies and processes in all of its subsidiaries and operating businesses, and joint ventures in which it has management control, and that P uses reasonable endeavours to ensure that the joint ventures in which it does not have management control, together with key subcontractors and representatives, are familiar with and are required to abide by its code of conduct to the extent possible;.

xii. procedures compatible with money laundering regulations;

xiii. policies regarding charitable and political donations;

xiv. terms related to external controls, e.g. procedures for selection of appropriate charities;

xv. policies relating to internal investigative resources, employee disciplinary procedures; and compliance screening of prospective employees;

xvi. policies relating to the extent to which senior management takes responsibility for implementing relevant practices and procedures;

xvii. mechanisms for review of the effectiveness of relevant policies and procedures across business and jurisdictions in which P operates;

xviii. compensation structures that remove incentives for unethical behaviour.

7.22 In designing a monitoring programme regard should be had to contemporary external guidance on compliance programmes.[10]

---

10 At the time of publishing guidance can be found in the Ministry of Justice Bribery Act 2010: Guidance to help commercial organisations prevent bribery, the OECD Good Practice Guide on Internal Controls, Ethics and Compliance, the BS 10500 Anti-Bribery System Standard, the US Sentencing Commission's Federal Sentencing Guidelines Manual, in particular its guidance on effective compliance and ethics programmes, and the guidance on corporate compliance programmes in the US Department of Justice's Principles of Federal Prosecution of Business.

Appendix 8 *Deferred Prosecution Agreements Code of Practice*

8. FINANCIAL PENALTY

8.1. The prosecutor represents the public interest, and should assist with the identification of appropriate terms by drawing the judge's attention where possible and relevant to the following information:

   i. any victim statement or other information available to the prosecutor as to the impact of the alleged offence on the victim;

   ii. any statutory provisions relevant to the offender and the offences under consideration;

   iii. any relevant Sentencing Council Guidelines and guideline cases; and

   iv. the aggravating and mitigating factors of the alleged offence under consideration.

8.2. Such information where available and relevant should form part of the agreed written application to be provided to the court at the final hearing.

8.3. Any financial penalty is to be broadly comparable to a fine that the court would have imposed upon P following a guilty plea.[11] This is intended to enable the parties and courts to have regard to relevant pre-existing sentencing principles and guidelines in order to determine the appropriate level for a financial penalty in an individual case. This should include consideration of P's means and where compensation is appropriate, this should be given priority over a penalty.

8.4. The extent of the discretion available when considering a financial penalty is broad. The discount for a guilty plea is applied by the sentencing court after it has taken into account all relevant considerations, including any assistance given by P. The level of the discount to reflect P's assistance would depend on the circumstances and the level of assistance given, and the parties should be guided by sentencing practice, statute and pre-existing case law on this matter. A financial penalty must provide for a discount equivalent to that which would be afforded by an early guilty plea. Current guidelines provide for a one third discount for a plea at the earliest opportunity.

8.5. To be considered as voluntary and therefore mitigating, co-operation should be over and above mere compliance with any coercive[12] measures.

---

11 Schedule 17, Paragraph 5 (4).
12 Such as notices under s 2(1) Criminal Justice Act 1987 issued by the Serious Fraud Office.

Application for Approval

9. PRELIMINARY HEARING(S)

9.1. The Criminal Procedure Rules make provision for the contents of the application.[13]

9.2. The prosecutor should contact a court designated to approve DPAs in order to request a listing and in doing so provide a realistic time estimate for a preliminary hearing.

9.3. The draft proposed application and any supporting documents must be submitted on a confidential basis to the court before the preliminary hearing.

9.4. The application must explain why the agreement is in the interests of justice and fair, reasonable and proportionate. In so explaining the prosecutor must address issues such as concurrent jurisdiction, on-going and/or subsequent ancillary proceedings, any conduct outwith the scope of the DPA which P has disclosed to the prosecutor but which does not form part of the draft indictment on account of the test at paragraph 1.2 above not having been satisfied.

9.5. Consideration should be given at the preliminary hearing to additional relevant issues such as timing of subsequent hearings.

9.6. The appropriate manner and timing of a preliminary hearing will vary on a case by case basis, and the court may adjourn a preliminary hearing if it requires more information about the facts or terms of a proposed DPA before it can make the full declaration under paragraph 7(1) of Schedule 17 to the Act.

10. APPLICATION FOR APPROVAL

10.1. The Criminal Procedure Rules make provision for the contents of the application for final approval.[14] They further provide that an application for final approval should be sought as soon as practicable once the court has made a declaration under paragraph 7(1) of Schedule 17 to the Act and the parties have settled the terms of the DPA.

10.2. The basis of the DPA and its terms will be explained in an agreed written application accompanied by the proposed final terms of the DPA, agreed case statement with any supporting documents and the prosecutor's confirmation of which evidential test has been met. These documents must be submitted to the court on a confidential basis before the application for approval.

---

13 Crim PR 12.
14 Crim PR 12.

Appendix 8 *Deferred Prosecution Agreements Code of Practice*

10.3. Issues germane to whether the DPA is in the interests of justice and its terms being fair, reasonable and proportionate such as concurrent jurisdiction, on-going and/ or subsequent ancillary proceedings, must also be addressed by the prosecutor in the application for approval.

10.4. The application for approval of the DPA may be in private. This is likely to be almost always necessary as the prosecutor and P will be uncertain as to whether the court will grant a declaration under paragraph 8 (1). For the parties to make an application in open court which was refused might lead to the uncertainties and destabilisation that private preliminary hearings are designed to avoid.

10.5. The court may adjourn an application for approval if it requires more information about the facts or terms of a proposed DPA before it can make the declaration under paragraph 8(1) of Schedule 17 to the Act.

11. DECLARATION IN OPEN COURT

11.1. If a DPA is approved, the court must make a declaration to that effect along with reasons in an open hearing.[15]

11.2. Once the declaration has been made in open court the prosecutor will, unless prevented from doing so by an enactment or by an order from the Court, publish on its website:

    i.   the DPA;

    ii.   the declaration of the court pursuant to paragraph 8 (1) of Schedule 17 to the Act with the reasons for making such a declaration;

    iii.   the declaration of the court pursuant to paragraph 7 (1) of Schedule 17 to the Act with the reasons for making such a declaration; and

    iv.   if appropriate, any initial refusal to make such a declaration with reasons for declining.

11.3. Immediate publication may be prevented by any enactment or order that postponement is necessary to avoid a substantial risk of prejudice to the administration of justice in any legal proceedings. P's offence and the sanctions provided for in the DPA will be made public as soon as it is safe to do so.

---

15 See paragraph 15.4 in respect of listing.

12. BREACH OF A DPA

12.1. Paragraph 9 of Schedule 17 to the Act deals with the situation where P is, or is believed by the prosecutor to be, in breach of a term of a DPA that has been approved at a final hearing.

ALLEGING AND PROVING BREACH OF A DPA

12.2. If, prior to the expiry of the DPA, it is believed that P is in breach of it, where possible the prosecutor should ask P to rectify the alleged breach immediately. In cases of minor breaches, it may be possible for a solution to be reached efficiently in this way, without the need for either an application under paragraph 9 of Schedule 17 to the Act or a variation of the DPA under paragraph 10 of Schedule 17 to the Act. The prosecutor will nevertheless still be required to publish details of the breach pursuant to paragraph 9 (8) of Schedule 17 to the Act. The prosecutor should also notify the court of any such developments.

12.3. If the prosecutor is unable to secure a satisfactory outcome in this way, it may apply to the court seeking a finding that P is in breach of the term as alleged, and explaining the remedy it seeks as a result. The question of whether or not there has been a breach of a term is to be judged on the balance of probabilities. The successful party may seek its costs of an application under paragraph 9 of Schedule 17.[16]

12.4. If the court finds that P is in breach of a term of the DPA it may invite the parties to agree a suitable proposed remedy. If agreement can be reached, that proposed remedy must then be presented to the court by way of an application in accordance with paragraph 10 of Schedule 17 to the Act. The court will approve the variation only if that variation is in the interests of justice and the terms of the DPA as varied are fair, reasonable and proportionate. It is anticipated that this mechanism should generally be used to rectify relatively minor breaches of a DPA where the parties have been unable to agree a remedy without the involvement of the court.

TERMINATION FOLLOWING BREACH OF A DPA

12.5. Where the alleged breach is more material or the parties are unable to agree a suitable remedy or the court does not approve a proposed remedy, the court may order that the DPA be terminated. If the court makes such an order the DPA shall cease to take effect from that point onwards, and the prosecutor may apply to have the suspension of the indictment covered by the DPA lifted in accordance with paragraph 2 of Schedule 17 to the Act.

---

16 Crim PR 76.1 (c).

Appendix 8 *Deferred Prosecution Agreements Code of Practice*

12.6. Where a DPA has been terminated in this way, P is not entitled to the return of any monies paid under the DPA prior to its termination, or to any other relief for detriment arising from its compliance with the DPA up to that point (for example the costs of a monitoring programme). The prosecutor may seek from P the costs of an application under paragraph 9 of schedule 17 to the Act.[17]

POST TERMINATION PROCESS

12.7. Should the DPA be terminated it will be usual for the prosecutor to apply for the suspension of the indictment to be lifted and P to be prosecuted. The application to lift the suspension need not be made at the time that the DPA is terminated.

12.8. The lifting of the suspension would reinstitute criminal proceedings. Given the manner in which the earlier investigation was concluded and/or the passage of time since the DPA was concluded the prosecutor may not be in a position to commence criminal proceedings immediately. Further investigation and preparation may be needed in order for the prosecutor to be trial ready.

12.9. Before re-opening proceedings, the prosecutor must be satisfied that the Full Code Test under the Code for Crown Prosecutors is met in relation to each charge. The court will have been informed at the final hearing if the original charge was pursuant to the second limb of the evidential stage at paragraph 1.2 i b) above, in which case the prosecutor will now need to be satisfied that the more stringent evidential stage of the Full Code Test is met. Furthermore the public interest position will need reassessing in light of the breach.

12.10. If the prosecutor requires time before being in a position to re-open proceedings the court should be informed of the prosecutor's proposed course of action and then kept informed of progress.

13. VARIATION OF A DPA

13.1. Paragraph 10 of Schedule 17 to the Act deals with the situation where it becomes necessary to vary the terms of a DPA that has been approved.

13.2. There are two possible situations in which variation may be necessary.

    i. The first is where a breach has occurred in respect of which the prosecutor has applied under paragraph 9 of Schedule 17, and the court has invited the parties to agree a solution to that breach, which the court then has to consider whether to approve.

---

17 Crim PR 76.1 (c).

ii. The second situation is where a breach has not yet occurred, but, absent the variation, is likely to. A variation in this category will only be approved by the court if it arises from circumstances that were not, and could not have been, foreseen by the prosecutor or P at the time that the DPA was agreed.[18] What circumstances a court considers to be adequate in these types of cases will have to be decided on a case by case basis. Variation of a DPA is not a mechanism that exists for mere convenience or efficiency. A DPA is a serious sanction for criminal conduct and will have been approved by the court on that basis. In the vast majority of cases the terms of a DPA that are approved at a final hearing should be strictly complied with in their entirety, failing which P risks prosecution.

13.3. In both situations, it is the prosecutor that must apply to the court to seek a declaration that a variation is acceptable. P does not have a right to apply to the court for a variation; it may only ask the prosecutor for a variation.

13.4. If a variation is approved, the court must give its declaration to that effect in an open hearing. Costs of an application under paragraph 10 of Schedule 17 to the Act may be sought.[19]

14. DISCONTINUANCE

14.1. On expiry of the DPA, the prosecutor should give notice to the court that it does not want proceedings to continue, in accordance with paragraph 11(1) of Schedule 17 to the Act.

14.2. Where considered necessary, consultation with the investigator and any monitor should take place prior to discontinuance.

14.3. Discontinuance notices should be sent to the court as soon as practicable after the decision to discontinue, and copies should be sent to P and the investigator.

14.4. The notice should state:

i. The effective date of discontinuance;

ii. The offences to be discontinued;

iii. Confirmation that the DPA has expired.

14.5. A DPA will ordinarily expire on the date specified in the agreement. However, this will not always be the case, and prosecutors should be

---

18 Paragraph 10(1)(b) of Schedule 17 to the Act.
19 Crim PR 76.1(c).

aware of the various circumstances under paragraph 11 of Schedule 17 to the Act in which a DPA is to be treated as having or not having expired.

14.6. No notice of discontinuance is needed where the court terminates the DPA: see paragraph 11(5)(b) of Schedule 17 to the Act.

14.7. In contrast to discontinuance under the section 23A of the Prosecutions of Offences Act 1985, once proceedings are discontinued under paragraph 11(1), fresh proceedings against P for the same offence may not be instituted unless the conditions specified in paragraph 11(3) of Schedule 17 to the Act (provision of inaccurate, misleading or incomplete information by P) are satisfied.

15. APPLICATIONS IN PRIVATE

15.1. Where an application in private is contemplated all parties should consider whether the hearing can be heard in public as a starting point and if not, whether as much as possible of the hearing can be heard in public.

15.2. An application for a private hearing might be made for example where it is necessary to avoid a substantial risk of prejudice to the administration of justice in any legal proceedings.

15.3. The court will not identify the parties to a private application.

15.4. Where the application to approve the DPA is in private it would be normally appropriate for reasons of transparency and open justice for the parties to request the court to delay the making of a declaration approving a DPA in open court so that a listing might be publicised in the normal manner.

15.5. All communications with the court in respect of a DPA will be confidential and the use of secure email should be the preferred means to maintain confidentiality.

16. PUBLISHING DECISIONS AND POSTPONEMENT

16.1. Transparency remains a key aspect of the success and proper operation of DPAs, and accordingly Schedule 17 of the Act requires in prescribed circumstances the prosecutor to publish on its website orders made by the court or decisions made by the prosecutor.

16.2. All requirements to publish under this section are subject to any enactment or order of the court under paragraph 12 of Schedule 17 to the Act preventing such publication from being made.

16.3. There is no requirement to publish a conclusion reached by a prosecutor alone that no breach has in fact occurred so that no application to the court has been made.

Appendix 9

Control and Management of Heavy Fraud and Other Complex Criminal Cases

A PROTOCOL ISSUED BY THE LORD CHIEF JUSTICE OF ENGLAND AND WALES (22 March 2005)

INTRODUCTION

There is a broad consensus that the length of fraud and trials of other complex crimes must be controlled within proper bounds in order:

(i) To enable the jury to retain and assess the evidence which they have heard. If the trial is so long that the jury cannot do this, then the trial is not fair either to the prosecution or the defence.

(ii) To make proper use of limited public resources: see *Jisl* [2004] EWCA Crim 696 at [113]–[121].

There is also a consensus that no trial should be permitted to exceed a given period, save in exceptional circumstances; some favour 3 months, others an outer limit of 6 months. Whatever view is taken, it is essential that the current length of trials is brought back to an acceptable and proper duration.

This Protocol supplements the Criminal Procedure Rules and summarises good practice which experience has shown may assist in bringing about some reduction in the length of trials of fraud and other crimes that result in complex trials. Flexibility of application of this Protocol according to the needs of each case is essential; it is designed to inform but not to prescribe.

This Protocol is primarily directed towards cases which are likely to last eight weeks or longer. It should also be followed, however, in all cases estimated to last more than four weeks. This Protocol applies to trials by jury, but many of the principles will be applicable if trials without a jury are permitted under s. 43 of the Criminal Justice Act 2003.

The best handling technique for a long case is continuous management by an experienced Judge nominated for the purpose.

Appendix 9 *Control and Management of Heavy Fraud etc*

It is intended that this Protocol be kept up to date; any further practices or techniques found to be successful in the management of complex cases should be notified to the office of the Lord Chief Justice.

1. THE INVESTIGATION

i) **The role of the prosecuting authority and the judge**

    a) Unlike other European countries, a judge in England and Wales does not directly control the investigative process; that is the responsibility of the Investigating Authority, and in turn the Prosecuting Authority and the prosecution advocate. Experience has shown that a prosecution lawyer (who must be of sufficient experience and who will be a member of the team at trial) and the prosecution advocate, if different, should be involved in the investigation as soon as it appears that a heavy fraud trial or other complex criminal trial is likely to ensue. The costs that this early preparation will incur will be saved many times over in the long run.

    b) The judge can and should exert a substantial and beneficial influence by making it clear that, generally speaking, trials should be kept within manageable limits. In most cases 3 months should be the target outer limit, but there will be cases where a duration of 6 months, or in exceptional circumstances, even longer may be inevitable.

ii) **Interviews**

    a) At present many interviews are too long and too unstructured. This has a knock-on effect on the length of trials. Interviews should provide an opportunity for suspects to respond to the allegations against them. They should not be an occasion to discuss every document in the case. It should become clear from judicial rulings that interviews of this kind are a waste of resources.

    b) The suspect must be given sufficient information before or at the interview to enable them to meet the questions fairly and answer them honestly; the information is not provided to give the suspect the opportunity to manufacture a false story which fits undisputable facts.

    c) It is often helpful if the principal documents are provided either in advance of the interview or shown as the interview progresses; asking detailed questions about events a considerable period in the past without reference to the documents is often not very helpful.

iii) **The prosecution and defence teams**

    a) *The Prosecution Team*

        While instructed, it is for the lead advocate for the prosecution to take all necessary decisions in the presentation and general

The Investigation

conduct of the prosecution case in court. The prosecution lead advocate will be treated by the court as having that responsibility.

However, in relation to policy decisions, the lead advocate for the prosecution must not give an indication or undertaking which binds the prosecution without first discussing the issue with the Director of the Prosecuting authority or other senior officer.

'Policy' decisions should be understood as referring to non-evidential decisions on: the acceptance of pleas of guilty to lesser counts or groups of counts or available alternatives: offering no evidence on particular counts; consideration of a re-trial; whether to lodge an appeal; certification of a point of law; and the withdrawal of the prosecution as a whole (for further information see the 'Farquharson Guidelines' on the role and responsibilities of the prosecution advocate).

b) *The Defence Team*

In each case, the lead advocate for the defence will be treated by the court as having responsibility to the court for the presentation and general conduct of the defence case.

c) In each case, a case progression officer must be assigned by the court, prosecution and defence from the time of the first hearing when directions are given (as referred to in paragraph 3.iii)) until the conclusion of the trial.

d) In each case where there are multiple defendants, the LSC will need to consider carefully the extent and level of representation necessary.

iv) **Initial consideration of the length of a case**

If the prosecutor in charge of the case from the Prosecuting Authority or the lead advocate for the prosecution consider that the case as formulated is likely to last more than 8 weeks, the case should be referred in accordance with arrangements made by the Prosecuting Authority to a more senior prosecutor. The senior prosecutor will consider whether it is desirable for the case to be prosecuted in that way or whether some steps might be taken to reduce its likely length, whilst at the same time ensuring that the public interest is served.

Any case likely to last 6 months or more must be referred to the Director of the Prosecuting Authority so that similar considerations can take place.

v) **Notification of cases likely to last more than 8 weeks**

Special arrangements will be put in place for the early notification by the CPS and other Prosecuting Authorities, to the LSC and to a single designated officer of the Court in each Region (Circuit) of any case

Appendix 9 *Control and Management of Heavy Fraud etc*

which the CPS or other Prosecuting Authority consider likely to last over 8 weeks.

vi) **Venue**

The court will allocate such cases and other complex cases likely to last 4 weeks or more to a specific venue suitable for the trial in question, taking into account the convenience to witnesses, the parties, the availability of time at that location, and all other relevant considerations.

2. DESIGNATION OF THE TRIAL JUDGE

i) **The assignment of a judge**

  a) In any complex case which is expected to last more than four weeks, the trial judge will be assigned under the direction of the Presiding Judges at the earliest possible moment.

  b) Thereafter the assigned judge should manage that case 'from cradle to grave'; it is essential that the same judge manages the case from the time of his assignment and that arrangements are made for him to be able to do so. It is recognised that in certain court centres with a large turnover of heavy cases (eg Southwark) this objective is more difficult to achieve. But in those court centres there are teams of specialist judges, who are more readily able to handle cases which the assigned judge cannot continue with because of unexpected events; even at such courts, there must be no exception to the principle that one judge must handle all the pre-trial hearings until the case is assigned to another judge.

3. CASE MANAGEMENT

i) **Objectives**

  a) The number, length and organisation of case management hearings will, of course, depend critically on the circumstances and complexity of the individual case. However, thorough, well-prepared and extended case management hearings will save court time and costs overall.

  b) Effective case management of heavy fraud and other complex criminal cases requires the judge to have a much more detailed grasp of the case than may be necessary for many other Plea and Case Management Hearings (PCMHs). Though it is for the judge in each case to decide how much pre-reading time he needs so that the judge is on top of the case, it is not always a sensible use of judicial time to allocate a series of reading days, during which the

Case Management

judge sits alone in his room, working through numerous boxes of ring binders.

See paragraph 3 iv) e) below.

ii) **Fixing the trial date**

Although it is important that the trial date should be fixed as early as possible, this may not always be the right course. There are two principal alternatives:

a) The trial date should be fixed at the first opportunity – i.e. at the first (and usually short) directions hearing referred to in sub-paragraph iii). From then on everyone must work to that date. All orders and pre-trial steps should be timetabled to fit in with that date. All advocates and the judge should take note of this date, in the expectation that the trial will proceed on the date determined.

b) The trial date should not be fixed until the issues have been explored at a full case management hearing (referred to in sub-paragraph iv), after the advocates on both sides have done some serious work on the case. Only then can the length of the trial be estimated.

Which is apposite must depend on the circumstances of each case, but the earlier it is possible to fix a trial date, by reference to a proper estimate and a timetable set by reference to the trial date, the better.

It is generally to be expected that once a trial is fixed on the basis of the estimate provided, that it will be **increased** if, and only if, the party seeking to extend the time justifies why the original estimate is no longer appropriate.

iii) **The first hearing for the giving of initial directions**

At the first opportunity the assigned judge should hold a short hearing to give initial directions. The directions on this occasion might well include:

a) That there should be a full case management hearing on, or commencing on, a specified future date by which time the parties will be properly prepared for a meaningful hearing and the defence will have full instructions.

b) That the prosecution should provide an outline written statement of the prosecution case at least one week in advance of that case management hearing, outlining in simple terms:

   i) The key facts on which it relies.

   ii) The key evidence by which the prosecution seeks to prove the facts.

The statement must be sufficient to permit the judge to understand the case and for the defence to appreciate the basic elements of its case against each defendant. The prosecution may be invited to

Appendix 9 *Control and Management of Heavy Fraud etc*

        highlight the key points of the case orally at the case management hearing by way of a short mini-opening. The outline statement should not be considered binding, but it will serve the essential purpose in telling the judge, and everyone else, what the case is really about and identifying the key issues.

    c)   That a core reading list and core bundle for the case management hearing should be delivered at least one week in advance.

    d)   Preliminary directions about disclosure: see paragraph 4.

iv)   **The first Case Management Hearing**

    a)   At the first case management hearing:

        (1)   The prosecution advocate should be given the opportunity to highlight any points from the prosecution outline statement of case (which will have been delivered at least a week in advance).

        (2)   Each defence advocate should be asked to outline the defence.

        If the defence advocate is not in a position to say what is in issue and what is not in issue, then the case management hearing can be adjourned for a short and limited time and to a fixed date to enable the advocate to take instructions; such an adjournment should only be necessary in exceptional circumstances, as the defence advocate should be properly instructed by the time of the first case management hearing and in any event is under an obligation to take sufficient instructions to fulfil the obligations contained in S 33–39 of Criminal Justice Act 2003.

    b)   There should then be a real dialogue between the judge and all advocates for the purpose of identifying:

        i)   The focus of the prosecution case.

        ii)   The common ground.

        iii)   The real issues in the case. (Rule 3.2 of the Criminal Procedure Rules.).

    c)   The judge will try to generate a spirit of co-operation between the court and the advocates on all sides. The expeditious conduct of the trial and a focussing on the real issues must be in the interests of **all** parties. It cannot be in the interests of any defendant for his good points to become lost in a welter of uncontroversial or irrelevant evidence.

    d)   In many fraud cases the primary facts are not seriously disputed. The real issue is what each defendant knew and whether that

Case Management

defendant was dishonest. Once the judge has identified what is in dispute and what is not in dispute, the judge can then discuss with the advocate how the trial should be structured, what can be dealt with by admissions or agreed facts, what uncontroversial matters should be proved by concise oral evidence, what timetabling can be required under Rule 3.10 Criminal Procedure Rules, and other directions.

- e) In particularly heavy fraud or complex cases the judge may possibly consider it necessary to allocate a whole week for a case management hearing. If that week is used wisely, many further weeks of trial time can be saved. In the gaps which will inevitably arise during that week (for example while the advocates are exploring matters raised by the judge) the judge can do a substantial amount of informed reading. The case has come 'alive' at this stage. Indeed, in a really heavy fraud case, if the judge fixes one or more case management hearings on this scale, there will be need for fewer formal reading days. Moreover a huge amount can be achieved in the pre-trial stage, if all trial advocates are gathered in the same place, focussing on the case **at the same time**, for several days consecutively.

- f) Requiring the defence to serve proper case statements may enable the court to identify

    - i) what is common ground and
    - ii) the real issues.

    It is therefore important that proper defence case statements be provided as required by the Criminal Procedure Rules; Judges will use the powers contained in ss 28–34 of the Criminal Proceedings and Evidence Act 1996 (and the corresponding provisions of the CJA 1987, ss. 33 and following of the Criminal Justice Act 2003) and the Criminal Procedure Rules to ensure that realistic defence case statements are provided.

- g) Likewise this objective may be achieved by requiring the prosecution to serve draft admissions by a specified date and by requiring the defence to respond within a specified number of weeks.

v) **Further Case Management Hearings**

- a) The date of the next case management hearing should be fixed at the conclusion of the hearing so that there is no delay in having to fix the date through listing offices, clerks and others.
- b) If one is looking at a trial which threatens to run for months, pre-trial case management on an intensive scale is essential.

Appendix 9 *Control and Management of Heavy Fraud etc*

vi) **Consideration of the length of the trial**

   a) Case management on the above lines, the procedure set out in paragraph 1.iv), may still be insufficient to reduce the trial to a manageable length; generally a trial of 3 months should be the target, but there will be cases where a duration of 6 months or, in exceptional circumstances, even longer may be inevitable.

   b) If the trial is not estimated to be within a manageable length, it will be necessary for the judge to consider what steps should be taken to reduce the length of the trial, whilst still ensuring that the prosecution has the opportunity of placing the full criminality before the court.

   c) To assist the judge in this task,

   i) The lead advocate for the prosecution should be asked to explain why the prosecution have rejected a shorter way of proceeding; they may also be asked to divide the case into sections of evidence and explain the scope of each section and the need for each section.

   ii) The lead advocates for the prosecution and for the defence should be prepared to put forward in writing, if requested, ways in which a case estimated to last more than three months can be shortened, including possible severance of counts or defendants, exclusions of sections of the case or of evidence or areas of the case where admissions can be made.

   d) One course the judge may consider is pruning the indictment by omitting certain charges and/or by omitting certain defendants. The judge must not usurp the function of the prosecution in this regard, and he must bear in mind that he will, at the outset, know less about the case than the advocates. The aim is achieve fairness to all parties.

   e) Nevertheless, the judge does have two methods of pruning available for use in appropriate circumstances:

   i) Persuading the prosecution that it is not worthwhile pursuing certain charges and/or certain defendants.

   ii) Severing the indictment. Severance for reasons of case management alone is perfectly proper, although judges should have regard to any representations made by the prosecution that severance would weaken their case. Indeed the judge's hand will be strengthened in this regard by rule 1.1 (2) (g) of the Criminal Procedure Rules. However, before using what may be seen as a blunt instrument, the judge should insist on seeing full defence statements of all affected

Case Management

defendants. Severance may be unfair to the prosecution if, for example, there is a cut-throat defence in prospect. For example, the defence of the principal defendant may be that the defendant relied on the advice of his accountant or solicitor that what was happening was acceptable. The defence of the professional may be that he gave no such advice. Against that background, it might be unfair to the prosecution to order separate trials of the two defendants.

vii) **The exercise of the powers**

    a) The Criminal Procedure Rules require the court to take a more active part in case management. These are salutary provisions which should bring to an end interminable criminal trials of the kind which the Court of Appeal criticised in *Jisl* [2004] EWCA 696 at [113] – [121].

    b) Nevertheless these salutary provisions do not have to be used on every occasion. Where the advocates have done their job properly, by narrowing the issues, pruning the evidence and so forth, it may be quite inappropriate for the judge to 'weigh in' and start cutting out more evidence or more charges of his own volition. It behoves the judge to make a careful assessment of the degree of judicial intervention which is warranted in each case.

    c) The note of caution in the previous paragraph is supported by certain experience which has been gained of the Civil Procedure Rules (on which the Criminal Procedure Rules are based). The CPR contain valuable and efficacious provisions for case management by the judge on his own initiative which have led to huge savings of court time and costs. Surveys by the Law Society have shown that the CPR have been generally welcomed by court users and the profession, but there have been reported to have been isolated instances in which the parties to civil litigation have faithfully complied with both the letter and the spirit of the CPR, and have then been aggrieved by what was perceived to be unnecessary intermeddling by the court.

viii) **Expert Evidence**

    a) Early identification of the subject matter of expert evidence to be adduced by the prosecution and the defence should be made as early as possible, preferably at the directions hearing.

    b) Following the exchange of expert evidence, any areas of disagreement should be identified and a direction should generally be made requiring the experts to meet and prepare, after discussion, a joint statement identifying points of agreement and contention and areas where the prosecution is put to proof on matters of which

Appendix 9 *Control and Management of Heavy Fraud etc*

a positive case to the contrary is not advanced by the defence. After the statement has been prepared it should be served on the court, the prosecution and the defence. In some cases, it might be appropriate to provide that to the jury.

ix) **Surveillance Evidence**

a) Where a prosecution is based upon many months' observation or surveillance evidence and it appears that it is capable of effective presentation based on a shorter period, the advocate should be required to justify the evidence of such observations before it is permitted to be adduced, either substantially or in its entirety.

b) Schedules should be provided to cover as much of the evidence as possible and admissions sought.

4. DISCLOSURE

In fraud cases the volume of documentation obtained by the prosecution is liable to be immense. The problems of disclosure are intractable and have the potential to disrupt the entire trial process.

The prosecution lawyer (and the prosecution advocate if different) brought in at the outset, as set out in paragraph 1.i)a), each have a continuing responsibility to discharge the prosecution's duty of disclosure, either personally or by delegation, in accordance with the Attorney General's Guidelines on Disclosure.

ii) The prosecution should only disclose those documents which are relevant (i.e. likely to assist the defence or undermine the prosecution – see s. 3 (1) of CPIA 1996 and the provisions of the CJA 2003).

iii) It is almost always undesirable to give the 'warehouse key' to the defence for two reasons:

a) This amounts to an abrogation of the responsibility of the prosecution;

b) The defence solicitors may spend a disproportionate amount of time and incur disproportionate costs trawling through a morass of documents.

The Judge should therefore try and ensure that disclosure is limited to what is likely to assist the defence or undermine the prosecution.

iv) At the outset the judge should set a timetable for dealing with disclosure issues. In particular, the judge should fix a date by which all defence applications for specific disclosure must be made. In this regard, it is relevant that the defendants are likely to be intelligent people, who know their own business affairs and who (for the most part) will know what documents or categories of documents they are looking for.

v) At the outset (and before the cut-off date for specific disclosure applications) the judge should ask the defence to indicate what documents they are interested in and from what source. A general list is not an acceptable response to this request. The judge should insist upon a list which is specific, manageable and realistic. The judge may also require justification of any request.

vi) In non-fraud cases, the same considerations apply, but some may be different:

a) It is not possible to approach many non-fraud cases on the basis that the defendant knows what is there or what they are looking for. But on the other hand this should not be turned into an excuse for a 'fishing expedition'; the judge should insist on knowing the issue to which a request for disclosure applies.

b) If the bona fides of the investigation is called into question, a judge will be concerned to see that there has been independent and effective appraisal of the documents contained in the disclosure schedule and that its contents are adequate. In appropriate cases where this issue has arisen and there are grounds which show there is a real issue, consideration should be given to receiving evidence on oath from the senior investigating officer at an early case management hearing.

5. ABUSE OF PROCESS

i) Applications to stay or dismiss for abuse of process have become a normal feature of heavy and complex cases. Such applications may be based upon delay and the health of defendants.

ii) Applications in relation to absent special circumstances tend to be unsuccessful and not to be pursued on appeal. For this reason there is comparatively little Court of Appeal guidance: but see: *Harris and Howells* [2003] EWCA Crim 486. It should be noted that abuse of process is not there to discipline the prosecution or the police.

iii) The arguments on both sides must be reduced to writing. Oral evidence is seldom relevant.

iv) The judge should direct full written submissions (rather than 'skeleton arguments') on any abuse application in accordance with a timetable set by him; these should identify any element of prejudice the defendant is alleged to have suffered.

Appendix 9 *Control and Management of Heavy Fraud etc*

v) The Judge should normally aim to conclude the hearing within an absolute maximum limit of one day, if necessary in accordance with a timetable. The parties should therefore prepare their papers on this basis and not expect the judge to allow the oral hearing to be anything more than an occasion to highlight concisely their arguments and answer any questions the court may have of them; applications will not be allowed to drag on.

6. THE TRIAL

i) **The particular hazard of heavy fraud trials**

A heavy fraud or other complex trial has the potential to lose direction and focus. This is a disaster for three reasons:

a) The jury will lose track of the evidence, thereby prejudicing both prosecution and defence.

b) The burden on the defendants, the judge and indeed all involved will become intolerable.

c) Scarce public resources are wasted. Other prosecutions are delayed or – worse – may never happen. Fraud which is detected but not prosecuted (for resource reasons) undermines confidence.

ii) **Judicial mastery of the case**

a) It is necessary for the judge to exercise firm control over the conduct of the trial at all stages.

b) In order to do this the judge must read the witness statements and the documents, so that the judge can discuss case management issues with the advocates on – almost – an equal footing.

c) To this end, the judge should not set aside weeks or even days for pre-reading (see paragraph 3.i)b) above). Hopefully the judge will have gained a good grasp of the evidence during the case management hearings. Nevertheless, realistic reading time must be provided for the judge in advance of trial.

d) The role of the judge in a heavy fraud or other complex criminal trial is different from his/her role in a 'conventional' criminal trial. So far as possible, the judge should be freed from other duties and burdens, so that he/she can give the high degree of commitment which a heavy fraud trial requires. This will pay dividends in terms of saving weeks or months of court time.

iii) **The order of the evidence**

a) By the outset of the trial at the latest (and in most cases very much earlier) the judge must be provided with a schedule, showing the

The Trial

sequence of prosecution (and in an appropriate case defence) witnesses and the dates upon which they are expected to be called. This can only be prepared by discussion between prosecution and defence which the judge should expect, and say he/she expects, to take place: See: Criminal Procedure Rule 3.10. The schedule should, in so far as it relates to Prosecution witnesses, be developed in consultation with the witnesses, via the Witness Care Units, and with consideration given to their personal needs. Copies of the schedule should be provided for the Witness Service.

b) The schedule should be kept under review by the trial judge and by the parties. If a case is running behind or ahead of schedule, each witness affected must be advised by the party who is calling that witness at the earliest opportunity.

c) If an excessive amount of time is allowed for any witness, the judge can ask why. The judge may probe with the advocates whether the time envisaged for the evidence-in-chief or cross-examination (as the case may be) of a particular witness is really necessary.

iv) **Case management sessions**

a) The order of the evidence may have legitimately to be departed from. It will, however, be a useful for tool for monitoring the progress of the case. There should be periodic case management sessions, during which the judge engages the advocates upon a stock-taking exercise: asking, amongst other questions, 'where are we going?' and 'what is the relevance of the next three witnesses?'. This will be a valuable means of keeping the case on track. Rule 3.10 of the Criminal Procedure Rules will again assist the judge.

b) The judge may wish to consider issuing the occasional use of 'case management notes' to the advocates, in order to set out the judge's tentative views on where the trial may be going off track, which areas of future evidence are relevant and which may have become irrelevant (eg because of concessions, admissions in cross-examination and so forth). Such notes from the judge plus written responses from the advocates can, cautiously used, provide a valuable focus for debate during the periodic case management reviews held during the course of the trial.

v) **Controlling prolix cross-examination**.

a) Setting **rigid** time limits in advance for cross-examination is rarely appropriate – as experience has shown in civil cases; but a timetable is essential so that the judge can exercise control and so that there is a clear target to aim at for the completion of the evidence of each witness. Moreover the judge can and should indicate when cross-examination is irrelevant, unnecessary or time wasting. The judge

Appendix 9   *Control and Management of Heavy Fraud etc*

        may limit the time for further cross-examination of a particular witness.

vi) **Electronic presentation of evidence**

    a) Electronic presentation of evidence (EPE) has the potential to save huge amounts of time in fraud and other complex criminal trials and should be used more widely.

    b) HMCS is providing facilities for the easier use of EPE with a standard audio visual facility. Effectively managed, the savings in court time achieved by EPE more than justify the cost.

    c) There should still be a core bundle of those documents to which frequent reference will be made during the trial. The jury may wish to mark that bundle or to refer back to particular pages as the evidence progresses. EPE can be used for presenting all documents not contained in the core bundle.

    d) Greater use of other modern forms of graphical presentations should be made wherever possible.

vii) **Use of interviews**

    The Judge should consider extensive editing of self serving interviews, even when the defence want the jury to hear them in their entirety; such interviews are not evidence of the truth of their contents but merely of the defendant's reaction to the allegation.

viii) **Jury Management**

    a) The jury should be informed as early as possible in the case as to what the issues are in a manner directed by the Judge.

    b) The jury must be regularly updated as to the trial timetable and the progress of the trial, subject to warnings as to the predictability of the trial process.

    c) Legal argument should be heard at times that causes the least inconvenience to jurors.

    d) It is useful to consider with the advocates whether written directions should be given to the jury and, if so, in what form.

ix) **Maxwell hours**

    a) Maxwell hours should only be permitted after careful consideration and consultation with the Presiding Judge.

    b) Considerations in favour include:

        i) Legal argument can be accommodated without disturbing the jury;

ii) There is a better chance of a representative jury; iii) Time is made available to the judge, advocates and experts to do useful work in the afternoons

c) Considerations against include:

i) The lengthening of trials and the consequent waste of court time;

ii) The desirability of making full use of the jury once they have arrived at court;

iii) Shorter trials tend to diminish the need for special provisions eg there are fewer difficulties in empanelling more representative juries;

iv) They are unavailable if any defendant is in custody.

d) It may often be the case that a maximum of one day of Maxwell hours a week is sufficient; if so, it should be timetabled in advance to enable all submissions by advocates, supported by skeleton arguments served in advance, to be dealt with in the period after 1:30 pm on that day.

x) Livenote

If Livenote is used, it is important that all users continue to take a note of the evidence, otherwise considerable time is wasted in detailed reading of the entire daily transcript.

7. OTHER ISSUES

i) **Defence representation and defence costs**

a) Applications for change in representation in complex trials need special consideration; the ruling of HH Judge Wakerley QC (as he then was) in *Asghar Ali* has been circulated by the JSB.

b) Problems have arisen when the Legal Services Commission have declined to allow advocates or solicitors to do certain work; on occasions the matter has been raised with the judge managing or trying the case.

c) The Legal Services Commission has provided guidance to judges on how they can obtain information from the LSC as to the reasons for their decisions; further information in relation to this can be obtained from *Nigel Field, Head of the Complex Crime Unit, Legal Services Commission, 29–37 Red Lion Street, London, WC1R 4PP.*

Appendix 9 *Control and Management of Heavy Fraud etc*

ii) **Assistance to the Judge**

Experience has shown that in some very heavy cases, the judge's burden can be substantially offset with the provision of a Judicial Assistant or other support and assistance.

Appendix 10

Crown Prosecution Guidance: Proceeds Of Crime Act 2002, Part 7 – Money Laundering Offences

PRINCIPLE

Introduction to Money Laundering

Criminal confiscation and money laundering offences are inter-linked. In investigating what has happened to the proceeds of crime, money laundering offences are likely to be disclosed.

Money Laundering is the process by which criminal proceeds are sanitised to disguise their illicit origins. Acquisitive criminals will attempt to distance themselves from their crimes by finding safe havens for their profits where they can avoid confiscation orders, and where those proceeds can be made to appear legitimate.

Money laundering schemes can be very simple or highly sophisticated. Most sophisticated money laundering schemes involve three stages:

- Placement – the process of getting criminal money into the financial system;
- Layering – the process of moving money in the financial system through complex webs of transactions, often via offshore companies;
- Integration – the process by which criminal money ultimately becomes absorbed into the economy, such as through investment in real estate.

Prosecutions for money laundering can involve any of these stages in the money laundering process.

Code for Crown Prosecutors – considerations

Money laundering offences are invariably serious. In summary, money laundering

- Incentivises crime by rendering it profitable;

Appendix 10 *Crown Prosecution Guidance: Proceeds Of Crime Act 2002*

- Provides domestic and transnational organised crime with a cash flow to perpetrate further crimes; and
- Threatens the financial system and its institutions, both domestic and international.

Therefore, where there is sufficient evidence to meet the evidential test under the Code for Crown Prosecutors, the following Public Interest factors in favour of prosecution for offences of money laundering should be very carefully considered:

- The importance of making it more difficult for criminals to legitimise their ill-gotten gains;
- The importance of deterring professional launderers;
- The importance of protecting the integrity of financial institutions domestically and internationally.

Main types of Money Laundering prosecutions

There are 4 types of money laundering prosecution. There are, firstly, those 'mixed' cases in which money laundering can be charged or included on an indictment in which the underlying proceeds-generating predicate offence is included.

The subsets of this are:

- 'Own proceeds' or 'self laundering', where the defendant in a money laundering case may also be the author of the predicate crime;
- Laundering by a person or persons other than the author of the predicate offence.

Secondly, there are those cases where money laundering is the sole charge capable of proof or the easiest charge to prove. Again, there are two subsets:

- 'Own proceeds' laundering;
- Laundering by a person other than the author of the predicate offence.

GUIDANCE

Money laundering offences under the pre-POCA law

Under the pre-POCA law, there were separate offences for drug money laundering under the Criminal Justice Act 1988 and the Drug Trafficking Act 1994.

The relevant law is set out at (Archbold 2003 25–520).

Guidance

Transitional provisions

As the 2002 Act has substantially changed all principal money laundering offences and related definitions it will matter whether the conduct alleged to be the physical element of the offence was committed before or after the commencement of the Act. The provisions of the old legislation (DTA and CJA) will apply to conduct before the Act comes into force.

Part 7 of POCA came into force on 24 February 2003 and acts of money laundering begun on or after that date are offences under the new Act. When the predicate offence that generated the proceeds took place is immaterial in determining whether the Act applies.

S.340 (4) makes it clear that the new offences bite on the proceeds of criminal conduct that took place before commencement.

The new principle money laundering offences

General

The new principal money laundering offences are now found in sections 327, 328 and 329 of the Proceeds of Crime Act 2002. The legislation is set out in (Archbold 2006 33–8).

These offences come into force on 24 February 2003.

Money laundering is defined as an act which constitutes an offence under S.327, 328 and 329 or a conspiracy or attempt to commit such an offence. Money laundering includes counselling, aiding or abetting or procuring.

It should be noted that convictions for money laundering under sections 327 and 328 attract the use of the **lifestyle assumptions** under S.75 and schedule 2 Proceeds of Crime Act 2002.

Under the pre-existing law was that there were separate offences for drug money laundering under the Drug Trafficking Act 1994 and non-drug offences under the Criminal Justice Act 1988. The Crown sometimes had difficulties in pinpointing for the purposes of charging under the appropriate Act the source of the criminal proceeds, see *R v Ali & Others [2005] EWCA Crim 87*).

Offences under S.327, 328 and 329 replace the parallel drug and non-drug money laundering offences with single offences that do not distinguish between the proceeds of drug trafficking and other crime.

Criminal property

Under the Proceeds of Crime Act, the Crown has to prove that the laundered proceeds are **'criminal property'**, as defined in S.340 of the Proceeds of Crime Act: that is to say that the property constitutes a person's ***benefit*** from ***criminal conduct***.

Appendix 10   *Crown Prosecution Guidance: Proceeds Of Crime Act 2002*

Criminal conduct

'Criminal conduct' is all conduct which constitutes an offence in any part of the United Kingdom (which means that an 'all crimes' approach is adopted in respect of predicate crimes committed in the UK).

Offences which were committed abroad are relevant predicate crimes if laundering acts are committed within our jurisdiction where the predicate offence committed abroad (from which proceeds were generated) would also constitute an offence in any part of the United Kingdom if it occurred here (S.340 (2) b) (Archbold 2006 33–29).

It is immaterial whether the criminal conduct occurred prior to the Act becoming law so long as the laundering act takes place post commencement.

Proving that property is 'criminal property'

To prove that property is 'criminal property' (ie the proceeds of crime) the prosecutor must show the property:

- Constitutes benefit from criminal conduct or that it represents such a benefit (in whole or part and whether directly or indirectly) and;
- The alleged offender **knows or suspects** that it constitutes or represents such a benefit [section 340(3)].

The property which may comprise the benefit from criminal conduct is widely defined (see S.340 [9] and [10]) to include:

- Money;
- All forms of property or real estate;
- Things in action and other intangible or incorporeal property.

Property is obtained by a person if he obtains an interest in it.

Because of the definition of criminal property, there is **no distinction** between the proceeds of the defendant's **own crimes** and of **crimes committed by others** (see S.340 [4]). Thus laundering one's own proceeds is just as much money laundering, as similar activities performed by someone else, notably professional launderers on behalf of the authors of the predicate or underlying offences.

Own proceeds laundering applies to all 3 principal money laundering offences.

Proving that proceeds are the benefit from criminal conduct in money laundering prosecutions (proving the predicate offence).

Proving that proceeds are the benefit of **'criminal conduct'** will usually be done by circumstantial evidence.

Guidance

Where money laundering offences are proceeded with on the same indictment as the underlying crimes, the underlying criminal conduct will be proved as part of the proceedings to the requisite standard. Where the money laundering proceedings are 'standalone', there are two ways of proving criminal property, firstly by proving the type of offending that gave rise to the criminal property and secondly by relying upon circumstantial evidence (*R v Anwoir* [2008] EWCA Crim 1354).

It is **not** necessary in 'stand alone' money laundering prosecutions to wait for a conviction in relation to the 'criminal conduct' (ie the underlying or predicate offences giving rise to the criminal property).

Prosecutors are **not** required to prove that the property in question is the benefit of a **particular** or a **specific** act of criminal conduct, as such an interpretation would restrict the operation of the legislation. The prosecution need to be in a position, as a minimum, to be able to produce sufficient circumstantial evidence or other evidence from which inferences can be drawn to the required criminal standard that the property in question has a criminal origin.

Typically evidence of the criminal origin of proceeds may be provided in money laundering proceedings by:

- Accomplice evidence;

- Circumstantial evidence and/or other evidence;

- Forensic evidence (eg contamination of cash with drugs) from which inferences can be drawn that money came from drug trafficking;

- Evidence of complex audit trails, from which an accountancy expert may be able to conclude that the complexity of the transactions indicate that the property was the proceeds of crime. (Archbold 2006 10–66). While this was not a money laundering prosecution, by analogy, it would seem permissible for a witness to give expert evidence that the facts lead him to the conclusion that the property was the proceeds of crime);

- Evidence of the unlikelihood of the property being of legitimate origin – Where the prosecution proves D has no legitimate explanation for possessing the property in question a jury may be willing to draw an inference that it is proceeds of crime;

- Criminals often attempt to launder proceeds through a cash intensive business. Where the cash flows appear too large or the profit margins too high this may be capable of giving rise to expert evidence that the business will usually give rise to a particular level of profit and the profits are clearly excessive which together with other available evidence can be sufficient to prove the underlying criminality. See R. v. Boam 1998 Cr. Law Bulletin.

Appendix 10   *Crown Prosecution Guidance: Proceeds Of Crime Act 2002*

Section 327 offence – Concealing criminal property etc.

Section 327 simplifies and replaces S.49 of the Drug Trafficking Act 1994 and S.93C of the Criminal Justice Act 1988. See (Archbold 2006 33–11)

The actus reus of the offence under S.327 is:

- concealing criminal property;
- disguising criminal property;
- converting criminal property;
- transferring criminal property;
- removing criminal property from England and Wales.

It is an either way offence. A person convicted of an offence under this section is liable to imprisonment for 14 years or a fine or both.

Concealing or disguising criminal property is defined as concealing or disguising its nature, source, location, disposition, movement or ownership or any rights with respect to it [POCA section 327(3)].

As noted above the offender has to **'know or suspect'** that the criminal property represents a benefit from criminal conduct (by virtue of section 340 POCA). The prosecution can also rely on circumstantial evidence from which a jury can draw inferences that the defendant had the necessary knowledge or suspicion.

It is necessary therefore to prove:

- the act of concealing, disguising etc;
- in relation to property;
- which was a benefit from criminal conduct; and
- that the defendant knew or suspected that the property represented a benefit from criminal conduct.

Defences to section 327 offence

It should be noted that an offence is not committed if a person makes an 'authorised disclosure' under S.338 to a constable, a customs officer, or a nominated officer. This will absolve disclosures, such as suspicious transaction reports to the police and to designated compliance officers within companies made within the requisite timescales in S.338. The defence also applies to those who intended to make such a disclosure but had a reasonable excuse for not doing so.

S.327 also exonerates acts done in carrying out a function relating to enforcement of any provision of the Act, or of any other enactment relating to

Guidance

criminal conduct or benefit from criminal conduct. It is not uncommon for the police or other enforcement authorities to take possession of criminal property in the course of their official duties and to convert or transfer it, eg into an interest bearing account pending further investigation.

Section 328 offence – Arrangements

Section 328 simplifies and replaces S.50 of the Drug Trafficking Act 1994 and S.93A of the Criminal Justice Act 1988. This offence potentially catches a large range of involvement in money laundering offences usually at the layering and integration stages. See (Archbold 2006 33–12).

This is the offence which will often be apt for the prosecution of those who launder on behalf of others. It can catch persons who work in financial or credit institutions, accountants etc, who in the course of their work facilitate money laundering by or on behalf of other persons. For legal advisers, please see the case of Bowman & Fels [2005] EWCA Civ 226, in which it was held that steps taken in court proceedings are not 'acts' for the purposes of s328.

The language of the physical acts is deliberately wide.

Thus the prosecution has to prove that:

- the defendant enters into or becomes concerned in an arrangement;
- which he knows or suspects facilitates (by whatever means) the acquisition, retention, use or control;
- of criminal property;
- by or on behalf of another person.

The offence is either way and carries the same maximum penalty as offences under S.327.

The criminal origin of proceeds can be proved in the same ways as set out at Proving that proceeds are the benefit from criminal conduct (the predicate offence) above.

Defences to section 328 offence

The same defences against committing the offence as are included in S.327 are included in S.328. See Defences to section 327 offence above.

Section 329 offence – Acquisition, use and possession

S.329 unifies and replaces S.51 Drug Trafficking Act and S.93B of Criminal Justice Act 1988.

Section 329 appears at (Archbold 2006 33–13). This offence can be committed if a defendant:

Appendix 10 *Crown Prosecution Guidance: Proceeds Of Crime Act 2002*

- uses criminal property;
- or (passively) possesses criminal property.

Similarly, it is an either way offence attracting the same maximum penalties as offences under sections 327 and 328.

It does **not** attract the lifestyle assumptions on conviction.

The prosecution has to prove:

- acquisition use or possession;
- of property;
- which was the benefit of criminal conduct;
- and that the defendant had the necessary knowledge or suspicion that the property represented a benefit from criminal conduct.

Possession means having physical custody of criminal property.

The Section 333 'Tipping off' offence (see below) may be available to the prosecution where the evidence is insufficient to prove the predicate offence against the defendant.

Defences to section 329 offence

These are set out in section 329(2).

The same defences as applying to offences under section 327 and 328 are provided for by section 329 (2) (a) and (b).

However, additionally a person does **not** commit an offence under this section if he acquired, used or had possession of the property for 'adequate consideration.' The defence replicates that available under the offences in S.93 B of the Criminal Justice Act 1988. It is available to cover those cases where the funds or property have been acquired by a purchase for a proper market price or similar exchange and to cater for any injustice which might otherwise arise: for example, in the case of tradesmen who are paid for ordinary consumable goods and services in money that comes from crime.

This defence will also apply where professional advisors (such as solicitors or accountants) receive money for or on account of costs (whether from the client or from another person on the client's behalf). This defence would not be available to a professional where the value of the work carried out or intended to be carried out on behalf of the client was significantly less than the money received for or on account of costs.

If a person pays proper consideration but it can be shown that he knows or suspects that such payment may help another to carry out criminal conduct he is not treated as having paid proper consideration (Section 328 (3)(c). There is a definition of inadequate consideration in sub-section (3).

Guidance

Failing to disclose, tipping off etc

Some countries underpin their preventive anti-money laundering regimes with administrative sanctions only. The UK has chosen to underpin the preventive regime with criminal sanctions to emphasise the importance of proper systems of reporting and control. The FSA now has strong powers to prosecute criminally breaches of the money laundering regulations, though the general criminal prosecuting authorities (CPS, SFO, Customs and Excise etc) are responsible for offences under Sections 330–333.

S.330 Failure to disclose: regulated sector

This offence is new and was controversial during the passage of the legislation. It is set out at (Archbold 2006 33–14).

The failure to disclose relates to money laundering offences under the Proceeds of Crime Act 2002 (section 327–329) so by its very nature it can only apply to information about laundering carried out after commencement date, ie 24 February 2003.

It places a **duty** on employees in a business in the regulated sector (ie a sector that has a supervisory or other appropriate regulatory regime – such as the banks) to make reports where they 'know or suspect' that another person is engaged in money laundering and where (even if they do not know or suspect) they 'have reasonable grounds for knowing or suspecting' that a person is engaged in money laundering.

The *'reasonable grounds for knowing or suspecting'* standard (ie a 'should have known' or negligence test) is new. The rationale for this is that a higher standard of diligence is expected in anti-money laundering prevention in the regulated sector, where comprehensive preventive systems (in line with international standards), are required to be in place. These include requirements to have in place internal systems for reporting and control, and education and training programmes.

The offence is either way and carries a maximum term of 5 years imprisonment or a fine or both on indictment.

To prove the offence it is necessary to show that:

- **information came to a person in the course of business in the regulated sector.** Schedule 9 as amended by the Money Laundering Regulations 2003 S.I. No. 3075 of 2003 and the Proceeds of Crime Act 2002 (Business in the Regulated Sector and Supervisory Authorities) Order 2003, S.I. No. 3074 of 2003, provides a list which determines what is a business in the regulated sector and what are the supervisory authorities. Bureaux de change, cheque cashing, money transfer stations, casinos, estate agents, insolvency practitioners, tax advisers, company and trust formations, accountants, lawyers (in connection with financial

Appendix 10 *Crown Prosecution Guidance: Proceeds Of Crime Act 2002*

or property transactions) and dealers in goods to a value of 15,000 euros or more now form part of the regulated sector;

- the information was information which the employee knew, suspected or caused the employee to have reasonable grounds for suspecting that another person is engaged in money laundering;
- **the employee failed to make the disclosure to a nominated officer** (usually the specially appointed compliance officer in a regulated business) or to the Suspicious Transaction Report Receiving Agency (NCIS).

Broadly the regulated activities covered are:

- accepting deposits;
- insurance;
- dealing in investments as principal or agent;
- arranging deals or investments;
- managing investments;
- safeguarding and administering investments;
- sending dematerialised instructions;
- establishing collective investment schemes;
- advising on investments;
- issuing electronic money.

Section 22 of the Financial Services and Markets Act 2000 gives greater assistance on the meaning of accepting deposits and carrying out contracts of long term insurance.

Where a business carries out some activities that are listed in Schedule 9 and some which are not, then only employees carrying out the listed activities will be caught by the offence.

Defences to section 330 offence

A person does not commit an offence under this section if:

- he has a reasonable excuse for not disclosing the information or other matter;
- he is a professional legal adviser and the information or other matter came to him in privileged circumstances (see below);
- he does not know or suspect that another person is engaged in money laundering; and

Guidance

- he has not been provided by his employer with such training as is specified by the Secretary of State by order for the purposes of this section.

In deciding whether a person has committed an offence under this section the court must consider:

- Whether he followed any relevant published Treasury approved guidance drawn up by the industry. Thus, when considering prosecutions a prosecutor must be familiar with the relevant supervisory guidance for the appropriate part of the regulated sector issued by the industry's Joint Money Laundering Steering Group.

In the case of legal advisers attention is drawn to S.331 (10) and (11) as to whether disclosures need to be made which potentially breach legal professional privilege. See *Bowman v Fels* [2005] EWCA Civ 226.

Section 330(10) sets out the circumstances in which legal professional privilege applies.

Section 330(11) provides that the protection afforded by legal professional privilege does not apply where 'the information or other matter is communicated or given with the intention of furthering a criminal purpose'.

Where a solicitor believes that information is communicated to him by his client in privileged circumstances and, therefore, does not make a disclosure but, unknown to the solicitor, the client is consulting him or her with the intention of furthering a criminal purpose, legal professional privilege would not apply. In these circumstances, where the solicitor had no reason to be aware of the client's secret purpose, he would have the defence of reasonable excuse under section 330(6)(a) of POCA.

In considering a case on these facts, prosecutors should be aware that during the passage of the Proceeds of Crime Bill, Lord Rooker said:

> 'The criminal law is quite clear: where a criminal offence is silent as to its mental element, the courts must read in the appropriate mental element. Therefore, in circumstances where a legal advisor did not know that information was not legally privileged, the courts would read in a requirement that he could not be convicted unless he did know.'

Offences under S.330 can be prosecuted by the Crown Prosecution Service where the police have investigated or where the Financial Services Authority (FSA) has passed information to the CPS or police. Evidence of an offence may become available to the FSA during their inspection processes. The FSA cannot bring a criminal prosecution under S.330.

Section 331 Failure to disclose offence: nominated officers in the regulated sector

See (Archbold 2006 33–19)

Appendix 10 *Crown Prosecution Guidance: Proceeds Of Crime Act 2002*

Section 331 creates a separate offence of failure to disclose in respect of nominated officers (ie compliance officers) who receive disclosures based under S.330 and who do not pass the information to the National Criminal Intelligence Service (NCIS) as the disclosure receiving agency when they:

- know or suspect; or
- have reasonable grounds for knowing or suspecting that another person is engaged in money laundering.

The offence is triable either way with the same maximum penalty on indictment as an offence under section 330 (up to 5 years imprisonment).

Section 332 Failure to disclose offence: other nominated officers

Section 332 creates a further offence of failure to disclose by nominated officers **outside** the regulated sector.

The offence is also either way and carries the same maximum penalty on indictment as an offence under section 330.

It cannot be committed by negligence. The mental element of this offence is knowledge or suspicion.

Section 333 Tipping off offence

(Archbold 2006 33–20)

Section 333 creates the offence of making a disclosure likely to prejudice a money laundering investigation being undertaken by law enforcement authorities. It replaces S.53 Drug trafficking Offences Act 1994 and S.93D of the Criminal Justice Act 1988.

This is an either way offence with a maximum penalty on indictment of 5 years imprisonment or a fine or both.

It is a defence to a charge under S.333 that a person;

> did not know or suspect that the disclosure was likely to prejudice an investigation;
>
> that the disclosure was made in connection with a function relating to enforcement; Or
>
> if the information is passed on in circumstances that amount to legal privilege, but not if the information is passed on to further a criminal enterprise.

CHARGING PRACTICE, PLEA ACCEPTANCE AND OTHER ISSUES

'Mixed cases' (where the author of the predicate offence can also be charged with laundering)

This is an area where careful exercise of prosecutorial discretion is required, particularly with regard to the possession offence under S.329.

It is suggested that in considering whether to add money laundering charges generally the following factors should be borne in mind:

- Parliament has decided money laundering offences are very serious carrying a maximum of 14 years. All the 3 principal money laundering offences potentially carry heavier penalties than most predicate offences. Theft, for instance, carries 7 years. Money laundering will therefore often be the most serious offence available.

- The underlying offence ought normally to be proceeded with, as it represents the conduct which gives rise to the criminal proceedings.

- Money laundering and the underlying criminality are separate offences. Money laundering activities should not be seen simply as 'part and parcel' of the underlying criminality. As the courts have often said in connection with theft and receiving – receiving is the more serious offence because, without handlers and receivers there would be no thieves. However prosecutors should recall that the practice of charging theft and handling in the alternative is followed where the evidence is unclear as to whether the defendant is a thief or a handler. In these types of case both offences (the underlying crime and the money laundering offence) will be capable of proof.

- A money laundering charge ought to be considered where the proceeds are more than de minimis in any circumstances where the defendant who is charged with the underlying offence has done more than simply consume his proceeds of crime.

- A charge under section 329 of possession of laundered proceeds, however, may not be necessary, for instance where proceeds were simply 'kept under the bed'. An application for confiscation of the actual benefit of the offence may be sufficient in those circumstances.

- Where, however, there is any **significant attempt to transfer or conceal ill-gotten gains money laundering should normally be considered as an additional charge**, in part because the purpose of the concealment will be to defeat or avoid prosecution and confiscation.

- A careful judgement will need to be made as to whether it is in the public interest to proceed with the money laundering offence in the event of a

Appendix 10 *Crown Prosecution Guidance: Proceeds Of Crime Act 2002*

plea to the underlying criminality by a defendant who is also indicted for laundering his **own** proceeds. The prosecutor should take into account whether the laundering activity involves such a significant attempt to conceal ill-gotten gains that a court may consider a consecutive sentence. Prosecutors should not simply proceed with a money laundering charge in this situation to trigger the lifestyle assumptions in respect of convictions for money laundering under S.327 or S.328. To do so, for no other reason, could attract abuse of process arguments.

- In a 'mixed' case, where the laundering is done by X on behalf of Y (the author of the predicate offence), it may be appropriate to proceed against Y for the underlying crime and X in relation to the laundering offence in the same indictment. This mirrors the position where a thief and handler are prosecuted in the same indictment in relation to the same stolen goods. Where the investigation has followed the money trail and there is sufficient nexus between the underlying offences and the money laundering then the case may benefit from being run together in one indictment, if it enables the prosecution to be presented in a clear and simple way. The jury will be able to take a global view of the evidence and the inclusion of the launderer on the indictment may strengthen the prosecution case. Care should be taken not to overload the indictment, which could lead to a successful application to sever.

Handling stolen goods

It is important to note that money laundering offences are not confined to cases involving money. Under the Proceeds of Crime Act, the prosecution must prove that the laundered proceeds are **'criminal property'**, as defined in section 340: that is to say that the property constitutes a person's **benefit** from **criminal conduct.**

Therefore, there will need to be a careful judgement in those cases where the prosecution could charge money laundering based on possession or an offence of handling stolen goods.

Prosecutors may consider charging a money laundering offence where either a defendant has possessed criminal proceeds:

- in large amounts; or
- in lesser amounts, but repeatedly and where assets are laundered for profit.

Prosecutors should take into account that charging money laundering will trigger the lifestyle provisions of POCA.

Reference should be made to the section on Handling Stolen Goods in Theft Acts elsewhere in the Legal Guidance manual.

It is permissible to draw compendious indictments that allege acquisition, possession or use Indictment Precedent Manual.

Prosecutors are advised to particularise alternative counts or charges where the evidence supports each of the relevant mental elements of the offence, so the court understands the basis of a jury's decision.

PROCEDURE

The CPS is required to report how it has contributed to the overall national Assets Recovery Strategy. Accordingly, Areas are required to keep records of money laundering prosecutions as instructed and submit quarterly returns (via Area Business Managers).

Appendix 11

Attorney General's Guidelines for Prosecutors on the Use of the Common Law Offence of Conspiracy to Defraud*

SUMMARY

1 – This guidance concerns the issues which the Attorney General asks prosecuting authorities in England and Wales to consider before using the common law offence of conspiracy to defraud, in the light of the implementation of the Fraud Act 2006. It may be supplemented by departmental-specific guidance issued by individual directors of the prosecuting authorities.

BACKGROUND

2 – When the Fraud Act 2006 comes into force on 15 January 2007, the prosecution will be able to use modern and flexible statutory offences of fraud. The 2006 Act replaces the deception offences contained in the Theft Acts 1968–1996 with a general offence of fraud that can be committed in 3 ways:

- fraud by false representation
- fraud by failing to disclose information
- fraud by abuse of position.

It also introduces other offences which can be used in particular circumstances, notably:

- new offences to tackle the possession and supply of articles for use in fraud
- a new offence of fraudulent trading applicable to sole traders and other businesses not caught by the existing offence in section 458 of the Companies Act 1985

---

* This guidance was issued by the Attorney General's Office on 29 November 2012. First published 2007.

Appendix 11 *Attorney General's Guidelines*

3 – The new offences are designed to catch behaviour that previously fell through gaps in the Theft Acts and could only be prosecuted as conspiracy to defraud. Indeed the Act is based on a Law Commission report (Cm 5560) which also recommended the abolition of the common law offence of conspiracy to defraud. The argument is that the offence is unfairly uncertain, and wide enough to have the potential to catch behaviour that should not be criminal. Furthermore it can seem anomalous that what is legal if performed by one person should be criminal if performed by many.

4 – However, consultations showed a widespread view in favour of retention of common law conspiracy to defraud, and the government decided to retain it for the meantime, but accepted the case for considering repeal in the longer term. Whether there is a continuing need for retention of the common law offence is one of the issues that will be addressed in the Home Office review of the operation of the Fraud Act 2006, which will take place 3 years after its implementation.

5 – In 2003, 14,928 defendants were proceeded against in England and Wales for crimes of fraud; 1018 of these were charged with the common law crime of conspiracy to defraud of which 44% were found guilty (compared with 71% for the statutory fraud offences). The expectation now is that the common law offence will be used to a significantly lesser extent once the Fraud Act 2006 has come into force.

ISSUES TO BE CONSIDERED IN USING THE COMMON LAW OFFENCE

6 – In selecting charges in fraud cases, the prosecutor should first consider:

- whether the behaviour could be prosecuted under statute – whether under the Fraud Act 2006 or another Act or as a statutory conspiracy
- whether the available statutory charges adequately reflect the gravity of the offence

7 – Statutory conspiracy to commit a substantive offence should be charged if the alleged agreement satisfies the definition in section I of the Criminal Law Act 1977, provided that there is no wider dishonest objective that would be Important to the presentation of the prosecution case in reflecting the gravity of the case.

8 – Section 12 of the Criminal Justice Act 1987 provides that common law conspiracy to defraud may be charged even if the conduct agreed upon will involve the commission of a statutory offence. However, Lord Bingham said in *R v Rimmington and R v Goldstein* [(2005) UKHL 63]:

> 'I would not go to the length of holding that conduct may never be lawfully prosecuted as a generally expressed common law crime where it falls within the terms of a specific statutory provision, but good practice and respect for

the primacy of statute do in my judgment require that conduct falling within the terms of a specific statutory provision should be prosecuted under that provision unless there is good reason for doing otherwise.'

9 – In the Attorney General's view the common law charge may still be appropriate in the type of cases set out in paragraphs 12–15, but in order to understand the circumstances under which conspiracy to defraud is used prosecutors should make a record of the reasons for preferring that charge.

RECORDS OF DECISIONS

10 – Where a charge of common law conspiracy to defraud is proposed the case lawyer must consider and set out in writing in the review note:

- how much such a charge will add to the amount of evidence likely to be called both by the prosecution and the defence
- the justification for using the charge, and why specific statutory offences are inadequate or otherwise inappropriate

Thereafter, and before charge, the use of this charge should be specifically approved by a supervising lawyer experienced in fraud cases. Equivalent procedures to ensure proper consideration of the charge and recording of the decision should be applied by all prosecuting authorities in their case review processes.

11 – Information from these records will be collected retrospectively for the review to be conducted in 3 years. It will enable the identification of where and why the common law offence has been used. It could then also form the basis for any future work on whether. and if so how, to replace the common law or whether it can simply and safely be repealed. It is expected that in 3 years the government will be able to review the situation in the light of the practical operation not only of the new fraud offences, but of other relevant changes. These include the Lord Chief Justice's protocol on the control and management of heavy fraud cases, and the sample count provisions in the Domestic Violence, Crime and Victims Act 2004. Any actual or proposed changes to the law on assisting and encouraging crime in the light of the Law Commission's study of that issue [Cm 6878, published in July 2006] will also be taken into account.

A – *Conduct that can more effectively be prosecuted as conspiracy to defraud*

12 – There may be cases where the interests of justice can only be served by presenting to a court an overall picture which cannot be achieved by charging a series of substantive offences or statutory conspiracies. Typically, such cases will involve some, but not necessarily all of the following:

Appendix 11 *Attorney General's Guidelines*

- evidence of several significant but different kinds of criminality
- several jurisdictions
- different types of victims, eg individuals, banks, website administrators, credit card companies
- organised crime networks

13 – The proper presentation of such cases as statutory conspiracies could lead to:

- large numbers of separate counts to reflect the different conspiracies
- severed trials for single or discrete groups of conspiracies
- evidence in one severed trial being deemed inadmissible in another

14 – If so, the consequences might be that no one court would receive a cohesive picture of the whole case which would allow sentencing on a proper basis. In contrast a single count of common law conspiracy to defraud might, in such circumstances, reflect the nature and extent of criminal conduct in a way that prosecuting the underlying statutory offences or conspiracies would fall to achieve.

B – Conduct that can only be prosecuted as conspiracy to defraud

15 – Examples of such conduct might include but are not restricted to agreements to the following courses of action:

- the dishonest obtaining of land and other property which cannot be stolen such as intellectual property not protected by the Copyright, Designs and Patents Act 1988 and the Trademarks Act 1994, and other confidential information – the Fraud Act will bite where there is intent to make a gain or cause a loss through false representation, failure to disclose information where there is a legal obligation to do so, or the abuse of position
- dishonestly infringing another's right; for example the dishonest exploitation of another's patent in the absence of a legal duty to disclose information about its existence
- where it is intended that the final offence be committed by someone outside the conspiracy
- cases where the accused cannot be proved to have had the necessary degree of knowledge of the substantive offence to be perpetrated

Index

Abuse of position
generally, 1.18–1.20
terminology, 1.21
Abuse of process
common law, 8.2–8.3
damage,
definition, 8.4–8.7
delay
  case law, 8.16
  complexity, 8.20
  documents, 8.19
  duration, 8.15
  factors, 8.14–8.15
  generally, 8.10–8.13
  guidance, 8.17
  justification, 8.15
  prejudice, 8.15
  trial process, 8.18
fairness test
  delay, 8.10–8.20
  generally, 8.8
  introduction, 8.5
  other issues, 8.21
  relevant issues, 8.9
good faith, 8.21
human rights, and
  delay, 8.10–8.13
  generally, 8.3
  introduction, 8.1
inadvertence, inefficiency or deliberate conduct, 8.21
introduction, 8.1
judicial controls at trial, 8.22
relevant issues, 8.9
right to a fair trial, 8.1
Accountants
insider trading, and, 3.236
mortgage fraud, and, 3.44

Acquisition of criminal property
see also **Money laundering**
'criminal conduct', 3.269
criminal property, 3.266–3.268
generally, 3.302
inadequate consideration, 3.303
'property', 3.268
Appeals
preparatory hearings, 6.20–6.21
terminating rulings, 6.27–6.29
'Article'
definition, 1.27
Articles for use in frauds
making or supplying 1.25–1.27
mortgage fraud, and, 3.27–3.28
possession, 1.22–1.24
ATM machines
articles for use in frauds, and, 1.27
Attempts
money laundering, and, 3.281–3.282
Attorney-General's guidance
conspiracy to defraud, and, 2.5
disclosure, and
  background, 7.10
  commencement date, 7.41
  general principles and practices, 7.43
  introduction, 7.12
  overview, 7.1
  purpose, 7.42
Missing Trader Intra-Community fraud, and, 3.143
Authorised disclosures
money laundering, and
  generally, 3.304
  introduction, 3.295

Index

Bank account information
  mortgage fraud, and, 3.54
Bank managers
  mortgage fraud, and, 3.42
Bar code labels
  articles for use in frauds, and, 1.27
Becoming concerned in an arrangement to facilitate
  see also **Money laundering**
  acts preparatory, 3.300
  generally, 3.299
  legal professionals, and, 3.301
Benefit fraud
  money laundering, and, 3.294
Birth certificates
  articles for use in frauds, and, 1.27
'Black boxes'
  articles for use in frauds, and, 1.27
Body corporate
  offences, and, 1.33
  sentencing, and, 9.19–9.28
'Boiler Room' fraud
  breach of general prohibition on carrying out regulated activity,. 3.87–3.97
  charges, 3.85
  conspiracy to defraud, 3.86
  dealing in investments as principal/agent, 3.91
  defences, 3.98–3.100
  financial promotion, 3.95
  overview, 3.80–3.84
  Regulation S shares, 3.84
  regulatory offences, 3.87–3.97
  share sales, 3.83–3.84
Breach of general prohibition on carrying out regulated activity
  'Boiler Room' fraud,. 3.87–3.97
  'Ponzi' frauds, and, 3.69–3.75
Brokers
  mortgage fraud, and, 3.42–3.43
Buy to let
  mortgage fraud, and, 3.9

Carbon credit fraud
  carbon credit certificates, 3.178–3.180
  certified emission reductions (CER), 3.179
  environmental background, 3.177
  introduction, 3.175–3.176

Carbon credit fraud – *contd*
  regulation of trading by FCA, 3.180
  trading, 3.181–3.183
  voluntary emission reductions (VER), 3.179
Cautions
  conditional police cautions
    DPP guidance, 5.14
    either-way offences, 5.15
    financial penalties, 5.17
    generally, 5.14
    indictable-only offences, 5.16
    PACE Code of practice, 5.14
  deferred prosecution agreements
    behaviour, 5.21
    cessation, 5.28
    consequences, 5.25
    content, 5.27–5.30
    Crime and Courts Act 2013 Sch. 17, 5.20
    Criminal Procedure Rules, 5.18, 5.64–5.66
    designated prosecutors, 5.24
    disclosure, 5.32–5.35
    DPP/SFO Code, 5.18, 5.31–5.63
    expiry date, 5.28
    general principles, 5.36–5.63
    guidance, 5.31–5.66
    introduction, 5.18–5.19
    operation, 5.24–5.26
    relevant offences, 5.22–5.23
    requirements, 5.29
    Sentencing Council guidelines, 5.31
    statement of facts, 5.27
  introduction, 5.1–5.2
  police cautions
    College of Policing Gravity Factors Matrix, 5.8
    conclusion, 5.13
    either-way offences, 5.7
    evidential test, 5.9
    factors, 5.4
    generally, 5.3–5.8
    indictable-only offences, 5.5–5.6
    matters to which regard be had, 5.6
    MoJ guidance, 5.4
    National Decision Model, 5.8
    procedures, 5.11–5.12
    public interest test, 5.10

432

Certificates
articles for use in frauds, and, 1.27
CHAPS payments
fraud offence under s.1, and, 1.9
Charges
'Boiler Room' fraud, and, 3.85
Missing Trader Intra-Community fraud, and, 3.137–3.141
mortgage fraud, and, 3.6
'Ponzi' frauds, and, 3.66
Cheating the public revenue
introduction, 3.184
nature of offence, 3.185
Civil recovery
mortgage fraud, and, 3.62
Companies House
mortgage fraud, and, 3.49
Company credit cards
fraud offence under s.1, and, 1.9
Compensation
sentencing, and, 9.16
Complex fraud cases
disclosure, and, 7.10
preparatory hearings, and, 6.13–6.17
Computer programmes
articles for use in frauds, and, 1.27
Concealing criminal property
see also **Money laundering**
generally, 3.298
Conditional police cautions
see also **Cautions**
DPP guidance, 5.14
either-way offences, 5.15
financial penalties, 5.17
generally, 5.14
indictable-only offences, 5.16
PACE Code of practice, 5.14
Confidence frauds
fraud offence under s 1, and, 1.9
Confiscation
Missing Trader Intra-Community fraud, and, 3.168–3.174
sentencing, and, 9.16
Conspiracy to defraud
Attorney-General's guidance, 2.5
'Boiler Room' fraud, and, 3.86
introduction, 1.4
jurisdiction, 2.6–2.8
money laundering, and, 3.283
overview, 2.1–2.5

Conspiracy to defraud – *contd*
'Ponzi' frauds, and, 3.67
scope of offence, 2.9–2.13
sentencing, 2.1
Contracts for difference (CFD)
insider trading, and, 3.231
Convention on the Protection of the EUROPEAN Community's Financial Interests 1995
generally, 1.5
Converting criminal property
see also **Money laundering**
generally, 3.298
Council tax records
mortgage fraud, and, 3.51
'Crash for cash'
fraud by false representation, and, 1.13
Credit card skimming devices
articles for use in frauds, and, 1.27
'Criminal conduct'
money laundering, and, 3.269
'Criminal lifestyle'
money laundering, and, 3.296
Criminal Procedure Rules
deferred prosecution agreements, and, 5.18, 5.64–5.66
Missing Trader Intra-Community fraud, and, 3.143
preparatory hearings, and, 6.11–6.12
Criminal property
'criminal conduct', 3.269
disguising, 3.298
generally, 3.266–3.267
'property', 3.268

Data
articles for use in frauds, and, 1.27
Dealing in investments as principal/agent
'Boiler Room' fraud, and, 3.91
Dealing in securities
insider trading, and, 3.218–3.219
Defence statements
disclosure, and, 7.11
Defences
'Boiler Room' fraud, and, 3.98–3.100
insider trading, and, 3.240

Index

Defences – *contd*
  Missing Trader Intra-Community fraud, and, 3.123–3.136
  possession of criminal property, and, 3.209–3.211
Deferred prosecution agreements (DPAs)
see also **Cautions**
  balancing exercises, 5.38
  behaviour, 5.21
  breaches of terms, 5.53–5.56
  cessation, 5.28
  consequences, 5.25
  content, 5.27–5.30
  Crime and Courts Act 2013 Sch. 17, 5.20
  Criminal Procedure Rules, 5.18, 5.64–5.66
  designated prosecutors, 5.24
  disclosure, 5.32–5.35
  discontinuance, 5.59–5.60
  DPP/SFO Code, 5.18, 5.31–5.63
  expiry date, 5.28
  final hearings, 5.49–5.52
  financial penalties, 5.47
  general principles, 5.36–5.63
  guidance, 5.31–5.66
  introduction, 5.18–5.19
  model process, 5.63
  operation, 5.24–5.26
  preliminary hearings, 5.48
  private hearings, 5.61
  procedure, 5.39
  relevant offences, 5.22–5.23
  requirements, 5.29
  Sentencing Council guidelines, 5.31
  statement of facts, 5.27, 5.43
  terms, 5.44–5.46
  test to be considered, 5.37
  unused material, 5.42
  use of information obtained, 5.40–5.41
  variation, 5.57–5.58
Delay
  abuse of process, and
    case law, 8.16
    complexity, 8.20
    documents, 8.19
    duration, 8.15
    factors, 8.14–8.15
    generally, 8.10–8.13

Delay – *contd*
  abuse of process, and – *contd*
    guidance, 8.17
    justification, 8.15
    prejudice, 8.15
    trial process, 8.18
Directors' disqualification
  fraudulent trading, and, 3.261
  sentencing, and, 9.39–9.42
Disclosure
  Attorney-General's Guidelines
    background, 7.10
    commencement date, 7.41
    general principles and practices, 7.43
    introduction, 7.12
    overview, 7.1
    purpose, 7.42
  common law, 7.4
  complex fraud cases, 7.10
  Criminal Procedures and Investigations Act 1996, and 7.5–7.15
  defence statements, 7.11
  deferred prosecution agreements, and, 5.32–5.35
  Disclosure Protocol
    background, 7.10
    generally, 7.12–7.15
    overview, 7.1
  e-disclosure, 7.16–7.25
  effectiveness, 7.38–7.40
  encryption, 7.26
  examination of material, 7.27–7.32
  guidance
    generally, 7.10–7.13
    introduction, 7.1
  human rights, and, 7.3
  importance, 7.2
  introduction, 7.1–7.3
  Missing Trader Intra-Community fraud, and
    'creeping disclosure', 3.146–3.148
    difficulties, 3.144–3.161
    generally, 3.142
    'kept in the dark', 3.149–3.152
    Operation Venison, 3.149–3.152
    Operation Vitric, 3.146–3.148
    public interest immunity, and, 3.144

Index

Disclosure – *contd*
Missing Trader Intra-Community fraud, and – *contd*
source of guidance, 3.143
systematic failures, 3.153–3.161
practice, in, 7.33–7.37
public interest immunity, 7.59–7.68
record keeping, 7.31–7.32
RIPA 2000 Part III, and, 7.26
right to a fair trial, and, 7.3
scheduling, 7.32
sentencing, and, 7.69
sifting material, 7.27–7.32
statutory basis, 7.5–7.15
third parties, by
generally, 7.44–7.53
held overseas, 7.54–7.58
unused material, 7.10
Disguising criminal property
see also **Money laundering**
generally, 3.298
Drug trafficking
money laundering, and, 3.307
Due diligence defence
Missing Trader Intra-Community fraud, and, 3.120
'Ponzi' frauds, and, 3.78

E-disclosure
generally, 7.16–7.25
Electricity meter devices
articles for use in frauds, and, 1.27
Electronic data or program
articles for use in frauds, and, 1.27
Electronic tags
sentencing, and, 9.18
Encryption
disclosure, and, 7.26
Entering into an arrangement to facilitate
see also **Money laundering**
acts preparatory, 3.300
generally, 3.299
legal professionals, and, 3.301
Estate agents
mortgage fraud, and, 3.53
EU law
Fraud Act 2006, and, 1.5
Expert evidence
insider trading, and, 3.241

Failure to disclose information
generally, 1.15–1.17
terminology, 1.21
Failure to pay tax
money laundering, and, 3.270–3.276
Fairness
abuse of process, and
delay, 8.10–8.20
generally, 8.8
introduction, 8.5
other issues, 8.21
relevant issues, 8.9
Fake documents
articles for use in frauds, and, 1.27
False accounting
mortgage fraud, and, 3.31–3.34
False representation
generally, 1.10–1.14
'representation', 1.12
terminology, 1.21
Financial promotion
'Boiler Room' fraud, and, 3.95
Financial reporting orders
generally, 9.32–9.34
introduction, 9.16
First-tier Tribunal
background reading, 5.74
case law, 5.75–5.76
closing speeches, 5.73
denial of claim for repayment of VAT, 5.67
examination in chief, 5.71
introduction, 5.67–5.68
knowledge, 5.74
opening statements, 5.70
practice and procedure, 5.69–5.73
representation, 5.69
s. 276 notices, 5.67
witnesses. 5/72
Framework Decision of 28 May 2001
generally, 1.5
Fraud (s 1 offence)
generally, 1.6–1.9
'Ponzi' frauds, and, 3.68
Fraud Act 2006
'article', 1.27
articles for use in frauds
making or supplying 1.25–1.27
possession, 1.22–1.24
background, 1.3

435

Index

Fraud Act 2006 – *contd*
  body corporate, and, 1.33
  commencement date, 1.1
  conspiracy to defraud, 1.4
  EU law, and, 1.5
  fraud (s 1 offence), 1.6–1.9
  fraud by abuse of position
    generally, 1.18–1.20
    terminology, 1.21
  fraud by failing to disclose information
    generally, 1.15–1.17
    terminology, 1.21
  fraud by false representation
    generally, 1.10–1.14
    terminology, 1.21
  fraudulent trading by non-corporate offenders, 1.28–1.30
  'gain', 1.21
  introduction, 1.1–1.5
  liability of company officers, 1.33
  'loss', 1.21
  making or supplying articles for use in frauds
    generally, 1.25–1.26
    terminology, 1.27
  mortgage fraud, and
    fraud by failing to disclose information, 3.25–3.26
    fraud by false representation, 3.20–3.24
    introduction, 3.19
    making or supplying articles for use in frauds, 3.27–3.28
  objective, 1.2
  obtaining services by dishonesty, 1.31–1.32
  offences
    articles for use in frauds, 1.22–1.27
    fraud, 1.6–1.9
    fraud by abuse of position, 1.18–1.21
    fraud by failing to disclose information, 1.15–1.17
    fraud by false representation, 1.10–1.14
    participating in fraudulent business, 1.28–1.30
  participating in fraudulent business, 1.28–1.30

Fraud Act 2006 – *contd*
  possession of articles for use in frauds
    generally, 1.22–1.24
    terminology, 1.27
  'property', 1.21
  purpose, 1.3
  scope, 1.2
Fraud by abuse of position
  generally, 1.18–1.20
  terminology, 1.21
Fraud by failing to disclose information
  generally, 1.15–1.17
  mortgage fraud, and, 3.25–3.26
  terminology, 1.21
Fraud by false representation
  generally, 1.10–1.14
  mortgage fraud, and, 3.20–3.24
  'representation', 1.12
  terminology, 1.21
Fraudulent trading
  any fraudulent purpose, 3.257
  'carrying on a business', 3.249
  case examples, 3.248
  creditors, 3.255–3.256
  definition, 3.247
  directors' disqualification, 3.261
  extent of participation, 3.250–3.252
  intent to defraud, 3.253–3.254
  introduction, 3.247
  land banking, 3.248
  nature of offence
    any fraudulent purpose, 3.257
    'carrying on a business', 3.249
    creditors, 3.255–3.256
    extent of participation, 3.250–3.252
    intent to defraud, 3.253–3.254
  non-corporate offenders, and, 1.28–1.30
  penalties, 3.259–3.260
  sentencing, 3.259–3.260
  unincorporated entities, 3.258

'Gain'
  definition, 1.21
Guilty plea
  sentencing, and, 9.10–9.14

HMRC records
  mortgage fraud, and, 3.55

Human rights
  abuse of process, and
    delay, 8.10–8.13
    generally, 8.3
    introduction, 8.1
  disclosure, and, 7.3

Impossibility
  money laundering, and, 3.282
Income of borrowers
  mortgage fraud, and, 3.15
Insider trading
  accountants, and, 3.236
  background, 3.212
  commission of offence
    'dealing', 3.227–3.229
    generally, 3.217–3.219
    'inside information', 3.220–3.223
    'insider', 3.224–3.226
    territorial scope, 3.230
  consent of DPP or Secretary of State, 3.216
  contracts for difference, 3.231
  Criminal Justice Act 1993 Pt V, and, 3.212
  'dealing', 3.227–3.229
  dealing in the security, 3.218–3.219
  defences, 3.240
  disclosing inside information, 3.218–3.219
  encouraging another person, 3.218–3.219
  examples, 3.233–3.234
  expert evidence, 3.241
  'inside information', 3.220–3.223
  'insider', 3.224–3.226
  instituting proceedings, 3.216
  professional intermediaries, 3.229
  proof, 3.242–3.243
  purpose of legislation, 3.213–3.215
  regulated market, 3.228
  reverse burden of proof, 3.239
  role of professionals
    accountants, 3.236
    introduction, 3.235
    solicitors, 3.237–3.238
  sentencing, 3.245–3.246
  solicitors, and, 3.237–3.238
  spreadbetting, 3.232

Insider trading – *contd*
  summary of issues, 3.244
  territorial scope, 3.230
Insurance frauds
  fraud by false representation, and, 1.13
Interlocutory appeals
  preparatory hearings
    appeals, 6.20–6.21
    background, 6.1
    case management, 6.12
    complex fraud cases, 6.13–6.17
    Criminal Justice Act 1987 ss. 7-10, and, 6.13–6.17
    Criminal Procedure and Investigations Act 1996, and, 6.18–6.19
    Criminal Procedure Rules, and, 6.11–6.12
    discretion of judges, 6.7
    interlocutory appeals, and, 6.2
    introduction, 6.1–6.6
    ordering, 6.7–6.9
    overriding objective, 6.11–6.12
    pre-trial rulings, 6.10
  terminating rulings
    appeals, 6.27–6.29
    generally, 6.22–6.24
    jurisdiction, 6.22
    prosecutor's responsibilities, 6.25–6.26
    'ruling', 6.23
Investigations
  mortgage fraud, and
    bank account information, 3.54
    Companies House, 3.49
    Council tax records, 3.51
    estate agent details and records, 3.53
    generally, 3.16
    HMRC records, 3.55
    introduction, 3.48
    misrepresentation, and, 3.7
    receipts, 3.52
    sales screen applications, 3.56
    seller records, 3.53
    solicitors' files, 3.50
    utility records, 3.51

'Lebanese loops'
  articles for use in frauds, and, 1.27

Index

Liability of company officers
offences, and, 1.33
'Loan sharking'
Consumer Credit Act 1974 s 39(1), and, 3.194–3.204
Financial Services and Markets Act 2000, and, 3.188–3.193
nature of offence, 3.188–3.1
offence from 1 April 2014, 3.188–3.193
offence pre-1 April 2014, 3.194–3.204
overview, 3.186–3.187
pay day lending, and, 3.186
possession of criminal property
defences, 3.209–3.211
generally, 3.205–3.208
Proceeds of Crime Act 2002 s 329, and, 3.205–3.211
'Loss'
definition, 1.21

Making or supplying articles for use in frauds
generally, 1.25–1.26
mortgage fraud, and, 3.27–3.28
terminology, 1.27
Misrepresentation
mortgage fraud, and
buy to let mortgages, 3.9
identity of the borrower, 3.8
introduction, 3.7
methods, 3.7
property for owner occupation, 3.9
purchase price, 3.11
rental yield and tenancy, 3.10
Missing Trader Intra-Community (MTIC) fraud
Attorney-General's guidelines, 3.143
'badges'
'back to back', 3.114
defence, and, 3.123–3.136
high speed banking, 3.119
insufficient due diligence, 3.120
introduction, 3.113
no due diligence, 3.120
no insurance, 3.116
no price negotiations, 3.118
no stock records, 3.117
no trading history, 3.121

Missing Trader Intra-Community (MTIC) fraud – *contd*
'badges' – *contd*
no written contract, 3.115
third party payments, 3.122
'back to back' arrangements, 3.114
banking arrangements, 3.119
charges, 3.137–3.141
confiscation proceedings, 3.168–3.174
Criminal procedure Rules, 3.143
defences, 3.123–3.136
disclosure
'creeping disclosure', 3.146–3.148
difficulties, 3.144–3.161
generally, 3.142
'kept in the dark', 3.149–3.152
Operation Venison, 3.149–3.152
Operation Vitric, 3.146–3.148
public interest immunity, and, 3.144
source of guidance, 3.143
systematic failures, 3.153–3.161
due diligence, 3.120
extent, 3.111–3.112
indicators, 3.113
insurance, 3.116
introduction, 3.101
nature, 3.102–3.110
price negotiations, 3.118
public interest immunity, and, 3.144
sentencing, 3.162–3.167
stock records, 3.117
third party payments, 3.122
trading history, 3.121
VAT, and, 3.101
written contract, 3.115
Money laundering
acquisition of criminal property
'criminal conduct', 3.269
criminal property, 3.266–3.268
generally, 3.302
inadequate consideration, 3.303
'property', 3.268
attempts, and, 3.281–3.282
authorised disclosures, and
generally, 3.304
introduction, 3.295
becoming concerned in an arrangement to facilitate
acts preparatory, 3.300

438

Index

Money laundering – *contd*
  becoming concerned in an
    arrangement to facilitate – *contd*
    generally, 3.299
    legal professionals, and, 3.301
  belief, 3.280
  benefit fraud, and, 3.294
  commission of specific offence,
    3.287–3.289
  concealing criminal property, 3.298
  conspiracy to commit, and, 3.283
  converting criminal property, 3.298
  'criminal conduct', 3.269
  'criminal lifestyle', 3.296
  criminal property
    'criminal conduct', 3.269
    disguising, 3.298
    generally, 3.266–3.267
    'property', 3.268
  disguising criminal property, 3.298
  drug trafficking, and, 3.307
  entering into an arrangement to
    facilitate
    acts preparatory, 3.300
    generally, 3.299
    legal professionals, and, 3.301
  evidence of underlying crime
    need for particulars, 3.290–3.291
    proof of commission of specific
      offence, 3.287–3.289
  failure to pay tax, 3.270–3.276
  impossibility, and, 3.282
  indirect benefit, 3.275
  inferences, 3.286
  interest in property, 3.276
  introduction, 3.262–3.265
  joinder with predicate offences,
    3.306–3.307
  knowledge, 3.277–3.280
  lawful profits, 3.270–3.276
  mens rea, 3.277–3.280
  mortgage fraud, and, 3.17–3.18
  no case to answer, 3.286
  offences
    acquisition, use and possession,
      3.302–3.303
    becoming concerned in an
      arrangement to facilitate,
      3.299–3.301
    concealing, disguising etc, 3.298

Money laundering – *contd*
  offences – *contd*
    'criminal lifestyle', 3.296
    entering into an arrangement to
      facilitate, 3.299–3.301
    general matters, 3.295–3.296
    limitations on scope, 3.297
  particulars, 3.290–3.291
  pecuniary advantage
    benefit fraud, and, 3.294
    generally, 3.292–3.293
  possession of criminal property
    'criminal conduct', 3.269
    criminal property, 3.266–3.268
    generally, 3.302
    inadequate consideration, 3.303
    'property', 3.268
  proof, 3.305
  proof of commission of specific
    offence, 3.287–3.289
  'property', 3.268
  removing criminal property, 3.298
  reporting suspicious activities, and
    generally, 3.309–3.313
    penalties, 3.314
  sentencing
    generally, 3.308
    introduction, 3.297
    reporting suspicious activities, 3.314
  submissions of no case to answer,
    3.286
  suspicion, 3.277–3.280
  territorial scope, 3.297
  transferring criminal property, 3.298
  use of criminal property
    generally, 3.302
    inadequate consideration, 3.303
  use of offences, 3.284–3.285
Money Laundering Directive of
  November 2005
  generally, 1.5
Mortgage fraud
  accountants, and, 3.44
  articles for use in frauds, 3.27–3.28
  bank account information, and, 3.54
  bank managers, and, 3.42
  brokers, and, 3.42–3.43
  buy to let mortgages, 3.9
  charges, 3.6
  civil recovery, and, 3.62

439

Index

Mortgage fraud – *contd*
- Companies House, and, 3.49
- conduct, 3.7
- context, 3.4
- Council tax records, and, 3.51
- estate agent details and records, and, 3.53
- false accounting, 3.31–3.34
- Fraud Act 2006, and
  - fraud by failing to disclose information, 3.25–3.26
  - fraud by false representation, 3.20–3.24
  - introduction, 3.19
  - making or supplying articles for use in frauds, 3.27–3.28
- fraud by failing to disclose information, 3.25–3.26
- fraud by false representation, 3.20–3.24
- generally, 3.3
- HMRC records, and, 3.55
- identity of the borrower, 3.8
- income of borrowers, and, 3.15
- investigation
  - bank account information, 3.54
  - Companies House, 3.49
  - Council tax records, 3.51
  - estate agent details and records, 3.53
  - generally, 3.16
  - HMRC records, 3.55
  - introduction, 3.48
  - misrepresentation, and, 3.7
  - receipts, 3.52
  - sales screen applications, 3.56
  - seller records, 3.53
  - solicitors' files, 3.50
  - utility records, 3.51
- making or supplying articles for use in frauds, 3.27–3.28
- misrepresentation, by
  - buy to let mortgages, 3.9
  - identity of the borrower, 3.8
  - introduction, 3.7
  - methods, 3.7
  - property for owner occupation, 3.9
  - purchase price, 3.11
  - rental yield and tenancy, 3.10
- money laundering, and, 3.17–3.18

Mortgage fraud – *contd*
- multiple frauds in respect of same property, 3.14
- obtaining a money transfer by deception, 3.37–3.38
- obtaining property by deception, 3.35–3.36
- obtaining services by deception, 3.39
- prevalence, 3.5
- procuring execution of valuable security by deception, 3.39
- property for owner occupation, 3.9
- purchase price, 3.11
- receipts, and, 3.52
- registration of property, and, 3.13
- rental yield and tenancy, 3.10
- role of professionals
  - accountants, 3.44
  - bank managers, 3.42
  - brokers, 3.42–3.43
  - introduction, 3.41
  - solicitors, 3.45–3.46
  - surveyors, 3.47
- sales screen applications, and, 3.56
- seller records, and, 3.53
- sentencing
  - consecutive sentences, 3.59
  - generally, 3.57–3.58
  - multiple offences, 3.59
  - no loss sustained, 3.59, 3.61
  - successive mortgages on same property, 3.60
- solicitors, and, 3.45–3.46
- solicitors' files, and, 3.50
- supplying articles for use in frauds, 3.27–3.28
- surveyors, and, 3.47
- Theft Act 1968, and
  - false accounting, 3.31–3.34
  - introduction, 3.29–3.30
  - obtaining a money transfer by deception, 3.37–3.38
  - obtaining property by deception, 3.35–3.36
  - obtaining services by deception, 3.39
  - procuring execution of valuable security by deception, 3.39
  - relevance, 3.29
- utility records, and, 3.51

Index

No case to answer
money laundering, and, 3.286

Obtaining a money transfer by deception
mortgage fraud, and, 3.37–3.38
Obtaining property by deception
mortgage fraud, and, 3.35–3.36
Obtaining services by deception
mortgage fraud, and, 3.39
Obtaining services by dishonesty
generally, 1.31–1.32

Participating in fraudulent business
generally, 1.28–1.30
Pay day lending
and see **Loan-sharking**
generally, 3.186
Payroll
fraud offence under s 1, and, 1.9
Pecuniary advantage
money laundering, and
benefit fraud, and, 3.294
generally, 3.292–3.293
'Phishing'
fraud by false representation, and, 1.13
Police cautions
see also **Cautions**
College of Policing Gravity Factors Matrix, 5.8
conclusion, 5.13
Crown Prosecution Service, and, 5.5–5.6
either-way offences, 5.7
evidential test, 5.9
factors, 5.4
generally, 5.3–5.8
indictable-only offences, 5.5–5.6
matters to which regard be had, 5.6
MoJ guidance, 5.4
National Decision Model, 5.8
procedures, 5.11–5.12
public interest test, 5.10
Superintendent, and, 5.5–5.6
'Ponzi' frauds
background, 3.63
'badges', 3.64–3.65
breach of general prohibition on carrying out regulated activity, 3.69–3.75

'Ponzi' frauds – *contd*
charges, 3.66
conspiracy to defraud, 3.67
defences, 3.77–3.79
'due diligence' defence, 3.78
fraud (s 1 offence), 3.68
overview, 3.63–3.65
regulatory offences, 3.69–3.75
taking of deposits, 3.70
Possession of articles for use in frauds
generally, 1.22–1.24
terminology, 1.27
Possession of criminal property
money laundering, and
'criminal conduct', 3.269
criminal property, 3.266–3.268
generally, 3.302
inadequate consideration, 3.303
'property', 3.268
unlicensed money-lending, and
defences, 3.209–3.211
generally, 3.205–3.208
Power of entry
generally, 4.1–4.2
Programs
articles for use in frauds, and, 1.27
Preliminary hearings
deferred prosecution agreements, and, 5.48
Preparatory hearings
appeals, 6.20–6.21
background, 6.1
case management, 6.12
complex fraud cases, 6.13–6.17
Criminal Justice Act 1987 ss 7–10, and, 6.13–6.17
Criminal Procedure and Investigations Act 1996, and
generally, 6.18–6.19
pre-trial rulings, 6.10
Criminal Procedure Rules, and, 6.11–6.12
discretion of judges, 6.7
interlocutory appeals, and, 6.2
introduction, 6.1–6.6
ordering, 6.7–6.9
overriding objective, 6.11–6.12
pre-trial rulings, 6.10
Pre-trial rulings
generally, 6.10

Index

Procuring execution of valuable security by deception
mortgage fraud, and, 3.39
'Property'
definition, 1.21
Public interest
simple cautions, and, 5.10
Public interest immunity
disclosure, and, 7.59–7.68
Missing Trader Intra-Community fraud, and, 3.144
Purchase price
mortgage fraud, and, 3.11

Receipts
mortgage fraud, and, 3.52
Registration of property
mortgage fraud, and, 3.13
Regulation S shares
'Boiler Room' fraud, and, 3.84
Regulatory offences
'Boiler Room' fraud, and, 3.87–3.97
'Ponzi' frauds, and, 3.69–3.75
Removing criminal property
see also **Money laundering**
generally, 3.298
Rental yield and tenancy
mortgage fraud, and, 3.10
Reporting suspicious activities
money laundering, and
generally, 3.309–3.313
penalties, 3.314
Right to a fair trial
abuse of process, and
delay, 8.10–8.13
generally, 8.3
introduction, 8.1
disclosure, and, 7.3

Sales screen applications
mortgage fraud, and, 3.56
Search and seizure powers
Criminal Justice and Police Act 2001, s 50, under
admissibility, 4.27
generally, 4.21–4.23
post-arrest powers, 4.26
production of material, 4.28
retention of material, 4.24–4.25

Search and seizure powers – *contd*
Department of Business, Innovations and Skills, and, 4.54
Financial Conduct Authority, and, 4.55–4.56
HMRC, and, 4.49–4.53
introduction, 4.1–4.8
PACE Code of Practice B, under
electronic material, 4.18–4.20
full and frank disclosure, 4.11
general power to seize, 4.16–4.17
generally, 4.9–4.11
information requirements, 4.10
legal professional privilege, 4.13
privileged material, 4.12–4.15
power of entry, and, 4.1–4.2
Proceeds of Crime Act 2002, under, 4.29–4.37
Serious Fraud Office, and, 4.38–4.48
Seller records
mortgage fraud, and, 3.53
Sentencing
ancillary orders
directors disqualification orders, 9.39–9.42
financial reporting orders, 9.32–9.34
generally, 9.16
introduction, 9.31
serious crime prevention orders, 9.35–9.38
assistance given or offered to a prosecutor, 9.9
body corporate, and, 9.19–9.28
compensation, 9.16
confiscation, 9.16
conspiracy to defraud, and, 2.1
culpability, 9.6
directors disqualification orders, 9.39–9.42
disclosure, and, 7.69
electronic tags, and, 9.18
elements, 9.1
explanation of effect, 9.17
financial reporting orders
generally, 9.32–9.34
introduction, 9.16
fixing the starting point, 9.7–9.8
fraudulent trading, and, 3.259–3.260
guilty plea, 9.10–9.14
harm, 9.6

442

Sentencing – *contd*
  insider trading, and, 3.245–3.246
  introduction, 9.1–9.2
  just and proportionate, 9.15
  Missing Trader Intra-Community
    fraud, and, 3.162–3.167
  money laundering, and
    generally, 3.308
    introduction, 3.297
    reporting suspicious activities,
      3.314
  mortgage fraud, and
    consecutive sentences, 3.59
    generally, 3.57–3.58
    multiple offences, 3.59
    no loss sustained, 3.59, 3.61
    successive mortgages on same
      property, 3.60
  previous Court of Appeal authority,
    9.29
  proportionality, 9.15
  reasons, 9.17
  reduction for guilty plea, 9.10–9.14
  Sentencing Council's guideline,
    9.2–9.18
  serious crime prevention orders
    generally, 9.35–9.38
    introduction, 9.16
  starting point for the offence, 9.7–9.8
  totality of sentence, 9.15
Serious crime prevention orders
  generally, 9.35–9.38
  introduction, 9.16
'Share scams'
  breach of general prohibition on
    carrying out regulated activity,.
    3.87–3.97
  charges, 3.85
  conspiracy to defraud, 3.86
  dealing in investments as principal/
    agent, 3.91
  defences, 3.98–3.100
  financial promotion, 3.95
  overview, 3.80–3.84
  Regulation S shares, 3.84
  regulatory offences, 3.87–3.97
  share sales, 3.83–3.84
Solicitors
  insider trading, and, 3.237–3.238
  mortgage fraud, and, 3.45–3.46, 3.50

Spreadbetting
  insider trading, and, 3.232
Submissions of no case to answer
  money laundering, and, 3.286
Supplying articles for use in frauds
  mortgage fraud, and, 3.27–3.28
Surveyors
  mortgage fraud, and, 3.47

Taking deposits
  'Ponzi' frauds, and, 3.70
Templates
  articles for use in frauds, and, 1.27
Terminating rulings
  appeals, 6.27–6.29
  generally, 6.22–6.24
  jurisdiction, 6.22
  prosecutor's responsibilities, 6.25–
    6.26
  'ruling', 6.23
Theft Act 1968
  false accounting, 3.31–3.34
  introduction, 3.29–3.30
  obtaining a money transfer by
    deception, 3.37–3.38
  obtaining property by deception,
    3.35–3.36
  obtaining services by deception,
    3.39
  procuring execution of valuable
    security by deception, 3.39
  relevance, 3.29
Third party disclosure
  generally, 7.44–7.53
  held overseas, 7.54–7.58
Transferring criminal property
  see also **Money laundering**
  generally, 3.298

Unlicensed money-lending
  Consumer Credit Act 1974 s 39(1),
    and, 3.194–3.204
  Financial Services and Markets Act
    2000, and, 3.188–3.193
  nature of offence, 3.188–3.1
  offence from 1 April 2014, 3.188–
    3.193
  offence pre-1 April 2014, 3.194–3.204
  overview, 3.186–3.187
  pay day lending, and, 3.186

Index

Unlicensed money-lending – *contd*
  possession of criminal property
    defences, 3.209–3.211
    generally, 3.205–3.208
  Proceeds of Crime Act 2002 s.329, and, 3.205–3.211

Unused material
  Attorney-General's Guidelines, 7.41–7.43
  deferred prosecution agreements, and, 5.42
  e-disclosure, 7.19
  guidance, 7.10
  introduction, 7.1
  practical disclosure, 7.33–7.37

Unused material – *contd*
  sifting and examining, 7.30, 7.32
  statutory basis, 7.8

Use of criminal property
  see also **Money laundering**
  generally, 3.302
  inadequate consideration, 3.303

Utility records
  mortgage fraud, and, 3.51

VAT
  and see **Missing Trader Intra-Community fraud**
  generally, 3.101